ALARMSTART SOUTH AND FINAL DEFEAT

About the Author

Having retired after a career as a university lecturer in geology, Professor Patrick G. Eriksson has devoted many years to research for this book, the last part of a trilogy following titles on north-western Europe 1939–44 and the Eastern Front 1941–45. He returned to primary sources and, crucially, as an associate member of the German Air Force Veteran's Association since 1974, he has interviewed and corresponded with more than a hundred former members of the *Luftwaffe*, from junior NCOs to *Geschwader* commanders. Such primary material is unavailable anywhere else and can never be gathered again.

ALARMSTART SOUTH AND FINAL DEFEAT

The German Fighter Pilot's Experience
in the Mediterranean Theatre, 1941–1944
over Normandy, Norway and Germany 1944–1945

Patrick G. Eriksson

AMBERLEY

First published 2019
This edition published 2022

Amberley Publishing
The Hill, Stroud
Gloucestershire, GL5 4EP

www.amberley-books.com

Copyright © Patrick G. Eriksson, 2019, 2022

The right of Patrick G. Eriksson to be identified
as the Author of this work has been asserted in
accordance with the Copyrights, Designs and
Patents Act 1988.

ISBN 978 1 3981 1237 7 (paperback)
ISBN 978 1 4456 9333 0 (ebook)

British Library Cataloguing in Publication Data.
A catalogue record for this book is available
from the British Library.

Typesetting by Aura Technology and Software
Services, India.
Printed in India.

CONTENTS

PREFACE

This volume follows *Alarmstart*,[1] complementing that book's focus on the air war over Western Europe, and equally the Eastern Front focus of the second book in the series, *Alarmstart East*[2] with its examination of aerial warfare and the German fighter pilot experience over the Eastern Front, against the Russians. *Alarmstart South and Final Defeat* examines what befell the *Jagdflieger* in the various war zones around the Mediterranean Sea, their experiences over Normandy with the Allied Invasion and subsequent conquest of occupied France, as well as the last year of the air battle over Germany, and flying in the Norwegian theatre. The volume ends with how some of the *Luftwaffe* pilots experienced the end of the war, and imprisonment for most of them.

The first major Mediterranean campaign for the Germans was the invasion in April to May 1941 of the Balkan countries of Yugoslavia and Greece, including the large island of Crete. Hitler considered Germany the rightful leader of Europe and had already, before the war, dismembered the Czechoslovakian state by absorbing the Sudetenland, forming the Protectorate of Bohemia and Moravia (under the harsh hand of the leading architect of the Holocaust, Reinhard Heydrich) and leaving a rump 'independent' Slovakia. The latter was a Nazi vassal-state and had sent small forces to serve on the Eastern Front.[3] Hungary was another German ally, and both Bulgaria and Romania fell within the Nazi-dominated orbit.[4] German troops occupied

Poland, whose conquest had precipitated the Second World War. The dictator was essentially satisfied with this situation as these conquered, subjugated or allied territories provided the requisite path to the Soviet Union, whose invasion lay at the core of his war and broader political aims. He did not have intentions to add Greece to his 'empire' and was not at all enamoured with the prospect of extensive naval warfare, which any military ventures abutting the Mediterranean Sea would almost certainly have encouraged. Germany had historically been a country focussed on land warfare.

Mussolini, the Italian dictator, on the other hand, fostered a vision of the Mediterranean becoming an Italian domain and he had a fairly large and modern navy which, with the demise of France in May to June 1940 and its necessarily deactivated fleet, left the British somewhat vulnerable in the region. It was Mussolini's ill-considered invasion of Greece in October 1940, launched from his earlier conquest, the tiny adjoining country of Albania, which precipitated a crisis. In retaliation, the British established bases in Crete, with Greek connivance, thus putting the Romanian oil fields at risk of air attack.[5] The Germans were thereby forced to eliminate the island of Crete and with it, obviously, Greece itself.[6] For the second time in the war, the *Luftwaffe*'s airborne forces were to be employed, and just like during the invasion of France and the Low Countries in May 1940, catastrophic losses were to be suffered, this time over Crete.[7] The remaining Balkan country, Yugoslavia, also fell into the maw that thus developed: having joined the Axis alliance in March 1941, a coup later that month ousted the pro-German government.[8] In time the war's most significant resistance movement would develop in Yugoslavia with the merciless struggle absorbing significant German ground forces and even involving *Luftwaffe* aircraft.[9]

The Mediterranean campaigns often tended to overlap with each other chronologically, the main ones being over the Western Desert (Egypt, and modern-day Libya, then known as Cyrenaica in the east and Tripolitania in the west, both parts under Italian colonial rule), and over and around the small island of Malta (actually three islands and a few islets, Malta being the main one).[10] Malta was a British possession with a major naval base and several airfields, which was under Italian attack from 11 June 1940 till late in 1942 with, additionally, three major *Luftwaffe* 'blitzes', the first running from January to May 1941, the second from December 1941 to May 1942, with a final 'blitz' in October 1942.[11] The second German aerial campaign in the first half of 1942 was the main attempt to subjugate the island and eliminate its potential as a naval and air base for British attacks on Italian/German sea supply traffic to their armies in the Western Desert.[12] These British attacks tended to devastate Axis logistics into North Africa, but the *Luftwaffe* continued to carry out episodic attacks on Malta as major air assets became available from other theatres, mainly from Russia and to a lesser extent the 'Desert', to suppress the island for several months. While the intense German attacks beat down RAF activities and forced naval forces to leave the island, as soon as the German aerial forces departed or were greatly reduced, so the British sea and air interdiction on sea transport arose time and again like a phoenix.[13] The *Luftwaffe* faced tough choices between supporting advances of General Rommel's *Afrikakorps* and Italian allied forces in the Desert, or trying to lance the Mediterranean boil that was Malta. There were never enough aircraft to do both jobs, never mind the demands of other, far-removed theatres.

An invasion of Malta to eliminate this constant threat to Axis North African logistics, logically by airborne forces, never took place, at least partly as a result of Hitler's reluctance to hazard his sorely depleted airborne elite troops again, after what the Anzac (New Zealand and Australian) and British defenders had done to them in Crete.[14] In the end, *Luftwaffe* resources were never enough to win either over the Desert or Malta. The naval war in the Mediterranean ebbed and flowed throughout, with hard aerial battles being fought over British convoys that were bringing much needed supplies to Malta, from both eastern and western ends of the sea; not least among these supplies were food, naval and aviation fuel, and aircraft.[15] On many convoys, flying in fighters off aircraft carriers into Malta was an inherent part of these large, complex and bloody operations.[16] The parsimonious British only supplied Spitfires (Mark V models) from March 1942, before that leaving the defence of Malta up to Hurricanes; a similar policy pertained in the Desert as well, with Hurricanes and various marks of the American P-40 being pitted against E, F and G models of the significantly better Me 109 before limited Spitfires arrived at the beginning of June 1942.[17]

The Mediterranean air war was one with strong participation of Commonwealth air (and ground) units encompassing fighters, bombers and other types as well, particularly from the South African, as well as Australian, Free French, Greek, Yugoslav and, towards the end, also American squadrons.[18] In addition the Desert campaign was one where ground, naval and air fighting were strongly inter-linked and many operations encompassed strong mutual dependency of these diverse forces. The air-ground cooperation so critical for winning battles was crafted by the British in North Africa first, where the so-called Desert Air Force and 8th Army became brothers in arms.[19] No Mediterranean theatre was ever that far from the sea, and many a pilot or crew ended up in 'the drink', only some being fortunate enough to be rescued (one example detailed in this book being the experiences of Dr Felix Sauer of *10/JG 53* who survived eight days in a raft, miraculously). The ground war in the Desert ebbed and flowed back and forth several times, depending which side had managed to accumulate enough materiel (especially armoured forces and fuel) for a successful counter-offensive.[20] Successful advances by either side greatly lengthened supply lines and logistic shortages, thereby granting a reprieve to the retreating enemy and enabling a comeback from their side as their own supply lines were shortened.[21] In all of this, the potential effect of an active Malta-based British offensive capability remained critical, particularly for the fuel-starved Axis divisions.[22]

In the Western Desert it was largely *Jagdgeschwader* 27 under the outstanding leadership of 'Edu' Neumann (whose views are included in this book) that bore the brunt of the German fighter battles, supported for shorter periods by *7/JG 26, III/JG 53,* and parts of *III/ZG 26*; right at the end, *JG 77* was withdrawn from the Russian front to replace an exhausted and depleted *JG 27*.[23] It was also over the Desert that the greatest German ace, in terms of victories claimed against Western opponents, achieved this distinction; the inimitable Hans-Joachim ('Jochen') Marseille.[24] The nature of his war and his struggle against increasing exhaustion are examined later in some detail, including valuable material from *Luftwaffe* psychologist Dr Paul Robert Skawran. By a strange coincidence, probably the top scorer of the war among British/Commonwealth pilots also flew in the Mediterranean region, over the Desert and later over Greece; the South African Squadron Leader 'Pat' Pattle, who lost his life in a hopeless battle over Piraeus harbour on 20 April 1941.[25] Marseille also paid the ultimate price, dying in an accident on 30 September 1942, at least partly a result of exhaustion and the strain of intensive combat flying.[26]

While the Greek and Cretan campaigns were over within less than two months (6 April to 1 June 1941),[27] the guerrilla war in Yugoslavia that had erupted after the country's rapid fall to invasion from 6 April 1941 would go on for years and reach an extent which necessitated commitment of German and Italian troops on the scale of divisions.[28] In the same time interval as the 1941 Balkan campaign, a pro-Axis coup in Iraq in April led to combat between British forces there, mainly belonging to the RAF, and Iraqi ground and limited air forces. A small *Luftwaffe* contingent flew in via Vichy French Syria and fought against the RAF and invading ground troops, but was soon destroyed.[29] Syria itself was invaded by British, Commonwealth and Free French forces on 8 June 1941 and, following some stiff fighting also by the Vichy French air force, the country was subjugated by 11 July.[30] In August 1941, the British and the Soviets jointly occupied the oil-rich nation of Iran to prevent any overt or covert Axis moves against that critical military asset.[31] German aircraft were not involved in action over either Syria or Iran.[32]

With General Montgomery's major victory over the Axis at El Alamein (23 October to 4 November 1942), the alternating retreats and advances of the two sides that had previously characterised the Desert war came to an end; Montgomery's defeat of Rommel was a decisive victory that so depleted the *panzer* army and its infantry that a stand could not be made at the far-western position at El Agheila again (which the British had reached twice before and then lost again).[33] Ground operations to stop the German advance at Alam el Halfa before the main Battle of Alamein, and victory in the latter conflict owed much to the contributions of the light-medium bombers of the Desert Air Force, many manned by members of the South African Air Force. Montgomery might have been slow and might have prepared for all battles very carefully and with great logistic strength before moving, but he kept going, kept winning and the Germans were driven back westwards along the North African littoral at a rapid pace.[34] Within days of the end of Alamein, on 8 November 1942, United States and British troops invaded Vichy-held North Africa, taking over Morocco and Algeria (and intending to advance into Tunisia, furthest east) against, in places, stiff Vichy French opposition.[35] This was rapidly overcome and French troops soon joined the Allies facing east approximately along the western boundary of Tunisia with Algeria. Essentially, the Western Desert and Tunisian campaigns graded into each other, and each supported the other by imposing a two-front war on the Axis in North Africa.[36] While the fighting in Tunisia raged on until 13 May 1943, with terrain and climate creating further difficulty, Allied ground and air forces overcame the opposition, trapping the bulk of the Axis army in the north of the country.[37] *Luftwaffe* attempts to fly in supplies and reinforcements by air, and to evacuate wounded and key personnel at the end of the campaign, suffered catastrophic losses to roving Allied fighters – once more the transport arm was decimated.[38]

Rommel's retreating *Afrikakorps* and Italian allies left Cyrenaica behind and entered southern Tunisia under a fighter umbrella provided by *JG 77*.[39] In northern Tunisia, *JG 53* gave cover; further fighter units encompassed *II/JG 2*, *II/JG 51* (operated in north and south), two ground attack *Gruppen*, as well as *II* and *III/JG 27* flying mainly from Sicily.[40] The American Army Air Force also operated in strength alongside RAF units and small French aerial forces over Tunisia.[41] What made the fighting there particularly interesting was that the RAF (and some USAAF squadrons also) operated the first advanced Spitfire IXs over North Africa, while the Germans, as always, employed only their best equipment, the most up-to-date marks of the Me 109 and Fw 190.[42] American strategic bombing with four-engined and twin-engined machines also played a significant role and pounded Axis airfields effectively, a portent of worse things to follow over Sicily later that same year.[43]

Luftwaffe fighters leaving Tunisia were now mostly based on Sicily, Sardinia or southern Italy, ready to defend Sicily from a possible invasion. These fighter units were all pretty run down, tired and demoralised from their defeat in Tunisia, and the bombing endured on most air bases in that theatre.[44] These same *Jagdgruppen*, although re-equipped to a certain extent, were given little chance to rest and recuperate as US Army Air Force and Desert Air Force heavy and medium bombers pounded the German air bases in Sicily endlessly; for the first time in the Mediterranean theatre German fighter units faced really large four-engined bomber formations (albeit this had already begun to a degree over Tunisia also) and performed poorly.[45] They were over-tired and unmotivated, had no proper experience of dealing with these leviathans, had poor support from ground controllers, and aircraft, personnel and equipment were regularly smashed on the ground. In addition to the bombers operating from North Africa and Malta, incessant fighter sweeps and fighter bomber raids took place.[46] *Reichsmarschall* Göring made things considerably worse by accusing the *Jagdflieger* of cowardice and even had some random pilots arrested for this.[47] The result was that *Luftwaffe* fighter defences in Sicily were already in a parlous state when that island was invaded on 10 July 1943. The invasion followed a crescendo of airbase attacks and German fighters had all been withdrawn to southern Italy by the end of the day on 13 July, from whence they, together with limited *Schlachtgruppen* (ground attack units), attempted with little success to intervene further over the island until its final evacuation on 17 August 1943.[48] Despite preponderant Allied air power over Sicily, massed German flak over the Straits of Messina enabled effective evacuation of troops and even some vehicles from Sicily, a tribute to the always highly efficient anti-aircraft arm of the *Luftwaffe*.[49]

It didn't take the Allies long to move into adjacent southern Italy (3 September 1943) with the large Salerno landings near Naples taking place only six days later.[50] This battle, which was touch-and-go for some time, was over by 18 September.[51] German fighter *Gruppen* opposing the landings were limited to only five who, between them, could field a meagre 51 serviceable Me 109s;[52] there had been no time for the *Luftwaffe* to recover from

Sicily. However, German ground attack and bomber aircraft performed well over Salerno, where the deadly German remote-controlled glider bombs also made their operational debut against Allied shipping.[53] By the beginning of October 1943, the Allies had taken the large airfield complex on the Foggia plain, situated close to the eastern coast of southern Italy, virtually opposite Naples.[54] A month later the 15th US Army Air Force (USAAF) began operations from this new airfield cluster, which gave them strategic bomber reach into Romania (Ploiesti oilfields), Hungary, Austria and southern Germany.[55] Further fighting up the Italian peninsula thereafter must be viewed as questionable, as little strategic gain resulted from this difficult, costly and slow campaign. Allied landings at Anzio in late January 1944 were supposed to put an end to the sluggish progress and enable Rome to be taken, but early opportunity after successful landings was squandered and a vicious battle ensued right into June 1944; *Luftwaffe* performance was much less effective than at Salerno.[56] The equally protracted battle on the main front line at Monte Cassino (January to May 1944) raged in parallel to the Anzio debacle.[57] As the Italian campaign dragged on, retaining German fighter *Gruppen* in that theatre made less and less sense as the demands of the Home Defence and then the Invasion of Normandy in June, became critical. *Jagdgruppen* were reduced from seven (March 1944) to four by June and only one by August, the last few German fighters being removed by September 1944.[58] With the Italian armistice in September 1943, the previous *Regia Aeronautica* had split into a pro-Allied part (which only operated over the Balkans to avoid combat with pro-Fascist fellow-Italians) and the *Aeronautica Nazionale Repubblicana* (ANR) which supported Mussolini's rump Italian Social Republic in the North.[59] When the *Luftwaffe* fighters pulled out, these latter units were the only remaining Axis fighters in the theatre, operating under direct *Luftwaffe* control.[60]

The Balkan countries remained largely a backwater through much of the conflict over Malta and North Africa, but the Ploiesti oilfields of Romania, and minor deposits in Hungary, were always in the Allies' thoughts. Once the Foggia airfields in Italy were in Allied hands, four-engined bomber raids by the 15th USAAF on Romania, Hungary and Bulgaria followed, and these necessarily passed over Yugoslavia and Greece.[61] Elements of *JG* 27 operated over Greece and its many islands following the loss of the Western Desert in late 1942 and later *II/JG* 51 took over.[62] With the Italian surrender on 8 September 1943, Italian-occupied Aegean islands switched sides but many were rapidly retaken by the Germans.[63] British and Commonwealth forces had occupied Kos, Samos and Leros with limited Spitfires to cover them being stationed on Kos, but the Germans assembled superior aerial weight and retook them during October and November 1943.[64] The Ploiesti oilfields were the main Balkan target for the Allies, with the first big raid on 1 August 1943, carried out at low level, being a disaster. Heavy bomber losses occurred due to flak, Romanian fighters, *I/JG* 4 over Romania and *IV/JG* 27 operating over Greece as the bombers flew out back to North Africa.[65] Not until April 1944 did the American bombers return, now flying from Foggia; 43 big raids were made on Romania until late August 1944, when the country succumbed to the Russians and changed sides.[66] The *Luftwaffe* pilots defending these Balkan countries had not benefitted unduly from the experience of their colleagues over north-western Europe, who had long battled the four-engined bomber menace, and had to learn from scratch and rapidly develop their own counter-measures, as described by some of the witnesses in this volume.

In illustration number one, the percentages of German fighter *Gruppen* stationed in the different main theatres from June 1941 till the end of the war are shown. From this it can be seen that the North African-Malta campaign was a significant though not dominant drain on *Luftwaffe* resources from late 1941 till April to May 1943 when the Tunisian campaign ended. Thereafter the aerial fighting over Sicily and Italy involved fewer *Gruppen* and had tailed off by mid-1944. June to August 1944 saw a massive spike in fighter units transferred to Normandy, at the expense of the Home Defence. From late 1942 till late 1944 the Balkans region absorbed a constant yet not over-significant number of fighter assets. Following the German defeat in Normandy the Home Defence once more became the prime theatre where the *Jagdgruppen* were stationed, approximate parity with Eastern Front transfers only being reached in 1945.

The German fighter arm was concentrated in the Home Defence from about middle 1943 and on into 1944, when it was defeated and reduced to such an extent as to enable the Invasion of Normandy to take place with effective Allied air superiority.[67] When the landings began on 6 June 1944, only two of the six *Luftwaffe Jagdgruppen* in France were placed so as to be able to react.[68] Although 17 fighter *Gruppen* were sent from the Home Defence to Normandy within days,[69] in a move long planned and prepared for, their decreased quality allied to massive Allied superiority in numbers ensured rapid defeat and catastrophic casualties over Normandy. As an example, in June 1944 the Allies were able to put up almost 10 times the number of German fighter sorties over the beachheads.[70] By the end of July, German fighter losses exceeded their own claims total,[71] and by early September the German armies in Normandy had been largely destroyed along with their fighter cover, and the Seine had been crossed, Paris liberated and the Belgian capital of Brussels as well thereafter.[72]

The final year of combat over Germany itself, from June 1944 to May 1945, was a period of stark combat with losses rapidly becoming unsustainable as the remaining experienced leaders at all levels fell victim to Allied qualitative and quantitative superiority. While the bulk of the Home Defence units were flying over Normandy, a rump Home Defence kept going, largely comprised of the *Wilden Sau* fighters (now converted to day fighting) and *Zerstörer* units, now mainly equipped with the improved Me 410, plus a few mainstream *Jagdgruppen* to fly high cover.[73] The chances of survival for any *Jagdflieger* were now very slim. Karl-Heinz Hirsch of *III/JG* 27 describes how, each morning, the fighter pilots began their day facing an unwanted breakfast, but with a bottle of cognac beneath each chair. Even on the ground, the entire fighter control system, never mind high casualties to fighter aircraft on the ground from strafing American fighters, itself became embroiled in direct combat. *Oberst* Hanns Trübenbach, senior controller in charge of a large headquarters near Darmstadt, and his large staff, were bombed out, and he was narrowly missed by a marauding P-51 Mustang strafer in this final year. Even the RAF bombers began to fly more day missions as the *Luftwaffe* fighter arm faded away, *Feldwebel* Rudolf Hener of *JG 3* providing a noteworthy eye-witness account of fighting against Lancasters. This was in addition to massive incursions by the England-based 8th and Italian-based 15th United States Army Air Forces.

These desperate times brought forth equally desperate attempted counter-measures. Foremost amongst these were the *Sturmgruppen*, operative from July 1944 onwards.[74] The concept was for *Gruppen*-strength mass attacks on the four-engined bomber formations by heavily armed and armoured Fw 190s, sporting 3 cm cannons in addition to their standard armament.[75] Again, Hanns Trübenbach was witness to the creation and operations of these fighters, which were the brainchild of Hans-Günther von Kornatzki: the latter led one of the three *Sturmgruppen* created (*II/JG 4*; the other two were *IV/JG 3* and *II/JG 300*) and lost his life in the battle.[76] On 1 January 1945 came the long-awaited '*Grosse Schlag*' (big blow) which Fighter General Galland had wanted to launch against the four-engined bombers but was forced to apply in reduced form in massed strafing attacks against Allied airfields at dawn on New Year's Day (*Operation Bodenplatte*). It was another desperate measure: in excess of 900 German fighters took part in the mission but suffered the loss of about one third of their number (plus 214 pilots killed, missing, POW) for about the same number of Allied aircraft destroyed, mainly on the ground.[77] The Allies were able to shrug off such losses and maintain their attack in all its forms. The final and most desperate measure of all was *Sonderkommando Elbe*. Whereas in the *Sturmgruppen* pilots were expected to destroy a four-engined bomber on each mission, even to the point of ramming them, these were never seen as suicide missions. With the *Elbe* pilots this changed, with all being expected to ram their opponents, and to bail out if at all possible. Once again Trübenbach was a well placed witness to these events. When they were finally launched on 7 April 1945, 45 of the 143 participating German fighters were lost (and 32 of their pilots) for only 14 downed bombers.[78]

The only bright spot on the *Luftwaffe* horizon late in the war was the Me 262 jet fighter. Any radically new design – and this one also had totally new technology for its two engines – takes time to be developed from an experimental prototype to an operational aircraft, and training of suitable pilots also takes a lot of time. So it was with the Me 262. *Erprobungskommando* 262 had already been launched in autumn 1943, under the command of *Hauptmann* Thierfelder, with the express purpose of developing it as a fighter. Horst Geyer, who figured in both companion volumes to this book,[79] became its commander in July 1944 after Thierfelder had been killed. The well known *Kommando Nowotny* was detached from this initial unit, tasked to test the Me 262 operationally in combat and to derive the best tactics. The balance of the original unit became *III/EJG* 2 led initially by Geyer and then by Heinz Bär.[80] With the death in action of Nowotny, a famous Eastern Front ace, on 8 November 1944,[81] little success in combat had yet been achieved by either it or *III/EJG* 2. While *Kommando Nowotny* then became the nucleus for *III/JG* 7 (expanded to an entire jet *Geschwader*, led first by Johannes Steinhoff and then by Theo Weissenberger), *III/EJG* 2 later became part of *JV* 44 (*Jagdverband* 44), formed and led by the discharged *General der Jagdflieger*, Adolf Galland until he was wounded, when Heinz Bär became its final leader.[82] However, the jets, while having had the potential possibly to turn the Battle of Germany around, came too late and in too limited numbers. Even in the best of circumstances this reality would have been little changed, despite much written on Hitler-imposed delays on its adaptation as a fighter. The radically new aircraft took time to be introduced into ordinary line units for aerial combat. The very high speed of the Me 262 needed special tactics in attacking four-engined bomber formations and enemy fighters, and it had a major weakness related to poor acceleration despite the high top speed; landing operations were always fraught with danger and the aircraft's engines readily burst into flames if throttled up too fast, as related by several of the veterans in this book.

The final theatre addressed here is Norway. The second volume in this series, dealing with the Eastern Front,[83] details operations against the Russians by *JG* 5 on the White Sea front and along the Finnish-Soviet border. Here, only operations against the RAF in Norway are examined. British incursions over Norway, mainly consisting of small formations and rare large ones including aircraft carrier raids, continued from 1941 till the end of the war.

Günther Scholz, who has featured in both previous volumes of the series, also appears in this theatre, as the *Jagdfliegerführer* Norway. Me 110s in small numbers also featured through much of the Norwegian campaign, as related by another veteran, Karl-Friedrich Schlossstein. Finally, the Norwegian operations of *16/JG 5* in the final period of the war, from late 1944 onwards, are described in some detail by Karl-Heinz Erler, who flew the Me 109 G-14, the best model of this famous aircraft according to him. By then, officer pilots were in such short supply that Erler's *Staffel* was led by a *Feldwebel*.

The end of the war brought short-lived relief to most *Luftwaffe Jagdflieger* but was certainly not a time of joy for them (unlike the Allies); they were faced either by long and harsh imprisonment in the East or poverty and devastation if released from often brief captivity in the West. However, those wartime POWs who had been moved to Canada or the USA often took much longer to reach home and more than a year of labour service in post-war Britain was by no means uncommon. Some of the veterans who are cited here remained prisoners in either North America or the United Kingdom (or both) until 1946, 1947 and even on into 1948. Rudolf Miese, shot down over Britain in November 1940 and badly injured, was repatriated later in the war, only to be taken prisoner a second time at the end of the war. Hans-Ulrich Kornstädt, who was shot down and bailed out over the Mediterranean in 1943 and miraculously rescued by a passing destroyer, was incarcerated for years in a French camp in the Sahara Desert; even if one managed to get out of the camp, the surrounding desert would have done for even the strongest man. He got back to a ruined Germany only in February 1948.

Once back home, or released after even longer and much harsher treatment from Russian confinement, returning prisoners found themselves often considered as pariahs and ex-officers were banned from most universities. No one was interested in the war or its veterans after 1945, a lack of regard which has lasted right until the present day. While all members of the German armed forces implicitly supported the war aims of a genocidal and murderous, oppressive Nazi regime through their wartime service, most were as brave and steadfast soldiers as those to be found in the ranks of the other side. Certainly, Hitler's SS, his *Einsatzgruppen* murder squads, the concentration camps and Holocaust were embodiments of prime evil, and not all 'ordinary' soldiers, sailors and airmen were innocent of these horrible activities.[84] Most of the fighter pilots fought a hard and clean war, however, and did not deserve their post-war relegation to a deliberately forgotten past in Germany. This book (and its two companion volumes)[85] attempts to present their side of the story, honestly and including discussion of contentious issues, and will hopefully stand as a realistic memorial for the many lives sacrificed and life-changing injuries (mental and physical) suffered by those who fought in the German fighter arm. Additionally, we hope it stands as a memorial to the enormous sacrifice of all sides in a terrible conflict.

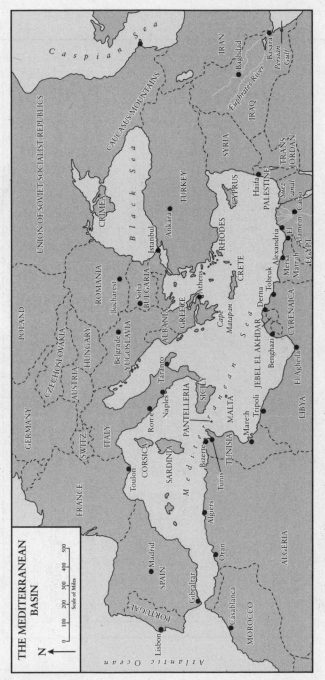

Mediterranean Sea and surrounding countries where various campaigns took place.

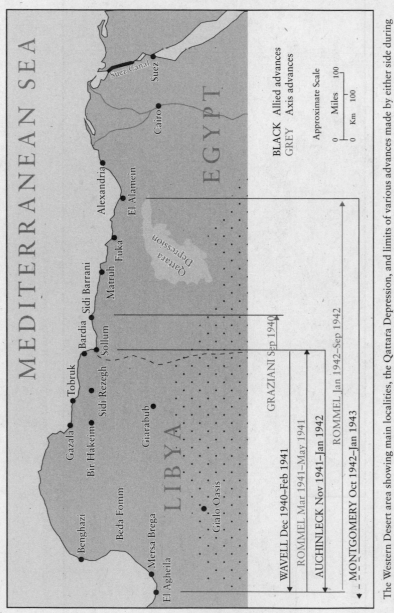

The Western Desert area showing main localities, the Qattara Depression, and limits of various advances made by either side during a campaign of almost 2½ years.

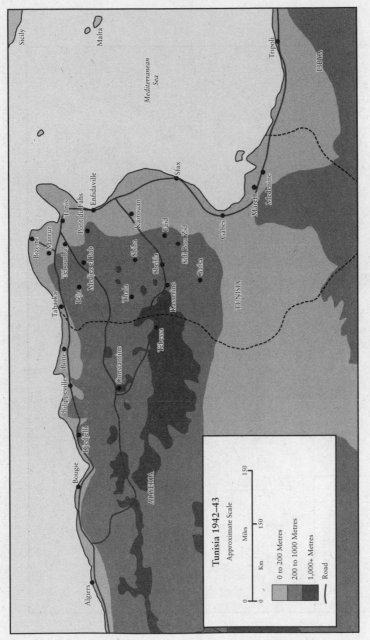

Basic map of Tunisia showing mountainous massif, main localities, as well as Malta and Sicily.

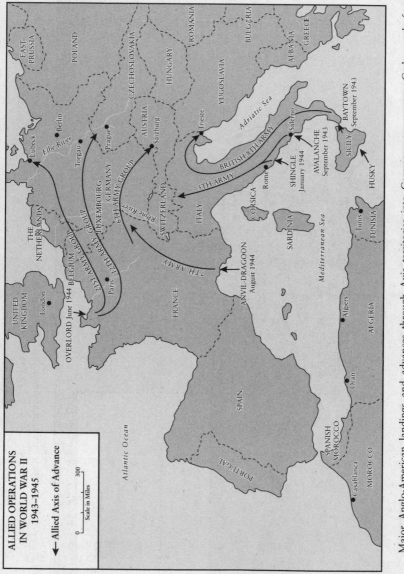

ALLIED OPERATIONS IN WORLD WAR II 1943–1945

← Allied Axis of Advance

0   300
Scale in Miles

Major Anglo-American landings and advances through Axis territories into Germany, 1943–1945. Code words for invasions/landings: Husky = Sicily; Baytown = toe of Italy; Avalanche = Salerno; Shingle = Anzio; Anvil/Dragoon = southern France; Overlord = Normandy.

I

THE BALKAN CAMPAIGN, APRIL–MAY 1941

The German invasion of the Balkans was not a planned campaign to begin with, and it was Mussolini's ill-considered invasion of Greece from his conquered Albanian base on 28 October 1940 that precipitated it. In retaliation the British occupied bases on Crete the next day (with Greek government agreement), thereby putting the strategically vital Ploiesti oilfields in Romania in range of British bombers.[1] The conquest of Crete was thus already on the German horizon by November 1940 and necessarily would have to be preceded by an invasion of Greece. The latter was planned to take place from Bulgaria into northern Greece,[2] and the addition of the British expeditionary force in Greece in late March 1941[3] just made this more inevitable. Such an invasion would outflank the major Greek forces which faced west/northwest against the Italians along the Albanian front. By the middle of March 1941, *Luftflotte* 4 in Bulgaria had assembled *c.* 400 aircraft, based at Bulgarian bases at Sofia, Plovdiv, Krumovo, Krainitzi and Belitza, which were to be utilised for the planned invasion of Northern Greece.[4]

Yugoslavia, which had joined the Axis alliance on 25 March 1941, was supposed to have supported this general military venture, but a coup ousting the pro-German government of the regent Prince Paul two days later forced a change of plan, and in late March 1941 *c.* 600 additional *Luftwaffe* aircraft were assembled on Austrian, Bulgarian and Romanian bases to counter a changed strategic situation.[5] These combined German aerial forces fell under the umbrella of *Luftflotte 4*.

Luftflotte 4 (Generaloberst Löhr) in the Balkans campaign; as at 5 April 1941[6] (reconnaissance, transport, army cooperation units not shown)

Under direct command *Luftflotte 4*, Vienna and south (eastern Austria):

Stab, I and *III/KG 2* (Do 17s)
III/KG 3 (Do 17s)
II/KG 4 (He 111s) (mainly mine-laying)
Stab, I, II and *III/KG 51* (Ju 88s)

Fliegerführer Graz (southeastern Austria) (*Kommodore StG 3*):

Stab/StG 3 and *II/StG 77* (Ju 87s)
Stab/JG 54, 5 and *6/JG 54, I/JG 27* (Me 109s)

Fliegerführer Arad (eastern Romania) (*Kommodore StG 77*):

Stab, I and *III/StG 77* (Ju 87s)
I/ZG 26 (Me 110s)
Stab, II and *III/JG 77, 4/JG 54* and *III/JG 54* (Me 109s)

Fliegerkorps VIII (south-southeastern Bulgaria) (*General* von Richthofen):

I/LG 1 (Ju 88s)
Stab, I and *III/StG 2, I/StG 3* (Ju 87s)
II/LG 2 and *10/LG 2* (*Schlacht* Me 109s and Hs 123s), *7/LG 2* (Me 110s)
II/ZG 26 (Me 110s)
Stab, II and *III/JG 27, I/LG 2* (Me 109s)

(In addition, *5* and *6/ZG 76* (Me 110s) served over Crete, while *III/JG 52* (Me 109s) stationed in Bucharest also became involved over Crete; briefly, *7/JG 26* (Me 109s) flew over Yugoslavia from its base in southeastern Italy. *III/ZG 26* (Me 110s) flew over Yugoslavia briefly, also from Italian bases.)[7]

Simultaneous assaults were thus to be made on both Yugoslavia and Greece, and these were launched on 6 April 1941. There were clear instructions from Hitler for the *Luftwaffe* forces ranged against Yugoslavia to destroy the Yugoslavian air force ground organisation as well as the capital city of Belgrade.[8] In general not much aerial opposition was expected over Yugoslavia and Greece, and thus fighter units utilised were those equipped with the Me 109 E, as opposed to the Channel-based *Geschwadern* by now operating the much improved F-model.[9] Opposing the *Luftwaffe* forces about to attack Greece was only weak opposition.

The Royal Hellenic Air Force itself, never strong or well equipped, had after months of fighting the Italians over the Albanian front been reduced to an effective 28 fighters and seven bombers.[10] The fighters were mostly Polish-built PZL P.24s along with British-supplied Gladiators. The British air forces in Greece were also weak, by the beginning of April comprising nine squadrons (Hurricanes, Gladiators, Blenheims and Lysanders) and two detachments of Wellington night bombers, together numbering less than 200 aircraft, of which only 82 were serviceable.[11] The RAF was to lose 151 of its aircraft over Greece, with 64 falling in combat and 87 damaged aircraft left behind; in return they claimed 164 victories against German and Italian opponents in the brief April 1941 campaign.[12]

The Royal Yugoslav Air Force was quite large and equipped with reasonably modern aircraft in the main, but these were from a wide variety of manufacturers and supplier countries: Britain, France, Italy, Germany, and their own indigenous aircraft industry, which supplied licence-built foreign as well as local designs.[13] Bomber and fighter aircraft were organised into two mixed brigades, one bomber and one fighter brigade, apart from minor forces directly under air force headquarters. Total aircraft available in April 1941 before the invasion (excluding communications, reconnaissance aircraft, seaplanes, trainers etc.) are given below:[14]

Fighters: 38 Hurricanes; 57 Me 109 E-3s; eight IK-2s and six IK-3s (good local design); one obsolete Avia; 30 obsolete Fury biplanes;
Bombers: 48 Blenheims; 54 SM-79s; 60 Do 17Ks.

In addition, during the fighting from 6 to 17 April 1941, Yugoslav workshops and factories were able to contribute an additional eight Hurricanes, six Do 17s, four Blenheims, two IK-2s, one IK-3, and one Me 109 E-3.[15]

Despite the total of Greek, Yugoslav and British aircraft numbers (effective frontline machines) being relatively high (*c.* 419), they were opposed by *c.* 1,000 German machines, with a cohesive German plan and full coordination among units as opposed to no plan and no cooperation between their various opponents. The latter Allies were quite simply rapidly over-whelmed by the *Luftwaffe*, and although they fought bravely, it was to no purpose in the end, except to cause casualties to the German air force. One interesting aspect was German Me 109 Es flying against Yugoslav-manned Me 109 Es.

Yugoslavia

The *Blitzkrieg* that descended on Yugoslavia at dawn on 6 April 1941 had all the ferocity and ruthless efficiency typical of a German invasion. Using their superior numbers in highly concentrated attacks largely on air bases and the capital city of Belgrade, they relatively easily overwhelmed the outnumbered defenders and were able to write off a considerable portion of the Yugoslavian air force on day one. *Fliegerkorps VIII* concentrated its attention on the 3rd Mixed Air Brigade in southeastern Yugoslavia, with dawn bombing and strafing attacks mainly by Me 110s and Me 109s on several airfields, which resulted in the effective destruction of a Fury squadron (11 shot down and one destroyed on the ground; eight aerial victories to I/LG 2 and three to II/ZG 26; II/LG 2 strafed the field), a Dornier wing (13 strafed and one shot down, 10 damaged on the ground), and an army reconnaissance squadron (16 aircraft strafed and destroyed by Me 109s).[16] This devastating opening assault was followed up by a second wave, of mainly Ju 87/Ju 88 attacks, with at least three more Me 110/109 strafing assaults during the rest of the day. During these, the 10 damaged Dorniers from the dawn raid were destroyed, as were 15 Dorniers of the second wing so equipped.[17] In return for these successes, *Fliegerkorps VIII* lost 14 aircraft (including seven Me 109s and two Me 110s) and the German army in the southeast another.[18] By the end of this first day, most of the Yugoslav aircraft in the southeast of the country had thus already been eliminated.

Soon after dawn on 6 April, Belgrade was subjected to a massive bombing attack by 74 Ju 87s (*StG 77*), 160 He 111s and Do 17s (*KGs* 4, 2 and 3), escorted by the Me 110s of *I/ZG 26*, the Me 109s of *Stab, II* and *III/JG 77*, and also *III/JG 54*.[19] They were met by 34 Yugoslav fighters, mostly Me 109 Es (and a few Hurricanes towards the end of the raid) of the 1st Fighter Air Brigade in the Belgrade region, who lost five shot down and seven seriously damaged for claims of 10 destroyed by the *JG 77* escorts; three further heavy raids on the Yugoslav capital followed, further depleting Yugoslav fighter defences and further devastating an already badly hit city.[20] *Oberleutnant* Günther Scholz, *Staffelkapitän 7/JG 54*, was struck by the weak anti-aircraft defences over Belgrade and remembered with some pathos providing conversion training to one of the aspirant Yugoslavian Me 109 pilots before the war.[21] In total the *Luftwaffe* claimed 19 Me 109s shot down over Belgrade and four other aircraft during 6 April 1941 (including three victories by *III/JG 54* and at least two by *I/ZG 26*); Yugoslavian losses were 10 fighters shot down and 15 damaged against a German loss of three bombers, four Stukas, five Me 110s and an Me 109.[22] The latter Me 109 was in fact shot down by ground fire flying over Croatia, as part of the *Stabschwarm* of *JG 54*, the pilot (*Oberleutnant* Otto Kath, adjutant of the *Geschwader*) managing a risky crash-landing into a river near the Yugoslavian-Austrian border, where he was lucky enough to be hauled out by a pro-German local sitting in a boat on the water nearby, who later delivered him through the Yugoslav lines to German forces.[23]

This incident raises a broader problem experienced by the Yugoslav people and their armed forces in resisting the invaders. This rather unique aspect of the Yugoslavian campaign was the divided loyalties of different parts of the country; in particular the inhabitants of Croatia, who were largely pro-German and anti-Serbian. Shortly before the assault on Yugoslavia began, *Major* Hannes Trautloft, the *Kommodore* of *JG 54* stationed at a base in the Graz area, learnt of an old Potez aircraft flown by a Croatian captain who managed to land on their airfield undetected in broad daylight; the man was a deserter and gave away valuable intelligence on air bases and flak defences in Croatia.[24] As a result, on 6 April, Trautloft led his four-man *Stabschwarm* in a low-level attack on one of the betrayed bases where they claimed seven aircraft destroyed on the ground and experienced only weak anti-aircraft defences, and no Yugoslav fighters at all. It was during this mission that the adjutant was shot down as related above.[25] With the fall of the Croatian capital, Zagreb, on 10 April 1941, Croat nationalist leader Ante Pavelić was able to declare a separate state, run by the Ustase movement, one just as fascist, genocidal (Jews, Serbs, Gypsies being their main victims) and dictatorial as the Nazi German regime.[26] In time Croat forces, including a fighter squadron later attached to *JG 52*, became operational on the Russian front.

Other major raids this first day included two devastating attacks by *II/StG 77* on army cooperation airfields that destroyed two squadrons.[27] The 1st Fighter Air Brigade around Belgrade had been hit very hard, but the 4th Bomber Air Brigade (equipped with Blenheims and SM 79s),[28] stationed essentially to the southwest of the fighters, was still largely intact. The Yugoslav Hurricane fighter units were also relatively unscathed, and the survival of both Blenheims and Hurricanes from the opening assaults on the first day might explain Erwin Leykauf from *8/JG 54*, replying to the question of whether there was much in the way of aerial combat with the Yugoslavian air force, with: 'Yes, with Yugoslavian Hurricanes and Blenheim bombers!' Günther Scholz was one of the *III/JG 54* pilots who scrambled against some Yugoslavian Blenheims which attacked their base later that day, hitting some of their aircraft on the ground, but losing a Blenheim to *Gruppenkommandeur Hauptmann* Lignitz.[29] The remaining Yugoslavian brigade, 2nd Mixed Air Brigade in the northwest of Yugoslavia, suffered some casualties from *Luftwaffe* units stationed in Italy on 6 April, including losses to *III/ZG 26* which strafed an airfield, destroying two Yugoslav SM 79 bombers and damaging three more.[30]

On the second day of the campaign, *Luftwaffe* attacks broadened in scope and in dispersion, but again with several devastating strafing attacks on training and army cooperation air bases. Army support operations were ramped up, while Yugoslav bomber formations mounted a number of attacks in their turn; two major air combats fell to II/JG 54, their 4th *Staffel* claiming four Yugoslav Me 109s in the Belgrade area (eight were actually shot down or seriously damaged), while 5th *Staffel* claimed six Blenheims from a formation of these bombers, five actually being lost.[31] By the end of 7 April 1941, almost 60% of the Yugoslav air force had been destroyed.[32] Only 10 days later, Yugoslavia surrendered.[33] Although the remnants of their air force fought bravely throughout, they never recovered from the devastating initial onslaught and the end was a foregone conclusion. Relatively few German fighter pilots experienced intense combat with the Yugoslav air force, and those that did were mainly from JG 77.[34] For many of the pilots of III/JG 54, ground attack and strafing missions are what they remember, along with some rather accurate shooting from some of their intended victims, as recounted below by *Leutnant* Max Clerico of 7/JG 54:

After the Battle of Britain came the Yugoslavian campaign; I had only one contact with enemy aircraft there, and flew mostly low level attacks against ground targets, very unpleasant encountering flak from quadruple light gun mountings! Finally, we relocated from Yugoslavia to eastern Germany. I had only the one aerial combat, I believe it was a Hurricane. Anyway, I gave him the works. Strangely enough the pilot made no attempt to manoeuvre out of the line of my fire and then dived into the clouds. Either the pilot was dead or completely apathetic, otherwise I believe I might possibly have been shooting past him the whole time! I had another unusual experience in Yugoslavia: we were making a low level attack on a light flak column (very unpleasant having to fly into the fire of 2 cm flak!). Then I saw to the side and about 50 m away a Yugoslav soldier standing, and aiming with his rifle at my aircraft. I gave him a tired little laugh, but then I heard the sound ('flop') of a bullet hitting my aircraft and I smelt fuel. He had actually put a bullet from his rifle right through my fuel tank 10 cm behind my back. One thousandth of a second slower (flying at 700 km/h in a low level attack), and he would have hit me in the throat! I am still grateful to him today (writing in 1994) that he did not succeed in this!

Known *Luftwaffe* fighter claims over Yugoslavia total at least 54: 30 falling to *JG* 77 (including *I/LG* 2), 16 to *II* and *III/JG* 54, at least six to *ZG* 26 and two to 7/*JG* 26.[35] The Royal Yugoslav Air Force had fought bravely, flying more than 1,400 sorties and claiming about 90 German and Italian aircraft shot down plus another *c.* 10 by flak defences.[36] German losses in the air numbered about 60 aircraft, at least 70 aircrew, the Italians losing another *c.* 10 machines, and the Hungarians six more; Yugoslav aircraft losses encompassed 49 shot down by the Axis air forces and flak (with many more damaged and beyond repair; aircrew lost numbered 27 fighter pilots killed and 76 bomber aircrew) plus another 85 aircraft destroyed on the ground by bombing and strafing.[37] Losses identified reasonably as directly combat-related (excluding operational accident losses) from the German Quartermaster General Loss Returns[38] total 44 aircraft (14 bombers, four Ju 87s, five reconnaissance aircraft, nine Me 110s, six Me 109s and six ground attack machines) of which 35 were lost in the first two days, after which the Yugoslav air force was a spent opponent.

Greece

While the units of *Fliegerkorps VIII* stationed in southern Bulgaria were available to fly over both northern Greece and Macedonia (southeastern Yugoslavia), much of their effort in the first few days went into operations in the latter area: amongst the fighters it was largely *II* and *III/JG* 27 that flew over northern Greece.[39] *Luftwaffe* losses over Greece from 6 to 12 April 1941 totalled 18 aircraft recorded in the Quartermaster General's Loss Returns, the only fighters lost being four Me 109s of *III/JG* 27 on the opening day of the campaign.[40] The latter combat is illustrative of the complexities of research into specific aerial engagements from the Second World War, or any other aerial conflict for that matter. Led by the redoubtable Squadron Leader M.T. StJ. 'Pat' Pattle, 12 Hurricanes of 33 Squadron bounced eight Me 109s of *8/JG* 27 over the Rupel Pass in Northern Greece in the early afternoon; Pattle himself claimed two Me 109s shot down, with a further three being claimed by his colleagues.[41] It is the losses to *8/JG* 27 that are something of a puzzle: the *JG* 27 history records *Staffelkapitän Oberleutnant* Arno Becker having been killed in this action and *Leutnant* Klaus Faber being shot down and taken prisoner west of Gefyroudi, and soon after two more pilots killed from *III/JG 27*, *Oberfeldwebel* Adolf Faltings and *Oberfähnrich* Eckard.[42] In the major history of the 1941 aerial fighting over the Balkans by Christopher Shores and co-authors, the first two losses of Becker and Faber are also recorded, along with *Oberfeldwebel* Gerhard Frömming who was wounded and crash-landed, seriously damaging his aircraft, while a fourth Me 109 was shot down as well, its pilot returning later on foot.[43]

The *JG 27* unit history also records Frömming being wounded on this day, but only in an appendix. Faltings was indeed killed on 6 April in his Me 109, at Belica-North airfield, but this aircraft belonged to the ground attack unit *II/LG 2* (clearly shown in the Quartermaster General Loss Returns) and not to *III/JG 27*, while *Oberfähnrich* Heinz Eckhardt (note different spelling to 'Eckard' in the *JG 27* history) was killed on this same day, but as a member of *I/LG 2*, over Yugoslavia.[44] The *Luftwaffe* Quartermaster General's Loss Returns[45] show four Me 109s of *III/JG 27* as being lost on 6 April 1941, with Becker killed, Faber missing, Frömming wounded (and his aircraft a 100% loss, not just seriously damaged) and with the fourth pilot also missing and shot down in the Gefyroudi area. Just to complicate things further, another source (Aircrew Remembered website)[46] has Adolf Faltings as having been shot down near Gefyroudi as a member of *8/JG 27*, and uninjured, and notes that Frömming was taken prisoner until his release in late April at the end of the campaign. It would appear, on balance, that *8/JG 27* thus lost four Me 109s shot down in this action against 33 Squadron RAF: Becker who was killed, Faber and Frömming who were taken prisoner, the latter wounded also, and a fourth pilot, not identified, who returned to his unit soon after on foot.

While one *Staffel* could be hammered in a single bounce and only a few minutes of combat, as happened to *8/JG 27* on the first day of the campaign, pilots in another *Staffel* from the same *Gruppe* never saw any enemy fighters during the fighting over Greece. Losses to enemy flak were a cardinal part of the Balkan operations for the German Me 109 and Me 110 pilots, and *Oberleutnant* Erhard Braune, *Staffelkapitän 7/JG 27*, also remembers captured British equipment very clearly: 'In the Balkan campaign there were hardly any combats with fighters from the British expeditionary corps – at least I cannot recall any. We flew Stuka escorts, free chases without meeting the enemy, and low level attacks. A low-level attack on the airfield at Tanagra (on 20 April 1941)[47] cost my *Staffel* its only loss of the campaign. Another memory of the Balkans: lots of captured materiel from the British stocks, for example outstanding tropics-style tents of a quality we had not ever seen before.'

With the core of the Yugoslavian air defences largely defeated in the first two days of that campaign, and following the surrender of Yugoslavia on 17 April 1941, a concentration of *Luftwaffe* units was rapidly assembled in Bulgaria and Macedonia by about the middle of April, to finish off the next victim, Greece: this comprised five *Gruppen* each of bombers, Stukas, Me 109s (II and III/JG 27; I/LG 2, II and III/JG 77) and two Me 110 *Gruppen* (I and II/ZG 26).[48] *Stab*, II and III/JG 54 remained behind in the Yugoslavian area.[49] From 13 April *Luftwaffe* activity over Greece intensified, and on this day a complete formation of six Blenheims was shot down by *Hauptmann* Hans-Joachim Gerlach, *Feldwebel* Herbert Krenz and *Unteroffizier* Fritz Gromotka of 6/JG 27; three other Blenheim raids during the day remained unscathed due to a Hurricane escort, but none was available for this lost formation.[50]

RAF and Greek aircraft had little chance for organised activity in Greece once the Germans concentrated on that country after the defeat of Yugoslavia: strafing attacks mainly by Me 109 units were common and created havoc. As examples, on 15 April Larissa was strafed twice and up to 14 Hurricanes may have been lost, while on 19 April, 18 out of 21 Greek fighters were destroyed on their field at Amphikia/Lodi by strafing Messerschmitts.[51] Also on 19 April 1941, there was a combat between seven Hurricanes from 33 Squadron RAF, again led by Squadron Leader Pattle, and five Me 109s, three from 8th and two from 9th *Staffeln* of JG 77.[52] South of Lamia, the two formations met literally head-on as they followed the curves of a deep valley at relatively low level;[53] there was thus no advantage of height or ambush to either side and opposing numbers of aircraft were close. The two small fighter formations flashed past each other with only a few opening fire as they did so, and thereafter dogfights erupted all over the sky: Pattle claimed two Me 109s and his pilots another two.[54] The *Staffelkapitäns* of both 8th and 9th *Staffeln* were shot down, *Oberleutnant* Armin Schmidt of the latter unit being killed, while *Oberleutnant* Kurt Ubben force-landed behind enemy lines and managed to get away, later being rescued by a Fieseler Storch aircraft which landed in a Greek village.[55] A third Me 109 was damaged and belly-landed at Korinos airfield;[56] 33 Squadron lost one Hurricane whose pilot was killed with another two damaged, which nevertheless managed to force-land at airfields.[57] Kurt Ubben and *Leutnant* Schopper of *8/JG 77* each claimed a Hurricane shot down, as did *Feldwebel* Riehl of *9/JG 77*.[58] Honours were thus very even in this brief confrontation, attesting to the quality of the pilots on both sides. Despite the small numbers of aircraft involved in this action, both sides over-claimed, underlining how pervasive involuntary over-estimation of successes was in most combats.

Pattle is recognised widely as the RAF's most successful fighter pilot of the war, with a score probably somewhere between *c.* 40 and 50 claimed victories, but loss of British records during the chaotic Greek campaign makes clarification difficult.[59] Suffering badly from influenza and running a high temperature, Pattle was killed next day (20 April 1941) in a large and complex air battle over Piraeus harbour, when he dived into a melee of Me 110s to try and help a fellow pilot.[60] *5/ZG 26* claimed five Hurricanes in this action and may have been responsible for his loss; one each by *Hauptmann* Theodor Rossiwall, *Oberleutnant* Sophus Baagoe, *Oberfeldwebel* Hermann Schönthier, *Unteroffizier* Fritz Muller and *Oberfeldwebel* Theodor Pietschmann.[61] This final battle over the Athens area involved 15 Hurricanes from 80 and 33 Squadrons RAF (six would be lost with three pilots killed and three wounded) and large numbers of Me 110s, Ju 88s, Do 17s and Me 109s.[62] During the day the *Luftwaffe* claimed a total of 14 Hurricanes (five by *5/ZG 26* as noted above; four by *II/JG 27*, three of them by *Oberleutnant* Rödel and one by *Oberfeldwebel* Schulz; one by *Stab/JG 27*; the other four might have been claimed by the rest of *II/ZG 26*) while losing four Me 109s, three Me 110s, two Ju 88s and four Do 17s.[63] Most of this action took place over the Athens area. British Hurricane losses totalled eight shot down and one seriously damaged, with five pilots killed, for the day.[64]

Despite claiming three victories on this last day of intensive fighting against the RAF, *Oberleutnant* Gustav Rödel, *Staffelkapitän* 4/*JG* 27 stressed that support of the German ground and naval forces remained their prime duty over the Balkans. 'On the operations of my Geschwader (*JG* 27) in the Balkan realm it can briefly be said that we took part in the fighting to occupy Greece, Crete, Albania (*sic*, already occupied by Italy in April 1939) and Yugoslavia as part of *Fliegerkorps VIII* under *General* von Richthofen. The emphasis lay in supporting our land and sea forces.' While some Me 110 pilots in *ZG* 26 did experience air combat, as described above over Piraeus harbour on 20 April, many saw only missions flown against ground targets. *Unteroffizier* Josef Neuhaus remembered: 'With *ZG* 26 there followed (after the Battle of Britain) *Zerstörer* operations over the Balkans, specifically over Greece and Crete. The missions were almost exclusively low level attacks on ground targets, troops and their logistical support.'

Losses over Greece which can be identified reasonably as directly combat-related (excluding operational accident losses) from the German Quartermaster General's Loss Returns[65] total 82 aircraft (29 bombers, 14 Ju 87s, 10 reconnaissance and one weather reconnaissance aircraft, six Me 110s, 21 Me 109s and one ground attack machine). More than three quarters of these German losses post-dated the shift of *Luftwaffe* units from Yugoslavia to Greece, with 64 aircraft lost between 15 and 27 April.[66] Amongst the Me 109 pilots lost was *Hauptmann* Franz-Heinz Lange, *Gruppenkommandeur* II/*JG* 77, who fell to flak in the Athens area on 23 April.[67]

On 23 April 1941, all three *Gruppen* of *JG* 77 (including I/*LG* 2) attacked Athens on a day marked by the departure of the last RAF aircraft from Greece; in the evening of the next day evacuation of British troops from Greece's southern coast began, an operation which was completed by 29 April with the loss of five transports and two destroyers to *Fliegerkorps VIII*'s aircraft.[68] Amongst the fighter units it was particularly 7/*JG* 77 that was involved in attacking ships of the evacuation fleet, and its *Staffelkapitän Oberleutnant* Wolf-Dieter Huy was the star fighter-bomber performer, hitting two transports on 25 April and two more on 27 April.[69] One of his pilots, *Leutnant* Günther Schwanecke, distinctly remembers these missions: 'I was in the 7/*JG* 77 during the Balkan campaign (Yugoslavia, Greece etc.) but scored no victories there, as we were operating as *Jabos* (fighter-bombers, with 250 kg bombs), that is attacking shipping targets mainly.'

Invasion of Crete

Air forces assembled for the invasion of Crete included: 493 Ju 52s and 80 gliders (*Fliegerkorps XI*) stationed in southern Greece, supported by the Greek-based bombers of *I* and *III/KG 2*, *III/KG 3*, *II/KG 4* (mine laying unit) and the Italian-based *II/KG 26* (part of *Fliegerkorps X* primarily engaged against Malta), Ju 87s from the whole of *StG 2* plus *I/StG 3*, and fighters from *II* and *III/JG 77*, *I/LG 2* (Me 109s) and *I* and *II/ZG 26* (Me 110s).[70] In addition, witness statements make it clear that *5* and *6/ZG 76* as well as elements (only 9th *Staffel* probably) of *III/ZG 26* also flew over Crete. *III/KG 30* and *I/StG 1* were transferred in as reinforcements on 22 May 1941 to enable simultaneous attacks on both ground targets on the island and Royal Navy ships at sea around it.[71] With the exception of *II/KG 4* (directly under *Luftflotte 4* headquarters), the gliders and Ju 52s, and *II/KG 26*, these aircraft were grouped under *Fliegerkorps VIII* which had a strength of 180 (110 serviceable) bombers, 132 (101 serviceable) Stukas, 110 (84 serviceable) Me 110 fighters and 112 (97 serviceable) Me 109s, plus 40 reconnaissance aircraft at the outset.[72]

The attack on Crete was originally planned for 15 May 1941, but was postponed to 18 and then 20 May due to delays in the seaborne arrival of aviation fuel for the Ju 52s and its further transport inland to the bases of these aircraft. Preparations were also hindered by British air attacks, one on the night of 17 May by an estimated 15 twin-engined fighters destroying five and damaging 38 machines on fields around Athens.[73] Throughout the battle for Crete, *Fliegerkorps VIII* suffered from ammunition, fuel and particularly bomb supply shortages; most of this materiel had to be flown in by a separate set of Ju 52 transports.[74]

Attacks on the airfields and troops stationed on Crete began on 3 May and continued until the early morning of 20 May when the airborne landings began. Due to their low speed and the low dropping height for paratroopers, the transporting Ju 52s were extremely vulnerable to anti-aircraft fire and interdiction against this threat was a first priority, followed by troop concentrations and emplacements, and road communications.[75] Despite heavy attacks on the British anti-aircraft defences on the island, these assets were handled intelligently, as experienced by some of the Me 110 pilots. One of these was *Leutnant* Werner Ludwig, *III/ZG* 26 who described it thus: 'In May 1941 we were assigned to the conquest of Crete. We took off from Hauplia (Argos) in the Peloponnese, and flew three missions over Iraklion in Crete. On the first two attacks we had to put up with heavy defensive fire from light flak guns. By the third mission there was "heavenly peace"; not a shot was experienced. We had the impression that the English were lying doggo. Thus the resistance offered when the paratroopers landed on 20 May 1941 was that much greater.'

British fighter opposition on the island, a potentially lethal threat to the transport fleet, was soon removed by the *Luftwaffe*. On 1 May only six Hurricanes and 17 essentially obsolete machines were observed by German reconnaissance but two days later a total of 12 Blenheims, six Hurricanes, 12 Gladiators and six Fulmars was seen, mainly on Iraklion airfield, with lesser use of the other two fields, Malemes and Rethymon.[76] Only a few incursions of Beaufighters and Hurricanes appear to have been made into German airspace over Greece, but Cretan anti-aircraft fire was intense, particularly over Suda Bay, the only sizable harbour on the island's north coast.[77] On 18 May three bomber *Gruppen* made a heavy attack on this harbour, and intense attacks on the RAF aircraft on the three airfields were made on the same day, 15 aircraft being claimed destroyed on the ground. These attacks were such that the RAF was withdrawn to Egypt next day, prior to the assault of the airborne troops.[78]

There is, however, more to this story than generally appears in the history books. On 1 May 1941, the remnants of 33 and 80 Squadrons RAF evacuated from Greece counted, respectively, four Hurricanes and eight pilots, and four Hurricanes and three pilots at Maleme airfield (there were also some 112 Squadron Gladiators at Heraklion). The Maleme machines were grouped together as the 'Hurricane unit' and on 14 May Squadron Leader Edward Howell arrived at Maleme as the new commander of this motley crew, bolstered by the arrival of six fresh pilots (and machines) to replace weary veterans, followed by two more Hurricanes from Egypt the next day.[79] Although there were supplies of fuel and ammunition, there were neither spares nor maintenance facilities (and thus damaged aircraft were cannibalised), so their fate was effectively sealed anyway. On 18 May most of the ground crews were flown out by Sunderland and at dawn on the 19th, the remaining serviceable fighters, three Hurricanes and four Gladiators, flew out to Egypt.[80] The 'Hurricane unit' lost about 55 men and two pilots missing, as well as four pilots taken prisoner on Crete.[81] John Dillon's website[82] records the incredible story of S/L Howell's short combat career; on arrival (14 May) he was sitting in the cockpit of a Hurricane trying desperately to acquaint himself with its controls (never having flown one before!) when events overtook him as the other two serviceable Hurricanes scrambled and he took off as well, only to find himself pulling up into a formation of five Me 109s at low level who fired at him head-on. As if that was not enough, he was also struggling fiercely with the unfamiliar controls, to raise the 'undercart', switch on the gun site, close the hood and find coarse propeller pitch, and then he was in his first dogfight. Attacking two of the Messerschmitts he claimed one shot down and the other damaged, and was the only machine of the three to return to the airfield.[83] A large raid on Suda Bay on 16 May by *c.* 30 Ju 87s and Ju 88s escorted by 15 to 20 Me 109s was met by three Hurricanes (flown by Blenheim pilots from 30 Squadron) who, for the loss of two of their number (and both pilots), claimed three Me 109s shot down plus one more probable, as well as a Stuka probable.[84] Edward Howell claimed a further Ju 52 transport and a Ju 87 during five days of chaotic combats over the island but did not depart to Egypt when the last remaining serviceable fighters left on 19 May; instead he joined the infantry. He was seriously wounded on the opening day of the airborne landings and lay helpless in the open for several days before German paratroopers rescued him, and an Australian prisoner and surgeon saved his life with an emergency operation.[85] He was flown out to Athens and POW camp sometime later in a Ju 52 and, after recovering, made a successful escape via Turkey back to Egypt.[86]

The German account of Edward Howell's remarkable combat initiation on 14 May describes a strafing attack on Maleme by *Stab, II* and *III/JG 77*, a mass of about 60 Me 109s, on their first mission over the island.[87] Planning and leadership were poor, as they attacked into the early morning sun (rather than out of it), yet they claimed five aircraft destroyed on the ground, with four more claimed shot down, one each by *Feldwebel* Baumgartner, *Leutnant* Eichel and *Hauptmann* von Winterfeldt of III/JG 77, the fourth possibly credited to *Hauptmann* Henz of II *Gruppe*.[88] Two Me 109 pilots were lost: *Unteroffizier* Willi Hagel of 4/JG 77, killed despite bailing out, and *Gefreiter* Hans Gabler of 6/JG 77 who went missing.[89] III/JG 77 returned for a second strafing run over Maleme in the late afternoon, claiming a further three victims on the ground, but *Leutnant* Diethelm von Eichel-Streiber (nephew of *Gruppenkommandeur* von Winterfeldt) was hit by flak and was lucky to get back over the 160 km of sea separating Crete from Greece.[90] The strain of flying combat missions into the Cretan defences over such a long sea crossing would have been considerable, especially in a damaged machine.

Preliminary bombardment of the three airfields and planned paratroop landing areas early on 20 May was followed by the landing of the first wave, which lost only 1.4% of the Ju 52s used, and from 08h00 to 11h00 these Ju 52s returned to their Greek bases.[91] However, take-off of the planned second wave became increasingly disorganised due to the dry and dusty airfields, confusion related to crowded bases, and crash-landed returning Ju 52s blocking runways, and delays of up to three hours were experienced as this wave was despatched in dribs and drabs.[92] Coordination of the transport aircraft with operations of *Fliegerkorps VIII* was thus disrupted and by the end of the day none of the three airfields had been taken yet.[93] JG 77 lost five Me 109s to flak on this day, four pilots becoming POWs, including *Oberleutnant* Berthold Jung, *Staffelkapitän* of 5/JG 77.[94] Vicious fighting on the ground continued for several days as the Germans were gradually able to land more troops and weapons, until the British and Commonwealth defenders (mostly New Zealand and Australian troops), exhausted and continuously attacked from the air, were forced to retreat towards the southern coast. All the while, the wastage through combat, operational losses and just plain accidents to the Ju 52 transport fleet continued unabated, and daily operationally available machines dropped rapidly[95] – as can be seen from illustration number five, it was a near-run thing.

Only by 25 May was Maleme airfield secure enough for the first German fighters to land there and lend welcome local support: a *Schwarm* from *II/JG 77* put down there after lunch.[96] Despite the RAF having pulled out of Crete before the German airborne assault on the island began, there was significant air support offered from Egypt between 23 and 31 May 1941 (table below), even including two attempts to base a few Hurricanes at Maleme again.

Summary of RAF daylight operations over Crete, May 1941, operating from Egyptian bases[97]					
Date	Details of operation launched from Egypt	RAF Losses	RAF claims	German claims	German losses
23 May	Five Marylands, four Blenheims, two Beaufighters attack Maleme	One Blenheim	Ten Ju 52s on ground	Two Blenheims, by 2/LG2 and 9/JG 77	Six Ju 52s on ground
	Seven Hurricanes land at Heraklion, two briefly attack bombing Ju 88s	One Hurricane strafed		By Me 110s	
24 May	Six Hurricanes leave Heraklion for Egypt	Two Hurricanes missing, ran out of fuel			
25 May	Six Marylands, 22 Blenheims attack Maleme	3 Blenheims by Me 109s, one Maryland by AA		Four Blenheims (b) by II/JG 77	One Me 109 (a)
	One reconnaissance Maryland		One Ju 52		One Ju 52
	Three Hurricanes to land at Heraklion, two shot down, one crash-landed	Three Hurricanes	One Ju 88, two Ju 52s	Two Hurricanes (b), by 5/JG 77	Two Ju 52s

Date	Details of operation launched from Egypt	RAF Losses	RAF claims	German claims	German losses
26 May	Six Marylands, six Blenheims attack Maleme	One Maryland (c), two Blenheims (c) shot down, by Me 109s		One Maryland by 8/JG 77, two Blenheims by 6/JG 77	
	Eight Hurricanes attack transports, Maleme airfield	Three Hurricanes (d), one damaged (d) and force-landed Egypt	Six Ju 52s shot down, one on ground	Two Hurricanes by 6/JG 77 and I/LG 2	Four Ju 52s, two damaged and crash-landed
27 May	Six Blenheims to attack Crete				
	Two Hurricanes, one Blenheim to intercept transports		Two Ju 88s, one probable		One Ju 88
28 May	Two Blenheims attack Maleme				
29 May	21 Hurricane sorties over ships returning south of Crete, also some Blenheim and Maryland sorties over the ships	One Hurricane, message-dropping, Crete	One Ju 88	One Hurricane (e) by Stab/JG 77	One recce. Ju 88
30 May	30 Hurricane sorties over ships returning south of Crete, also some Blenheim and Beaufighter sorties over the ships		Two He 111s, one Ju 88		One recce. Ju 88, one Do 17, one He111 (f)

31 May	44 Hurricane sorties over ships returning or operating south of Crete, also total of 32 Blenheim, Maryland, Beaufighter & Fulmar sorties over the ships	One Hurricane missing (by Ju 88s or Me 110s?)	Three Ju 88s and one Me 110	Four Hurricanes (by Me 110s?)	One Ju 88, one Me 110 (2/ZG 26)
Totals (excludes ground losses)	At least 208 sorties	Six Blenheims, two Marylands, 10 Hurricanes	20 German aircraft	At least 18 RAF aircraft	15 aircraft

Notes: Above excludes all non-directly combat-related losses, which were considerable – for example, on 27 May, six Blenheims were lost in this way. Abbreviation: recce. = reconnaissance. (a) – *Hauptmann* Helmut Henz, *Gruppenkommandeur II/JG 77*, killed by Blenheim gunners from three shot down by his pilots with the loss of all nine crewmen; (b) – *Unteroffizier* Rudolf Schmidt, *5/JG 27*, shot down two Blenheims and one Hurricane; (c) – Maryland by *Leutnant* Emil Omert *8/JG 77*, Blenheims by *Oberleutnant* Walter Höckner *6/JG 77*; (d) – one Hurricane and the damaged claimed by *Oberleutnant* Höckner *6/JG 77* and *Leutnant* Fritz Geisshardt *I/LG 2*, one Hurricane fell to anti-aircraft fire and fourth was missing; (e) – by *Oberleutnant* Erich Friedrich, *Stab/JG 77*; (f) – He 111 *en route* to North Africa.[98]

On 27 May, *III/JG 77* was relieved by *III/JG 52*, transferred into southern Greece from Romania. Although they flew some ground attack missions the new arrivals saw no air combat over the island.[99] During four of the nights during this same period (28–31 May), the majority of the British troops were evacuated by the Royal Navy from the island, and by 1 June the battle was effectively over.[100] The Royal Navy suffered the loss of three cruisers and six destroyers in the battle for Crete, with numerous other ships damaged, including two battleships and a carrier: in the entire Balkan campaign the British lost 44 transport vessels.[101]

German losses in the invasion of Crete were staggeringly high: 3,674 dead and missing, 2,504 wounded paratroopers and air-landed troops as well as further casualties amongst the Ju 52 and glider crews, comprising 185 dead and missing and 90 wounded; 151 Ju 52s were destroyed and 120 seriously damaged out of the force of almost 500 such transport aircraft engaged.[102] The effect on Hitler was even more important as he never risked his airborne troops again in a major air landing operation, and this was particularly relevant to the planned invasion of Malta later on, which, of course, never took place. 28 German fighter claims during operations over the island, all by *JG 77* (including *I/LG 2* as its third *Gruppe*) have been traced,[103] but those of the Me 110-equipped units are not known; 12 aircraft were claimed destroyed on the ground,[104] although this total appears too low.

German aircraft losses at Crete identified reasonably as directly combat-related (excluding operational accident losses) from the German Quartermaster General's Loss Returns total 184 aircraft (24 bombers, 11 Ju 87s, seven reconnaissance aircraft, 24 Me 110s, 20 Me 109s, one ground attack machine, one marine aircraft, and 96 Ju 52s). The much greater total Ju 52 losses given above reflect operational (mostly) and ordinary accidents in addition to directly combat-related losses. The 92 Ju 52 combat losses suffered during the landing operations (20–28 May 1941) are ascribed in the 'Returns' to the following causes:

Artillery fire on ground – 13
Enemy fire *('Feindbeschuss')* – 28
Anti-aircraft fire – 12
Crash-landing with combat damage – 11
Unknown – 8
Bombed on ground – 11
Fighter combat – 1
Other causes – 8

One other mission fell to the *Luftwaffe* during the Balkans campaign, supporting the Arab rising in Iraq against the British occupying forces, as briefly described by *Feldwebel* Joachim Robel of *6/ZG 76*: 'In 1941 we took part in the Balkan campaign, up till the occupation of Crete. One *Staffel* (4/ZG 76) moved to Iraq, flying via Rhodes and Aleppo (Vichy French Syria) and in Iraq supported the rising of the Arabs against the British. The venture however was not a success and they were defeated. The main fighting in the Balkan campaign was over Crete. Here our main tasks were to support the paratroopers by low level attacks on ground targets.'

An Operational Side-Show: Iraq, May 1941

This brief and relatively small-scale campaign (impressively detailed by Christopher Shores[105] on which source this brief account is based) resulted from a *coup d'etat* in Iraq which brought a pro-Axis leadership into power. It led to hostilities (begun on 18 April 1941) between Iraqi forces and British forces in the country (soon followed by more from outside), particularly at the large RAF base at Habbaniya, west of Baghdad, which suffered a siege and saw desperate action by local ill-equipped RAF forces. The poorly equipped Iraqi air force put up a lacklustre performance and was virtually destroyed by the British, and some weeks later small numbers of German aircraft were dispatched to help the Iraqis, comprising 14 Me 110s (the full complement of 12 aircraft of 4/ZG 76 and two from ZG 26), five of seven He 111s of 4/KG 4 which actually arrived, 20 Ju 52 transports, a few Ju 90 large transport aircraft, and minimal technical support staff.[106] These began arriving on 11–12 May 1941, flying into bases in northern Iraq; by 31 May all fighting between the RAF and the new Iraqi regime and its German supporters was over. Action had mainly encompassed raids on each other's bases with British attacks also being made into Syria, through which country the Germans had their aerial supply route; the He 111s bombed Habbaniya once and most attacks on British airbases and troops were performed by strafing Me 110s. Most aircraft casualties to both sides were also on the ground, with only limited aerial combat between the Me 110s and British Gladiators and Hurricanes; all the German Me 110s and He 111s were either destroyed or abandoned damaged and left behind.[107] *Leutnant* Martin Drewes, one of the few remaining witnesses from the erstwhile 4/ZG 76 provided an account to the author of this short-lived campaign, detailed below:

The operations of the 4th *Staffel* of *Zerstörergeschwader 76* (part of the *Haifischgruppe* – Shark's Mouth *Gruppe*, *II/ZG 76*) with 12 aircraft in Iraq was tough. Firstly, not all

12 aircraft made it. One crashed in Palmyra, a second crashed while landing in a sandstorm in Mosul, and a third landed in the sandstorm at Mosul on one engine, perfectly, but we had no spare parts; however, we were happy that we could at least cannibalise the two damaged aircraft in Mosul for spare parts. Our operations were directed against the air base at Habbaniyah and against vehicle columns on the Rutba-Baghdad caravan route. I have no records from this time and have thus not written a book about these experiences. Today (writing in September 1990) only three crew members are still alive as far as I know: Franz Eisenach (*Oberstleutnant* retired, *Bundesluftwaffe*), Dr Leo Baro (in Canada – he was a radio-operator/air-gunner) and myself, here in Brazil. Bernd Philipp Schröder wrote a book, *Irak 1941....* but it is full of mistakes and describes only the experiences of the one group of three aircraft during their few operations. Our group (also three aircraft) flew many more operations and after receiving new machines in Athens, returned to operations in Iraq and in Syria (flying from Aleppo). Many have written of what occurred in Iraq behind the curtains. For myself, I was in contact with the Grand Mufti of Jerusalem (he was in Berlin), with the ex-minister president Rashid Ali El Gailani and with the ex-minister of war Fawzi al-Kaukiji, and met them occasionally in Berlin. Fawzi was an interesting man, and as an officer in the First World War on the German side (in Turkey), he was awarded the Iron Cross First Class, Legion d'Honneur etc; he was sentenced to death more than once and pardoned each time – a courageous man.

2

WESTERN DESERT, FEBRUARY 1941–JANUARY 1943

The campaign in the Western Desert began with the move of elements of the first *Luftwaffe* units to Tripolitania in January 1941, together with the first troops of General Rommel's *Afrikakorps*; the first *Luftwaffe* aircraft was lost on 15 February 1941 and the first victory claimed (by *III/ZG 26*, the first fighter unit to reach Africa in January-February) on 19 February 1941.[1] In April 1941, Me 109s of *JG 27* started to arrive, their first victory being claimed on 19 April.[2] German fighter units and the approximate dates of their service in the Desert are listed below; these dates are approximate as individual *Staffeln* and the *Stab* making up a full *Gruppe* tended to arrive and depart over several days; ground elements might take much longer to catch up with their flying elements, or might precede them.[3]

Stab/JG 27	10 December 1941 to 13 November 1942
I/JG 27	21 April 1941 to 2 October 1942
II/JG 27	24 September 1941 to 6 December 1942
III/JG 27	6 December 1941 to 12 November 1942
III/JG 53	8 to17 December 1941 and 24 May 1942 to 27 October 1942
7/JG 26	14 June 1941 to 24 September 1941
III/ZG 26	February 1941 to November 1942[4]

Individual *Staffeln* of III/ZG 26 moved freely between the Desert and Tripolitania, Sicily, Greece/Crete: periods in Tripolitania-Libya-Egypt as follows: 7/ZG 26 December 1941 to 5 August 1942; 8/ZG 26 13 February 1941 to December 1941, 22 February 1942 to 21 March 1942, and 24 May 1942 to November 1942; 9/ZG 26 June 1941, November 1941, and 24 May 1942 to 5 August 1942.[5]

JG 27 was thus the main 'African' *Geschwader* and made claims for 1,166 aerial victories during their campaign there, for the loss of 37 pilots killed, 25 missing and 27 POWs (air combat losses were 20 killed, 23 missing and 26 POW, flak victims being two killed, two missing, one prisoner; the balance were lost to operational accidents, enemy raids etc.).[6] Comparative figures for *III/JG 53* were 113 victory claims for 11 pilots killed, seven missing and three POWs (those lost to air combat were five dead, six missing; flak accounted for one killed and one missing pilot).[7] 7/JG 26 claimed 14 victories for no losses.[8]

The rather gypsy-like movements of units was very typical of *Luftwaffe* Mediterranean operations, as recalled by one of the veterans of *III/JG 53*, *Oberfeldwebel* Alfred Seidl of 8th *Staffel*: 'November 1941, we move to Catania in Sicily. In December, a further move, to Africa, for the protection of Benghazi. In air combats with English bombers I am lightly wounded. Then, we left our aircraft behind (for *JG* 27) and flew back to Sicily in transport aircraft. After operating over Malta, we returned to operations in Africa in May 1942. In August for some weeks I was *Staffelführer*, as an *Oberfeldwebel*. On 30 September 1942, I had to bail out and was seriously wounded. From a hospital in Marsa Matruh I was taken to Bari in Italy in another hospital ship; after that it was a hospital train to Rosenheim and at the end of November 1942 to Munich. After recovery, at the end of February 1943, I went back to the *III/JG 53* in Sicily, at San Pedro.'

This report of Alfred Seidl underlines an important difference in policy between the *Luftwaffe* and the RAF; German fighter pilots tended to remain tied to one specific unit for very long periods, while the British almost always shifted their pilots to new units after a tour, injury or wounds. A strange new world awaited the German pilots in North Africa; few had any experience of the continent or notions of the rigours ahead in this harsh setting.

More than half the victories claimed by *JG 27* fell to only 15 pilots, a typical performance by the *Luftwaffe*, with the incomparable Hans-Joachim ('Jochen') Marseille way out in front:[9]

Hans-Joachim Marseille*	151
Werner Schroer	61
Hans-Arnold Stahlschmidt*	59
Gustav Rödel	52
Gerhard Homuth	46
Otto Schulz*	42
Gunther Steinhausen*	40
Friedrich Körner	36
Karl-Heinz Bendert	36
Rudolf Sinner	32
Karl-Wolfgang Redlich	26
Ferdinand Vögl	25
Ludwig Franzisket	24
Karl von Lieres u. Wilkau	24
Horst Reuter	20

Four of the top seven aces died in the Desert (*) while Körner and Reuter became POWs.[10] Top ace in *III/JG 53* was Jürgen Harder on 16 claims, followed by Werner Stumpf on 15;[11] Joachim Müncheberg led *7/JG 26* with five claims.[12]

Several unique features characterised the aerial fighting above the Desert. Firstly, the typically parsimonious British only provided Spitfires late in the campaign with operational debut only on 1 June 1942.[13] Prior to that the Hurricanes and P-40s which predominated for much of the campaign in the Desert were outclassed by the performance of the Me 109s, E, F and G models, as recalled by *Oberfeldwebel* Josef Kronschnabel, *III/JG 53*. 'I flew over North Africa from May till August 1942. I cannot say much about the P-40 as an opponent, as I largely engaged them and shot them down while in pursuit of them (he shot down four P-40s there). The P-40 was also more manoeuvrable than our Me 109 and we avoided dogfights. We had the advantage that our aircraft were faster and we thus waited for other opportunities to make an attack. I may add that I was shot down by flak over Egypt on

31 August 1942. In autumn 1942 I was temporarily in South Africa in a prison camp at Pietermaritzburg (where the author resides) inland from Durban. Unfortunately I did not have the opportunity to see anything of the country, except for the inside of the camp.'

Jochen Marseille would become the top scoring German pilot of the entire war against the Western powers, and did this in the period from April 1941 to September 1942; he was described by no less a peer than Adolf Galland[14] as the 'unrivalled virtuoso' amongst the *Luftwaffe's* many aces. He is a very interesting person to study; much has been written about him, a good deal of it somewhat apocryphal as is normally the case for a person achieving legendary status. He will be discussed in some detail here and his true nature and unique flying and fighting abilities, repeatedly observed by many of his comrades, can perhaps better be understood through comprehension of the man himself, and through the contribution of *Luftwaffe* psychologist, or *'Selenspion'*, Dr. Paul Robert Skawran.

The Western Desert campaign was marked by a rich Commonwealth component amongst the RAF squadrons, particularly of South African units, as well as Australian squadrons, Free French, Greek, and others. While the Germans, as was their wont, concentrated on their top aces becoming established and shooting down as many victories as possible, their opponents put much more weight in strategic use of air power, especially of the medium bomber and in having squadrons manned by pilots where everyone would strive to fight and score within their abilities. Far too often in the *Luftwaffe* the accent on ace performance and success under-utilised the potential and real abilities of the 'ordinary' pilots; Marseille is a singular case in point, as his comrades tended to watch his flying and fighting, to guard his tail rather than establish themselves as effective cogs in the large strategic mill. The German failure to stop the RAF's medium bombers in the Desert was to prove a fatal one for the *Afrikakorps*.

The British achievement of air superiority and much more effective strategic application of air power was predicated on high losses to their fighter pilots flying aircraft of lower performance than the opposing Me 109s, until the arrival of the first Spitfires in mid-1942. Some very pertinent comments in this regard are offered by *Oberstleutnant* Edu Neumann, commander of *I/JG 27*, the first *Gruppe* to arrive in the Desert, and later the *Geschwader Kommodore* from 8 June 1942:[15] 'The English? Of all our enemies they were the hardest and also the fairest of opponents. Defensive circles were a necessity for the British fighters that were then in operation in North Africa, due to their inferiority to the Me 109. It was especially in the diving speed that the Me 109 was much superior, and thus when danger threatened could disappear downwards and then, having zoom-climbed to one side, attack from above once more. It is very difficult to shoot down an enemy aircraft from a defensive circle. Only *Hauptmann* Marseille managed this, all those who tried to copy him were themselves shot up or shot down. In any case, there were enough Spitfires, so that it was not necessary to have used the defensive circle – the English!' Henri Rosenberg, then a senior NCO in *9/JG 27*, echoed these sentiments: 'The Tommies in Africa were first class in their training, but unfortunately in the beginning technically inferior in their aircraft, also in the case of the Kittyhawk. The Me 109 was superior in its higher speed. We sped with high velocity through the large formations of fighters, shot one down and then pulled up and zoomed to begin a new attack. It was only Jochen Marseille who was able to take on dogfighting with success within such large masses of enemy machines. Shooting down an Englishman counted twice as much as shooting down a Russian amongst the German fighter pilots. The English and Australian pilots in North Africa were clever boys, also the Canadians. We often had those who were shot down and captured round to visit us so we could see how things were going.'

However, the Me 109 was by no means a perfect aircraft, nor one which could not be attacked successfully and shot down by skilled opponents. *Feldwebel* Gerhard Keppler, *1/JG 27*, had this to say about their aircraft: 'We spoke of the Me 109 as the "flying paving stone", and while it left something to be desired in being able to out-turn enemy machines, we laid emphasis on the possibility of letting ourselves "fall out of the fight", and then to use the power of our engines to place us in a favourable position again. Our *Staffelkapitän*, *Hauptmann* Ludwig Franzisket, was a much loved commander, who asked a lot of himself and was thus an excellent example to us. I learned a lot about flying from him. Günther Steinhausen was a comrade with whom I got on very well.

We lived in North Africa in the same tent and were thus together a lot of the time, so that a good friendship developed between us. He was open-minded, happy and always pleasant, but also very ambitious. This made him a good and aggressive fighter pilot, who had excellent flying control of his aircraft.' While the German strategic application of their fighter aircraft in the desert was poor, tactical leadership of *Staffeln* was generally excellent, and many of the top aces (although not Marseille, whose methods could not be imitated by others) were effective role models for new pilots, as described above by Gerhard Keppler.

Living conditions in the Western Desert added an extra element of hardship to the harsh realities of war.[16] Sandstorms and the persistent abrasive dust made engine life shorter than it already was in favourable climes; water was strictly rationed, food poor and never fresh, while the contrast between blistering hot days and freezing nights was compounded by swarms of flies.[17] *Oberfeldwebel* Heinrich Rosenberg of *JG* 27's 9th *Staffel* recalls an additional unpleasantness of the desert nights: 'In Africa our quarters were mostly somewhere in the desert, in tents, removed from the airfield to give some measure of quiet at night. The English "Desert Rats" however, came several times out of the night to lay explosives on the wings of our aircraft or attacked suddenly out of the darkness with heavy machine guns, decimating the already reduced machines available, caused by climate and desert dust, from the establishment strength of 12 machines to two-three-four per *Staffel*. A *Gruppe* which should have had 42 Me 109s was often only 12 aircraft strong.' It is interesting to note the negative effects on morale that the SAS (Special Air Service, then in its infancy) raids, inspired and led by David Stirling, founder of what has become a British institution, had; and this despite many failed raids as well. The 'Desert Rats' were in fact the famous British 7th Armoured Division.

A Detailed Log Book Record of Operations over the Desert

'Henri' Rosenberg persuaded his fellow desert pilot, *Feldwebel* Hans Fahrenberger of *8/JG* 27, to provide copies of a log book from this theatre, as his own was not available: 'Unfortunately I no longer have my log book from North Africa – it was lost in the flight from my house in Berlin, in the face of the advancing Russian army; before the war I had been a flying instructor there.' The Fahrenberger log book records flights from 1 April 1942 to 5 August 1942, detailing a total of 107 of his 116 *Feindflüge* in the Western Desert during Rommel's final advance, up to El Alamein (see graphic summary, illustration 12).

During this operational time in the Desert he flew 18 different individual aircraft, five from 8th *Staffel*, two each from 7th and 9th *Staffeln* and nine from the *Gruppe* not assigned to any specific *Staffel*. This underlines the shortage of serviceable machines in the desert for *JG 27*, and only very few pilots (the senior and very successful individuals) would have had an individual aircraft assigned to them. Fahrenberger had *Feindberührung* (combat; enemy met) nine times in the four-month period, seven of them indicated as with P-40s (numbers of P-40s engaged were only recorded for three of these events: two, five and 20). Fahrenberger was shot down and force-landed twice, both times by P-40s: 12 June 1942 and 16 June 1942. He claimed only one victory, a P-40 on 2 July 1942 for his seventh success (having scored six victories over Russia previously). Average mission duration is determined as 62 minutes (varied between 10 and 110 minutes). Average durations of different mission types (only where two or more were flown) were as follows:

Alarmstart (n=2)	41 minutes
Me110-*schutz* (n=5)	43 minutes
Aufklärerschutz (n=13)	57 minutes
Stukaschutz (n= 46)	63 minutes
Ju88-*schutz* (n=5)	66 minutes
Ju52-*schutz* (n=2)	68 minutes
Freie Jagd (n=23)	90 minutes

It makes sense that emergency scrambles (*Alarmstart*) were short (if no enemy met) and Ju 52 escorts longer (due to the slow speed of these lumbering transports). The Stukas were also slow and their flights were thus demonstrably only over the immediate battle lines and not deep into enemy territory as they were too vulnerable. The reconnaissance aircraft also had similarly short duration missions, even less than the Stukas, and were faster aircraft – again these escort missions can thus be deduced as only penetrating over battle line areas. Me 110 escort missions were even shorter, penetrating little into enemy territory (they were faster than Ju 88s). Ju 88 missions with their higher speed than either reconnaissance or Stuka aircraft were slightly longer, suggesting they flew a bit deeper into enemy territory. *Freie Jagd* (free chase) missions were the longest of all, and by a significant margin as well; one can well understand pilots enjoying these to the maximum duration as they offered the best chances for action from a favourable tactical position and potential victory claims as well. Missions flown per day for Fahrenberger varied between one and four (on active days – he did not fly on every day – viz. 107 operations in 126 days) – 32 days with one mission each, 20 days with two each, seven days with three each and four days with four missions on each.

From illustration 12, summarising Hans Fahrenberger's combat record over the Western Desert, it is clear that escort missions (*Schutz* in German) of various types dominated his flying: in four months of operations he only met the enemy 11 times (and had combat with them nine times), scoring one victory as against himself being shot down and force-landing twice. This suggests the possibility that some units and pilots were assigned more of the missions where chances to score were much reduced, and I put this question to some of the pilots who had flown in the Western Desert in *JG* 27. A spectrum of replies was received which are detailed below. Before giving these, it is perhaps fitting to provide some context for this point. The time period covered by Fahrenberger's log (1 April 1942 to 5 August 1942) was one of intense combat between the German fighters of *JG* 27 and *III/JG* 53 on the one hand and those of the British and Commonwealth squadrons on the other.

Victory claims for the German fighter units for this same period totalled 414 for *JG* 27 (one for *Stab/JG* 27, 195 for *I/JG* 27, 159 for *II/JG* 27, 59 for *III/JG* 27) and 61 for *III/JG* 53.[18] Examining the claims data from the relevant source in more detail, the top-scoring *Staffel* in this period was 2/*JG* 27 with 85 claims, followed by 3/*JG* 27 and 4/*JG* 27 with 61 claims each; however the latter

Staffel had begun severe over-claiming with proven falsification towards the end of the time under examination here.[19] In almost all *Staffeln* one or only a few ace pilots were responsible for the predominant proportion of the claims: 'Jochen' Marseille was top in the Desert campaign (*3/JG 27* – he claimed 49 of their 61 successes between 1 April 1942 and 5 August 1942), while three pilots in *2/JG 27* together claimed 75 of that unit's 85 claims for the period.[20] The *III/JG 27* pilots with only 59 nine claims for the period were far behind the other two *Gruppen,* but very close in their success to *III/JG 53*. Perhaps the fact that *III/JG 27* was the last *Gruppe* of this *Geschwader* to reach the Desert in late 1941 and thus had less experience of that theatre, as did *III/JG 53* also (served there 20 May 1942–27 October 1942),[21] might explain this at least partially. However, even for them, leading pilots dominated the claims: Henri Rosenberg of *9/JG 27*, one of the pilots quoted in this chapter, claimed nine of the 18 victories accredited to his *Staffel* for the 1 April to 5 August 1942 period.[22] *Feldwebel* Hans Fahrenberger's *Staffel,* the *8/JG 27* was the least successful unit in its parent *Geschwader* in the period examined here, having only claimed five victories between 1 April 1942 and the end of June 1942. Next day, Werner Schroer was transferred in from *Stab I/JG 27* to take over the unit as the new *Staffelkapitän,* replacing *Oberleutnant* Hans Lass. He rapidly changed the score, adding 20 victories of his own by 5 August 1942, to which were added two more by his comrades including Fahrenberger's only claim from the period covered in his logbook.[23]

Certainly (illustration 12), Hans Fahrenberger flew more Stuka escort missions than operations of any other type. *Oberfeldwebel* Heinrich Rosenberg, *9/JG 27* revealed that Stuka escorts were in fact fairly complex, multi-part affairs, with escort and free chase components. 'Escorts for Stukas, amongst our main tasks, consisted of four parts: (1) *Freie Jagd* ahead; (2) high cover; (3) direct cover; (4) *Freie Jagd* behind. The direct cover meant protection of the Stukas before any possibility of trying to get a victory, that means that one had to do your best to bring the Stukas home safely and rather forget about scoring victories; one was only allowed to defend, not shoot down. There were also other escort missions flown, for He 111s and Ju 88s, as well as for reconnaissance Me

109s over Alexandria and Cairo. Normally, these escort missions comprised direct escort only.' Although it is not clear from Fahrenberger's log book whether all Stuka formations escorted actually bombed or were sometimes intended as bait, some such missions might well have served to increase the chances of other German fighter pilots scoring while *III/JG 27 Staffeln* did the dirty work, as might be surmised from the view expressed by its *Gruppenkommandeur, Hauptmann* Erhard Braune, who led this unit for the entire period covered by the logbook.[24] 'The point of many a mission in 1941–1942 in North Africa can in retrospect be questioned. For example, the "bait tactic", when we approached the lines with a Ju 87 unit, when enemy fighters were to be lured into an unfavourable tactical situation, and where the Ju 87s were to turn back without dropping any bombs. Mostly, these were a waste of time; after the second such mission the enemy would have figured it out. More useful were escorts for supply ships (also for Rommel), but uselessly wasted fuel worsened the greatest shortage we had. The fuel barrel-carrying Ju 52s could not fulfil this requirement.'

However, another *JG 27* pilot of the time, *Oberleutnant* Rudolf Sinner (*Stab I/JG 27* and, from 4 June 1942, *Staffelkapitän 6/JG 27*), vehemently denied that any particular *Staffel* or pilot would have been assigned more or less of any specific mission type when reacting to my query about mission assignments not being equal for all pilots:

> Your classification of pilots into 'ordinary fighter pilots' and 'aces' ('*Experten*') is striking and prejudiced. Such a class structure of pilots or the supposed protectionism in mission assignments never existed. Experienced pilots obviously also flew escort missions, while green pilots also took part in *Freie Jagd* assignments. The leadership position in all the operational formations (*Rotte, Schwarm, Staffel* or *Gruppe*) was naturally filled by the most experienced flier available. Your presumption of frustration amongst pilots due to too many escort or other less glamorous assignments while '*Experten*' had many more opportunities to engage in combat and score victories, has no credibility, and in fact creates a false impression. What is true is that every '*Experte*' started

out as an 'ordinary frontline pilot' and only gained leadership duties in the air (which provided more opportunities to score victories) when he had assembled enough experience and had also proven himself in combat. The following extract from my own log book (same time period and same theatre of war) might show you that my comrade from *III/JG 27* (i.e., *Feldwebel* Hans Fahrenberger) whose record you quote, began in the same way as all who later might have become aces, with mission duties that were less exacting (I also was no absolute beginner when I came to Africa):

Comparison of mission types flown: pilots Fahrenberger and Sinner, *JG* 27, Western Desert		
Type of mission	Your example, *III/JG* 27 (Fahrenberger; period 1 April 1942–5 August 1942)	Sinner, *I/JG* 27 (period 19 June 1941–22 October 1941)
Escort missions	72	17
Freie Jagd	31	23
Other missions	7	70
Enemy contact	11	11
Victory claims	1 (in four months of operations)	1 (in four months of operations)

Your claim also that escort operations were 'frustrating' because they gave no opportunities to score victories is not justified, as demonstrated by my own victory claims in Africa: 32 victories, of which 16 were scored on *Freie Jagd* missions and 16 on other types of operation (of them, eight during escort missions, five from scrambles, three during armed reconnaissance assignments). The duty of the fighter arm was primarily to protect our own forces and facilities. To harm the enemy – say through shooting down his aircraft – was a secondary duty. Effective escort seldom resulted in reward to an individual, but was in no way less valuable than the shooting down of an enemy aircraft, which could bring fame to an individual in time! The only ones getting frustrated in this connection, in my view, are those – unfortunately much in fashion – who regard our fighter arm as a bloody theatre that was intended to give opportunity to an ambitious clique to play the roles of heroes. You thus see how problematic it is, from second-hand information like documents and witness viewpoints (that are often decidedly false or prejudiced), to reach logical conclusions or to compile meaningful interpretations.

With that, the author of this book was thoroughly put in his place! While in no way wishing to denigrate the views of a brave and successful fighter pilot (who ended the war as a *Major* with 39 victories, and in command of *III/JG* 7 flying the Me 262), it must be said that the two time periods (1 April 1942 to 5 August 1942 for the Fahrenberger log book, 19 June 1941 to 22 October 1941 for Sinner) are not readily compatible, the tempo of operations for the former period being much more intense.²⁵ For the 1 April 1942 to 5 August 1942 period covered by Fahrenberger's log book, Sinner in fact scored 17 victories, 16 of them after he had taken command of *6/JG* 27. Rudolf Sinner's valuable views should also be taken with those expressed by Henri Rosenberg and Erhard Braune; a more balanced view is perhaps offered by a fourth participant, *Feldwebel* Gerhard Keppler, flying in *1/JG* 27 at the time. 'I believe that one can compare a fighter *Staffel* on a fundamental level with a soccer team. Such a team needs not only good attacking players, but also middle field players and defenders. There were people in fighter units who were very good shots; naturally these were appropriately assigned to duties where their talents could best be applied, while others had to take over the lion's share of the escort duties. I myself flew many missions in Africa as '*Katschmarek*' (wingman) of *Staffelkapitän* Franzisket; he shot down enemy aircraft, I guarded his tail. One must thus see many victories as the result of teamwork. In addition, I flew a lot of low level attacks and fighter-bomber missions. The mission assignments were certainly thus divided up according to the capabilities of the individual pilots.'

Death of a German Ace; Demise of a British General

Despite having spent some months on the Russian Front before arriving in Africa, *Feldwebel* Henri Rosenberg of *III/JG* 27 was shocked by the stark realities of the consequences of war when he met an old comrade while on his way to the new theatre. 'Erbo Graf von Kageneck was *Staffelkapitän* of the 9/JG 27 and I was with him in Russia in 1941. He was a youthful and enthusiastic pilot, as we all were in those days. He was a hero, if one can be allowed to use such an expression. Sadly in Africa on 24 December 1941, in the afternoon on Christmas Eve, he was shot down by "Killer" Caldwell from Australia in a completely unconventional way. The Australian merely pulled his Kittyhawk vertically onto its tail and shot straight up into the *Schwarm* of Me 109s flying past above him. In this way Erbo was badly wounded in the genitals and lower body. He died later in Naples; perhaps he also helped in this, as he could not easily face his future as an emasculated man. I was stuck with my aircraft in Athens after a stone had damaged my propeller (on his way to North Africa, where his *Staffelkapitän* had preceded him) when I saw him for the last time in a transport aircraft being evacuated, a completely broken man and one marked for death. This was a great shock to me as a "young" fighter pilot. Up to that stage I had not yet flown any operations, as I had been wounded on the ground in Russia during the advance, in a swampy area. During my honeymoon world tour in 1978 I met Caldwell in Australia; later August Graf von Kageneck, Erbo's brother, wrote to me and asked for Caldwell's address. Caldwell then wrote to August and gave him an account of what happened, including an excerpt from his logbook.'

Sometimes a supposedly minor action of a single pilot can have significant consequences. *Oberfeldwebel* Emil Clade of 5/JG 27 was actually responsible in a way for the appointment of the famous General Mongomery to command of the British 8th Army in the Western Desert, as he admits with wry humour in the account below. His role in the events described has not been included in several of the previously published accounts:

In the unit history of *JG 27*[26] and in the Shores/Ring book *Fighters over the Desert*[27] the shooting down of Lieutenant General Gott is described. My name is not mentioned in these accounts, but I can tell more about this event than is written in those sources. On 7 August 1942 I had the mission of flying *Freie Jagd*; I was flying with my *Schwarm* at 6,000 m over the airfield of Burg el Arab when I saw a twin-engined machine below me starting to take off. It took an approximate course for Cairo. I waited until the aircraft was far enough away from the base, then I dove 6,000 m, still maintaining wireless silence as the Tommy listened to our signals, and attacked the Bombay aircraft. The crew was totally taken by surprise, as the rear gunner's position was unmanned. After the first short burst of fire, due to my much higher speed I could only manage a short burst, the Bombay pilot cut his throttles and landed in the desert. While the aircraft was still moving, the passengers jumped out of the machine. Once it had stopped moving I told my wingman *Unteroffizier* Schneider to attack and burn the force-landed aircraft; on the way home I told him that the victory belonged to him, in order to motivate him. Naturally thus the name of pilot Schneider was recorded in the war diary of *III/JG 27*. We did not have the shared victory practice as applied in the RAF. About an hour after landing I learned from our headquarters that the newly appointed commanding general Gott was killed in this combat. The only living (in April 1990) witness to this event is Gerhard Holzhauer, retired *Oberst* resident in Oldenburg. The successor to Gott was the well-known Montgomery and he then chased us back to Tunis. Seen in retrospect, this victory was a mistake on my part.

Hans-Joachim Marseille: A Controversial, Much Discussed Personality Re-evaluated

An awful lot has been written on Marseille. He is often portrayed as an almost serial womaniser, a drinker, an anti-Nazi, and is described as turning up late for parades during basic training, with a disciplinary history of excessive proportions.[28] A young and as yet unknown *Luftwaffe* recruit allowed to get away with such behaviour without getting thrown out of flight school is hard to imagine. That he was a young, lively and typically bohemian youth from Berlin[29] can hardly be doubted, as this is supported by almost all sources on his life and character. However, his family had some rather strong Nazi connections. His father, who left the German army after the First World War, became a policeman and, having reached the rank of *Oberst* by the mid-1930s, transferred to the army once more, later rising to *Generalmajor*. He was killed fighting partisans on the Eastern Front in January 1944 as commandant of a garrison behind the German lines.[30] The connections between the German police, *Gestapo*, the *Einsatzgruppen* who massacred the Jews in the East, rear area security troops (generally active as anti-partisan units) and other Nazi institutions are well known. Marseille's stepfather, Carl Reuter, in whose house he grew up, was an early Nazi Party member from the 1920s, later joined both SA (*Sturmabteilung*, or 'Brown Shirts') and SS, and served in various political functions, culminating in being a Nazi member of the *Reichstag* (cf. parliament) from 1933 to 1936.[31] After this his trail becomes faint but he appears to have become active in police circles. As a typical teenager, and one growing up with an absent father and living with a stepfather, Marseille would almost certainly have rebelled anyway against paternal authority, the 'Party' and the establishment as it then was: this would not necessarily imply that he was a convinced anti-Nazi.

That some fellow pilots would have been jealous of Marseille goes without much explanation. He was very gifted as a pilot, had outstanding eyesight, extraordinarily fast reactions, and was an outstanding shot in the air; allied to this was the bumptious behaviour of an immature youth seeking his place in a harsh wartime world. Being outspoken, disrespectful to his elders, and boastful are hardly unusual traits in a youngster who joined the *Luftwaffe* at 18. The young pilot who drank, and often to some excess, is far rather the norm than the exception, as applies to all nations in the Second World War. Fighter pilots were also singled out as objects of admiration and attraction to females, and most of them happily embraced these enhanced chances of romantic success; again, Marseille does not stand out as a 'bad boy' in this regard either. As to his disciplinary record being very poor, what documentation has so far been made public does not support this. It is perhaps pertinent to examine his early record in this regard, culminating in two official evaluation reports on Marseille written by his immediate superiors during and after his first exposure to combat in the Battle of Britain.

He joined the *Luftwaffe* on 7 November 1938 as a *Flieger* for his stint of basic military training, followed by a move on 1 March 1939 to *Luftkriegsschule* 4 for basic flight training. Regular promotions followed: on 13 March 1939 to *Fahnenjunker* (officer cadet), on 1 May 1939 to *Fahnenjunker-Gefreiter* and on 1 July 1939 to *Fahnenjunker-Unteroffizier*.[32] Having learnt to fly he was transferred on 1 November 1939 to *Jagdfliegerschule* 5 for fighter pilot training with simultaneous promotion to *Fähnrich* (officer candidate) and was given an 'outstanding' evaluation on leaving.[33] On 18 July 1940 he moved to *Ergänzungsgruppe Merseberg* for a final polish of operational-type training prior to a posting to an active fighting *Geschwader*.[34] Thus far there is hardly evidence for serious disciplinary offences – the promotions were regular and the path to an appointment as an officer open; his evaluation from the fighter training school would hardly have been 'outstanding' if he was such a disciplinary nightmare. He was posted to *I/LG* 2 on 10 August 1940 and actually arrived there on 12 August, joining 1st *Staffel* as wingman to an experienced old sweat, *Oberfeldwebel* Goedert.[35] His first operation followed the very next day;[36] no soft introduction to the harsh reality of war and aerial combat, and the Battle of Britain was no picnic for a green beginner, not from either side. Not only did Marseille manage to survive the very dangerous introduction period to war flying (which accounted for so many pilots in all air forces, theatres and campaigns of the Second World War and beyond), he also started to score victories, showing a built-in and natural talent for aerial combat, albeit one as yet rather rough around the edges, with almost as much loss caused to the *Luftwaffe* as the RAF: first victory on 24 August 1940; second on 2 September over a Spitfire but his own aircraft was damaged and he crash-landed near Calais-Marck, 50% damaged; Iron Cross 2nd Class (EK 2) awarded on 9 September; another Spitfire claimed on 11 September 1940 for his third victory, but again his own aircraft was damaged in combat and he force-landed near Wissant, his Me 109 being 75% damaged and a write-off; a Hurricane claimed on 15 September and a Spitfire on 18 September 1940 were his 4th and 5th victories; awarded EK 1 on 17 September 1940.[37] On 23 September he was shot down after combat near Dover and bailed out into the Channel, being rescued by a German floatplane and requiring a brief stay in hospital to recover; a Hurricane was claimed for his 6th victory on 27 September and next day he had an emergency landing after engine failure, near Theville; a Spitfire on 28 September was his 7th success[38] – related to above emergency landing? He served in I/LG 2 till 30 September 1940, and apparently only three of his seven claims in the Battle of Britain were confirmed by the *Reichsluftfahrtministerium* (RLM).[39] A letter from his brother makes it clear what an impact his Channel bailout had on him and that a lasting fear of a repetition remained with him thereafter.[40]

In the first volume of the *JG 77* unit history[41] are copies of two positive reports on Marseille. The one by his *Gruppenkommandeur Hauptmann* Herbert Ihlefeld, dating from December 1940 by which time Marseille was in 4/JG 52, praised his '*Rottenkameradschaft*' (his performance as a wingman) as outstanding and also described his later role as a *Rottenführer* as outstanding as well; Ihlefeld goes on to say he has a talent to handle any situation and perform the tasks assigned to him fully. The other evaluation, by his *Staffelkapitän Oberleutnant* Buhl of 1/LG 2, dated 6 September 1940, describes him as displaying good soldierly behaviour. Both reports praise him as a pilot and as intelligent and brave. Ihlefeld does mention his being seen as cheeky due to remarks he made which upset older comrades, which were ascribed to his free and open character. Poor discipline is not mentioned nor any problems with drinking, women, turning up late for missions etc. In fact, that Marseille was especially praised for being both a good wingman ('*Rottenkameradschaft*') and a good *Rotten*-leader speak for good flying discipline and a responsible attitude; similarly, it is significant that Buhl notes his good soldierly behaviour, hardly the sort of comment for someone with an inordinately long disciplinary record.

Marseille was posted to *II/JG 52* on about 1 October 1940 (but definitely in October 1940), apparently to the 4th *Staffel* of JG 52, led by *Oberleutnant* Johannes Steinhoff, later a major ace (mainly eastern victories) and a leading post-war General in the new *Bundesluftwaffe*.[42] In the text of the published version of an interview long after the war,[43] Steinhoff stated that Marseille was in his 4/JG 52 from just before the Battle of Britain, and criticised him for being involved with women to a degree that affected his flying and operations, that Marseille had no understanding of being a *Rottenflieger* (note the direct contrast with the two documented reports from superiors in I/LG2 who said exactly the opposite) and that he, Steinhoff, had to fire him, leading to his transfer to JG 27. However one needs to bear in mind that this interview was conducted decades after the war and human memory is fallible.

To balance what one might term a very typical description of Marseille's supposed peccadillos, some documentary data are available from the *Traditionsgemeinschaft Jagdgeschwader 52* website (www.jg52.net)[44] where two wartime documents dealing with the young Marseille's time in II/JG 52 are shown. One is a review of Marseille's service, character and suitability for promotion to the next rank (he was then an officer candidate, *Fähnrich*), and the second is an excerpt from the *Strafbuch* (literally, the disciplinary record for those serving in the unit) for 6/JG 52. Both documents are signed by the *Staffelkapitän* of 6/JG 52, *Oberleutnant* Resch, appointed to that position from 6 October 1940.[45] Marseille thus appears, firstly, to have been a member of 6/JG 52 and not of *Oberleutnant* Steinhoff's 4/JG 52, as also intimated in the unit history of II/JG 52;[46] secondly, he joined the 6th *Staffel* only late in the Battle of Britain. The *Strafbuch* contains all disciplinary infractions for an individual, including a copy of all those brought with the person from previous units. In the case of Marseille, there are only three infractions noted, all from early in his career while still in training:

(1) Strong reprimand for inappropriate answer to an instructor, and inappropriate behaviour which disturbed instruction, on 4 September 1939 – punishment dated 14 September 1939. At basic flying school.[47]

(2) Three days of simple confinement given on 17 November 1939, for taking a day of non-sanctioned leave during a cross-country/transfer flight – served on 21–24 November 1939. At fighter pilot school.[48]

(3) Five days of confinement to quarters for calling a *Fahnenjunker-Gefreiter* (lower rank than himself) '*Du duslige Sau*' (befuddled or stupid pig) on 10 February 1940; punishment given on 14 February and served on 15–20 February 1940. At fighter pilot school.[49]

These punishments can be graded in severity from the mildest (reprimand; *strenger Verweis*) through confinement to quarters (*Stubenarrest*) followed by the somewhat more severe simple confinement (*milder Arrest*); all fell within the purview of a commanding *Oberleutnant* or company commander who could impose them on senior NCOs, which included officer candidates (*Fähnrich*),[50] as Marseille was at the time of incidents two and three above. His rank for incident one was even lower. These are all mild offences, none of them necessitating a court martial;[51] and upon leaving the fighter pilot school where offences two and three above were recorded, he still received an 'outstanding' evaluation. Thereafter, no other disciplinary matters are recorded. Taken together, this is hardly the record of someone with a list of disciplinary offences as long as your arm. It would appear to be a case of part of the 'Marseille legend' bearing little resemblance to the truth as read from documentary evidence. *Oberleutnant* Resch, *Staffelkapitän 6/JG 52*, stated in his evaluation of Marseille on 11 December 1940, that he showed keenness to redress shortcomings noted in previous career evaluations, that he had a good attitude to his superiors, was comradely to the NCOs lower in rank to him as an officer cadet, displayed keenness in operations against England along with prudence and reliability; finally, Resch supported his suitability for promotion to the next rank (officer, *Leutnant*).[52] This is a very positive evaluation of Marseille and one which shows him to be serious and professional about his duties as a fighter pilot, and belies the cited comments of Steinhoff.

All of this raises the question, what had Marseille really done to earn the negative images of him and his behaviour, as a dutiful soldier, given from many post-war sources and quotes from former fellow pilots and superiors? Perhaps, once again, some facts might be pertinent. When Marseille was transferred from *I/LG2* to *II/*

JG 52, the move might have been to boost the latter unit rather than to get rid of a troublemaker; *III/JG 52* had a brief and dismal introduction to the Battle of Britain in late July 1940 where, over a few days, they lost several pilots including most of the leadership of the *Gruppe* and *Staffeln* and had to be withdrawn and posted back to Germany.[53] In addition, one of their shot-down pilots who was taken prisoner spilled his guts in no uncertain terms, as can be read from the very extensive report on his interrogation by RAF intelligence officers in Britain (so-called 'K report').[54] *II/JG 52*'s performance in the Battle of Britain was not much better: they flew missions on the Channel from 12 to 18 August 1940, were then withdrawn to Holland, returning to the Channel again on 20 September until 5 November 1940, followed by return to Germany for Christmas; back to Holland on 26 December 1940, and the Channel once again on 10 February 1941.[55] During the period 12 August 1940–10 February 1941 the *Gruppe* made 23 victory claims (approved at *Geschwader* level) and lost, in action, an equal 23 aircraft with seven pilots missing/killed, 12 POWs and two wounded.[56]

When Marseille was posted in to *II/JG 52* in early October 1940 he had seven victories which had been approved by his own *Geschwader* (four were not confirmed by the RLM, a not uncommon occurrence).[57] This gave him a higher score than any member of *II/JG 52* at that time. *Oberleutnant* Steinhoff, who was very critical of Marseille, as noted above, had four victories to his name at that stage and scored his 5th on 30 September 1940 and his 6th on 14 February 1941, a week before Marseille left *II/JG 52*.[58] It is distinctly possible that the young and rather brash youth, who only left his *Ergänzungsgruppe* in August 1940 to begin his career as a fighter pilot in *I/LG 2*, coming into a new unit in early October with a higher score than any pilot there, would have been rather resented, especially by the senior and experienced pilots of *II/JG 52* – after all, they, including Steinhoff, had been flying fighters for years and had seen action long before Marseille left training establishments. It is an alternative explanation for why Marseille was posted from *II/JG 52* so soon, and apparently under a cloud, to join *JG 27* in February 1941. However one interprets this further move, Marseille was posted to *I/JG 27* on

21 February 1941, immediately at the end of his leave, spent at home (from 16 January–20 February 1941).[59]

Marseille thus came to *JG* 27, which was to be the crucible of his meteoric career as a fighter pilot, and which likely further fired the heat of jealousies in some contemporaries and further enhanced the so-called Marseille legend, much of it greatly exaggerated, as already seen above. Within days of joining *JG* 27, Marseille was promoted to *Oberfähnrich* (senior officer candidate) on 1 March 1941. *I/JG* 27 were transferred to North Africa in April 1941, after a very brief Balkan mission, and soon after arriving in Africa while flying from Tripoli on 20 April 1941, Marseille had an engine failure on the way to the front line base and force-landed, his Me 109 being 35% damaged.[60] These same sources allow a brief reconstruction of his initial combat experiences in the Western Desert. On 23 April he shot down his first North African victory but was himself again shot down and belly-landed near Tobruk, his aircraft a write-off. He shot down a Blenheim on 28 April and two Hurricanes on 1 May (11th victory). On 21 May 1941 he was again shot down in combat and made another emergency landing near Tobruk, with 40% damage to his Me 109. On 14 June, he had his aircraft damaged and force-landed (and was shot down and force-landed again, by anti-aircraft fire, not long after), and got two more victories, two Hurricanes on 17 June 1941 (13th victory). A day earlier his commission as *Leutnant* became effective.

A number of factors are to be noted in this early time in *I/JG* 27. Firstly, his commanding officer, *Hauptmann* Eduard 'Edu' Neumann, was someone of finely developed judgement of human talent and a commanding officer who realised that different personalities needed to be handled differently; he was one of the few *Geschwader Kommodoren* (appointed to command the entire *JG* 27 on 8 June 1942) to gain such a post in the period after 1940 who was not also a major ace, underlining his leadership talents.[61] Neumann had first scored in Spain and by the time he led *I/JG* 27 to North Africa, had nine victories to his credit.[62] Marseille was a member of *3/JG* 27, commanded by *Oberleutnant* Gerhard Homuth (15 victories on reaching Africa) with another role model in the *Staffel* being *Oberleutnant* Ludwig

Franzisket (then 14 victories).[63] Marseille would no longer be seen as the brash, outspoken and inexperienced interloper with a higher score than anyone else in his *Gruppe*; in contrast he was now amongst comrades who would support him, leaders who would mould and encourage him, and who would provide an environment where he would teach himself to maximise his talents, while overseeing his weaknesses.

The second factor of this early time in Africa was that Marseille was continuing his combat approach as applied over the Channel – charging fearlessly into combat with little thought or cunning, and being shot down almost as much as he shot down others: six victory claims as against himself coming to grief four times in combat with damaged or written-off Me 109s. Wisely, Neumann saw there was need for a change of attitude for Marseille and encouraged him to take time and trouble to work out more effective personal combat philosophies and to teach himself better fighting tactics. And he also posted Marseille home for a long break first, from 18 June–25 August 1941, not many months after his previous leave; this was also the first of regular leave breaks granted to him by Neumann throughout his time in the Desert.[64]

Back in the desert again, things began to change with Marseille's combat approach:[65] he shot down a Hurricane on 28 August 1941 for his 14th claim. Two Hurricanes followed on 9 September, another on 13 September and yet another the next day (18th victory). He took to heart the advice given to him by Neumann and spent a lot of time and effort perfecting his flying, tactics, and deflection shooting, and from 24 September 1941, when he claimed four Hurricanes and a Maryland (23rd victory), he had begun to fly and fight in his own unique style and with ever-increasing success.[66] Two P-40s followed on 12 October 1941 (25th claim).[67] Now he was steadily increasing his effectiveness and was no longer being regularly shot down himself. From 15 October to 3 December 1941 he was posted to Germany for conversion onto the Bf 109 F-4, with some reports of him being ill again at this time;[68] Neumann was no fool and was learning how to handle his best thoroughbred. The *Ehrenpokal* was awarded on 3 November 1941, and the German Cross in Gold three weeks later, during this period away.[69] After that it was back to the desert once more, now flying the superb Me 109 F model, considered by many pilots as its finest version and vastly superior to the Hurricanes and P-40s of the opposing side. Between 5 and 17 December 1941 he shot down four Hurricanes and seven P-40s to bring his score up to 36 victories.[70] Then he was in hospital in Athens followed by a short visit home from 26 December 1941 to 6 February 1942. However, this was no happy time for Marseille: his sister, to whom he was devoted, was murdered in late December 1941, apparently by a jealous SS officer.[71] Once again he returned to North Africa and claimed a further 16 victories between 8 and 27 February 1942 (13 P-40s and 3 Hurricanes) to bring his score to 52 victories; on 13 February his own aircraft was damaged in combat and he force-landed.[72] The *Ritterkreuz* was awarded on 22 February 1942, followed by yet another period of home leave, 28 February–24 April 1942 (and some time in hospital also).[73] His commanding officer was continuing to treat Marseille sympathetically, and as a result his protégé was now a famous and established ace. But much more spectacular success was now to follow, in a remarkably short time.

Back at the desert front once more, a remarkable series of 49 victories followed between 25 April and 17 June (100th–101st on the latter date); his own aircraft was hit and damaged on 13 May 1942.[74] Promotion to *Oberleutnant* was effective from 8 May and then Marseille was awarded the *Eichenlaub* (6 June) and *Schwerten* (18 June) within less than two weeks of each other,[75] a truly outstanding achievement. His was now a household name across Germany; Neumann's mentoring and support had paid off. As Marseille's fame and prestige grew, so did that of the entire *Geschwader* and the entire *Jagdwaffe*. On 8 June 1942 he was given command of 3/JG 27.[76] Once again, an extensive home leave was granted, partly also to receive his new and very rarely awarded decorations, from 19 June to 21 August 1942. It was during this visit that he is described as having played jazz on the piano with Hitler present and, on another occasion, to have overheard some details of the atrocities in Lidice (in what is today the Czech Republic, in retaliation for the assassination of Heydrich) and against the Jews.[77]

By 23 August he was back at the front and began his last series of remarkable victory claims. Between 31 August and 26 September 1942 he claimed 57 successes, including 17 on 1 September.[78] That same day he was promoted to *Hauptmann* and the *Brillanten* to the *Ritterkreuz*, the then highest German decoration, was awarded two days later.[79] Thereafter things began to go wrong: on 3 September his own aircraft was hit in combat and damaged, and on 6 September his good friend Steinhausen (40 victories, posthumous *Ritterkreuz*) was killed in action, and another good friend, Stahlschmidt (59 victories, *Ritterkreuz* and posthumous *Eichenlaub*), the next day.[80] After this he started suffering visibly from stress and even sleep-walking; on 15 September he injured his arm in a force-landing and scored no victories until the 26 September.[81] Having brought his score to a phenomenal total of 158 victories against Western aircraft, the highest such total of the entire war, the great Marseille was killed on 30 September 1942; he bailed out of a new Bf 109 G-2 returning from a mission, which had caught fire due to an engine fault, hit the tailplane and did not open his parachute.[82] The 158 victory claims were made on 388 operational missions; the *Bundesarchiv* has records for 109 of them.[83] Thus died the 'Star of Africa'; while the morale effect of such a champion on his fellow pilots and the entire German forces in Africa was hugely positive, his death was equally catastrophic in lowering combat effectiveness, and his *Gruppe*, I/JG 27, had to be withdrawn from Africa a few days later, on 2 October 1942.[84]

Marseille's performance against Western opponents in the desert must have caused some very serious concern to Nazi sympathisers in the *Luftwaffe* upper ranks, and must have exacerbated earlier jealousies of his abilities. With his 100th victory in June 1942, he was very closely tracking the successes scored by the great German aces on the Eastern front – only a month earlier had Gollob, Bär and Graf themselves obtained their 100th victories (as had Ihlefeld, Marseille's old commander from I/LG 2, in April 1942).[85] By the time that Marseille's 100th fell in June 1942, none of these four leading German aces had many more Eastern victories to their name. Gollob's 150th victory claim (as the first such in the *Luftwaffe*, and mostly Russian victims) in August 1942, was closely followed by Marseille's 150th Western claim in

September 1942. Here once again, was a 22-year-old pilot who was actively competing with the great aces of the Eastern Front, but doing it against Western opponents; this made a mockery of the arrogant, assumed superiority of the Germans over the Russian *Untermenschen*, a cornerstone of the Nazi creed. How could this have happened? It is noteworthy that soon thereafter, also in September 1942, Hermann Graf's 200th claim was made, all of them in the East,[86] thereby putting an end to any notions that a youngster in North Africa could so easily embarrass leading Nazi tyros such as Gollob and Graf and cast doubts on the superiority of the German race in the East. With the death of Marseille, the greatest performer against the Western Allies for the entire war had already come and gone; no one would ever top his achievements. But this once more provided fuel for jealousy and for the already growing and skewed Marseille legend. A lengthy comment on Marseille follows by *Oberst* Edu Neumann, *Geschwaderkommodore JG 27*. He deals with the oft-quoted over-claiming Marseille's record is supposed to have encompassed in the opinion of many Allied-orientated writers, and the unique nature of the Marseille method of air fighting and deflection shooting – never successfully imitated by anyone else:

I am fully aware that it is a universal problem, with over-claiming. Roughly, one can say that where many fighter units – irrespective of whether they are friend or enemy – fight within a restricted airspace, the error quota is understandably high; when fewer units are involved, this means fewer mistakes are made in adjudging successes. In North Africa in 1941 it was most of the time, on the German side, only *I/JG 27* that was present. In addition, the ground surface lacked any forests or swamps which gave a good means of visual control on aircraft shot down and hitting the ground. In 1942 for a long time there was only the one *Geschwader*, JG 27, just three *Gruppen*. In the book of Shores and Ring[87] the victory claims of both sides are given and analysed – meticulously in my opinion – and the mistakes found were almost all of small import. For me also, I was always able to note, that the good fighter pilots of my *Geschwader* were each other's hardest critics. And in this regard, in the case of Marseille, there was never the least utterance of any doubt about his claims. Naturally I understand that the high victory claims of German fighter pilots have caused raised eyebrows of our enemies. However it is generally overlooked that the German fighter pilots – in comparison with those of their opponents – universally were sent into action much more frequently; that brings many victories but in equal proportions, also high losses. I do not want to exclude the likelihood that with other pilots in Africa, mistakes were made in claiming victories, but with Marseille the watchful eye of his comrades was very strict. What good fighter pilot would watch without envy, how another is more successful? Never once during the entire time that Marseille was in Africa did I have the least doubt about the accuracy of the claims made by him. Another successful pilot was the then *Oberleutnant* Franzisket (after the war a world renowned biologist), to whom it was of no concern at all whether someone was better than him. An exception! He told me in Africa that, when one found oneself nearby at the same time as Marseille joined combat, you could only watch in awe, as he had his own way of flying and fighting that was absolutely fascinating. I experienced this over Bir Hacheim in 1942 also! Marseille was not some holy cow to be protected, when – but only when – there was any doubt about his claims. He was a uniquely good fighter pilot, but he had the disadvantage to be much too fast. His reaction times were unbelievably short, in the air and on the ground. He would get really happy, when one of his *Staffel* comrades achieved an aerial victory, which happened only seldom, his reaction speed could not be superseded.

So where does this all leave us with Marseille? Using the first compendium volume on the air war over the Western Desert by Shores and Ring,[88] one can compare Marseille's claims with Allied losses and make a well-motivated estimate that for 150 of his 151 Desert claims, 78 are definitely confirmed, 24 are to be rejected and 48 considered possible (i.e. there were more German and Italian claims than there were available Allied victims shot down). Assuming that 50% of Marseille's 'possibles' were in fact shot down by him would give an overall figure of 102 confirmed victories. This is very close to the 109 victory claims for which documents are available in the *Bundesarchiv* (these documents for his confirmed victories came originally from the *Reichsluftfahrtministerium* or RLM, during the war). Turning to another analysis of this controversial field (not just for Marseille or the German aces of 1939–1945, but for all aces over the past century), the greatest authority on the North African air war, Christopher Shores, concludes that although there is good evidence for some over-claiming by Marseille in his last two months of operations (August-September 1942) due to his extreme self-confidence and excellent shooting (which was not always fully lethal due to the speed with which victims were supposed to have been dispatched), for two-thirds to three-quarters of his claims, there is an identifiable Allied victim, destroyed, force-landed or heavily damaged, giving an overall score of about 100 confirmed.[89] There is thus something of a consensus in approximate score, and these estimates and their basis do not seriously conflict with the views of Marseille's commanding officer and mentor, *Oberst* Edu Neumann quoted above.

Neumann obviously perceived that Marseille was someone who flew and fought very intensively, and who put his entire available energy and indeed almost his soul into every combat, leaving him exhausted after most missions and unable effectively to function without regular breaks from fighting. This is reflected in illustration 13, showing just how perceptive a mentor and leader Neumann was and how he was responsible to a large degree for the successful employment of Marseille as an instrument of combat and of war. There is also almost a trend of increasing need for rest as Marseille's successes grew, possibly evidence that a glowing candle was burning itself out more thoroughly with every stint of intense combat. This possible perception is borne out also by Professor Paul Robert Skawran, the *Luftwaffe*'s '*Seelenspion*', the trained psychologist experienced in analysing what made pilots tick, and who spent much of the war observing them on active service. As Professor Skawran lived in the same city as I did in his later life, I was able to meet him several times and engage him in long and fascinating discussions on the topic of fighter pilots, the personalities of the famous among them that the Professor knew well. He also gave me a copy of his 1969 book *Ikaros*,[90] not well known amongst English-speaking readers or writers, nor easy to obtain any more. I was privileged to have extensive explanations of Professor Skawran's methods of analysis and the basis of the definition of his groups of fighter pilot types; he had written extensively about Marseille.

Skawran places Marseille amongst his defined group of the 'ambitious-sensitive' (*Ehrgeizig-Feinnervigen*) fighter pilots, where 'sensitive' implies high emotive sensibility;[91] Marseille is seen almost as the typical example of such a pilot. These pilots are very ambitious, driven, very determined to achieve their aims, mostly loners who like to fight alone – they are not leaders (such as Edu Neumann). When they fly and fight they are essentially in another world, with total concentration on the job at hand.[92] Marseille was really an extreme example of this type of personality; he took his duties so seriously that he practised flying, fighting and shooting until he had developed a unique style of attacking the enemy from almost any position, and was particularly and uniquely able to penetrate their defensive circles effectively; he often flew slowly, with lowered flaps, and throttled down, carrying out manoeuvres others could never emulate, his actions easily visible in the air due to the white condensation trails marking his wingtips due to the extreme manoeuvres he performed.[93] When such pilots fly in action, the intensity of their activities and of their concentration is enormous and they essentially reach a state almost of ecstasy when in action; once they land, they are totally exhausted, as Marseille so often was, unable often to get out of his aircraft or celebrate his successes until some minutes had passed.[94] Then he would get out of the machine and the stern mask that came down at the start of a mission would be lifted, and his normal happy personality would replace it; the fighting, ecstatic Marseille thus hid behind this surficial layer of the jolly, Bohemian personality.[95] Thus the intensity of each period of combat, in between the frequent leave periods that were needed to keep him from total exhaustion and loss of all effectiveness, grew as time passed and the candle was indeed burning out.

Edu Neumann understood at least some of this and what was needed to keep Marseille going, but in his masterful use of the fighting machine that was 'Jochen' Marseille, lay also the seeds of Marseille's own destruction; his end was therefore almost inevitable, whether through combat, accident or total exhaustion. The happy, playboy image that so many saw as the essential Marseille merely hid the real, intense and totally dedicated person beneath; the boasting and the stories of affairs with women and famous actresses were part of a complex almost two-part (yet not schizophrenic) persona and one most often misunderstood. However, women could more easily see through Marseille's surficial layer to appreciate the true vulnerability of the intense person beneath; this was the basis for his supposed success with the opposite sex. In many ways he was really a shy and retiring personality,[96] but one with enormous dedication and ambition to achieve his aims, masked with a relatively frivolous exterior.[97] He flew and fought himself into the ground and his destruction was inevitable. The greatest 'virtuoso' amongst the fighter pilots (as described by Adolf Galland)[98] was in reality but a brief, bright comet who largely managed to conceal his real self from those around him, on the Channel coast and in the Western Desert.

Flying the Zerstörer over the Desert: Heavy Fighters and Fighter-Bombers

Elements of III/ZG 26 were the first German fighters to operate over the Western Desert and continued to do so almost through to the end. They tended to shuttle regularly between North Africa, Sicily and Greek airfields, operating as long-range escorts of supply convoys across the Mediterranean, as well as fighters and fighter-bombers in the desert. In between they were also sent over Malta with similar duties (as discussed elsewhere). Below, the then-*Hauptmann* Georg Christl, *Staffelkapitän* of 7/ZG 26 provides an excellent account of *Jagdbomber* (*Jabo*) tactics applied in the desert:

After my transfer to ZG 26 the next stop was Sicily – here we flew cover for ships. In this, the Me 110 showed itself to be very well suited to the task, due to its endurance.

The crews gained confidence in their aircraft again. When things took off in North Africa (*III/ZG 26* began arriving there in January 1941),[99] we flew in the first instance, low level attacks to stop the enemy advance, and then especially the strong armament of the aircraft proved itself. However, it should be noted that in the beginning there was hardly any enemy fighter defence, and when there was, we could handle it ourselves. Very effective were low level attacks in the enemy hinterland – airfields, fuel dumps etc. – we hardly had any losses, but caused great distress to the enemy. These missions should have been emphasised more as the Me 110 with drop tanks was ideally suited to them. These missions to attack deep into enemy territory were ordered by the *Fliegerführer* (*Fliegerführer-Afrika*; essentially the staff who ran the tactical air war in the desert) following prior aerial reconnaissance. We were delegated to attack a specific airfield and, after a single low level attack, could pick our own further targets. These were mostly lorry convoys, which were easy to identify from the dust they raised. I remember on one mission that the English shot rockets with small parachutes on them that were connected to a cable. However the rockets were launched too late and we only saw them as we were leaving the field we had just attacked. In these attacks we flew very early in the morning, and north of the coast for about 50 km, with radio silence and at low altitude, and on turning south and reaching the coast, we dropped our plywood long range tanks. When we reached the chosen enemy airfield, every pilot had to pick out his own target and then fire was opened from all barrels and the four 50 kg bombs were dropped. After the attack the aircraft were reassembled into a loose formation and then we flew back through the enemy hinterland. The crews enjoyed these missions a lot as the '110' was very well suited to them and each pilot could develop his own initiative. Later on the circus began again with escorts for Stukas (Ju 87s). In the meantime the enemy had greatly reinforced their fighter defences and we were once again in the soup as we had been over England in 1940. In the Battle of Britain we had successfully used the defensive circle to reduce losses; in North Africa the British took over this tactic with their fighters, which was forced on to them by the superiority of the Me 109.

Similar experiences are related by the next witness, from the same *Zerstörer Gruppe*, *Feldwebel* Werner Ludwig, but with dive-bombing added to the range of expertise expected of the crews of the Me 110s. 'After the Battle of Britain we were retrained as dive-bombers: approach flight at 4,000 m height, dive to 2,000 m at an angle of 45° and then drop two 10 cm bombs; aiming was done with the reflection gun sight available in the Me 110; 800 km/hr could not be exceeded in the dive as otherwise the aerodynamic properties of the aircraft could be affected. For example, the leading edge of the wings could be pushed in by a series of hammer-like blows. Our tactic in North Africa, from Tripoli to El Alamein was always the same: approach at 4,000 m, dive to 2,000 m, drop the bombs and then make a low level strafing attack on the enemy airfield or troops (mainly tanks). In attacking airfields use was made of cluster bombs (four packs of 40 cluster bombs) to increase the scatter effect. The cluster bomb packs were attached, two to a side, under the wings. On a mission with *c.* 20 Me 110s, already a fairly large formation, we were provided with an escort of a few Me 109s. We had orders to avoid combat if attacked by enemy fighters. The Me 110 was too heavy and clumsy when pitted against a Spitfire or Curtiss P-40. Living conditions in the Desert varied from accommodation mostly in houses (Derna area), while on the advance into Egypt tents were prepared for us. We also often lived in rocky cliffs, near the Egyptian border (Gambut) but still within Libya.'

JG 27 is Finally Withdrawn from Africa and Replaced by JG 77

Following the death of its star pilot, Marseille, *I/JG 27* had to be withdrawn at the beginning of October 1942 (to fly over

Malta briefly, before a short-term return to North Africa from 25 October till 13 November 1942). In the following month *Stab* and *III/JG 27* departed, with the last unit, *II/JG 27*, leaving on 6 December 1942.[100] As the *JG 27 Gruppen* moved out so those of *JG 77* moved in; they entered combat in the Western Desert at a very difficult time, just as the Battle of Alamein reached its climax, sending the German *Afrikakorps* into a headlong retreat towards Tunisia. Professor Paul Robert Skawran, while visiting *I/JG 77* in Italy after the end of the Tunisian and Sicilian debacles, copied a part of the war diary of this *Gruppe* and kindly provided a copy to the author.[101] A summary of the experiences of this unit as recorded in their *Kriegstagebuch* is given in the table below, and paints a vivid picture of the impossible task these pilots had in trying to stem a powerful offensive, supported by powerful and strategically focussed, well led air forces. Such documents are very rare and this fragment preserved by Prof. Skawran is thus very valuable; almost all *Luftwaffe* unit war diaries (*Kriegstagebücher*) were destroyed at the end of the war. The *I/JG 77* war diary reflects many interesting details, amongst others:

(1) It is very short and to the point, reflecting a very hectic experience for the newly arrived *Gruppe*, during the precipitate retreat of the German-Italian army after the heavy defeat at El Alamein – this began on 5 November 1942 within days of their arrival in the Desert.

(2) The decisive nature of the El Alamein defeat is very evident in the speed with which towns and strategic locations were abandoned, and the British 8th Army appears to have been seen by the *Gruppe* as being in close pursuit throughout (contrary to what many published studies have indicated) while Allied air forces (largely RAF) kept up a ruthless and continuous attack on the coast road and airfields.

(3) Montgomery's famous pause of almost a month at the Agedabia position (from whence 8th Army had itself been driven twice previously and which greatly worried

everyone outside the Army) is also very evident, but once the advance began again, a second set of retreats followed for the Axis army and air forces.

(4) Only the *Gruppenkommandeur*'s (*Hauptmann* Heinz Bär) victories are named to a specific pilot, reflecting the *Luftwaffe's* obsession with the ace and the almost exclusive appointments of such pilots to command units.

(5) There is a graduation from what might be considered the end of Western Desert operations and the commencement of those over Tunisia proper; the first contact with American P38s on 21 January 1943 indicates combat with Tunisia-based air forces, and the fall of Tripoli on 23 January 1943 was really the end of the Western Desert campaign – soon after two rapid moves were made into Tunisian airfields.

The German spelling of well-known place names from the original document has been retained: for example (more familiar English spelling in brackets): Mersa Matruk (Mersa Matruh); Gambus (Gambut); Bengasi (Benghazi); El Daber (El Daba). The entry for 17 January 1943 under 'details' below is also interesting: 'POWs report enemy air force ordered to avoid all combats. Enemy morale strongly weakened by activity of *JG 77*'. This was a serious case of wishful thinking.

And thus the famous Western Desert air war came to an end. In many ways it was a microcosm of that over the Eastern Front. The German fighters displayed their common obsession in obtaining victories and were thus happy to tackle the Allied fighters (which were largely inferior in performance to the Me 109 F and G models) escorting their medium bomber formations, rather than going for the bombers. On the Eastern Front, German *Jagdflieger* often concentrated on bouncing Russian fighters rather than the much more destructive Il-2 ground attack aircraft. In both cases, for the German ground forces, the tactical success in the air of their fighters was at the cost of significant contributions to the strategic defeat of those forces by the highly effective enemy bombers.

	Summary of operations, Western Desert (25 October 1942–3 February 1943), from copy of *Kriegstagebuch* I/JG 77 (via P.R. Skawran)[102]						
Date	Base	Missions Flown	Sorties Flown	Victories claimed	Losses	Attacks on own base	Details
25 October	San Pietro	0	0	0	0	0	Transfer to Bir El Abd
26 October	San Pietro	0	0	0	0	0	*Hauptmann* Bär leads three Me 109s to new base
2 November	Bir El Abd	?	?	1	0	0	During daylight enemy fighter-bomber attacks on highway and *Panzer* Army. Lots of activity over front. *Gruppenkommandeur* Bär 1 Spitfire (118th victory).
3 November	Bir El Abd. (After fourth operation relocate to Gutorifia; prior to this, Spitfires, P-39s & Bostons seen over base, front)	6	?	7 (incl. five P-40s by *Hauptmann* Bär)	0	By 24 Bostons and 12–16 escorts; three Me 109s damaged	Heavy pressure by enemy armour; heavy and costly battles but line held. Few enemy armoured cars get within 8 km of base. Heavy enemy air attacks on *Panzer* Army. Continuous bomber and fighter-bomber attacks on highway at Fuka and El Daber.
4 November	Gutorifia (retreat to Quasabar)	?	?	5	0	0	*Increasingly stronger enemy armoured attacks. Continuous enemy air attacks on airfields, highway and panzers by day and night. Continuous low level attacks by I/JG 77.*

Date	Location						
5 November	El Quasabar	?	?	4 (incl. 124th & 125th of Bär)	0	Two fighter and fighter-bomber attacks on Quasabar-East. Two further attacks of strong bomber formations with light escort on retreat route at Quasabar	*Panzer Army retreats to Fuka, British armour follows closely, Ramke Brigade trapped at El Alamein. Heavy enemy air attacks on retreat route day and night.*
6 November	Gambus (12h00 to Bir El Aria)	0, no fuel	0	0	0	0	*Panzer Army retreats further, to Marsa Matruk*
9 November	Bir El Aria	?	?	1 (Bär's 126th)	0	0	*Panzer Army retreats to Halfaya Pass; much air activity over Panzers. I/JG 77 flew Freie Jagd in area Sidi El Barani – Sollum.*
10 November	"	5	28	5 (Bär's 127th–128th)	1	0	*Panzers S of Sollum; enemy fighter-bomber and low level attacks on highway and airfields. Freie Jagd over panzers and roadblocks; combat with 30–40 P-40s and Spitfires.*
11 November	Bir El Aria (move to Mar Juba)	4	16	11 (Bär's 129th–130th)	0	0	*Panzers retreat further, British armour 40 km SW of Sollum; continuous fighter-bomber and low level attacks on retreat roads and airfields. Freie Jagd with 50 P-40s and combat with 10 P-39s.*

Date	Base	Missions Flown	Sorties Flown	Victories claimed	Losses	Attacks on own base	Details
13 November	Mar Juba (move to Bengasi)	0	0	0	0	0	*Tobruk abandoned*
14 November	Bengasi (move to Magnis)	0	0	0	0	0	*Derna abandoned.* Sandstorm.
16 November	Arco	0	0	0	0	0	*Bengasi abandoned.* Sandstorm.
17 November	Arco (move to Magnis-Arco)	0	0	0	0	0	*After battle at Agedabia, slow retreat to the Marsa el Brega position.*
25 November	Arco	1	9	0	0	0	Escort Stukas; *Hauptmann* Bär destroys armoured car. Almost completely overcast; no air activity.
27 November	"	0	0	0	0	0	Kesselring commends JG 77 for excellent successes in low level attacks.
1 December	"	?.	?.	0	0	0	Six armoured cars, six lorries, five armoured personnel carriers destroyed by II/JG 77.
7 December	"	?.	?.	4 (Bär's 131st– 132nd)	0	Two fighter-bomber attacks on Arco	*Freie Jagd* of 19 Me 109s vs. nine P-40s, 14 Spitfires, one Baltimore, El Agheila-El Brega area.
8 December	"	4	?.	3 (Bär's 133rd– 134th)	0	One fighter-bomber attack by strong US fighter forces	*Infantry broke off contact with enemy without battle.* Scramble and combat with 30 P-40s.

82

Date	Location						
10 December	"	6	30	7 (Bär's 135th–136th)	1	One fighter-bomber and one fighter attack; second attack warded off before reaching base	Combat with 50–60 P-40s and Spitfires.
11 December	"	7	29	1 (Bär's 137th)	0	0	Combat with 35–40 P-40s, Hauptmann Bär gets 800th Luftsieg of I/JG 77.
14 December	"	4	17	7 (Bär's 138th–139th)	0	0	*Enemy advance on El Agheila position from Mata Giofr area.*
15 December	Arco (move to Wadi Tamit)	0	0	0	0	0	
18 December	Wadi Tamit (move to Tanorga)	0	0	0	0	0	
24 December	Tanorga	0	0	0	0	0	*Enemy south of Syrte with c. 4,000 vehicles.* Call from *Reichsmarschall* on new tasks. Recognition for achievements of fighters in Africa in last two months.
25 December	Tanorga (move to Bir Dufan)	0	0	0	0	0	
3–5 January	Bir Dufan	0	0	0	0	0	Sandstorm

Date	Base	Missions Flown	Sorties Flown	Victories claimed	Losses	Attacks on own base	Details
14 January	"	6	53	11 (Bär's 140th–144th)	4	0	*Enemy advances farther, new offensive expected* Strong enemy fighter activity, c. 240 aircraft. Combat with 62 P-40s, 18 Mitchells, 29 Bostons.
17 January	Bir Dufan (move to Castel Benito)	0	0	0	0	0	POWs report enemy air force ordered to avoid all combats. Enemy morale strongly weakened by activity of *JG 77.*
18 January	Castel Benito (move to Ben Gardane)	0	0	0	0	Strong night bomber attack – nine Me's damaged, two destroyed. Two fighter-bomber attacks. Second raid by 12 bombers, 30 P-38s	Ben Gardane covered by sand – many damaged propellors.
21 January	Ben Gardane	4	7	2 (Bär's 145th–146th)	0	0	*Panzer Army performs fighting retreat in area northwest of Tachuma.* Strong enemy fighter-bomber and low level activity. Escort mission, combat with 20 P-38s.
23 January	"	5	16	1 (Bär's 147th)	0	0	*Tripoli falls to British.* Combat with 30 P-40s.

							Low level attack on base – four Me's seriously damaged	
24 January	"	o	o	o	o	o	o	Combat with 20 P-4os.
25 January	"	4	20	c	2 (Bär's 148th–149th)	o	o	
27 January	"	2	18		3 (Bär's 150th–152nd)	o	o	*Enemy advances to Juara.* Combat with 12 P-4os.
29 January	Ben Gardane (move to Mat Mata)	o	o	o	o	o	o	New base sand-covered
3 February	Mat Mata (move to Fatuassa)	o	o	o	o	o	o	

Notes: italics in last column at right denote major ground events. When no claims and losses recorded, this relates to the copy made from the *Kriegstagebuch* of I/JG 77 not recording any, but does not necessarily mean that no claims or losses actually occurred.

3

MALTA,
JANUARY 1941–OCTOBER 1942

The aerial battles over Malta raged for a very long time and in due course this small island (actually three islands, Malta itself, Gozo and tiny Comino) became the most bombed place on earth. The raids began on 11 June 1940 on the day after Italy's declaration of war on Britain (and France), and they continued until late in 1942. The Allied invasion of French North Africa ('Torch') which began on 8 November 1942, effectively put an end to this long and intense campaign, as German and Italian attention shifted elsewhere.[1] Of course there were more raids during the Tunisian and later Sicilian and even Italian campaigns that followed, but the aerial siege and sea blockade were over with the onset of Operation Torch and the victory of the British 8th Army at Alamein just before that.

For the entire Malta campaign the *Regia Aeronautica* was constantly in action, and as demands from other theatres (particularly Russia and North Africa) allowed, major German concentrations of aircraft joined them. At such times the Italian participation tended to decrease, only to increase once more after German departure or decrease of the German contribution. The aerial struggle formed part of a greater picture as Malta's strategic location in the central Mediterranean placed it astride the main supply routes for the Axis forces, from Italy to North Africa. Airborne and seaborne strike forces from the George Cross island were thus able to interdict, often to critical effect, supplies to the

Axis forces in the Western Desert, and prior to the great battle at Alamein in fact achieved a fatal stranglehold on General Rommel's fuel supplies. These British attacks from Malta were beaten down when major forces of the *Luftwaffe* came into the Maltese picture, but no sooner had the German air fleets departed or been radically weakened by the needs of other theatres, than Malta's interdiction became resurgent once again.

This complex see-saw of airborne activities was intrinsically linked to the many convoys, launched from both east (Alexandria in Egypt) and West (Gibraltar) that brought the supplies to maintain Malta's civilian and military populations. These convoys saw major air battles over the ships at sea, as well as related naval engagements, and the survival of the island often hung in the balance as convoys were decimated, or even turned back with no ships getting through.[2]

The supply of fighter aircraft, mainly from aircraft carriers sailing from Gibraltar, was repeated many times, often in concert with supply convoys; about 525 fighters reached Malta safely, 94% via carriers (thus demonstrating the critical importance of sea power to Malta's survival and concomitant Axis defeat in the desert),[3] the balance being flown in from North Africa. Details are provided in the two tables below.

British fighter deliveries to Malta (by aircraft carriers sailing from Gibraltar)[4]			
Month and year	Number of delivery operations	Fighters launched from carrier(s)	Fighters which arrived in Malta
August 1940	1	12 Hurricanes	12
November 1940	1	12 Hurricanes	4
April 1941	2	36 Hurricanes	35
May 1941	1	48 Hurricanes	46
June 1941	4	156 Hurricanes	143
September 1941	2	60 Hurricanes	59
November 1941	1	37 Hurricanes	34
March 1942	3	31 Spitfires	31
April 1942	1	47 Spitfires	46 (1 defected to Algeria)
May 1942	1	17 Spitfires	17

Month and year	Number of delivery operations	Fighters launched from carrier(s)	Fighters which arrived in Malta
June 1942	2	63 Spitfires	59 (2 of which crash-landed)
July 1942	2	64 Spitfires	59
August 1942	2	70 Spitfires	65
October 1942	1	29 Spitfires	29

Notes: of the total of 333 Hurricanes which arrived on Malta by this means during 1940–1941, approximately 150 were dispatched on to the Western Desert.[5] Of the 304 Spitfires which arrived safely on Malta by this means during 1942, 12 Spitfires (601 Squadron) transferred from Malta to the Western Desert on 22–24 June 1942.[6] On 25 October 1942, two Spitfires fitted with extra-long range tanks flew into Malta directly from Gibralter.[7]

British fighter deliveries to Malta (flown in direct from Western Desert)[8]			
March 1941	1	6 Hurricanes	6
March 1942	1	10 Hurricanes	10
April 1942	2	16 Hurricanes	16 (1 of which crash-landed)
May 1942	2	6 Hurricanes	6

There were three distinct periods of intense German participation in the Malta campaign:[9]

(1) *Fliegerkorps X* in Sicily (units also in North Africa), 10 January to 26 May 1941;
(2) *Fliegerkorps II* in Sicily, 19 December 1941 to 18 May 1942;
(3) A short-term 'blitz', 11 to 27 October 1942.

German fighter units stationed in Sicily and operating over Malta encompassed essentially *7/JG 26* and short-term participation of parts of *JG 27* in the first blitz (number 1 above). The second blitz was the major one and reached its crescendo in March-May 1942, when Spitfires finally joined the Hurricanes of Malta, opposition being provided predominantly by the entire *JG 53* (including its new *Jabostaffel, 10/JG 53*) and by *II/JG 3* for a while. The final, October blitz was supported by *I, II* and *Stab/JG 53*,

I/JG 27 and *I/JG 77*; *Stab* and *II/JG 53* remained in Sicily in the period between the second and third blitzes (numbers 2 and 3 above) and elements of *III/ZG 26* served for the longest period.[10]

The First Blitz: 10 January to 26 May 1941

Fliegerkorps X, experienced in shipping attacks, assembled on Sicilian airfields from mid-December 1940 to early January 1941. It had been moved from Norway, and comprised two Ju 87 *Gruppen*, three of bombers, with *III/ZG 26* to escort them; within about a month, however much of this strength was moved to the Western Desert.[11] A complex British convoy and naval operation from both ends of the Mediterranean came to a climax on 10 January to the west of Malta when, in its first major operation, *Fliegerkorps X* attacked the Royal Navy carrier *Illustrious*, obtaining five hits with Stukas, followed later by another Stuka bomb from an Italian-crewed aircraft. Seriously damaged, the vessel made it to Malta that night.[12] From 16 to 19 January 1941 furious German and Italian attacks failed to cause further serious damage to the carrier undergoing emergency repairs in La Valetta harbour, after which she slipped away to Alexandria, but needed major repairs which kept her out of the war for a long period.[13] In early February an Me 109 *Staffel* was added to *Fliegerkorps X*, *7/JG 26*, commanded by 22-year-old *Oberleutnant* Joachim Müncheberg, who had 23 victories to his credit and the *Ritterkreuz*.[14] He was amongst the *Luftwaffe's* leading fighter pilots, a position he maintained until his death over Tunisia in 1943. Müncheberg was an expert exponent of the typical German fighter tactic of the bounce from on high, followed by a zoom climb back to safety. This tactic suited the Me 109 perfectly as it used its superior qualities and avoided its weaknesses against the more manoeuvrable RAF fighters.

Leutnant Otto Stammberger recalls this notable pilot and ace: 'I knew "Jochen" Müncheberg as *Staffelkapitän* of the 7th *Staffel*. I myself was in the 9th *Staffel* in the years 1940 and 1941. Müncheberg was a good comrade and outstanding shot. In early 1941 he went to Sicily and later that year to Africa.' The Me 109s arrived in Gela, Sicily on 7 February 1941 and flew their first mission over Malta five days later.[15] Between 12 February and 13 May 1941, *7/JG 26* claimed 36 known victories plus very likely another two (from unknown *Staffel* pilots), as well as three more credited as 'probables'.[16] Exactly half of these, 18 accredited victories, fell to Müncheberg, with six going to the next most successful pilot, *Oberleutnant* Klaus Mietusch.[17] 35 of these claims can be matched with RAF losses, 34 of which were Hurricanes.[18] Not a single Me 109 was lost or even seriously damaged,[19] underlining the fine leadership and skills of this *Staffel*'s commander and dominant ace, and the superiority of the Me 109 E over the Hurricane Is and IIs when the bounce tactics were so well employed and dogfighting avoided.

Müncheberg also had much greater experience than any of his opponents, as amply demonstrated on 16 February 1941. Six Hurricanes of 261 Squadron led by Flight Lieutenant James MacLachlan, an established ace with eight victories to his name, had planned to form a defensive circle if attacked by the redoubtable Me 109s.[20] Flying at 20,000 feet, the Hurricanes were indeed attacked by six Messerschmitts lead by Müncheberg, who made an initial diving attack. The circle of British fighters then formed and the Germans zoomed back up for another dive; this time only four came down and MacLachlan was tempted into going for them as they overshot him.[21] Despite looking carefully behind him and into the sun, he was surprised and shot down by a further attack (presumably the remaining two Me 109s who had stayed up), being seriously wounded, bailing out and losing his arm in surgery a few days later; his victor appears to have been Müncheberg.[22] It is an outstanding example of the favourite German fighter tactic in operation, and one used with a good deal of success for a very large part of the entire war, on all fronts. On 26 February, Müncheberg again shot down a leading RAF ace, seven-victory Flying Officer Eric Taylor of 261 Squadron, who desperately tried to keep on attacking a Ju 87 despite having already been hit heavily, and he was killed.[23] This illustrates also the different philosophies of the two air forces: while the *Luftwaffe* fighter arm had an almost obsessional focus on scoring victories and supported and boosted the *Experten* (major aces) at all turns, their RAF counterparts frowned somewhat on the ace concept and saw it as their prime duty in battles such as those over Malta (as previously in the Battle of Britain) to shoot down the bombers even at the cost of knowingly exposing themselves to fighter attack from the escorts. For the *Luftwaffe*, their aces greatly outscored their British, American and Russian opponents, establishing records that still stand today, but the Allied approach was in the long term a war-winning philosophy.

I/JG 27 was only in Sicily for a few days (1–10 March 1941)[24] and claimed one victory there, by *Leutnant* Willy Kothmann,[25] which is confirmed by British losses.[26] While *III/ZG* 26 made a total of five claims over Malta and three more over the Mediterranean against British carrier-borne naval aircraft, only one can be confirmed, plus three damaged Fulmars.[27] *III/JG* 27 flew in the theatre a bit longer (2–24 May 1941)[28] making five victory claims,[29] all again confirmed by RAF casualties.[30] *Oberleutnant* Erbo Graf von Kageneck (see also Chapter 2) was their most successful pilot, claiming four of the five successes.[31] Despite this *Gruppe* only spending a few weeks in Sicily, *Oberleutnant* Erhard Braune, *Staffelkapitän* 7/JG 27, remembered several rather unique aspects of the experience remarkably clearly:

The flying parts of the *III/JG* 27 were transferred immediately after the end of the Greek campaign to Sicily (Gela). The most immediately necessary mechanics were, as far as I remember, flown across also, with Ju 52s. I can remember that we had to fly with captured British fuel, as our own supplies in Greece had not arrived. Only in Sicily could we once again fill up our aircraft from drums. I remember this situation well as the octane value of the British fuel did not equate to that which was used for our engines (N-series) and the sounds the cylinders made did not give the pilots much confidence for the long flight over the Greek mountains and then over the Mediterranean Sea. Our operations over Malta took place at a time when the airborne defence of the island was low; the 7/JG 26 (Müncheberg) had taken the sting out of it. In contrast, the flak was operating in fine fettle. Sometimes the He 111s we were escorting (they were more likely Ju 88s) flew into the detonation clouds of the heavy flak only to disappear completely. Our operations over Malta only lasted for three weeks. We flew exclusively escorts for the bomber units of

Fliegerkorps X (headquarters at Taormina). Pilots of these He 111s would be able to report on these missions better than the fighter pilots. In the middle of May 1941 we moved to Germany and flew over Russia from the first day of that campaign.

The Critical Blitz: 19 December 1941 to 18 May 1942

This was the period of really critical aerial fighting over Malta, and also the time when Spitfires were first brought to the island (in March 1942; see table of fighter deliveries to the island). The fighting intensified from January and reached a crescendo in April to May 1942 (see chart of losses shown in illustration 24).[32] *JG 53* was the major *Luftwaffe* fighter unit present during this blitz, with its entire strength present for most of this period.[33] A new *Jabostaffel*, *10/JG 53* was activated in February,[34] and *II/JG 3* came in as reinforcement from mid-February till late April.[35] While *I/JG 53* departed for Russia at the end of April, and *III/JG 53* for the Desert in late May, *Stab* and *II/JG 53* remained on Sicily until November 1942.[36] Dr Felix Sauer, serving as an *Unteroffizier* with *6/JG 53*, was transferred in February 1942 to the fighter-bombers of *10/JG 53*, and recalled his experiences over Malta during this major blitz:

We kept absolute command of the air over the Island of Malta for quite a time, till about April 1942. But Malta possessed an excellent flak defence, and it was therefore always rather dangerous to fly over in the lower regions. This situation changed considerably when the English – with the assistance of the aircraft carriers *Eagle* and *Wasp* – managed to land Spitfires on the island, flown by seasoned pilots, who had collected their experiences over England in the 'Battle of Britain'. From that date – *c.* April 1942 – our losses increased. From that time the 'Tommies' replaced their Hurricanes – which had been inferior to our types – by the manoeuvrable and well-armed Spitfires. Comparing the Me 109 and the Spitfire, one might say that the Spitfire was somewhat better in the 'dogfight' (*Kurvenkampf*), whilst the Me 109 was faster in breaking away (*Wegkurven*), which was advantageous when attacking. We attacked from behind, from a greater height, and with the sun at the back. Among our pilots were many who scored more than 100 'downings' (*Abschüsse*), though many of these successes were also Russian front victories. I do not know of anyone with over 100 victories on the English side. That means that the Me 109 must have been of good quality, though everything depended on the pilots themselves.

Fighting over Malta in this new and most catastrophic blitz began in December 1941, the first victory claim on 19 December, fittingly, being made by the *JG 53 Kommodore, Major* Günther Freiherr von Maltzahn,[37] one of the war's great fighter leaders, and a man beloved by his *Geschwader's* pilots and groundcrew. As an example, Dr Felix Sauer, 6 and *10/JG 53* paid him the following tribute. 'As a man and as a soldier, *Kommodore* Günther von Maltzahn was a model in every respect, and for everybody. He was "noble" not only by name. What counted with him was the inner value of people – the service rank was of no account to him. I have known him in many situations, and I have always regarded him as a model pilot, chief, and especially as a man. His soldiers just loved him. When on 11 April 1942 he was shot down near Malta and was drifting in the sea, we flew a protective barrier round his rubber boat; he was rescued in no time. If, in this action, an Englishman had interfered, we'd have done with him, so much did we love and revere our *Kommodore* Günther von Maltzahn. He should be quoted in the same breath with the (probably) greatest German fighter pilot Werner Mölders. His human, as well as his professional personality is mentioned far too rarely, though he deserves the highest appreciation.' On 25 January 1942, von Maltzahn led five Me 109s of *Stab/JG 53* in a classic bounce of RAF Hurricanes, first attacking the top cover machines, and then following zoom climbs back to altitude, repeated the bounce twice more, on lower flying Hurricanes; they claimed five victories and actually appear to have got four.[38] Following another successful bounce, by *II/JG 53*, which dispatched three Hurricanes and their pilots on 4 February 1942, two pilots from *6/JG 53* strafed an RAF rescue launch searching for the British pilots, killing four of the crew and badly damaging the craft.[39] The combat was turning vicious and thereafter use of these rescue launches was curtailed when German aircraft were about,[40] thereby also raising casualties among downed German aircrew. Amongst the *JG 53* fighter pilots who experienced the regular missions over the island was *Oberfeldwebel* Josef Ederer of the 3rd *Staffel* whose recollections are detailed below:

> After the first tour in Russia I came to Sicily in early 1942; we were stationed there at Gela and Comiso. Our main task in regard to Malta was to hinder the English who were trying to strangle supplies to Africa through operations from their Maltese base. We also had to watch La Valetta and the eastern approaches to the harbour. As opponents, the English were fair and in some ways superior to us, as they were fighting over their own territory and as we had to fly over *c.* 100 km of ocean between Sicily and Malta, to get there. When there was aerial combat over Malta and one was shot up by the English, and you then had to break off combat and try to return home, the English had fighters waiting off Sicily to finish off the damaged German aircraft that could no longer defend themselves properly. As I had good vision and was also a good pilot, I generally flew as wingman to the *Staffelkapitän* (at that time *Oberleutnant* Tonne) or on large missions I led the *Holzaugenrotte* (high cover pair of Me 109s). In the Malta missions I was not able to gain any victories. But today I do not regret this. At Comiso (on 23 February 1942)[41] I suffered a crash during a landing approach, due to a forgotten ammunition case left on the runway. The result was that my Me 109 turned over, and I spent five months in hospital.

With the arrival of the first Spitfires on Malta, flown off an aircraft carrier, on 7 March 1942,[42] a new chapter in the long history of air combat over the island began. On 10 March the Spitfires flew their first operation, successfully bouncing *JG 53* Me 109s escorting Ju 88 bombers, and killing *Feldwebel* Heinz Rahlmeier of *8/JG 53*;[43] in return one Hurricane pilot was killed (probably by *Hauptmann* Karl-Heinz Krahl, *Gruppenkommandeur II/JG 3*) and another crashed when caught landing by *Unteroffizier* Hans

Schade of *8/JG* 53.[44] Another nine Spitfires delivered via carrier arrived on Malta on 21 March, by which stage only two of the first 15 were still serviceable, and soon after their arrival a massive raid on Takali airfield was delivered by *c.* 70 Ju 88s; five RAF fighter pilots were killed, and nine aircraft destroyed (including two Spitfires and four Hurricanes) and 26 damaged (including five Spitfires and 15 Hurricanes), all these casualties being suffered on the ground.[45] Although seven more Spitfires arrived on 29 March (and more Hurricanes were flown in directly from the Western Desert – table above),[46] attrition amongst these and all aircraft on Malta was essentially more rapid than the pace of such deliveries as aircraft succumbed to bombing and air combat.

On 20 April the US carrier *Wasp* flew off 47 new Spitfires of which 46 reached the island safely, but the Germans were fully aware of this reinforcement and launched 272 bomber sorties against the Malta fighter fields, with the net result that five Spitfires were lost, two on the ground and a further 11 damaged, nine on the ground, all on that same day.[47] So the intense fighting in the air over Malta was matched by ferocious bombing of the small island, most of it aimed in this blitz on the RAF airfields. The continued resistance of the British pilots and the advent of the Spitfires impressed their opponents, amongst them *Oberfeldwebel* Josef Kronschnabel, *9/JG* 53 who made one claim for an RAF fighter over Malta[48] and paid tribute to his enemy. 'The English were, as always, impressive as opponents and fighters over Malta. They tried to repel the attacks of the bombers that we fighters were escorting, but which they seldom achieved as we were then superior in numbers to them. In dogfights they were superior to us, as the Spitfire was more manoeuvrable. We hardly ever allowed ourselves to get into dogfights and utilised other opportunities to get into shooting positions. The English pilots were brave enemies, despite their inferiority in numbers.'

Despite the Spitfires now available to the defenders, the Me 109s continued to bounce the British fighters, as they had the time and distance between taking off from Sicily and arriving over Malta to gain enough height for surprise attacks from above, for which the Me 109 F was so well suited. The intense fighting and continuous bombing of airfields meant that RAF defending fighter formations remained relatively small, and attacking Me 109s were often not just in superior tactical positions over the island, but also many times were present there in superior numbers. The tasks of the German fighter pilots in the second Malta blitz were many and varied, as summed up by the next witness, *Feldwebel* Alfred Seidl of 8/JG 53 who made two confirmed claims for British fighters[49] over the island. 'January to May 1942: attacks on Malta; operated as *Schwarmführer*, and flew escort for German and Italian convoys, as well as bomber escorts and low level attacks on Malta itself.'

The climax of this, the second Malta blitz, came on 20–22 April 1942, marked by the loss of seven defending Spitfires and two Hurricanes, with four Me 109s also downed; a second peak occurred from 9 to 12 May, when 13 Spitfires and five Me 109s were lost.[50] Altogether, from 19 December 1941 to 18 May 1942, JG 53 claimed a total of 195 victories over Malta, with the top scorers for this period shown below:[51]

Major Günther Freiherr von Maltzahn, *Kommodore*, Stab/JG 53 – 14

Hauptmann Helmut Belser, *Staffelkapitän* 6 and later 8/JG 53 – 14

Oberfeldwebel Rudolf Ehrenberger, 6/JG 53 – 14

Hauptmann Gerhard Michalski, *Staffelkapitän* 4/JG 53 – 9

Oberfeldwebel Herbert Rollwage, 5/JG 53 – 8

In its turn, *JG 53* lost seven pilots killed, 11 missing and 10 POW over Malta and surrounds, with seven wounded in combat; in addition eight more pilots died in accidents with one more wounded.[52] Notable pilots lost included *Leutnant* Hermann Neuhoff of 7/JG 53, victor in 40 combats, who was taken prisoner on 10 April 1942; *Feldwebel* Hans Schade of 8/JG 53 with 13 victories to his name was killed on 1 April in action, and *Leutnant* Siegmund Hosnedl of 7/JG 53, 10 victories, died in an accident on 15 May 1942.[53] II/JG 3 claimed only six victories over Malta, and lost two pilots killed, two POW and one killed in an accident; among the dead was 24-victory *Ritterkreuzträger* and *Gruppenkommandeur*, *Hauptmann* Karl-Heinz Krahl, shot down by flak on 14 April 1942.[54]

One German pilot who was shot down over Malta and landed in the sea like so many others, German, Italian and British, only survived by a miracle after eight days in his dinghy; many of the others were not that lucky and many were not rescued and disappeared in the vastness of the Mediterranean Sea. This lucky survivor was *Unteroffizier* Dr Felix Sauer, originally a member of 6/JG 53, and from February 1942 with the *Jabo-Staffel*, 10/JG 53: 'In December 1941 I was sent to Sicily – to fly sorties over Malta until May 1942. There, I flew 90 sorties as a fighter pilot, until I was shot down on 16 May 1942 – followed by a spectacular rescue by the Italian torpedo boat (small destroyer) *Turbine*, after eight days drifting about in the Mediterranean. This "happening" has appeared in numerous newspapers, books and films, on the air and on TV. I am still being asked (written in 1990) in a variety of enquiries for my impressions of this eight days' odyssey in the Mediterranean. It remains to be said that the one-time enemies (in the air) have long made friends and have visited one another. In 1992 a grand reunion is scheduled in Malta, of all the pilots, their ground staff and the flak. For myself, I hope for a reunion and reconciliation with the four survivors of an American bomber, shot down by myself later, over Germany.'

Dr Sauer sent me a copy of an Italian newspaper article (in English) on his eight-day ordeal at sea: 'I am sending you the version of the late Italian writer Dino Buzzati, which appeared in the newspaper *Corriere della Sera*, which you may use if you like. It was written in 1942, immediately after my rescue. In case you use it, I should be grateful to you if you would include an honourable mention of my rescuers – the brave Italian officers and sailors of the *Turbine*. In 1943 this vessel exploded and was sunk after an attack by the Americans and English on Sicily.' Excerpts from this article (given in quotation marks)[55] are combined with brief summary linking texts, giving a shortened and edited version of the newspaper story: 'He landed on the sea by parachute, spent eight days in a tiny rubber boat without food or drink, accompanied by a fly and a seagull, and followed by strange kinds of fishes. With an admirable endurance and consideration he manages to keep away despair and Death who, apparently, is in no hurry, being sure of his prey. Above all, however, he trusts in the power of Heaven, and his faith is so strong that the miracle happens: as he is about to give up, an Italian warship, which is crossing the Mediterranean, makes for the shipwrecked pilot, a fact which would amount to the same as discovering an ant in the heart of a desert. But here are the details of the event – comparable only to the happenings in old adventure tales.'

His adventure began with a sortie over Malta and consequent air combat. 'Dr S., teacher of biology and chemistry at a German high school – it is of some importance to know this fact for the better understanding of the whole adventure – is an airman and sergeant in reserve. After fighting a long time on the Channel coast, he came to Sicily, from where he flew more than 90 sorties over Malta. On May 16, he and four other fighters escorted a heavy bomber over the airfield of Hal-Far. During this attack four Spitfires suddenly appeared in the sky. S. moves to counter-attack. But as he gives the gun, there is an explosion in the engine, which goes dead. He dives and escapes his enemies. He knows that there is nothing left to do now. So he descends from 3,000 m to 700 m and parachutes himself out. His comrades fly some circles around him and make him understand that they have seen him and that they will try to help him. While bailing out he hurts his chin. For a while he is stunned, but the cold water soon restores him to his senses. He detaches himself from the parachute and inflates his small rubber boat. Every member of a fighter squadron carries such a boat with him, fixed to his shoulder.' Confidently expecting early rescue by the German air-sea rescue units, Felix Sauer settles down to wait. 'Our flying biologist settles down in his boat and begins to wait (and see). He is now 15 km east of Marsa Sciroco on Malta. It is about four pm. Somebody is sure to come to his aid. And, actually, after an hour and a half, there appears a sea rescue aircraft, escorted by fighters. While it is trying to land, five Spitfires attack it, though its markings are perfectly visible. This unfair attack is avenged at once. One of the Spitfires is shot down at the same moment. But the rescue aircraft has to turn back as well. Dr S. finds himself alone again.'

While still in sight of Malta, Felix Sauer had to endure a heavily escorted, second rescue aircraft appearing and flying right over him, but despite firing off all his signal flares they did not see him in the dusk. As darkness set in he examined his provisions: three chocolate bars (of little use as they would merely increase his thirst), some Pervithin lozenges, and an aluminium film holder with sugar in it, but alas, no water. Later as the breeze blows him back towards Malta he is able to witness a night raid on the island. Soon after, two small boats emerge from the gloom and are obviously looking for someone – him? – their lights straying over the waves. To avoid being taken prisoner, he lies low and as some more bombers approach, the lights are extinguished and they disappear. Soon after his first dawn at sea yet another rescue aircraft flies within 50 m of him but again he is not seen. 'Unfortunately (for him) the day before a reconnaissance plane had come down exactly in the same area. The crew must have perished, for there is only an empty rubber boat floating about – the same type as his boat. The crew in the rescue plane notice the empty boat. "Pity", they think, "S. must be dead or captive!" So they give up the search. Now the biologist realizes: the comrades won't come back. He will have to see how he can help himself (with a miniature boat 2 m long and 1 m wide, and three bars of chocolate?).' During this second day the capricious breeze drives him first south, and towards the end of the day he notices the small island, Filflar, just off the south coast of Malta. In the gathering dusk five British MTBs (motor torpedo boats) are seen and he uses a last signal flare found during the day in his dinghy, to attract their attention, but the fast boats disappear again. Later the two small boats with searchlights of the previous night, return, this time much closer, but he shouts in vain, they do not see him. No more qualms about being taken prisoner, rescue by anyone would now be welcome.

'Felix Sauer refuses to be discouraged. Courage pays! The pilot is 30 years old, mobile and strong. Above all, his mental reserve is inexhaustible. Shipwrecked on a lonely island, he would outdo even Robinson Crusoe.' Cold hard logic tells him that his comrades are no longer looking for him and that the British have not found him in two nights. The breeze still blows and may help him to within visible range of Malta the next day, to be seen and rescued. He takes the yellow silk signal flag and uses the telescopic aluminium tube supplied with it to make a primitive sail, and the breeze takes him to the north once more. His thirst is, thank God, still manageable. 'The castaway is soaked with sea water, his teeth are chattering with cold. He finds some consolation watching five luminous jelly-fish which keep following him.' After a long night, dawn finally arrives, to reveal the mountains of Sicily on the horizon, but any hope of reaching Sicily and friends is soon dashed by the contrary wind which drives him away to the south again. He estimates his drift from a small piece of paper thrown into the sea, and judges he might be able to reach the African coast in four days, but then again, a wind change, sending him eastwards, and he thinks, calmly, this might deliver him to Crete in about seven days. 'God, he thinks will not forsake him.' His faith remains strong. 'No, no, our biologist and chemist isn't raving, not yet, not yet! He hasn't lost his self-control. In a small note-book, like a scientist, he takes down, by and by, all his calculations, observations and deliberations. He mentions the five jelly-fish, some species of flat fish, showing a comb; another strange creature reminding him of the monster of Loch Ness, as it stretched its long snake-like neck out of the water. (Yes, he decides – should he return home – to collect further information about this strange creature from a scientist who knows more than himself.) The tiny sail is moving towards Crete, with its miniature barque and the shipwrecked sailor – a nut-shell on the immensity of the ocean! There is nothing beyond water and sky, eternal monotony! Water and sky, and sky and water.'

As his thirst now, for the first time, really starts to torment him, he obtains a little relief from drops of dew that accumulated on the boat overnight in a calm sea. However, the next day, there is no such luck as the waves kept the boat in motion and no dew collected. He tries using a piece of gauze in an empty flare casing to facilitate condensation of salt from sea water but it does not work. Then he thinks further, still the consummate scientist: drinking small amounts of salt water makes one's thirst worse due to the effect of the salty taste more than anything else, so he takes a small amount in a flare case with a little sugar added; three cases quenches the raging thirst, so in the evening the dosage is repeated. Once more, he finds himself becoming optimistic again – this way he might still hold out. 'Like the capable practical chemist he is, he meantime ponders over certain pills which might serve to precipitate the salt from the sea water. There ought to be a solution to this problem. Back home, he will tackle the problem, for the benefit of all future castaways.' As he drifts helplessly and endlessly further eastwards, all alone, he sees distant RAF fighters and some German Ju 52 transports. He is feeling his strength ebb away and realises that in realistic terms, the odds of rescue are falling fast. He starts a last letter to his wife, on the back of her photo, and on some other scraps of paper. However, his faith in God remains as strong as ever. 'His face is black, scorched by the sun, and sore with the brine, his eyes are swollen and ache, heavy spasms torment his stomach, his limbs have become stiff and paralysed. Will he survive this night?'

He makes it through another night and as the sun rises once more he realises that this must be the last dawn he will see, but then: 'A MIRACLE! – considering that some 10 planes kept searching for big naval units, and in limited areas, without finding them. And here, in the midst of the Mediterranean, a solitary ship is heading straight for a small dinghy and its shipwrecked inmate. Strange! However, his faith never wavered and in some way he had always felt that this moment would come.' He raises his small flag/sail, but the ship has seen him anyway and even greater miracle, it is an allied Italian ship! He is among friends once again and as he is taken gently on board, almost totally helpless, he cannot avoid bursting into tears. 'And then he manages to open his lips and to ask in Italian – *Come state?* – How are you?' The sailors look after him devotedly and he is as one reborn, though on reaching port he can hardly stand. 'Now he is lying in a comfortable bed in the military hospital, awaiting complete recovery. His general has paid him a visit and presented him with the EK I (Iron Cross first class) for his more than 90 flights over Malta. His room is full of flowers. On the bed: the note book with his entries: the log-book of his terrible sea-trip. There are, moreover, the empty shell cases, the film-case with the sugar, one bar of chocolate – left over – (it would only have made him thirstier) and the letter to his wife – no more needed now. When he closes his eyes, he still feels like being in the rubber boat, gently rolling on the waves, together with his fly and his sea-gull.'

Flying the Me 110: Fighter-bombers over Malta
Stab III/ZG 26, and at least elements of the three *Staffeln* (which
served all over the Mediterranean area) flew over Malta from
January 1941 till May 1942, the longest serving unit in this theatre.
They were used as fighter-bombers rather than pure fighters due
to their vulnerability to Hurricanes and Spitfires in combat. Who
better to discuss these missions than the *Gruppenkommandeur*,
Hauptmann Georg Christl? 'I took part in almost all the operations
over Malta. We flew only bombing missions there – carrying two
250 kg and four 50 kg bombs – mostly dropped on the harbour of
La Valetta. These missions were flown at great heights, from the
south out of the sun. After dropping the bombs we dived away
at full speed to the north and thereby ended up flying only a few
metres above the sea. The flak defences around the harbour were
so strong that there remained no other way of carrying out these
bombing attacks. We had only a few losses over Malta.'

One of his men, *Leutnant* Werner Ludwig of the 8th *Staffel*,
remembers flying two fighter-bomber sorties over the Maltese
islands in early 1942 with a totally different attack technique,
and one more dangerous too. 'In early 1942 we flew two attacks
on the islands of Malta (Malta itself, Gozo and Comino). Malta
was mountainous. The harbour of La Valetta had enormous flak
protection and, as a result, was mainly attacked at night by the
bombers. On Gozo there was an airfield that we attacked. We took
off from the south coast of Sicily, from Gela. We attacked from
the north and dropped our bombs, then over the sea south of the
island we turned around at low level and made a second attack
with cannons and machine guns at low level. The defence of the
English light flak was very good, our losses too high, and thus
further such attacks were discontinued.'

Between the Blitzes
During this period (19 May 1942 to 10 October 1942), *Stab* and
II/JG 53 soldiered on over Malta. While III/JG 53 was in North
Africa, I/JG 53 arrived just in time (1 October 1942) back from
Russia to take part in the third blitz.[56] I/JG 77 were also withdrawn
from the Eastern Front to reinforce the German fighters over the
island, arriving in Sicily on 1 July 1942.[57] They were led by the

redoubtable *Hauptmann* Heinz Bär, 113 victory claims and the *Ritterkreuz mit Eichenlaub und Schwerten* to his credit, and one of the major unit leaders and *Luftwaffe* characters of the war.[58]

10/JG 53 Jabo left the Malta theatre on 13 June 1942 for North Africa,[59] but that stalwart Dr Felix Sauer did not go with them. In July 1942, having been discharged from hospital following his eight-day ordeal in a dinghy in the Mediterranean, he was given convalescent leave in Lorient, and promoted to *Feldwebel*. Thereafter he became an instructor for the rest of the war, except for some missions against the American four-engined bombers over Germany, but that is another story.

A newly joined pilot of *JG 53* in Sicily, *Leutnant* Heinz Riedel, was posted to the *Stab* upon arrival, where his *Kommodore* could take him under his wing and teach him the rudiments of being a fighter pilot. Alas, he was not to last longer than about six weeks: 'I am sorry that I cannot contribute much to your book, my time with *Jagdgeschwader 53* was too short. From the beginning of June 1942 until 11 July 1942 I flew in the *Geschwaderstab* of the *Pik-As* as the wingman to Freiherr von Maltzahn (*Kommodore*). On 11 July 1942 I was shot down over Luca on Malta and became a POW of the English on Malta. After about a week I was taken from our small prisoner community on Malta, together with my comrade from the *Pik-As* Dr Heiner Jörg, hailing from Bamberg in Germany, and flown by C-47 to Cairo.'

During this interim period (19 May 1942 to 10 October 1942), *Stab* and *II/JG 53* claimed 67 victories over and around Malta, while losing eight pilots in action and another three in accidents, two as POWs and three wounded; one more crewman was lost from an air sea rescue aircraft, in action.[60] Amongst the missing were two nine-victory aces, *Leutnant* Hans-Volkmar Müller (*5/JG 53*, 5 September 1942) and *Leutnant* Wilhelm Ruge (*5/JG 53*, 8 June 1942).[61] Top scorers with these JG 53 units were *Oberleutnant* Gerhard Michalski, initially *Staffelkapitän 4/JG 53* and then *Gruppenkommandeur* of *II/JG 53* from July 1942 (15 claims), *Oberfeldwebel* Herbert Rollwage *5/JG 53* (ten claims) and *Leutnant* Franz Schiess of the *Geschwaderstab* (six claims).[62] *I/JG 77* claimed 65 victories, top scorers being *Oberleutnant* Siegfried Freytag, *Staffelkapitän* of *1/JG 77* (11 claims),

Oberfeldwebel Walter Brandt of 2nd *Staffel* (ten claims) and *Leutnant* Edgar Berres of 1st *Staffel* (eight claims).[63] In return, they lost five pilots and one POW, plus one wounded pilot, all in action, and one pilot killed in an accident.[64]

The October Blitz: 11–27 October 1942

This was the final blitz on Malta, and though of short duration, was an intense period of aerial combat. The Germans had assembled a strong force in Sicily to try and beat down the offensive activities of Malta's aircraft against desperately needed seaborne supplies for Rommel's army in the Western Desert. Rommel was now facing an imminent British offensive in late October 1942 that was to see his catastrophic defeat in the Battle of Alamein, fought from 23 October to 5 November 1942. The *Luftwaffe* concentrated units from Crete, Russia and North Africa in Sicily: two full Ju 88 *Geschwadern*, KG 54 and KG 77, the similarly equipped II/LG 1, a *Gruppe* of night bombing He 111s as well as a *Schlachtgruppe*, I/SchG 2; Me 109s were from *Stab* and II/JG 53 as well as I/JG 77 (left 27 October 1942), all still based on Sicily, the newly arrived I/JG 53 (in Sicily from 1 October–25 November 1942) and I/JG 27 (5–23 October 1942).[65] These aircraft were sorely missed in the Desert, whence I/JG 27, I/JG 77 and I/SchG 2 departed in late October.[66]

The Germans were faced by a strong Spitfire fighter force of five well stocked squadrons, on better dispersed and blast-protected airfields, now under the control of that fighter expert, Air Vice-Marshal Keith Park of Battle of Britain fame.[67] The blitz itself occurred over only nine days, from 11 to 19 October 1942, and the losses due to air combat and anti-aircraft fire over Malta amounted to: German – 25 bombers and 10 Me 109s; Italian – six fighters; British – 27 Spitfires.[68] JG 53 Me 109s made 18 claims from 11–27 October 1942, while losing 12 Me 109s and six pilots (one a POW, five missing or killed) during the same period.[69] On 15 October, *Hauptmann* Gerhard Michalski, newly appointed *Gruppenkommandeur* of II/JG 53, was shot down on his 500th *Feindflug* (combat mission, meaning enemy contact or over enemy territory, as opposed to operational mission – *Einsatz* – which has a broader meaning also encompassing flights without contact and some of those over friendly territory). Michalski parachuted into the sea and was soon rescued by a Do 24 flying boat, escorted by Me 109s of 2/*JG* 53. Soon after the flying boat had to make a second sea landing to rescue *Feldwebel* Gerhard Stockmann, one of its escorting Me 109 pilots, who had just been shot down by Malta Spitfires.[70] The next day *Unteroffizier* Heinz Golinski of 3/*JG* 53, after making his 46th victory claim, was shot down and posted missing; he was posthumously awarded the *Ritterkreuz*.[71] I/*JG* 77 claimed almost twice the number of victories (11–27 October 1942) as the two *Gruppen* of *JG* 53 together, namely 35 while losing 11-victory ace *Leutnant* Wilhelm Scheib of 1st *Staffel* on 12 October; top scorer of the *Gruppe* was *Oberleutnant* Siegfried Freytag, *Staffelkapitän* of 1/*JG* 77, who made 10 claims.[72]

I/*JG* 27 claimed seven Spitfires for two Me 109s (both pilots lost) shot down over Malta (11–23 October 1942), before their departure back to Africa.[73] A witness from this *Gruppe*, *Feldwebel* Gerhard Keppler of the 1st *Staffel* probably assigned more importance to espionage than was warranted. 'The missions that I flew from Sicily over Malta, from 10 October to 5 November 1942 (*sic*, they were only there till 23 October), were mostly escorts for Ju 88 and Me 110 formations. I recall these missions as extremely unsatisfactory, as our take-offs in Sicily were continuously reported by agents to Malta and, as a result, the British fighter defence was always high up in the sun when we arrived, waiting for us. They could thus always attack us from very advantageous positions (often from head-on), which greatly exacerbated our fighter escort duty and also brought large losses to the bomber formations, without us being able to counterattack effectively.' It was far more likely that it was the efficient use of Malta's radar under the steady hand of Keith Park rather than a nest of Sicilian spies that resulted in the unsatisfactory missions detailed here by Gerhard Keppler.

JG 53, I/*JG* 77 and I/*JG* 27 claimed a total of 60 Spitfires over Malta (11–27 October 1942) while British losses amounted to only 31.[74] Obviously there is significant over-claiming here (not unusual in intense air combat over short time periods) and much of this needs to be laid at the door of I/*JG* 77, which made the most claims. Its top-scoring pilot in the October blitz, Siegfried Freytag, gained the nickname of the 'Star of Malta',[75] which must have been seen as at least a bit presumptuous by the *JG 53* veterans of the Malta theatre.

After 27 October 1942, fighting over Malta dwindled rapidly, only one Spitfire crash-landing following combat damage and a single Me 109 of *I/SchG* 2 being lost to British anti-aircraft fire from 28 October to 7 November 1942.[76] On 8 November the Allied invasion of French North Africa began and *JG 53* and *JG 77* rapidly became embroiled in the Tunisian campaign with Malta then largely out of the *Luftwaffe*'s mainstream. It is fitting that a pilot from *JG 53* should have the final word on the Malta campaign. As recounted before, *Oberfeldwebel* Josef Ederer of *3/JG 53* had been seriously wounded landing back at Comiso on 23 February 1942 when his aircraft turned over on landing: 'On 14 September 1942, after these five months in hospital I rejoined my *Staffel* in Pitomnik, Stalingrad. In the middle of November 1942 (*sic*, this transfer was at the end of September)[77] we left our Me 109 Gs behind and were flown out of Stalingrad with Ju 52s, over the Balkans, where we had a stopover in Tirana, and on to Sicily. Against the English we now had only old Me 109 Fs available. Now we were in Sicily for the second time and had a much better enemy in front of us than the first time.' Despite these privations over Malta, he had had a lucky escape in getting away from Stalingrad before that city and its largely German occupiers were surrounded and wiped out. His *Staffel* was the last unit of *JG 53* to see action over Malta, remaining behind in Sicily on 25 November 1942 when the rest of the *Gruppe* departed for North Africa, and remaining in Sicily until 15 December 1942.[78]

4

TUNISIA: THE END IN AFRICA, NOVEMBER 1942–MAY 1943

For the German fighter units sent to the Tunisian theatre, while individuals experienced success in air combat, the overall situation was rather negative with almost continuous retreats, especially for those flying in support of the *Afrikakorps*, entering southern Tunisia from the Western Desert and Tripolitania with the victorious 8th Army and Desert Air Force in hot pursuit. As *Oberfeldwebel* Johann Pichler, 7/JG 77 put it: 'In November 1942 we transferred to North Africa, and then experienced the retreat right back to Tunis; we flew to Sardinia on 10 May 1943.'

On 8 November 1942, the Americans and British landed in French North Africa, in Morocco in the West and in the Oran and Algiers areas in Algeria further to the East.[1] They were hoping to drive east from Algiers and to take Tunis and Bizerta in northern Tunisia, thereby cutting off Field Marshal Rommel's *Afrikakorps*, retreating westwards along the Cyrenaican coast after their massive defeat by the British 8th Army at the Battle of El Alamein (23 October to 4 November).[2] However, on 9 November, Hitler began pouring troops into the north of Tunisia, initially in the Bizerta area; the Allies responded by seizing the port of Bône (Annaba today) on 12 November, on the north Algerian coast about 70 km west of the Tunisian-Algerian border.[3] By 15–16 November, Allied forces (now including local French troops) had advanced further eastwards across the border into north-western Tunisia, taking the Tabarka-Beja-Souk el Arba areas.[4] By late November 1942, the Allies held a line running south to south-eastwards from the coast in northern Tunisia and about 50 odd kilometres west of Tunis at its nearest; further south, isolated forces held the Kasserine Pass area and south of that, the Gafsa area (north-west of Gabes).[5] The Allies were to remain largely stalled in northern Tunisia until May 1943.[6]

Meanwhile the victorious 8th Army advanced rapidly westwards, largely along the coast of Egypt and Libya, reaching the El Agheila position where they twice before had been halted and defeated, in late November 1942. This position was taken in a battle between 13 and 16 December, and then the advance continued westwards, with Tripoli falling on 23 January 1943, after a stiff preceding battle at Buerat (15–16 January).[7] General Montgomery's veteran army continued westwards, advancing across the Tunisian border at the beginning of February, and then taking Medenine on 17 February. That wily old fox, *Feldmarschall* Rommel took an opportunity now to assemble the three *panzer* divisions in Tunisia and fall on 2nd US Corps in the Kasserine Pass-Tebessa area (14–24 February), inflicting a sharp defeat.[8] He then came south again, intending to dish out the same medicine to the 8th Army, but was roundly defeated himself at the Battle of Medenine on 6 March 1943, followed by a further defeat in the Battle of Mareth from 20–27 March, further north-westwards into southern Tunisia.[9] Advancing eastwards in southern Tunisia, US forces took Gafsa on 17 March, while the advancing 8th Army took Gabes (on the coast to the southeast) on 29 March 1943.[10] After the Battle of Wadi Akarit in the Gabes Gap (6 April), US and 8th Army forces met on the Gafsa-Gabes road on the 7 April; subsequently, the 8th Army advanced rapidly northwards along the eastern Tunisian coast, taking Sfax (10 April), Sousse (12 April 1943), and meeting with British 1st Army (northern Tunisia) at Kairouen on 11 April.[11] By now the Germans had been squeezed back into north-eastern Tunisia and 1st Army, reinforced by units from the 8th, on 6 May 1943 made a major attack in the north, from the Medjez el Bab area towards Tunis (which fell on 7 May, as did Bizerta on the north coast, the latter to US 2nd Corps).[12] Within a few days German remnants surrendered in the Cap Bon Peninsula, north-east of Tunis.[13]

Luftwaffe Jagdgruppen, which served in the Tunisian arena included the whole of *JG 53* and *JG 77,* as well as *II/JG 2* and *II/JG 51,* plus two *Schlachtgruppen: III/ZG 2* (which became *II/SKG 210* in January 1943; flew Fw 190s) and *I/SG 2* on Me 109s and Hs 129 tank-busters.[14] While *JG 53* spent the entire campaign stationed in northern Tunisia in the Tunis-Bizerta area (*Stab/JG 53* – 9 November 1942–30 April 1943; *I/JG 53* – 25 November 1942–30 April 1943; *II/JG 53* – 9 November 1942–9 May 1943; *III/JG 53* – only for two brief periods, 9–30 November 1942 and 7–10 May 1943) as apparently did *III/ZG 2* also, *II/JG 51* (14 November 1942–4 January 1943) and *II/JG 2* (20 November 1942–11 January 1943) were stationed there only in the earlier few months.[15] Here these units supported German ground forces in northern Tunisia where hard fighting against 1st Army took place with little opportunity for a war of manoeuvre. *II/JG 51* and *I/SG 2* were transferred to the Gabes area in southern Tunisia in late 1942–early 1943, presumably in case 8th Army had burst unexpectedly through the struggling and retreating *Afrikakorps.*[16] *II/JG 2* and *II/JG 51* were moved to the Sousse region (respectively: 11 January–15 March 1943, and February–8 April 1943) to support German attacks against French troops in the Ousseltia-Robaa area from 18 to 23 January and a second attack against the French in the Sbeitla area (30 January–2 February 1943); following this, *II/JG 2* returned to France on 22 March.[17]

Feldwebel Alfred Rauch, *5/JG 51* was amongst those meeting the American air forces for the first time: 'In Africa we had to do with the American fighter the "Lightning". It was the equal of our Me 109. But the superiority of the Americans made itself much more felt through their greater numbers.' Meanwhile, far to the south and the east, the whole of *Jagdgeschwader 77* was flying against Desert Air Force and the British 8th Army as the latter two forces advanced from the El Agheila position westwards to Medenine (*Stab, II and III/JG 77* – mid-December 1942 to 15 February 1943; *I/JG 77* mid-December 1942 till 3 February 1943).[18] In January 1943 the rapidity of the retreat seems to have got to *Oberfeldwebel* Johann Pichler of *7/JG 77*: 'Eight days ago we lay almost 300 km east of Tripoli, while since the day before yesterday we are about the same distance to the west thereof.'

On 16 January 1943, Johann Pichler led one of two *Schwarme* in pursuit of a formation of Lightnings that had strafed their field base at Bir Dufan, but suffered engine problems about 120 km deep in the desert just as they neared their quarry, and had to force-land.[19] He was rescued by the *Gruppe's* Fieseler Storch several hours later, none the worse for wear.[20] The other *Schwarm* of 7/JG 77 on this occasion had been led by *Oberfeldwebel* Eduard Isken who had seen Pichler's forced landing, and who was the only one of the eight Me 109 pilots to claim one of the P-38s, but this was not confirmed.[21] In correspondence with the author, Isken noted that he had claimed a total of 15 victories over North Africa by the end of January 1943, to add to his 16 Russian claims; he would survive the war with a total score of 56 victories, including 17 of the feared four-engined bombers and in return was himself shot down nine times, bailing out on six of these occasions. He was awarded the *Ritterkreuz* in January 1945, still an *Oberfeldwebel*! *Unteroffizier* Werner Killer, unlike Isken and Pichler was no veteran and describes joining 9/JG 77 on 16 January 1943 just after finishing his training:

Now I was 20 years old, an *Unteroffizier* and qualified fighter pilot. After leave with my parents, my journey took me via Munich by train and on to Bari in Italy. Here we could, as available, take over aircraft assigned to us or alternatively ferry Bf 109-Gs to units at the front. As I enjoyed flying, I gladly took on this task, and thus I was able to take one machine to Sicily and another one to Gabes in Tunisia. The flights back took place in a Ju 52 and the Gigant Me 323. On 16 January 1943 I was allowed to take over a machine assigned to my *Geschwader*, a Bf 109 G trop (adapted for service under tropical conditions), yellow 12. My flight went from Reggio, via Trapani, Tunis, Gabes, Tripoli to El Asabaa. Seeing as this airfield was not shown on any map and all I had to go on were vague directions given to me by a lorry driver from Castell Benito, when I began this journey, I was thus glad when I managed to actually find the field. I certainly never belonged to the fighter aces, like *Hauptmann* Ubben, *Major* Harder, *Hauptmann* Bär, *Hauptmann* Clausen, or *Oberleutnant* Omert, to whom I handed over my machine. They were all *Ritterkreuz* winners, some even *Eichenlaub* winners, with over 50 and even 100 victories. I was assigned to the 9th *Staffel*, JG 77 of *Leutnant* Ernst. The most successful pilot in my *Staffel*, with 50 victories, was *Feldwebel* Kaiser. My first victory: On 2 February at 07h50 our *Schwarm* took off. Our task was to protect Ju 87s. After a short time we caught up with the formation, 12 Stukas. We had been ordered to provide indirect escort, 500 to 1000 m above the formation. I flew as wingman (*Kaczmarek*) to *Leutnant* Ernst. At *c.* 08h30 we reached the target: American positions, tanks and lorry concentrations. (As the Stukas made to drop their bombs, enemy fighters were reported below the Bf 109 *Schwarm*). With a dive we got behind a close-packed, totally unaware Kittyhawk formation. I reduced my excess speed through side-slips. My sights were switched on, the guns were loaded. Then *Leutnant* Ernst opened fire. (Werner Killer then attacked the Kittyhawk flying second from the right, getting so close the American markings appeared to be huge). I pressed the triggers, and machine guns and cannons delivered their load into the aircraft in front of me. Parts and fragments flew over my canopy. With a sharp left turn I avoided getting myself in front of one of the enemy aircraft. Straight away I had another Kittyhawk in front of me, a short burst of fire, and with a white smoke trail it went down, I wanted to follow it, but had one behind me myself (he escaped by pulling his 109 up into the sun). On the ground two burning aircraft could be seen! The return flight was trouble-free and we had no losses ourselves. I waggled my wings over our field, and landed at 09h05. I was greeted joyously by the mechanics and congratulated on my first *Abschuss*. While this might sound very pleasant, did we also see the unending suffering, the death and destruction we brought to others and that was brought to us? May God prevent another war from happening and may mankind become wiser.

Soon after this, on 4 March 1943, Werner Killer was himself shot down and made prisoner in Tunisia.[22] JG 77 had arrived in North Africa at a time marked by the long and final retreat of the *Afrikakorps* from deep within Egypt right back to Tunis. Two days after his forced landing in the desert (16 January 1943), *Oberfeldwebel* Johann Pichler, 7/JG 77 enjoyed a more positive experience: 'To add to my first two *Abschüsse* in Africa (two P-40s on 14 January)[23] I was able to score a third victory on 18 January 1943. It was a four-engined American bomber that I shot down during a raid on Tripoli.' This raid on Tripoli was made by 12 B-17s escorted by about 25 P-38s and was intercepted by *c.* 20 Me 109s of the *Geschwader* who became involved with the escort, claiming one of them; Johann Pichler was the only one to get at the bombers, having taken off late and on his own, and mortally damaged one before being chased away by the P-38 Lightnings,[24] as he recalled: 'I had initially not seen any of the Lightnings. Only when I was about to make my third attack on the hindmost three bombers, was I attacked and shot at by four Lightnings.' Johann Pichler shot down two more victories in Tunisia, a brace of B-25s on 4 and 5 April 1943 (bringing his total for the war to 33 victory claims at that stage, with more to follow later).[25]

Most of *JG 77* as well as *I/SG 2* were transferred to the area north–north-west of Sfax in central Tunisia to provide fighter and ground attack support for the German attack on US 2nd Corps in the Thelepte-Kasserine-Tebessa battle of 14–24 February 1943; *Stab* and *II/JG 77* arrived there on 15 February, *I/JG 77* on 3 February and they all departed between 6 and 8 April.[26] They were joined later by *III/JG 77* (which had been sent to, firstly the Gafsa area from 15–26 February, and then back to Medenine again, 26 February to 15 March 1943), also till 8 April.[27] Final movements of the remaining German fighter units were to the Tunis and Cap Bon Peninsula region at the end of the campaign, including all of *JG 77* (6–8 April till 7–8 May 1943) and II/JG 51 (8–19 April), where a final stand was made.[28] Most of these pilots, plus those of *JG 53*, finally got away but first did several trips to ferry out key ground personnel in the back of their Messerschmitt fighters which were cut open behind the cockpit to make their accommodation possible.[29]

A portion of the handwritten *Kriegstagebuch* (war diary) of *I/JG 77* during its time in Tunisia was copied by Dr Paul Robert Skawran, the *Luftwaffe* psychologist who spent a lot of time during the Tunisian operations with *JG 77* and *JG 53*.

Date (all 1943)	Base	Missions Flown	Sorties flown	Victories claimed	Losses	Attacks on own base	Details (sentences in italics reflect ground operations)
4 February	Fatnassa	1	7	2 (Bär's 153rd–154th claims)	0	0	Scramble and combat with 42 B17s, 12 P38s and 12 Bostons. Bär claims first four-engined victory of I/JG 77.
6 February	"	?	?	0	0	0	British reports claim 26 German fighters shot down 4 February in big British attack on Gabes – actually only three Germans shot down over own territory, and eight enemies claimed.
15 February	"	4	37	2 (Bär's 155–156)	0	0	*Enemy forces destroyed at Sidi bou Sid.* Low level attack on Telepte airfield, combat over field with 10 Spitfires and P40s.
26 February	"	5	35	10 (Bär's 157–161)	0	0	*Battles at Sidi bou Sid and Sbeitla.* Enemy fighter bombers attack Gabes. Combat with 60 P40s, Spitfires and Beaufighters.
27 February	"	?	?	2 (Bär's 162–163)	0	0	Enemy attack on Gabes. Apart from two claims, one Spitfire *wirksam beschossen.*

Summary of operations, data taken from copy of *Kriegstagebuch I/JG 77*: 4 February–8 May 1943 (via P.R. Skawran)[30]

Date (all 1943)	Base	Missions Flown	Sorties flown	Victories claimed	Losses	Attacks on own base	Details (sentences in italics reflect ground operations)
3 March	"	3	16	2 (Bär's 164–165)	0	Three US bomber attacks on Fatnassa – one by B17s, two by formations of Mitchells and Bostons. One Me destroyed, one lightly damaged, five soldiers killed.	Combat with 20–30 P40s.
5 March	"	2	34	1 (Bär's 166)	0	0	Combat with 20 P40s and Spitfires.
6 March	"	2	22	3 (Bär's 167–169)	0	0	Combat with 20 P40s and Spitfires.
7 March	"	3	37	1 (Bär's 170)	0	0	*Freie Jagd* in Medenine area. Combat with 36 Spitfires and 60 P40s.
10 March	"	?	?	1 (Bär's 171)	0	0	*Mareth position.* On an operation with 14 Me 109s escorting Stukas (Ksar-Khilane area) had combat with 20 P40s and 6 Spitfires.
13 March	"	?	?	0	0	0	Scramble and *Hauptmann* Bär, in Gabes area, attacked a P40 – *wirksam beschossen* (seriously damaged).
23 March	"	?	?	1 (Bär's 172)	0	0	*Major Müncheberg killed after 135th victory, unbeaten.* Apart from this victory, Bär also got a P39 *wirksam beschossen.*

24 March	"	?	7 (Bär's 173–174)	1	Two bomber raids, each by 18 Mitchells and c. 30 escorting fighters.	*Mareth front quiet.* Intense enemy air activity. Scramble at 09h40 led to combat of 13 Me 109s with 18 Mitchells, c. 30 P40s, Spitfires and P39s.
25 March	Fatnassa (moved to La Fauconnerie and Bou Thadi)	?	o	o	Prior to move two further bomber raids on airfield.	
6 April	Bou Thadi (moved to La Smala)	?	o	o	o	
8 April	La Smala (moved to Korba)	?	o	o	o	
14 April	Korba (moved to Soliman-South)	?	o	o	o	
16 April	Soliman-South	?	1 (Bär's 176)	o	o	*Freie Jagd* over convoy in area of Cape Bon, combat of two Me 109s with 12 Spitfires.

Records of the retreat from Africa to Sicily destroyed by enemy action. 20 April–11 May 1943: in this time interval the *Gruppe* flew fighter bomber escorts and *Freie Jagd* missions in the combat areas Pont-du-Fahs and Medjes El Bab. Cover for ships outside and within the Bay of Tunis seldom led to action or victories. Flew a few escorts for reconnaissance aircraft as far as south of Sousse and Kairouan, without meeting the enemy. Four bombing raids on own field at Soliman-South; four Me 109s destroyed. On the evening of 7 May and on 8 May 1943, 50 officers and other ranks from the ground staff ferried to Sicily with Me 109s in four repeat operations. New base at Chinisa near Marsalla, Sicily.

Once *I/JG 77* had withdrawn from North Africa and survived the following Sicilian campaign, in about August 1943 he was able to take the time to copy a part of this insightful document, for the period 4 February to 16 April 1943.[31] Details were few, and only the victory claims of *Gruppenkommandeur Major* Heinz Bär were recorded in the *Kriegstagebuch,* a common practice in the ace-obsessed *Luftwaffe.* The brief details of the daily combats provide a small window into the many different tasks facing a typical *Jagdgruppe* in the Tunisian theatre.

In addition to the fighter units operating directly in Tunisia, four others were stationed in Sicily to defend that island and southern Italy from American bomber attacks, to oppose aircraft from Malta and also to provide the escorts for the very hazardous German supply flights across the Mediterranean to Tunisia. These included *III/JG 53*, who also had a brief time in Tunisia as seen above; they flew from Sicily and temporarily also from Sardinia, from 30 November 1942–5 May 1943.[32] One of their pilots was *Oberfeldwebel* Alfred Seidl of 8th *Staffel* who recalled: 'After recovering from being shot down and wounded after bailing out (30 September 1942, Western Desert), at the end of February 1943 I was sent back to *III/JG 53*, in Sicily at San Pedro airfield. From March until May 1943 I flew missions to Tunis from almost all the airfields in Sicily.' Other Sicily-based *Gruppen* were *II/JG 27* (27 February to 20 June 1943), *III/JG 27* (March to May 1943) and *III/ZG 26* (November 1942 till June 1943).[33]

Unteroffizier Heinz Hommes was a newly qualified fighter pilot when he arrived in Sicily to join *9/JG 53*, and experienced his early combats mainly against Spitfires, as detailed below. As *III/JG 53* flew frequent escorts for ships (and later transport aircraft) carrying supplies to Tunisia, they were in Tunis often and had combat in that area also, quite apart from fighting the Malta-based Spitfires:[34]

I was no fighter 'ace', but I was an average fighter pilot. After my training – from October 1940 until December 1942 – I became operational in Tunis in North Africa. My unit was the 9th *Staffel*, III *Gruppe* of *JG 53* '*Pik-As*'.

My first opponents were the English in their Spitfires. As *Katschmarek* of my *Staffelkapitän* I survived the first few combats unharmed, but without any successes myself. We had great respect for the English, who were basically fair enemies. Their Spitfires by now were the equals of the Me 109s and even began to overtake the 109 in their flying characteristics. If during aerial combats we were attacked from behind, we used a tactic of pulling up steeply, as the 109 with the 'DB 601' engine had fuel injection. When the Spitfire tried to follow, its fuel supply cut out briefly and it would fall back. We would then pull round and change our role from hunted to hunter. When attacked we also pulled up into the sun, so that our opponents would become blinded and then fall away. The clouds also often saved us from being hit. Our attacking tactic was mostly – whether against the English in Tunisia or later the Americans (in 1944 over Romania) as well as the Russians (1944–1945 over Hungary) – from above, that is from above and behind. By diving down we gained a lot of speed and about 100 m below our targets we pulled up and opened fire from about 60 m distance. The excess speed was used to pull up, as the enemies were not without abilities. Often then a dogfight would begin that could end either way. The adopted attack method we used was not without its dangers. On the one hand the battles were happening at ever higher altitudes, at which the flying characteristics of the aircraft – due to the thin air – changed. On the other hand when hitting an enemy with a burst of fire, parts of the aircraft could break off and hit your own machine. An aerial combat necessitated the highest concentration and lightning-fast reactions.

I corresponded with Hans-Ulrich Kornstädt for some years and finally met him in May 1993 at a gathering of the *Gemeinschaft der Jagdflieger* in Munich. He very kindly supplied me with a copy of his self-published book on his adventures as a fighter pilot and prisoner of war, from which the following account of his experiences is derived.[35] Hans-Ulrich Kornstädt was a freshly-baked *Leutnant* when he joined *II/JG 27* in Düsseldorf at the end of December 1942, where they were resting and awaiting new pilots and aircraft; on 26 February 1943 they finally moved to the front, landing at Trapani in Sicily. Kornstädt was by now the Technical Officer of the 4th *Staffel*, and their tasks were now many: apart from local defence of their airfield, defence of the island (against escorted enemy bomber formations) also fell to them, and hardest of all, long escort flights for convoys, lone ships and German transport aircraft across the Mediterranean to Tunisia. Life was very hectic, few missions not leading to enemy contact and combat; in his first three months, Hans-Ulrich Kornstädt flew 124 *Feindflüge*,[36] a very heavy workload for a newly joined pilot. The first time he opened fire on the enemy was against a Spitfire on the return flight from escorting Ju 52s to Tunis, but unfortunately he was too far away from the Spitfire and failed to see his *Rottenführer*, who was closer to the Spitfire; his first shots in action thus damaged his own comrade's Me 109 but the pilot, an *Unteroffizier*, made it back to Sicily. The *Luftwaffe* used a very sensible system whereby the most experienced pilots led in the air irrespective of rank, and *Leutnant* Hans-Ulrich was subjected to quite a tirade from the *Unteroffizier* on landing! But he was also a kind comrade and reported the damage to his own aircraft as being 'enemy-inflicted'![37]

On 9 May 1943, a few days before the German and Italian forces now trapped in north-eastern Tunisia surrendered, Hans-Ulrich Kornstädt had his first encounter with a four-engined bomber formation and scored his first victory.[38] A massive raid was mounted on Palermo by B-17s as well as American medium bombers all with a strong fighter escort, together 211 aircraft.[39] Kornstädt was first off from Trapani and, his inexperience showing, attacked 36 B-17s on his own, making two lone head-on attacks, with the lead B-17 having two engines set on fire on the second pass, and crashing into the sea.[40] The excitement and terror in this first full-on encounter with an enemy formation was such that the young pilot soiled himself (a not uncommon ordeal for many a green pilot in all air forces) and on landing was congratulated by his *Kommodore*,

Oberstleutnant Gustav Rödel who pinned the Iron Cross 2nd Class on his uniform while complaining of the smell![41]

The last Axis forces in Tunisia surrendered on 13 May 1943.[42] In operations over Tunisia, Sicily and the Mediterranean from 8 November 1942 to 9 May 1943, *JG 53* had claimed 277 victories, but against this has to be balanced losses of 206 Messerschmitt fighters (60% plus grade of damage, 60% being the write-off level), with another 92 damaged; 75 pilots were lost (killed, missing, POW) and 36 wounded.[43] There had definitely been a turning point in the air war by now, with *JG 53*'s losses amounting to more than three quarters of their claim numbers. For *JG 77*, their victory claims were significantly higher at 376 between 15 December 1942 and 8 May 1943;[44] against this 170 aircraft were lost (60% damage and higher), 94 damaged, while pilot losses came to 60 killed, missing, POW and 14 wounded.[45] *II/JG 51* scored 121 victories for the loss of 14 pilots, eight wounded, plus 18 lost ground crew and another 22 wounded.[46] Finally, *II/JG 2* claimed about 150 victories for the loss of 18 pilots.[47] The Sicily-based *II/JG 27* made another 48 claims and *III/ZG 26* an additional minimum of 17 while *III/ZG 2/II/SKG 210* contributed at least another two claims; the two *JG 27 Gruppen* suffered 30 pilot losses to all causes, while *III/ZG 26* lost 28 crewmen and *I/SG 2*, 17 pilots.[48] Taking *JG 77*'s victories and losses as counting towards the Tunisian campaign (rather than that in the Western Desert) from 15 December 1942, a German claims total of at least 991 daytime victories is counted; total German losses amount to a minimum (as the *JG 27*, Me 110 and ground attack units' aircraft losses are recorded only where crew were lost) of 451 fighter-type aircraft (Me 109s, Fw 190s, Me 110s, and a few Hs 129 ground attack aircraft). Of course German bomber and especially transport aircraft losses were also very high; total German aircraft losses for the entire central Mediterranean theatre from November 1942 till May 1943 came to at least 2422 (the vast majority of which occurred over Tunisia), with total Allied losses over Tunisia (including Operation Torch – fighting against the French) of 849 aircraft.[49] Italian losses are not included in these totals.

Top scoring *Luftwaffe* fighter pilots over Tunisia (including Sicily-based units) – *JG* 77 claims counted from 15 December 1942, others from arrival in theatre in November 1942.[50]			
Name	Unit	Claims	Notes
Leutnant Ernst-Wilhelm Reinert	*II/JG* 77	51	
Oberleutnant Kurt Bühligen	*II/JG* 2	40	
Major Heinz Bär	*I/JG* 77	38	
Leutnant Erich Rudorffer	*II/JG* 2	27	
Oberleutnant Franz Schiess	*Stab* and *III/JG* 53	23	
Leutnant Wolfgang Tonne	*I/JG* 53	21	Killed accident 20 April 1943
Feldwebel Anton Hafner	*II/JG* 51	20	

Top-scoring German ace over Tunisia was *Leutnant* Ernst-Wilhelm Reinert, who already had over 100 successes in Russia before arriving in the theatre, and whom we shall meet again in later chapters; he was to survive the war. Kurt Bühligen, Heinz Bär and Erich Rudorffer would also survive, but not Schiess, Tonne and Hafner; Bär was one of the great characters in the *Luftwaffe* who flew in action for almost the entire war, ending up as the leading Me 262 ace amongst many other exploits.[51] He had many brushes with authority and was several times demoted in terms of his postings, but was always soon reinstated to senior command positions, as he was a natural leader of vast experience and great capabilities.

5

SICILY AND ITALY,
MAY 1943–SEPTEMBER 1944

After leaving Tunisia, just before its final fall to the Allies, German fighter units flew first of all to Sicily; *JG 53* was retained there and immediately became involved in its defence against an intense Allied bombing campaign, from 30 April for *Stab* and *I/JG 53*, and from 9–10 May 1943 for *II* and *III/JG 53*.[1] *JG 77* was much more fortunate, arriving in Sicily on 7–8 May but all being transferred within a few days to the relative quiet of Italy and in the case of *I/JG 77* even briefly to Germany.[2] *Stab*, *I* and *II/JG 77* would return after this break to Sicily (respectively, for the periods: 13 June to 13 July 1943; 8 June to 10 July 1943; 19 June to 13 July 1943) but *III/JG 77* was sent to Sardinia where most of the *Gruppe* remained for the entire Sicilian campaign.[3] *Stab*, *II* and *III/JG 53* flew out of Sicilian bases until all three units were withdrawn on 13 July, a few days after the invasion of the island began on 10 July 1943; *I/JG 53* left Sicily on 17 June already for southern Calabria where it stayed until withdrawal further north and out of the immediate Sicily battle zone on 16 July.[4] The units of *JG 77* stationed on the island also suffered from heavy Allied bombing attacks before the invasion as well as thereafter, before they left the island.[5]

Other units stationed on the island were *II/JG 27* (from February 1943 until 20 June when withdrawn to southern Italy, where they remained after the evacuation of Sicily), as well as *II/JG 51* but only for two brief periods: 19 April to 5 May, and then for four days when the invasion took place (10–13 July 1943).[6] Thereafter they moved to southern Italy till sometime in July before a further move to northern Italy.[7] *III/JG 27* were in Greece until 14 July 1943 and then moved to the Lecce-Brindisi area after the invasion had begun, before withdrawal to Austria during July.[8] *IV/JG 3*, though stationed near Lecce in the heel of Italy (20 June to 26 July, when withdrawn from the immediate battle zone), had most of their aircraft operating out of Sicily between 12 and 15 July just after the invasion took place.[9] After their withdrawal from Sicily on 13 July, *Stab, II* and *III/JG 53* remained stationed in southern Italy for some time (respectively: till sometime in August 1943; 31 July; 27 July).[10] *Stab* and *II/JG 77* were similarly based in southern Italy after leaving Sicily on 13 July, for the rest of the battle period (i.e. till Sicily fell on 17 August).[11] The movements of *I/JG 77* after leaving Sicily on invasion day (10 July) were more complex and these details can be followed from the *Kriegstagebuch* of this *Gruppe* – see table below.[12]

Defending Sicilian Airspace Prior to the Invasion: May to Early July 1943

Unlike the other fighter *Gruppen* exiting Tunisia in a depleted and exhausted state, those of the '*Pik-As*' *Geschwader* were not soon withdrawn to Italy to recuperate and build up strength in aircraft, equipment and pilots again, but were kept back to defend the island.[13] Together with *II/JG 27* they alone were tasked with the aerial defence of Sicily until approximately mid-June, when two *Gruppen* of JG 77 replaced *I/JG 53* and *II/JG 27* who were both moved back to southern Italy.[14] In this period, *JG 53* had to face a growing Allied aerial attack, mainly by fairly large four- and twin-engined bomber formations, heavily escorted by P-40s, P-38s and Spitfires, Allied fighter-bomber attacks on their airfields adding to the intense bombing of the 'heavies', as well as fighter sweeps over Sicily.[15] Up till 11 June when the Italian-occupied island of Pantelleria surrendered to a seaborne invasion without a shot, having been bombed into submission, *JG 53* also flew many sweeps and escorts over this island.[16] Up till 2 July 1943, *JG 53* claimed 66 enemy aircraft in these varied operations (53 fighters, five twin- and eight four-engined bombers) for the loss of 60 Me 109s, 53 more damaged while losing 15 pilots with 19 more wounded, to all causes.[17] Victory claims and operational losses were becoming perilously close, but the old failing of concentrating on enemy fighters rather than their bombers persisted.

II/JG 27 was exposed to the same combat conditions, as can be illustrated through one experience of Hans-Ulrich Kornstädt, who appeared in the previous chapter. *Leutnant* Kornstädt of 4/JG 27 and his wingman took off from Trapani in Sicily at about 11h00 on 7 June 1943, for a reconnaissance patrol over Pantelleria Island; when they got there, flying at 6000 m in glorious sunshine without a cloud in sight, they saw that the island was almost covered with white and black smoke from Allied bombs.[18] When they got closer they could see that the enemy (about 150 aircraft: B-17s, Marauders, Mitchells and Beaufighters escorted by P-40s, P-38s and Spitfires) were concentrating on the airfield and harbour of Pantelleria.[19] Calling to his wingman to get the hell out of there while they still could, having now completed their reconnaissance, he looked around for his comrade and saw instead two Spitfires coming in behind him. As the dogfight continued his enemies built up to eight Spitfires, and he tried to avoid them by turning very tightly at very slow speed with flaps and undercarriage down,[20] but to no avail. He was soon hit, the engine caught fire and he was spattered with hot glycol, bailing out rapidly and hitting his leg against the aircraft. He landed safely in the sea, out of sight of Sicily, Pantelleria and North Africa, inflated his mae west and then broke all swimming records retrieving his rapidly disappearing dinghy.[21] After an anxious afternoon and night of drifting in the vast sea, Kornstädt was extremely lucky to be rescued by a British destroyer in the early morning mist the next day; this landed him in North Africa and unfortunately for him he ended up as a POW of the French for five years.[22]

The experiences of *Stab, I* and *II/JG* 77 over Sicily between 8 June and 2 July were analogous to those of *JG 53*, with many bombing attacks (mostly on their airfields) by both four- and twin-engined Allied bombers, fighter sweeps, strafing attacks on airfields; in addition, over Sardinia there were a number of large bombing raids targeting harbours and airfields, opposed by *III/JG* 77.[23] As if this was not enough, *JG* 77 performed reconnaissance missions over Malta, Pantelleria and especially of the Tunisian ports of Bizerta and Sousse, as the danger of Allied invasion increased day by day.[24]

Göring, that peerless commander of the *Luftwaffe*, meanwhile caused another crisis amongst his fighter pilots in Sicily. During June 1943, *Generalmajor* Theo Osterkamp, the *Jafü* Sicily, experienced and good at his job, was sacked due to his many critical comments passed up the chain of command, and on 16 June *General der Jagdflieger* Adolf Galland was brought in as a somewhat less than enthusiastic temporary replacement, accompanied by *Oberst* Günther Lützow.[25] Despite initially being sympathetic to the tired and dispirited pilots of *JG 53* and *JG 77*, especially in their difficulties facing large four-engined bomber formations and lacking the experience of their Home Defence colleagues in dealing with these, Galland was upbraided by the *Luftflotte Kommandeur General* Wolfram von Richthofen and changed his tune radically.[26] The entire situation came to its crisis on 25 June when an exceptionally large B-17 formation of 124 aircraft attacked Messina, where *III/JG 53* intercepted and claimed two of them with another three falling to the flak defences of the city; the bombers, which were unescorted then flew off to the west.[27] Galland wanted a mass attack made on the retreating bombers and sent off 80-odd Messerschmitts in pursuit from *Stab, I* and *II/JG 77* as well as *II/JG 53*, but radar reports were soon lost as the bombers descended to sea level; as the fighters were reaching the end of their endurance over the sea, some pilots of *JG 77* sighted the B-17s and attacked, claiming two shot down, one *Herausschuss* (separation from formation) as well as eight B-17s '*wirksam beschossen*' (effectively shot-up).[28] Göring, safe and far away from the scene of action, was totally unsatisfied with the results and, as was his wont, responded emotionally with a message accusing the *Jagdgruppen* of cowardice and demanding that one pilot from each *Gruppe* be court-martialled for cowardice in the face of the enemy.[29] Galland, who should have known better and normally would have, had, however, been so affected by von Richthofen's pep talk that he actually had four *JG 53* pilots arrested, and in days to come regularly bawled out the Sicily defenders.[30] The effect of Göring's message was bad enough on an already demoralised group of pilots, but was made that much worse by Galland's behaviour; they had expected him to at least understand and be pragmatic.[31]

From 3 July 1943 onwards the Allied air raids, strafing attacks, fighter sweeps on German and Italian airfields, harbours, cities and military installations on Sicily reached a crescendo, before the invasion of the island itself on 10 July.[32] Jochen Prien's third volume of the *JG 77* history[33] summarises the available fighter-type aircraft in the Sicily region on the eve of the invasion: 165 serviceable Me 109s (78 on Sicily itself, 45 in Sardinia and 42 in Italy) – and this for a total of nine *Jagdgruppen*! It should be borne in mind here that northern France and Belgium had been successfully defended by only six *Jagdgruppen* in 1941–1942, and that the three *Jagdgruppen* of *JG 27* had dominated the Western Desert skies for much of 1941–1942. Now in the face of massed bomber and fighter attacks directed against the fighter defences of Sicily, nine *Jagdgruppen* were effectively swept aside. How times had changed for the once mighty *Luftwaffe*. In addition to the Me 109s there were 34 serviceable *Zerstörer* aircraft in southern Italy, and 79 *Schlacht* aircraft spread between the two islands of Sicily and Sardinia.[34] Even harder hit than the flying units themselves were the ground establishments of the *Luftwaffe*, with many airfields largely useless, ground equipment destroyed or damaged, and ground crews just as tired and combat-stressed by the incessant bombing (day and night) and strafing as their flying comrades.[35] Once more, the Allies' focus on strategic objectives gave them an enormous advantage.

The Invasion of Sicily and Subsequent Operations while Based on the Island: 10–13 July 1943

As would be the case in the Normandy landings slightly less than a year hence, paratroopers preceded the main landings the night before. What was it actually like for the German fighter pilots to finally face this enormous invasion force, land, sea and air? This is hard to imagine, but some idea can be gained from a direct witness, *Leutnant* Alfred Hammer, *6/JG 53*: 'On 10 July 1943 when I saw the invasion fleet approaching from Africa, the entire sea was covered by ships, large and small. Anyone who had seen this could not imagine any favourable result for the war any more. But we had to continue flying to the bitter end despite the enormous superiority (of the Allies).'

As can be seen from the *Kriegstagebuch* of *I/JG 77* below, this *Gruppe* had already left the island shortly before the invasion, leaving *Stab and II/JG 77*, as well as *Stab, II and III/JG 53* still on the target island, with *II/JG 51* due to fly in on this very day.[36] Within a few days the position of all these fighter units had become untenable and all were moved to southern Italy on 13 July.[37] In these four days of fighting from Sicilian bases, *Stab* and *II/JG 77* claimed five victories while losing six Me 109s with another 10 damaged, one pilot killed and one wounded, with 12 further aircraft abandoned and destroyed by their ground crews at Trapani.[38] On 12 July, the combined *II/JG 77*, *II/JG 51* and *II/SG 2* were able to put up the grand total of only 32 sorties on seven missions, and *Gruppenkommandeur II/JG 77*, *Hauptmann* Siegfried Freytag was shot down over Gela and bailed out wounded.[39] By 13 July, *I/JG 77* was back in southern Italy with new aircraft and lost one and its pilot over Sicily while another Me 109 was destroyed by bombing on their new base of Vibo Valentia in southern Calabria.[40] The 7th *Staffel* and, for a short while, parts of *8/JG 77*,[41] were moved from Sardinia to the embattled island on 12 July, as recalled by *Oberfeldwebel* Johann Pichler of the first-named *Staffel*: '10 May 1943 move to Sardinia (from Tunisia), and on 12 July 1943 transfer to Sicily. On 14 July 1943 shot down in air combat by a Spitfire – injured left foot on tail of aircraft bailing out.' On 13 July 1943 *III/JG 77* claimed two victories over Sicily but for the loss of five Me 109s, one pilot dead and three others wounded.[42]

Supporting the Sicily Battle from Southern Italy: 14 July to 17 August 1943

From 14 July until 17 August 1943, when the island was finally evacuated by the Germans (and their Italian allies), *Luftwaffe* fighter activities were launched from southern Italy, with units based essentially in Calabria (the 'foot') and in the 'heel'. *Oberfeldwebel* Alfred Seidl, just returned to *III/JG 53*'s 8th *Staffel* after a rest period from flying at the war school in Bordeaux, recalled: 'August 1943, back in Sicily again; landings of the Americans and then retreat to the Naples area; *Staffelführer* once more, wounded in bail-out.' The bail-out mentioned by Seidl was a lot more dramatic than the laconic comment above: this occurred on 23 August just after the island was evacuated by the Germans, just after he had taken off from Grazzaniese just northwest of Naples. When his engine failed he was forced to bail out at only 170 m; miraculously he survived with minor bruises.[43]

Even after the *Jagdgruppen* were withdrawn from Sicily itself, the bombing of their new bases continued, in southern Italy; thus, on 16 July 1943, Vibo Valentia in southern Calabria was raided by *c.* 100 four-engined bombers which destroyed the vast majority of the fighter aircraft stationed there.[44] *I/JG 53* had 21 Me 109s written off in this attack and had to be withdrawn from the battle zone for some weeks to re-equip.[45] Losses to *Stab*, *I* and *II/JG 77* were just as bad (estimated at about 30 Me 109s; other witnesses say all were destroyed), with, in addition, most ground equipment also wiped out.[46] They were also withdrawn to bases further north in Calabria.[47] This attack took out the guts of the southern Italian fighter defence and Allied air superiority was now assured.[48]

Also active in the battle were the *Stab* and three *Gruppen* of the Fw 190-equipped *SKG 210*, as well as two *Gruppen* of the similarly-outfitted *Schlachtgeschwader* 2.[49] Also largely involved in ground attack missions were the Me 110s of *II/ZG 1*, stationed at Monte Corvino near Salerno (outside Naples) during the Sicilian battle.[50] Despite the vulnerability of their rather cumbersome Me 110s to Allied fighters, it was once again the Allied bombers that knocked them right out of the fight. *Oberfeldwebel* Joachim Robel, Me 110 gunner in *III/ZG 26* – which despite being then stationed in the Rome area had elements serving over Sicily – was a witness to the power of the American bombers: 'From Italian bases we attacked shipping concentrations lying off Sicily with heavy bombs. The Americans were completely caught by surprise and made no response. A few days later the Americans attacked our airfield with heavy bombers and destroyed everything. Not a single Me 110 survived the bombardment.' Unlike over Tunisia where a drawn-out air battle had taken place with initial marked German success, that over Sicily was over quickly with Allied fighter strength ensuring that their bombers got through and annihilated their targets. Stationed further away from all this chaos, in the Brindisi area from 14 July until later that month, *III/JG 27* were still able to take part in more classic air fighting, as described by *Oberleutnant* Emil Clade, *Staffelkapitän 7/ JG 27*, who survived a terrifying bail-out:

Parachute jump over the Straits of Messina. We were flying defensive sorties over Sicily against the advancing American invasion troops. I was already on my return flight to our base on the Italian mainland (Brindisi) when I was attacked by an English Spitfire *Schwarm* over Mount Etna (3,000 m). They were probably from Malta. I remained without success in this encounter, but received some hits in my Me 109. This led to me immediately getting out of there and I dived towards the mainland. I had just crossed the Sicilian coast over Catania, when my engine began to burn. I had to give up my hope of reaching the mainland on the other side, and decided to get out as I could no longer see anything due to the smoke. In the excitement I forgot to disconnect my radio helmet. One could only disconnect this by pulling out the plug-in. If you only tugged on the leads, then nothing came loose. The helmet also did not come loose on its own, that was attached to the throat microphone with two press-studs. I climbed out of the 109 at about 1,000 m but remained hanging against the side of the fuselage by my helmet. The slipstream made it impossible to get back into the cockpit and to get at the plugged-in leads. I was diving down in a steep spiral towards the sea. With desperate strength I turned myself around on my body's axis to get rid of my 'chinese pot'. In about 500 m altitude I finally succeeded in this. I immediately pulled the ripcord and my parachute opened with a gigantic tug. In the same instant I saw a massive spout of water. My trusty 109 had just said goodbye. One can only judge height poorly over water. I thus shook off one of my fur-lined boots and watched its fall, counting off the seconds. I did not want to forget to take a deep breath before landing in the water. While I was still counting I did not keep an eye on the horizon and then I had already plunged into the water. My mae west quickly brought me up again, but I saw no sky above me as my parachute had fallen into the water exactly above me. With the help of my pocket knife I was able to free myself from this prison. Now I got my dinghy from behind my back. I remembered that one was supposed to only half inflate the dinghy to be still able to get on board it. Only then were you supposed to fully inflate it. It took maybe over half an hour before, exhausted but happy, I was lying in my one-man boat. Only now did I look around me. The coastline that had looked so close from the air was now so far away. I saw Mount Etna in the west and the Calabrian Peninsula in the east. Actually I would probably have landed on terra firma in due time anyway. After about an hour I heard voices and soon thereafter I saw a boat coming out from the direction of Sicily. I shouted as loudly as I could and the two occupants rowed towards me. This took too long for the young fisherman, and he swam with the crawl over to me as his father came closer. Soon I was back on land again in the house of my rescuers who were very hospitable. My clothes were soon dried in the sun and after about two hours I was able to start my journey back to my *Staffel*.

Kriegstagebuch of I/JG 77: An Unlucky Sicilian Campaign

This valuable and rare document[51] summed up below illustrates the combat experiences of just one of the Sicily fighter *Gruppen*. Only two days after arriving on Sicily, after getting out of Tunisia at the last moment, they were caught on the ground at Chinisia and lost most of their remaining aircraft in a bombing raid. After re-equipment and a break they returned to Sicily on 8 June, but a month later, just before the invasion, they once again moved to northern Italy for re-equipment.[52] A few days later they were back in the battle zone, but got caught in the Vibo Valentia bombing on 16 July 1943, once more losing almost all their new aircraft. Soon after, the *Gruppe* was effectively *hors de combat* due to widespread tropical illnesses. Interestingly, their move north to Bari for the first re-equipment was by road, as no Ju 52s were available to help. The catastrophic Stalingrad airlift and the coeval supplies airlifted into North Africa in November 1942 to January 1943 had gobbled up 659 Ju 52s; 177 more Ju 52s (and some additional larger transport machines) were lost in the final part of the Tunisian campaign (April to early May 1943).[53] The effect of the crew losses was to basically shut down *Luftwaffe* instrument training and bomber transition training,[54] both major strategic sacrifices affecting German war potential.

Summary of operations, Sicily, from copy of *Kriegstagebuch I/J.G. 77*: 9 May 1943–19 August 1943 (via P.R. Skawran)[55]					
Date (1943)	Base	Victories claimed	Losses (air)	Attacks on own base	Details
9 May	Chinisia (Sicily)	0	0	Bombing raid on base; most of remaining aircraft destroyed or damaged	
11 May	Chinisia (moved to Bari; no Ju 52s available, moved by road – arrived 16 May)				Commander in Chief South, Kesselring inspected the *Gruppe* at Chinisia and expressed his recognition for their efforts; awarded *EK* 2 to technical personnel
18 May	Bari (moved to Foggia)				Re-equipped; operational again from 20 June 1943
19 June	Foggia (moved to Sciacca, on Sicily, already bombed a week earlier)				Many tires damaged and many aircraft not operational (as a result of this raid); *Hauptmann* Bär promoted to *Major*; on leave; the new base was often bombed from then on
8 July	Sciacca				Only 10 operational aircraft left; these were turned over to the *II Gruppe*; *I/JG* 77 pilots flew to Vicenza in northern Italy to get new aircraft
14 July	Vibo Valentia (southern Calabria)	?	?		On 11 and 12 July to Lecci with 35 Me 109s, and on 13 and 14 July to Vibo Valentia; from there low level attacks and *Freie Jagd* missions flown

16 July	Botricello (middle of Calabria)			Bombing raid on field at Valentia; again most of the aircraft destroyed or damaged; runway unusable; moved to Botricello near Cotrone	Got new base organised and settled in; spare parts obtained; without billets and equipment, housed in tents; due to the ordeal of the retreat from Africa and furthermore working in Botricello without any protection from the sun, the *Gruppe* suffered a lot from sickness, mainly malaria, tropical illnesses and assorted fevers and stomach ailments
20 July	Botricello				56 officers and other ranks sick
31 July	"				128 sick personnel
19 August	"				*Hauptmann* Burkhardt takes over the *Gruppe*

The Sicilian operations came at great cost to the *Luftwaffe*; almost 40% of total German fighter production from the beginning of May to mid-July 1943 was eaten up by the Mediterranean operations.[56] Losses were appalling: 131 fighters and 72 bombers in June 1943; 246 fighters and 237 bombers (plus another 238 other types of aircraft) in July; 321 German aircraft lost in August 1943.[57] German fighter claims for the period 1 June to 17 August 1943 were: 124 for *JG 77*; 165 for *JG 53*; 85 for *II* and *III/JG 27*; 24 for *IV/JG 3*; and 22 for *II/JG 51*;[58] the grand total of 420 victory claims paled against the losses.

Italy: September 1943 to September 1944

The heavy losses inflicted on the German *Jagdgruppen* during the Sicilian operations were not lost on the *Luftwaffe* leadership in southern Italy in the next few months. *II/JG 53* at least were deliberately targeting the four-engined bomber formations that did so much damage. *Leutnant* Alfred Hammer, *6/JG 53* recalled: 'The main task (August to October 1943) was to shoot down as many four-engined bombers as possible. This was very hard, as the bombers always had a strong fighter escort.'

On 25 July 1943, as the Sicily battle progressed steadily in the Allies' favour, Italian dictator Benito Mussolini fell from power and was arrested (later rescued by German commandos and founded a northern, rump fascist state), and a new non-fascist regime emerged under Marshal Badoglio.[59] Following the evacuation of Sicily (17 August 1943) by the Axis, it was not long before the Allies moved on to the Italian mainland. On 3 September 1943 initial relatively limited landings were made in southernmost Italy with little opposition; the major landing followed at Salerno near Naples on 9 September and an intense battle took place there for the next nine days.[60] On the day before this major landing, an armistice between the Allies and Badoglio's government was announced.[61] The Salerno air battle was a major event in the Mediterranean theatre: German fighters from *IV/JG 3*, the entire *JG 53*, plus *Stab* and *I/JG 77* could only muster 51 serviceable Me 109s to oppose these landings.[62] However, a much more important role at Salerno fell to the ground attack and bombing units of the *Luftwaffe*. An equal number of Fw 190 *Schlacht* machines were serviceable (*II* and *III/SKG 10*, *II/SchG 2*) and *IV/JG 3* also flew ground attack missions.[63] German bombers (only operating by night), torpedo aircraft and the new remotely controlled bombs launched from bombers of *KG 100* (particularly the Hs 293 glider bomb) were effective; they managed to achieve 85 bomb strikes on Allied vessels lying off Salerno, which sank 12 large vessels including a heavy cruiser.[64] Operations both on the ground and in the air came close to repelling the landings but by 15 September the beachhead became more secure and within three days the Germans retreated northwards to the Gustav defensive line along the Volturno River.[65] By 1 October, Naples had fallen and, much more importantly, so had the airfield complex of the Foggia plain to the east; occupation of the latter was of critical strategic importance as heavy bombers were now placed within range of southern Europe – Germany, Austria, Romania and Hungary.[66] There was now actually no longer any strategic need for further Allied advances up the Italian peninsula but a long, dogged struggle lay ahead, from one German defensive line to the next, exacerbated by poor weather and rugged terrain.

The other major aerial battle of the Italian campaign was the Anzio landings (meant to break the slow slogging match up the peninsula), begun on 28 January 1944; unfortunately the total surprise achieved was wasted through complacent leadership, giving the Germans time to assemble a powerful confining force on high ground surrounding the beachhead.[67] Up till the end of February it was touch and go whether the beachhead would actually survive at all, as German counter-attacks almost succeeded; finally after a long stalemate, the Allies managed to break out of the landing area and this long and rather unnecessary slugging match was finally over by 5 June 1944.[68] German assembly of airpower to counter the Anzio landings was fast and efficient: for the fighter element *I/JG 4*, *II/JG 51*, *I* and *III/JG 53* as well as *Stab*, *I* and *II/JG 77* were already in Italy, and were joined in February by *I/JG 2* from France (see table below); three *Nachtschlachtgruppen* (night ground attack groups) as well as bomber reinforcements added to the weight of aerial attack.[69] Allied air power was much better placed and organised than at Salerno, however, forcing German bombing and ground attack missions to be flown largely at night, thereby also curtailing the effectiveness of the remotely launched bombs that had done so much damage in daylight earlier outside Naples.[70] The Battle of Monte Cassino (17 January to 18 May 1944), the main bastion along the Gustav defence line, ran in parallel with the fighting at Anzio;[71] *Leutnant* Alfred Seidl, flying with 8th and later with 7th *Staffeln* of *III/JG 53*, was involved in both battles. 'October to December 1943: again (after leave) with the *III Gruppe* in the Po Valley and in the area of Venice and Udine. January 1944: transfer to airfields north of Rome. The Americans land at Anzio and Nettuno, and we drop bombs on the beachhead. February 1944: after three years belonging to 8th *Staffel* I took over the 7th *Staffel* as *Staffelkapitän*. March 1944: in the Monte Cassino battle I was seriously wounded in air combat – six weeks in hospital in Florence, followed by leave to fully recover. May to June 1944: again stationed in the Udine area, heavy battles with the Americans.'

Luftwaffe fighter units stationed in Italian theatre (September 1943–September 1944)[72]		
Unit	Dates in theatre	Details
I/JG 2	20 February–8 April 1944	Equipped with Fw 190
IV/JG 3	August–28 September 1943	
I/JG 4	21 December 1943–1 August 1944	
II/JG 51	December 1943–March 1944	
Stab/JG 53	1 September 1943–27 June 1944	
I/JG 53	1 September 1943–9 May 1944	
II/JG 53	1 September–16 October 1943	
III/JG 53	1 September 1943–27 June 1944	
Stab/JG 77	1 September 1943–9 September 1944	
I/JG 77	1 September 1943–31 July 1944	
II/JG 77	1 September 1943–15 August 1944	Equipped with MC 205 from 24 September 1943–24 January 1944
III/JG 77	1 September–8 November 1943	Sardinia till 10 September 1943; Corsica till 25 September 1943; Italy till 8 November 1943
Unless otherwise noted, units equipped with Me 109		

As can be seen from the table above, *IV/JG 3* left the theatre after the Salerno battle while *II/JG 53* departed for Germany in October 1943; in late 1943, *II/JG 51* and *I/JG 4*, transferred into Italy from the Home Defence, replaced *II/JG 53* and *III/JG 77* (then went to Romania in November 1943).[73] Thus by the time of the Anzio landings *Jagdgruppen* in the Italian theatre were back to six in number; the transfer of *I/JG 2* from France as a reinforcement for the forces opposing Anzio raised the fighter *Gruppen* to seven in February to March 1944, but thereafter they declined rapidly, as can be seen in illustration 37.[74] By August 1944 they were down to a single *Gruppe*, and *Stab/JG 77*, the last German fighter unit (and a very small one at that) left in September 1944 (illustration 37).[75] After that, Axis fighter defences in northern Italy were limited to those from the small *Aeronautica Nazionale Repubblicana* of Mussolini's rump fascist state.

To illustrate the aerial combat experience of the *Jagdgruppen* over Italy, two graphs are shown in illustrations 38 and 39. These provide statistics of claims and losses for *Jagdgeschwader 53* '*Pik-As*' for the period 18 August 1943 to 30 June 1944 – in other words from just after the evacuation of Sicily to the end of June 1944 (there were neither claims nor losses for July to September 1944 for this *Geschwader*).[76] The first graph (illustration 38), which details the claims made, shows very clearly that while the fighting was intense in the few weeks after leaving Sicily, thereafter it tailed off considerably.[77] The Salerno landings in September 1943 resulted in relatively few claims, as did the onset of the Anzio landings in January to February 1944, but claims were measurably higher for the following two months of that battle. Claims against enemy fighters outnumbered bomber claims significantly.[78] The second graph (illustration 39) shows the losses suffered by *JG 53* for the same time period over Italy.[79] Here, while losses were high for the first few weeks after Sicily (balance of August 1943), they peaked significantly for the Salerno period immediately thereafter (September 1943), then remained relatively muted right through to June 1944, showing little influence from the Anzio fighting.[80]

While the fighting on the ground in Italy remained hard and bloody for both sides, with there being little strategic value in the campaign after the Foggia airfield complex had been overrun, aerial combat in this theatre was really a sideshow compared to the scale of the slaughter taking place (to both sides) in the Home Defence or that being meted out to the *Luftwaffe* fighter arm over Normandy in mid-1944. The Russian front also makes the aerial and even ground fighting in Italy appear of rather small moment, as for example when *Operation Bagration* wiped out German Army Group Centre in June to July 1944 and swept aside the German aerial support almost completely. However, none of these considerations would have affected the fighting experiences of troops and aircrew in the Italian campaign – they fought, suffered and died in numbers and were both unaware and probably also unimpressed by what was going on in any other theatre, and rightly so. Climatic conditions and topography in Italy made the fighting there extremely hard, often even bearing comparison with the arduous trench warfare of 1914–1918. A soldier, sailor or an airman's contribution and sacrifice should be judged equal, whatever the apparent importance or scale of the theatre he happens to find himself in.

6

SOUTH-EASTERN EUROPE AND THE BALKANS, 1943–1944

This is a complex area geographically and historically, and during the Second World War it experienced invasions and variable alliances: countries changed sides in some cases and remained loyal in others. The major air operations during 1943–1944 revolved principally around raids on the Ploiesti oilfields of Romania, lesser raids on the much smaller oil resources of Hungary, as well as more politically motivated bombing of large cities such as Sofia in Bulgaria or Budapest in Hungary with a view to encouraging regime changes. Territories such as Greece were areas over which attacking bomber formations largely passed, *en route* to and returning from deeper lying targets such as in Romania, Bulgaria and Hungary, and much the same applied also to Yugoslavia, although the latter region was also bombed directly. Romania, Hungary and Bulgaria also had native air forces which played leading roles in their defence in conjunction with *Luftwaffe* fighter *Gruppen*.[1] Throughout this large region of highly diverse nations and cultures, the greatest challenge in aerial combat was meeting and effectively combating the large formations of four-engined American bombers and their fighter escorts. The admittedly still early experiences in this regard of the Home Defence *Gruppen* appear not to have been made readily available to the fighters stationed in the Balkans, who had to work things out for themselves in the heat of desperate combat.

It is difficult to apply a simple chronological structure to airborne combat for this chapter; while operations began earliest over Romania, these continued in parallel with later missions against Bulgaria while many of those directed against Hungary and Yugoslavia were somewhat later still. For this reason a more geographic structure is used. As an example of the experiences of many *Luftwaffe* units in this theatre, the *Stab* of JG 27 was stationed in various parts of south-east Europe and the Balkans during 1943–1944: in Greece (July to October 1943), then in Montenegro (October 1943) and finally in southern Serbia (October 1943 to February 1944).[2]

The *Geschwader Kommodore*, *Oberstleutnant* Gustav Rödel recalled some of his experiences as part of this small unit: 'Operations in the Balkans in 1943–1944 were mainly about defending against the attacks by US bomber formations. *Abschüsse* and air combats in the Balkan area are a very wide-ranging theme. The aerial combats in this theatre initially were relatively problem-free, as the Germans almost always had an absolute air superiority; this however changed with the appearance of the four-engined bombers with their fighter escorts.'

Greece

At this stage in the war the German fighter presence in Greece was limited. *III/JG* 27 flew to southern Greece when they left the Western Desert, worn out and exhausted, in November 1942, being stationed firstly in Crete (until March 1943); thereafter they remained in southern Greece (near Athens, south-west of Corinth, and in the south-west on the island of Zakyntos) until March 1944, apart from two relatively short transfers to Sicily (March to June 1943 and 14 July to 23 September 1943).[3] The newly-formed *IV/JG* 27 was sent to Greece to cover their two absences, being stationed in the same southern Greek area from May 1943 till 28 October 1943.[4] After March 1944, for a while there appears to have been no formal German fighter presence in Greece, until in the summer of that year, parts of *II/JG 51* (*c.* two *Staffeln* in strength, but parts of these also operated over Serbia) arrived, to operate mostly over the Aegean islands, during at least June to

July, and with 6th *Staffel* flying escort for supply Ju 52s during September 1944 over the Aegean islands.[5]

A short-lived and relatively small-scale German-British war took place in the Greek islands soon after the Italian surrender on 8 September 1943, as most were garrisoned by Italian troops who had now changed sides.[6] The Germans moved rapidly and efficiently by taking the strategic islands of Cephalonia, Corfu and Split between 21 and 25 September to ensure safe sea communications with mainland Greece; the British intervention in contrast was rather piecemeal and forces applied somewhat weak.[7] They occupied Kos, Samos and Leros and three more small islands in the eastern Aegean close to Turkey,[8] but Rhodes with its strategically sited airfields had already been taken by the Germans on 12 September.[9] Using Ju 88s and the vulnerable Stukas effectively (illustration 41) in the absence of adequate British fighter opposition and with cover provided by *III* and *IV/JG* 27, Kos was retaken by the Germans on 3–4 October, who then attacked Leros continuously from the air, until it too fell to an assault over five days (12–16 November 1943); the British then evacuated Samos and Syros islands.[10] The *Luftwaffe* could thus still be effective at this stage of the war, but only where weak fighter opposition was experienced.

The British had first landed light forces on Kos on 13 September 1943 and within three days the first six Spitfires of 7 Squadron, South African Air Force (SAAF) moved in.[11] Despite putting up a very brave fight, the few fighters on Kos were outnumbered and subject to constant German strafing and bombing attacks. On 18 September, Antimachia airfield was attacked twice by Ju 88s and once by strafing Me 109s; during a second strafing attack on the airfield four Spitfires took off to engage but lost two aircraft and their pilots in return for two claimed Messerschmitts, but the Germans had also destroyed three Dakotas on the ground and another hit the sea avoiding Me 109 attack.[12] The next day a further small Ju 88 raid escorted by about a *Staffel* of Me 109s rendered the airfield unserviceable, and destroyed two more Dakotas on the ground; two 7 SAAF Squadron Spitfires that took off were both shot down by the Me 109s, with one pilot killed and one claim made in return.[13] Six more Spitfires of the SAAF squadron arrived on Kos on 20 September; five days later eight serviceable Spitfires were available on Kos, with four more under repair.[14] In a heavy Ju 88 raid on 27 September Antimachia again became unserviceable and two 7 SAAF Spitfires were shot down by escorting Me 109s, killing both pilots (III/JG 27 claimed three Spitfires, losing one pilot of their own);[15] the Spitfires moved to the Lampi strip, recently prepared on Kos.[16]

In action over Leros island that same afternoon, 7 SAAF Squadron shot down a Me 109 for the loss of a Spitfire.[17] By evening only four serviceable Spitfires remained and next day German bombers rendered Lampi unserviceable and escorts shot down two more Spitfires with one pilot killed.[18] On 28 September 1943 reinforcements of eight Spitfires from 74 Squadron RAF reached Kos; the next day Antimachia, from whence the Spitfires were perforce operating again, was bombed and also became unserviceable.[19] A third poorly prepared field was now used on Kos.[20] By 1 October only six Spitfires were serviceable on the island, one from 7 SAAF and five from 74 Squadron.[21] On 3 October the island was heavily attacked from the air, with both seaborne and paratroop landings overwhelming the defenders on the ground and by next day Kos had fallen; overall, 22 German aircraft had been claimed by AA defences, 7 SAAF Squadron (12 claims) and 74 Squadron while flying from the island.[22] IV/JG 27 claimed four victories over Kos during September 1943.[23] On 28 September 1943 III/JG 27 claimed four Spitfires over the island and surrounds, including the 2,000th victory of the *Geschwader*, which fell to the *Gruppenkommandeur*, Major Ernst Düllberg.[24]

Emil Clade, who had been with JG 27 since 1940 when he first served in III/JG 27, later flew in the Western Desert and Sicily with II *Gruppe*, before being appointed as *Staffelkapitän* 7/JG 27 in May 1943.[25] Based on six months service over Greece from September 1943 till March 1944, he has provided a fascinating account of their varied duties there, and of how they really struggled to work out the best tactics to deal with the four-engined bombers which began to fly over Greek territory on their way to and from other Balkan countries like Romania,

Bulgaria and Hungary. His account of solving certain supply shortages in a small way is also a classic:

At the time I was an *Oberleutnant* and *Staffelkapitän* of 7/JG 27. In North Africa and again over the Straits of Sicily I had bailed out into the sea, then in Greece I parachuted into a partisan area, and again later over Germany I was shot down two more times. Thus five times, but I always had a Guardian Angel. Against that I was able to achieve 27 *Abschüsse*, five of them bombers. In 1943 my home base was Kalamaki (near Athens). From there we were sent out in *Schwarm-* or *Staffel*-sized formations across the entire Aegean and were continually moving, sometimes more than once per day. Thus the available airfields were apparently always manned, so that enemy reconnaissance must have had the impression of the existence of a strong fighter defence. So we flew, for example, an escort mission starting in Athens and landing in Crete or Rhodes. Our tasks were many and varied: escort for bomber formations or for small convoys which supplied the many islands in the Aegean, free chases against reconnaissance machines or single bombers that mostly attacked our lone-sailing ships at low level. Towards the end of our time there, we experienced ever increasing, high-flying American four-engined bomber formations that gave us big problems at the time, as they flew in tight formations, were well armed and flew at *c.* 6,000 m. In the beginning we had heavy losses of good experienced pilots, until we were able to develop the correct attack tactics. The Liberator bombers flew in from North Africa and, as we often lost half of our fighters attacking them, hardly any of us had the confidence to get in close to another one, which was necessary to obtain a certain *Abschuss.* I was also shot down by return fire of their gunners.

I can describe two attack methods from the early stages of the bomber war, but both showed themselves to be unusable. (1) An Me 109 flew 500 m above the bomber formation and dropped a 250 kg bomb with a time fuse into the bomber formation, that flew in very tight formation. We only managed this once. Firstly we had to make contact with the formation very early and then the bomb-carrier and his height-measuring companion were subject to concentrated defensive fire from the bomber formation and often shot down. (2) We experimented with rockets (we called them launchers) that were fired from 21 cm open launching tubes beneath the wings of our fighters. But with these also we had to get closer than 1,000 m from the bombers and were subject to their defensive fire before being able to launch. These launchers were very unreliable. If they even ignited, the steering jets often malfunctioned, so that the rockets either flew in curved paths or tumbled. In both cases, the desired effect, namely to break up the bomber formation and thus decrease the effect of their defensive fire, was not achieved and attacks had to be broken off prematurely. As a result of these experiments, after that we flew only in close formations and attacked in *Staffel*-strength, from above against their flanks and at high speed. Already with the first such attack the bombers normally jettisoned their bombs and the formations broke up. Admittedly, our formations also broke up. Still, when a repeated attack was made the defensive fire was easier to bear. This method showed itself to be more effective, so that the Americans soon no longer came without fighter escort. The rest of the story is already known from the accounts of the Home Defence. A special complication in Greece was the addition that after a bail-out one either fell into the sea or landed in partisan-infested areas. Thus we always flew with sea rescue equipment and if at all possible also with pistols. We suffered greatly from the pressure of the Greek resistance movement. Thus at night only the defended localities were half safe, as they were well guarded. Although the resistance of the Greeks was caused primarily by the Italians, our relationship with the Greeks did not improve when, following the Badoglio putsch, the Italians left us. Temporarily then we even had to fight against the Italians also. Our supply position got steadily worse by the land routes. In Yugoslavia the partisans under Tito were always very well organised. This affected the civilian population very badly, they were always starving. The high command in Athens let the Allied Forces Command Mediterranean know that they wanted to grant safe passage to convoys with food supplies to Piraeus and that these supplies would be given entirely to the Greek population, but this offer was not taken up. Apparently, one did not trust the German *Wehrmacht* leadership.

An amusing illustrative episode is worth recounting. We really missed fresh meat, as we largely received tinned meat, as was already very familiar from the North African theatre. Almost every evening a shepherd and his flock went past our quarters. My *Staffel* cook, a clever man, held out a salad leaf to one of the sheep one evening and the sheep promptly followed him into the house. What happened then can be told swiftly, although we were forbidden under threat of severe punishment, to take anything away from the Greek population. 'Organising' something, the *Landser* (German version of the British 'Tommy') word for 'stealing', was widespread in the war and, depending on the need, was also tolerated. However, in Greece this was explicitly forbidden and the court-martials went on without favour. Hardly two hours had passed, and it was already dark, when a phone call from the commander in Athens came through which referred directly to this incident. My *Gruppenkommandeur* assured him quite truthfully that he knew nothing of the matter, and that he doubted if any such thing could happen in our unit. Our doctor, who was also the *Gruppenadjutant*, was informed through me. He told the *Kommandeur* that, sadly, the tale was true. Now very cross, the *Kommandeur* told the poor 'Doc', 'Watch how you come out of this affair'. As the commander in Athens insisted on a house to house search, my poor doctor had to work fast. He came roaring past me in an ambulance, told the cook to quickly pack the carcass in the ambulance and disappeared, not to return before midnight. The poor chap drove around half the night in an ambulance with a butchered carcass through the streets of Athens until he finally returned, and then there was a fine feast. But the *Kommandeur* would not partake of it, even though his tongue was hanging down to his knees. That's how strict the regulations were against different viewpoints.

Bulgaria

Bulgaria had declared war against Great Britain and the United States on 13 December 1941, but never entered hostilities against the Soviet Union, the country being strongly Russophile in its attitudes.[26] Action of Bulgarian fighters with overflying US aircraft occurred on 21 October 1943 for the first time, and Allied raids on Bulgaria took place in the period 14 November 1943 to 17 April 1944; there were four large raids on Sofia during 1943.[27] A German *Jagdgruppe, I/JG 5*, arrived on 9 January 1944 to assist the Bulgarians just in time for two major raids on Sofia the next day, but only remained in the country till February.[28] IV/JG 27 was posted in on 4 February and also stayed only a short time, till 23 March 1944.[29] Four more heavy raids on Sofia in March and another two in April 1944 brought to an end the series of attacks on the capital.[30] Thereafter till late in August, aerial action over Bulgaria was either with overflying formations on their way to and from Romania or attacking other targets in Bulgaria itself.[31] Bulgaria underwent a communist uprising at the end of August 1944[32] and the Russians soon after occupied the country, which then joined their new allies in fighting the retreating Germans in south-eastern Europe. The presence of part of *II/JG 51* (of about *Staffel*-strength and comprising elements of 4/JG 51 as well as *Stab II/JG 51*, posted to Bulgaria from 14 June 1944 to 31 August 1944)[33] could not alter this reality.

Yugoslavia

IV/JG 27 was dispatched to Yugoslavia in late 1943 (28 October 1943 to 3 February 1944)[34] to help defend south-east European airspace against the Allied bomber formations.[35] Particularly in December 1943 they were to suffer high losses: 11 pilots killed and one wounded, reducing them to only 11 serviceable Me 109s by the year's end.[36] On 17 December their famous *Gruppenkommandeur*,

Hauptmann Joachim Kirschner was shot down by Spitfires, bailed out but had the misfortune to be apprehended by the partisans, who murdered him; he had been able to claim 13 victories in this theatre, bringing his total score to 188.[37] By the end of 1943, *IV/JG 27* had brought their victory total from operations over Greece and Yugoslavia since May 1943 to almost 70; 23 of these claims were made by *Feldwebel* Heinz Bartels.[38]

II/JG 51 was stationed in Yugoslavia (mainly in Serbia) for most of the period March 1944 to 3 September 1944, apart from short postings to Ploiesti, Romania (6–17 April 1944) and Bulgaria (14 June to 31 August 1944).[39] During the first period in Yugoslavia (up till about the end of the first quarter of 1944) they mainly flew against the four-engined bomber formations crossing Yugoslavian airspace, but in the second quarter of the year they were closely involved in operations to oppose Allied support for Tito's partisan army, with significant Allied fighter incursions into Yugoslav airspace to attain air superiority and also to escort supply planes which were supporting the partisans.[40] Direct air raids on Belgrade itself in Serbia occurred on 16–17 April 1944.[41]

Hungary

The first contact between Hungarian air force fighters and overflying US forces took place on 17 March 1944, and bombing raids on Hungary began on 3 April.[42] The next day *IV/JG 27* was posted to Hungary to support their allies, and remained there until 6 June 1944.[43] In late April 1944, *Leutnant* Gerd Schindler was posted to *IV/JG 27*, joining 10th *Staffel*. Here he soon met his first four-engined bomber formation over Wiener-Neustadt and was able to shoot one up, and then had a long dogfight with two P-51s. After experiencing several other combats in the new theatre, one day while chasing after bombers near Vienna he was attacked by a P-47 and in his ignorance of Western aircraft, having recently moved from the Eastern Front (from *III/JG 52*), he tried to escape by diving away. A huge mistake – the much heavier Thunderbolt easily kept up with him, firing away but missing and then pulled away, its pilot waving (probably his guns jammed); this undoubtedly saved his life. He experienced both living conditions and rations on the ground as excellent. Following a second heavy raid on Hungary on 13 April, aerial action quietened down for a full six weeks before the period from 20 May 1944 to 21 August 1944 when it became prominent once again.[44] Soon after this, Hungary was invaded by Soviet troops and aerial action became concentrated against their air forces, as already related in one of the companion volumes to this book.[45] In the first week of November 1944, combat with raiding American aircraft flared up once more over Hungary, for the last time.[46]

Romania

Hitler's war machine was heavily dependent on the Ploiesti oilfields as their major supplier of fuel and lubricants, essential in any modern and mechanised warfare. It was oil that drove Hitler to his disastrous advance into the Caucasus and to Stalingrad on the Eastern Front, fatally over-extending an already stretched *Wehrmacht*. Apart from Ploiesti there were minor sources of natural oil in Hungary, and the German synthetic fuel plants. The Americans launched the very first bombing raid on Ploiesti, from Egypt, on 12 June 1942, by 13 B-24s flying at night and arriving over their target at dawn; 12 made it to Ploiesti. Due to cloud no damage was done, but all 13 crews made it back to either Allied territory in Iraq and Syria, or to neutral Turkey (four aircraft).[47] There was then a long wait until the next raid, on 1 August 1943, by 178 Liberators, flying from North Africa once more.[48] Attacking at extremely low level the B-24s suffered heavily from the massed flak defences of the oilfields and as they turned away, from the attentions of Romanian fighters and *I/JG 4*; much further south Me 109s of *IV/JG 27* in Greece claimed five of the retreating bombers.[49] A horrific total of 54 bombers was lost on the raid, 51 in combat or on the way back; Romanian flak claimed 15 and their fighters 25 definite or probable victories.[50]

The bombers did not come back to Romania till April 1944, when Bucharest was bombed for the first time on 4 April, and Ploiesti the next day; from then until 19 August 1944 another 19 large raids on Ploiesti followed, as well as 22 attacks on other Romanian targets.[51] After departing the Crimea in early May 1944, *II/JG 52* had been added to the Romanian air defences; *Fähnrich*

Heinz Ewald of the 6th *Staffel* recalled, rather tersely: 'Wounded on 24 June 1944, near Ploeczty in Romania; I was involved in an aerial combat against *c.* 180 four-engined Liberators and Fortresses accompanied by *c.* 120 escort fighters, and I had to bail out at a height of 6,600 m.' *Luftwaffe* fighter units stationed in Romania are summarised in the table below. Initially only a single German *Staffel* was there, but at the turn of 1942 to early 1943 this was built up to a full *Gruppe*, I/JG 4.[52] Several months after the great low-level raid of 1 August 1943 this *Gruppe* departed and was replaced by III/JG 77 (and briefly also by I/JG 5).[53] When heavy bombing resumed in April 1944 rapid reinforcement followed in April-May 1944.

German fighter units stationed in Romania, late 1942 to August 1944[54]		
Unit	Period in Romania	Remarks
I/JG 4	August 1942–26 November 1943	Only one *Staffel* present till end 1942–start 1943 when balance of *Gruppe* arrived
I/JG 5	15 November 1943–9 January 1944	
II/JG 51	6–17 April 1944	
II/JG 52	9 May–10 July 1944	
I/JG 53	9 May–26 August 1944	
III/JG 77	8 November 1943–28 August 1944	
II/JG 301	29 April-August 1944	
10/JG 301	Early April 1944–31 July 1944	This was the only operational unit of III/JG 301

Amongst the old hands with the 7th *Staffel* of III/JG 77 was *Leutnant* Johann Pichler. Below he describes some of his experiences there, culminating in his capture by the Russians while helpless in hospital:

I rejoined my *Staffel* on 2 January 1944 in Mizil, Romania (after having been shot down and wounded over Sicily,

14 July 1943). On 3 July 1944 about five waves each of
33–35 B-17s flew from Bari in Italy to attack Bucharest at a
height of 7,000 m. As escort they had P-38s and Mustangs
flying at 8,000 m to 10,000 m; their number was not known
to me. Our warning service was very good, the incursions
being reported shortly after they took off, at about 09h30 to
10h00. I was assigned to lead the *Gruppe* in this attack.
We were greatly inferior in numbers and had about 20 Me
109s. At an altitude of 7,500 m I made the first attack –
10 km north-west of Bucharest – with my *Schwarm*, from
exactly head-on, and was able to shoot down a B-17. At
the same time we were fired on from above by the escorting
fighters. My *Rottenflieger* was hit in the radiator and later
had to bail out due to being hit again. After I had got rid
of the fighters behind me, I was able once again to attack
a wave of B-17s, this time leaving Bucharest, from exactly
head-on and shoot down another B-17, from which six of
the crew bailed out. My third *Abschuss* followed far to the
west of Bucharest, but still over Romania, and this time
all 10 crew members bailed out after my burst of fire and
shortly after that this B-17 also dived down and crashed.
The entire combat lasted 20 minutes. For me this was the
perfect mission and one also marked by a lot of good luck.
Earlier, in about the middle of May 1944, another raid
had come in from Bari, of about 150 B-17s, on the Ploiesti
oil fields, this time without any escorts. Within about
15 seconds the entire area was covered up to 4,000 m by a
dark cloud of flak bursts. I flew into this flak cloud without
hesitation, made three attacks but not a single shot came
from my guns. This operation could have resulted in three
Abschüsse – jammed guns! On 22 July 1944 in an aerial
combat with a Mustang fighter my Me 109 was shot down
in flames. After bailing out I landed on a road and broke
both my legs, and ended up in the *Luftwaffe* hospital in
Bucharest. As a result of the putsch on 16 August 1944 by
the Romanian army, the *Luftwaffe* hospital was handed
over to the Russians on 30 August 1944 and thus I entered
Russian captivity, from which I was only released on

4 January 1950. I have no documents at all from my four years of front-line experience; some were burnt in two bail-outs and of the rest the Romanians took some and then the Russians robbed me of everything.

Another pilot flying over Romania with *III/JG 77* was *Unteroffizier* Martin Hain who came fresh from *Ergänzungsgruppe Süd* in France to Romania after Easter in 1944, where he was assigned to 8th *Staffel* of *III/JG 77*; in correspondence with the author he detailed his brief life as a front-line fighter pilot. He and several other newly arrived colleagues lacked the full 20 hours on the type of aircraft (Me 109 G) used by their assigned front-line units on joining *III/JG 77*, having only half of that time in their logbooks. The balance was supposed to be obtained in their unit, and when he first joined the *Gruppe*, stationed in Mizil near Ploiesti, things were quiet enough that some training could take place. However, soon the first incursions of American four-engined bombers from the Brindisi area in Italy began, and initially they lacked fighter escort, and were thus attacked successfully and generally kept from accurate bombing of the oilfields. However, there were losses to the German defenders as well, and the new pilots soon enough had to be sent on their first missions. For Martin Hain, his first experience of combat was on 6 June 1944 (the same day Normandy was invaded far to the West). By now the attacking formations of Liberators were accompanied by P-38 Lightnings and P-51 Mustangs and it became ever more difficult to get at the bombers.

On 10 June 1944 the entire *III/JG 77* took off to intercept a reported high-flying bomber formation, but this turned out to be a false alarm caused by a few aircraft dropping 'window' (aluminium strips to confuse radar returns) and the *Gruppe* was then ordered to drop to low level to search for P-38s. As the *Gruppe* formation started to break up with the descent, some P-38s were seen very low down and one conveniently flew into Martin Hain's sights. He opened fire but then saw that it was already being pursued and shot at by another Me 109, and the P-38 then belly-landed after its pilot had bailed out. 8th *Staffel* then managed to regroup and gained some height, Hain flying as the tail-end Charlie as more P-38s were sighted. Without waiting for orders, he broke away and dived on them. As one of the twin-engined fighters turned he hit it with a full burst of cannon and machine gun fire and it crashed in flames. His first victory was confirmed by several comrades, but he was being pursued by two more P-38s and, as he turned into their attack and was catching up on them in a tight turn, he discovered that his guns had jammed, so turned back for home. *III/JG 77* claimed three P-38 Lightnings on this day, all by beginner pilots who were each rewarded with the *EK 2* for their performances. Illustration 44 in the plates shows three 'real' fighter pilots, rather satisfied with themselves, after the three novices had each gained their first victories, as well as a copy of Martin Hain's certificate for the award of the Iron Cross 2nd class (*EK 2*).

Unteroffizier Hain's combat career was limited to five missions (*Feindflüge*) during which he was able to claim three successes. On his last mission on 3 July 1944 he was shot down himself and bailed out, being wounded; he did not see action again. The page from his *Leistungsbuch* (a short summary of his career as a pilot) shown in illustration 45 summarises his three combat claims (P-38 on 10 June 1944; B-24 '*wirksam beschossen*' [literally, well shot-up; thus seriously damaged] on 11 June, and another one shot down on 3 July 1944). On his fifth *Feindflug* on 3 July 1944, Martin Hain was scrambled along with other members of *III/JG 77* to meet enemies flying in towards the Bucharest-Ploiesti area, but was shot down about 60 km west of Bucharest. He was lucky to escape by parachute and survived wounded. In a Romanian hospital at Cervenia he was visited by a *Luftwaffe* officer and an Orthodox priest; this officer had flown to the crash site of a comrade from *7/JG 77* to identify the body before visiting Hain in hospital. Shown in illustration 46 is a copy of his Wound Badge (Black) – i.e. for a first wound – certificate.

Martin Hain's operational period lasted exactly one month, from 3 June to 3 July 1944 (see excerpt from his flying logbook below). That he managed to survive five *Feindflüge* and even score two victories and one seriously damaged bomber, was not at all a bad record for a freshly baked, relatively poorly trained fighter pilot at this stage of the war. He was lucky to get away with his life on being shot down; many others did not, the opposition being tough and heavily outnumbering the defenders of Romanian airspace. At least in his case there was some return for an average training period of *c.* two years. Others died on their first mission or during training itself.

Example of a fighter pilot's (brief) operational life, Romania, summer 1944, based on flying logbook, 21 May 1944–3 July 1944: *Unteroffizier* Martin Hain 8/JG 77 (based at Mizil near Ploiesti the entire time, but also using satellite fields) (Source: Martin Hain)

21 May: *Rotten* mission, 15h45–16h10

3 June: Scramble against reconnaissance aircraft, 13h55–14h25; enemy not found; landed at satellite field (returned to Mizil an hour later)

6 June: Scramble against bombers & fighters, 09h00–10h36 (1st *Feindflug*); combat with P-38s, one shot up

10 June: Scramble, 08h02–09h31 (2nd operational flight); combat with P-38s, one seriously damaged and one shot down (1st victory)

11 June: Scramble, 08h14–09h25 (3rd *Feindflug*); combat with B-24s, one seriously damaged; landed at satellite due to being hit in engine (returned to Mizil that evening)

28 June: Scramble, 09h00–10h31 (4th *Feindflug*); combat with B-24s and P-51s; hit 3 times in tail and once in wing

3 July: Scramble, 11h08–12h45 (5th *Feindflug*); combat with B-24s and P-51s, one B-24 shot down, self shot down and bailed out, wounded

---

Another freshly minted fighter pilot to join *III/JG 77* in summer 1944 was *Oberfähnrich* (senior officer cadet) Erich Sommavilla. As a totally inexperienced newcomer he was largely protected against tackling the large American formations (in contrast to Martin Hain of the same *Gruppe*), as discussed by him below:

> After completing my fighter pilot training I joined *III/JG 77* in summer 1944 at Mizil in Romania. This *Gruppe* flew mostly as part of a larger battle formation together with *I/JG 53* ('Pik-As') and a *Gruppe* of JG 52, exclusively against US bomber formations from Foggia in Italy,

that continuously attacked the oilfields at Ploiesti. These operations, in which *Major* Harder (*Kommandeur* of I/JG 53) was always the leader of our combined formation, brought us heavy losses, as the Americans came with very large fighter escorts, with a fighter-to-fighter ratio of about 1:10. We had only limited operational aircraft that had already been repaired often, while the Romanians received large supplies of new aircraft. The attacks of our fighters in the large battle formation led by *Major* Harder were carried out in strictly closed-up formation, and in critical situations we still stuck together, in defensive circles. When the escort was absent or when we were able to break through it, we attacked the bomber formation from head-on as a unit. Anyone who broke away from our formations was an easy prey for the many American fighters. I had no operational contact with the US bombers; either we missed each other or on such operations there was no serviceable aircraft for me to fly. We had installed a '*Staffelkommandogerät*' at our base that used large loudspeakers to broadcast the radio traffic of the pilots in action across the entire airfield, with all the emergency shouts, victory howls and the orders of *Major* Harder when he was advising the entire combat grouping, in action, changing formations used or ordering a defensive circle. At least, all of us on the ground could shiver in sympathy with them!

After the capitulation of Romania the US incursions ceased (late August 1944). In August 1944 we experienced that the American fighters over Romania began to shoot at German fliers hanging helpless beneath their parachutes or collapsed the 'chutes by flying just above them, with their slipstream, trying to make them fall to their deaths; then they also tried to shoot up belly-landed Me 109s and especially the force-landed pilots, with their guns. Luckily for us our emergency fields lay mostly in extensive maize or crop fields, even in vineyards, so that one could get away from a belly-landing reasonably hidden. In Romania, to our astonishment, when we arrived in Bucharest there was almost normal civilian traffic activity, and in the shops one could buy German cameras, radios, toilet articles and many luxury goods, that had long vanished in the *Reich*, and also food such as hams and salamis, and ice cream. Of course we had too little money for these things as higher authority paid our money in *Reichsmarks* into accounts held at our permanent registration stations (home headquarters) and we received only a pocket money allowance in Romanian *Leis*. But this was enough for an ice cream or some ham or salami of course.

Amongst the *I/JG 53* pilots who flew with *III/JG 77* and *II/JG 52* in large battle formations to tackle the big American bomber incursions was *Unteroffizier* Heinz Hommes, who had just recovered from a long illness after initial operational experience over Tunisia with *9/JG 53*. He recalled the savage nature of aerial combat over Romania in this time period. 'After a long period of illness from March 1943 till the end of that year and then not being allowed to fly due to intolerance of low-flying and strafing attacks, I was transferred to the 2nd *Staffel* of JG 53 in April 1944. I returned to operational flying in Romania, where I was confronted with the flying fortresses (Liberator and Boeing-Fortress). We still also had to fight against the escorts, the Lightnings, Mustangs and Thunderbolts. I had successes, but was myself shot down twice, trusting myself to my parachute each time. While the English had been fair enemies, the Americans were brutal. Their flying tactics were somehow different, one noticed it straightaway. They were always aggressive and only attacked in large numbers, odds of 1 to 8 being mostly the norm. If they had got one of us, and the pilot saved himself by bailing out, these "pigs" did not hesitate to shoot the helpless pilot on his chute. I saw this with my own eyes! Two days later it would also have happened to me, if my *Kommandeur* – *Major* Harder – despite the danger, had not thrown himself at four Mustangs.' Hommes had managed to claim three P-51s, one P-38 and a Liberator over Romania in June-August 1944.[55]

American air raids on Romania came to an end on 19 August 1944.[56] Soon after the fall of the pro-German Romanian government (23 August 1944) and its armistice with the Soviet Union, this country changed sides, and the Germans rapidly exited Romania in some chaos.[57] German fighter units still in Romania then left mainly for Hungary, where the fight continued, now mainly against the Soviets rather than the western Allies (but also against the Romanian air force) as recounted in a companion volume to this book[58] dealing with operations over the Eastern Front.

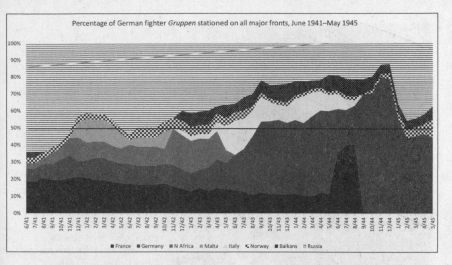

Percentage of German fighter *Gruppen* stationed on all major fronts, June 1941–May 1945

■ France ■ Germany ■ N Africa ■ Malta ■ Italy ↖ Norway ■ Balkans ≡ Russia

1. It is clear that the North African-Malta campaign absorbed significant fighter forces from late 1941 till the end of the Tunisian campaign (April–May 1943). Thereafter operations over Sicily and Italy locked up fewer *Gruppen* until about mid-1944 when they were essentially withdrawn. June–August 1944 saw a massive transfer of fighter units from German Home Defence to Normandy. From late 1942 till late 1944 the Balkans region was served by several *Jagdgruppen*, remaining relatively constant in number while never becoming over-significant. Home Defence became the prime theatre once more after defeat at Normandy, only reaching approximate parity with the Eastern Front in 1945.

2. *Oberleutnant* Günther Scholtz and *Leutnant* Max Clerico of 7/JG 54 enjoy a lighter moment during the Balkans campaign in 1941. Clerico: 'I still have a photo of *Oberleutnant* Scholtz (*Staffelkapitän* 7/JG 54) and myself wearing nightcaps, that we often wore when we had spare time to fly in open-cockpit sports aircraft (Kl 35 – wonderful!), which we wore as a joke so as not to appear so military! ... Mine had a tassel made of wood wrapped in textile (clearly visible in the picture) and this unfortunately bounced around in the Kl 35's slipstream and hit me on the back of the head often; that way I could not fall asleep.' (Dr Max Clerico)

Left: 3. A formal portrait of *Leutnant* Gűnther Schwanecke, 7/JG 77 taken in 1941. He flew mainly low level attacks on shipping in the Balkans campaign of that year. (Gűnther Schwanecke)

Below: 4. Formation flight practice over Germany for a *Schwarm* of four Me 110s from *III/ZG 26*. This *Gruppe* saw action over Yugoslavia and later over the island of Crete during the 1941 Balkan campaign. (Werner Ludwig)

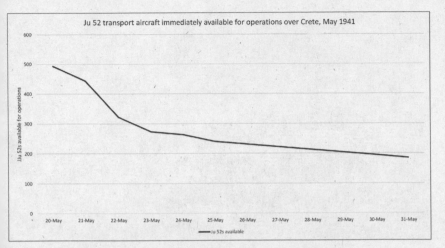

Ju 52 transport aircraft immediately available for operations over Crete, May 1941

5. The wastage evident here encompasses combat losses, operational losses and accidents. Very steep losses characterised the first few days of the operations, after which a steady decrease in operational machines continued. This situation would not have been able to continue for too much longer if the defenders of the island could have imposed some more delay on the invasion. For source of data, see note 71 for Chapter One.

6. *Unteroffizier* Johann Pichler of 7/JG 77 commented on this photograph: 'One of my hardest forced-landings, on 22 May 1941 on my airfield in the Peloponnese, during the operations over Crete.' This followed combat damage suffered during a *Schwarm* attack on the British battleship *Valiant* north of Crete, with the Messerschmitt evidently being destroyed (graded as 85% damage, some parts salvageable) with extensive damage to the cockpit area (note windscreen pointing vertically upwards in the middle of the photo) – his survival was a miracle. (Johann Pichler)

7. *Leutnant* Martin Drewes and his gunner flying to Iraq on 14 May 1941 as part of 4/ZG 76. Despite carrying Iraqi markings and the crews wearing Iraqi uniforms, the famous shark's mouth emblem on the nose of *II/ZG 76* ('*Haifischgruppe*') aircraft was maintained; note also the long range fuel tanks. (Martin Drewes)

8. *Hauptmann* Joachim Műncheberg who led *7/JG 26* over the Western Desert. Photo taken after his time in Africa, late 1941 or beginning of 1942, after the award of the *Eichenlaub*. (Lothair Vanoverbeke)

9a, 9b & 9c. New experiences for most German fighter pilots in North Africa: the Arabic people, palm trees, desert and camels. The touristic experience soon gave way to more serious pursuits. All three photos taken around Castel Benito airfield, south of Tripoli. *Feldwebel* Werner Ludwig of *III/ZG 26* gets close to a camel in the top left hand photo. (Werner Ludwig)

10. *Oberfeldwebel* Heinrich 'Henri' Rosenberg, *9/JG 27*, or as he put it, 'the "Phantom" in Africa, 1942'. Note the ubiquitous fighter pilot's scarf to reduce chafing around the neck with the constant swivelling of their heads looking for the enemy possibly approaching from above and behind. (Heinrich Rosenberg)

11. Gerhard Keppler, who flew in the Western Desert as a *Feldwebel* with *1/JG 27*. This shows him later in the war after promotion to *Leutnant*. He commented on the medal hanging next to his C-licence badge for gliding (three white swallows on a blue background, above the Iron Cross First Class): 'The badge hanging next to the C-licence is something Italian, whose name I can no longer remember.' The latter was likely the Italian Africa Service Medal. (Gerhard Keppler)

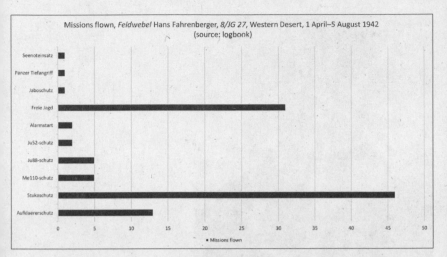

Missions flown, *Feldwebel* Hans Fahrenberger, *8/JG 27*, Western Desert, 1 April–5 August 1942
(source: logbook)

12. One of the *Aufklärerschutz* (reconnaissance escort) missions here was actually an *Aufklärung* (reconnaissance mission) by Fahrenberger himself near his own base. *Seenoteinsatz* = air sea rescue mission; *Panzer Tiefangriff* = low-level attack on tanks. He was already an experienced pilot before arriving in the Western Desert, his prior operations encompassing the following *Feindflüge*: Channel (cf., late Battle of Britain) – two; Balkan campaign – 10; Russia 1941 – 106; prior missions over Africa – nine. His grand total of operational missions had thus reached 234 by 5 August 1942.

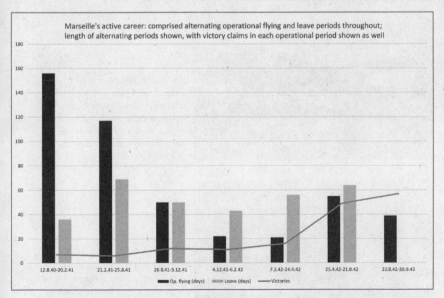

13. Note that the leave periods tended to become longer as time went on and as exhaustion became ever more prevalent. In the end the candle that was Marseille inevitably burnt itself out. Sources of data given in text and notes to Chapter 2.

14. Professor Paul Robert Skawran, the *Luftwaffe*'s '*Seelenspion*', a trained psychologist who spent much of the war observing German pilots on active service. (Paul Skawran)

15. A Me 110 N of *III/ZG 26* loaded with two 250 kg bombs and four 50 kg bombs, takes off on a fighter-bomber mission in the Western Desert. Note *Geschwader* badge on nose. (Georg Christl)

16. A Me 110 of *III/ZG 26* providing escort of supply convoy for Rommel over the Mediterranean Sea. The aircraft carries the *ZG 26* badge on its nose. (Georg Christl)

17. The sad remains of a Me 110 of *III/ZG 26*, burnt out after being attacked on the ground at Fuka in Egypt. (Werner Ludwig)

18. Take-off from Derna in the Western Desert, Me 110 of *III/ZG 26*. (Werner Ludwig)

Above left: 19. A Me 110 of *8/ZG 26* being warmed up on Cagliari airfield in Sardinia. *III/ZG 26* was the first *Luftwaffe* fighter unit to fly into Sicily for operations over Malta, arriving from 14 December 1940. (Werner Ludwig)

Above right: 20. *Unteroffizier* Dr Felix Sauer, then with *6/JG 53*, taken in Bergen, northern Holland in September 1941 three months before he moved to Sicily to fly over Malta. (Dr Felix Sauer)

21a & 21b. Two photographs of *Major* Gűnther Freiherr von Maltzahn, *Kommodore* of the '*Pik As*' (Ace of Spades) *Geschwader*, *JG 53*. In the right hand picture, *Major* von Maltzahn (second from left) and *Oberleutnant* Otto Böhner (at right; *Staffelkapitän* 6/*JG 53* over Malta, December 1941-March 1942; wounded over Malta 7 March 1942). Photographs taken in September 1941, Bergen airfield in northern Holland, before the move to Sicily. (Dr Felix Sauer)

22. *Oberstleutnant* Helmut Bennemann, who succeeded *Kommodore* von Maltzahn, and led *JG 53* over the Italian theatre from 9 November 1943 till 27 June 1944. (Helmut Bennemann)

23. *Oberfeldwebel* Josef Ederer, *3/ JG 53* captioned this photograph: 'Home leave, July-August 1942, after leaving hospital following my crash in Sicily.' (Josef Ederer)

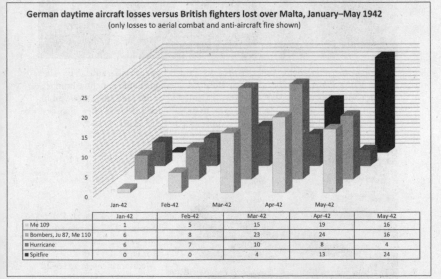

German daytime aircraft losses versus British fighters lost over Malta, January–May 1942
(only losses to aerial combat and anti-aircraft fire shown)

	Jan-42	Feb-42	Mar-42	Apr-42	May-42
Me 109	1	5	15	19	16
Bombers, Ju 87, Me 110	6	8	23	24	16
Hurricane	6	7	10	8	4
Spitfire	0	0	4	13	24

24. In May 1942, two 'other' type German and eight Italian aircraft were also lost, which are not included. Source of data: note 32 for Chapter 3.

25. The Italian destroyer *Turbine* which rescued *Unteroffizier* Dr Felix Sauer, *10/JG 53* from the sea after eight days, on 23 May 1942. (Dr Felix Sauer)

26. *Unteroffizier* Dr Felix Sauer, *10/JG 53* said of this photograph: 'The 10th *Staffel* of the *Pik-As-Geschwader* was the "*Jabo*" (*Jagdbomber*, fighter-bomber) *Staffel*. Four pilots of this *Staffel* next to the emblem of the unit, the *Jabo*-symbol, a bomb pointing towards Malta. Despite their primary *Jabo* role they also flew some ordinary fighter missions when required.' (Dr Felix Sauer)

27. *Unteroffizier* Dr Felix Sauer, *10/JG 53* posing in his dinghy: 'In my dinghy for eight days on the Mediterranean Sea, 16–23 May 1942. The yellow signalling flag also served as a sail.' (Dr Felix Sauer)

28. 'An original photo from the rescuing vessel: German fighter pilot *Unteroffizier* Dr Felix Sauer, drifting in the Mediterranean Sea for eight days, is found 200 km east of Malta and rescued on 23 May 1942 by the Italian destroyer *Turbine*.' (Dr Felix Sauer)

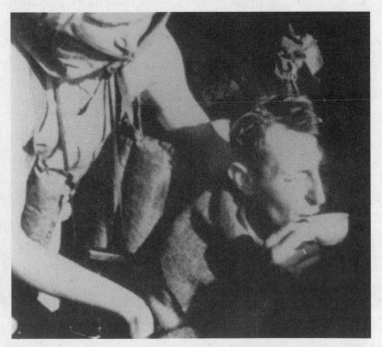

29. *Unteroffizier* Dr Felix Sauer, *10/JG 53*: 'The first drink after rescue, on board the destroyer *Turbine*.' (Dr Felix Sauer)

30. Me 110 with auxiliary fuel tanks on a Sicilian airfield (Gerbini or Catania) with a snow-covered Mount Etna in the background. (Georg Christl)

31. An interesting landing circuit with such high mountains so close to the airfield: Palermo airfield in Sicily. (Werner Ludwig)

32. Dr Felix Sauer convalesces in Lorient, July 1942, now promoted to *Feldwebel* also, after his 'adventure' in the Mediterranean. (Dr Felix Sauer)

33. *Oberfeldwebel* Eduard Isken, one of the senior NCOs who made up the backbone of *III/JG 77* and who saw significant action over Tunisia. This photo was taken in January 1945 after he had been awarded the *Ritterkreuz*. (Eduard Isken)

34. *Oberfeldwebel* Johann Pichler, 7/JG 77 merely captioned this photograph: 'April 1943 in Africa.' (Johann Pichler)

Above left: 35. Ex-*Leutnant* Hans-Ulrich Kornstädt, 4/JG 27, in an amusing pose taken in his Munich garden in 1989. (Hans-Ulrich Kornstädt)

Above right: 36. *Leutnant* Hans-Ulrich Kornstädt, 4/JG 27: 'Mother and son, 1942 in Berlin.' (Hans-Ulrich Kornstädt)

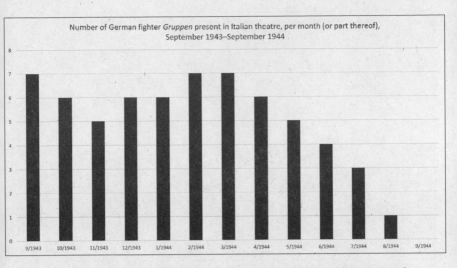

Number of German fighter *Gruppen* present in Italian theatre, per month (or part thereof), September 1943–September 1944

37. Allied landing and bridgehead operations at Salerno (September 1943) and at Anzio (January–February at peak, continued till early June 1944) resulted in relatively minor increases in German fighter allocations. Data source: notes 74 and 75, Chapter 5.

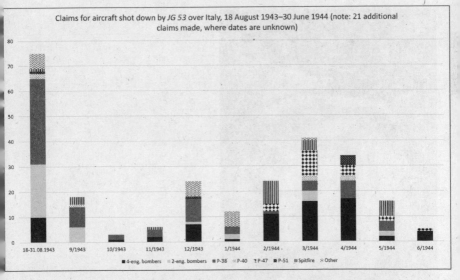

Claims for aircraft shot down by *JG 53* over Italy, 18 August 1943–30 June 1944 (note: 21 additional claims made, where dates are unknown)

■ 4-eng. bombers ▩ 2-eng. bombers ■ P-38 ⬙ P-40 ⬙ P-47 ■ P-51 ‖ Spitfire ✖ Other

38. The most intense fighting took place in the few weeks after leaving Sicily, after which victory claim numbers tailed off considerably. The Salerno landings (September 1943) and first two intense months of fighting at the Anzio bridgehead (January–February 1944) did not produce major increases, but claims were measurably higher for the following two months of the latter battle. *JG 53*'s claims against enemy fighters significantly outnumbered claims against Allied bombers. Data source: note 76, Chapter 5.

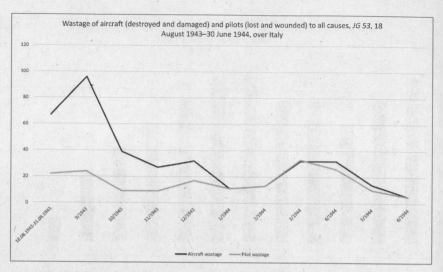

Wastage of aircraft (destroyed and damaged) and pilots (lost and wounded) to all causes, *JG 53*, 18 August 1943–30 June 1944, over Italy

— Aircraft wastage — Pilot wastage

39. High losses for the first few weeks after the loss of Sicily (balance of August 1943) increased to a peak for the Salerno period immediately thereafter (September 1943); after this relatively muted losses pertained through to June 1944, with little influence from the Anzio fighting. Data source: note 76, Chapter 5.

40. *Major* (*Oberst* by the end of the war) Gustav Rödel, *Geschwaderkommodore JG 27* titled this photograph: 'A photo from the war.' (Gustav Rödel)

41. The Balkans, 1943, *Oberfeldwebel* Johann Pichler, 7/JG77: 'Heavily laden Ju 87 dive bombers off on a new mission.' (Johann Pichler)

42. *Oberleutnant* Emil Clade, *Staffelkapitän* 7/JG 27, Greece 1943–1944. (Emil Clade)

43. One of the ever more scarce veterans flying over the Balkans in 1943–1944, *Oberfeldwebel* Johann Pichler, 7/*JG 77* in the foreground, in a photo from earlier in the war, taken in southern Russia in winter 1941/42. 'Shortly before departing on leave, with the Me 108, December 1941. The Me 108 could seat four people.' (Johann Pichler)

44a. 'Mizil/Romania, 10 June 44: after the first victory in air combat; in the middle is *Unteroffizier* Martin Hain 8th *Staffel*, JG 77'.

Right: 44b. Award certificate for the Iron Cross 2nd Class (*EK 2*) awarded to *Unteroffizier* Martin Hain for the aforementioned first victory. (Martin Hain)

Below: 45. *Unteroffizier* Martin Hain, *8/JG 77*: copy of a page from his *Leistungsbuch* showing his three claims. Columns headed, left to right: running number of claim; aircraft type shot down; date; time; grid square reference/place; height; witnesses (that for number 3 is a ground witness); remarks. (Martin Hain)

IM NAMEN DES FÜHRERS
UND OBERSTEN BEFEHLSHABERS
DER WEHRMACHT
VERLEIHE ICH
DEM

Unteroffizier

M a r t i n H a i n

8./ J.G. 77

DAS

**EISERNE KREUZ
2. KLASSE**

B u k a r e s t , 22. Juni 1944
Der Kommandierende General und Befehlshaber
der Deutschen Luftwaffe in Rumänien

(DIENSTSIEGEL)

(DIENSTGRAD UND DIENSTSTELLUNG)
Generalleutnant

lfd. Nr.	Typ	Datum	Uhr	Ort	Höhe	Zeugen	Bemerkungen
1	P38 Lightning	10.VI.44	0912	⊞ 55373	30 m	Ofw. Hackler, Uffz. Rosenberg	Aufschlagbrand.
	„Liberator"	11.VI.44	0915	⊞ Giurgiu	6000 m		
	Liberator	3.VII.44	12.45	⊞ 5427 24 Ost-Süd	6500 m	Uffz. O.B. Matei Marin Fab. Flic Batl. 2, Stamm.-Kp.	
							Die Richtigkeit der Eintragungen lfd. Nr. 1–3 bescheinigt: ..., den 28.7.44 Leutnant u. Staffelführer i.V.

Kopie des Leistungsbuches.
8/JG. Martin Hain

Dem

Hain, Martin Unteroffizier
Name, Dienstgrad

III./Jagdgeschwader 77
Truppenteil, Dienststelle

ist auf Grund seiner am 3.7.1944

erlittenen 1 maligen Verwundung oder Beschädigung das

Verwundetenabzeichen

in Schwarz

verliehen worden.

Im Felde , den 27.7. 19 44

Im Auftrage:

Unterschrift, Dienstgrad und Dienststelle
Hauptmann und Gruppenkommandeur.
m.d.W.d.G.b.

46. *Unteroffizier* Martin Hain, *8/JG 77*: award certificate for the *Verwundetenabzeichen* or Wound Badge (Black) signed by the acting *Gruppenkommandeur* of *III/JG 77*, *Hauptmann* Bresoscheck, an ethnic German from Yugoslavia. (Martin Hain)

An 2./J.G. 11

Der 2./J.G. 11
wird der Abschuß eines amerikanischen Jagdflugzeuges vom Typ
North American "Mustang"   am 7.6.44   08,oo Uhr
durch Oberleutnant Fritz E n g a u

RAMBOUILLET BEI PARIS
VERLEGUNGSFLUG AN
DIE INVASIONSFRONT!

als sechsundvierzigster (46.) Luftsieg der Staffel anerkannt.

                              I.A.
                    gez. Unterschrift

F.d.R.d.   schrift: z.U., 7.11.1944

                  Gau

          leutnant u. Offz. z.b.V.

47. Copy of official confirmation certificate (*Abschussbestätigung*) for a victory claim by *Oberleutnant* Fritz Engau, *Staffelkapitän* 2/JG 11, achieved on 7 June 1944 during the transfer flight of *I/JG 11* to the Invasion Front. Handwritten note added by Fritz Engau. The original certificate went to the *Staffel* (to whom the victory was always credited, not the individual pilot) and stayed there, the unit itself issuing a stamped copy of the certificate to the relevant pilot. Note that issue of the certificate post-dated the claim by three months. (Fritz Engau)

48. A *JG 26* pilot sits in his Fw 190. (*JG 26* veteran, via Lothair Vanoverbeke)

49. *Oberleutnant* Wilhelm Hofmann, in a photograph taken probably at either Wevelghem or Moorsele in Belgium, in about 1941; obviously in hot summer weather, during *Sitzbereitschaft* in his Fw 190. (*JG 26* veteran, via Lothair Vanoverbeke)

50. *Oberfeldwebel* Eduard Isken receives the *Ritterkreuz* on 14 January 1945; he ended the war as a *Leutnant*. (Eduard Isken)

51a & 51b. *Oberleutnant* Ernst Scheufele, *Staffelkapitän 6/JG 5* (and later of its successor *14/JG 4*): 'Two pictures from my Me 109 time.' (Ernst Scheufele)

52. One of the *Sturmgruppen* pilots: '*Unteroffizier* Ernst Schröder, 5th *Staffel JG 300*, in his Fw 190 A-8 R2, Red 19, field base at Löbwitz bei Bitterfeld, in about November 1944.' (Ernst Schröder)

53. '*Unteroffizier* Ernst Schröder, 5th *Staffel JG 300*; aircraft Red 19, Fw 190 A-8 R2, *Werkenummer* 172733 (with a *Kreisel* experimental gun sight installed!); full leather flying suit and Mae West, back parachute lying on wing; October/November 1944 in Löbwitz bei Bitterfeld.' The emblem and slogan below the cockpit were a personal marking derived from the Cologne Carnival, Schröder being a native of that city [note 38, Chapter 8]. (Ernst Schröder)

54a & 54b. Two late-war Fw 190 victims, at left near Liege and at right near Florennes, both in Belgium. (Lothair Vanoverbeke)

55. Belly-landed Fw 190, one of many late war *Jagdverband* casualties. Wrecks like this would have littered Belgium, north-eastern France and adjacent Germany after *Operation Bodenplatte* on 1 January 1945. (Lothair Vanoverbeke)

56. Fighter pilots often had personal emblems painted on their aircraft, as this pilot recalled: 'Blue 11 with *Unteroffizier* K-H. Erler, Stavanger-Norway, *16/JG 5*. I painted the coat of arms of all my fellow pilots' home cities/towns on their aircraft. My own coat of arms, for Freiburg/Saxony, is too fine-detailed, so that instead I painted the ancient symbol of the miners: crossed hammer and mallet.' (Karl-Heinz Erler)

57. Karl-Heinz Erler captioned this late-war photograph taken in Norway: 'Our readiness area with veranda, at Forus in southwest Norway, where we played "*Skat*". The Me 109 just beyond the hut is the "bird" of *Feldwebel* Heinz Halstrick (on the right, just below right hand window), who was our last *Staffelkapitän*. We did not have any officers left. I had the honour to be his wingman and we were friends then and still are today (writing in 1995). I am second from right leaning out the window. In the foreground with the cards in his hand is *Unteroffizier* Emil Seez, from Swabia, and next to Halstrick, on his right, is *Unteroffizier* Werner Müller.' (Karl-Heinz Erler)

58. Air and ground crew pose on their aircraft: 'Forus, Norway, 16th *Staffel* of *JG 5*; my Blue 11 with mechanic and armourer, plus *Unteroffizier* K.H. Erler on cowling. The photo was taken about the beginning of March 1945.' (Karl-Heinz Erler)

59. *Staffel* line-up, late-war Norway: '16th *Staffel JG 5*; from left: Ach, Eder, Steiner, Schmilewsky, Schüler, Smejkal, Erler.' (Karl-Heinz Erler)

60a & 60b. Karl-Heinz Erler drew these *JG 5* badges: 'The "*Eismeer*" badge was the official emblem of *Jagdgeschwader 5*; the other badge is the one for our 16th *Staffel* – I designed the latter myself. It represents, humorously, the day fighters with their weapon and flying helmet.' (Karl-Heinz Erler)

J.G.5 „Eismeerjäger"

16.JG.5

61. *16/JG 5* dispersal area at Forus, Norway, 1944 (headquarters at left). Note the boardwalk in foreground and wooden-paved parking places for individual aircraft, all to avoid the mud. (Karl-Heinz Erler)

62. One of the many *Luftwaffe* prisoners of war, *Oberleutnant* Heinz Altendorf, *Staffelkapitän* of 7th *Staffel, JG 53* – 'Pik As' in a photograph taken in September 1940. One tends to forget how young almost all the combat pilots were; at 23 in 1940, Heinz Altendorf was bordering on being considered 'older'! (Heinz Altendorf)

7

THE NORMANDY INVASION AND SUBSEQUENT ALLIED RE-CONQUEST OF FRANCE

Oberleutnant Fritz Engau, *Staffelkapitän* 2/JG 11, sums up the Normandy campaign experience in a brief recollection, which neatly encapsulates the odds against the *Jagdwaffe* in this long-awaited battle, which stemmed directly from their defeat in the Battle of Germany in the five-odd months leading up to the Invasion itself.[1] 'On the Invasion Front the superior numbers of the Allies were particularly large. The Mustangs circled over almost every cross-roads, junction and railway station, with some pairs low down, the others high above them as cover. Spitfires and other fighter types were also there in profusion. We suffered appalling losses, already on the transfer flight (actually on landing from it) from Germany to France on 7 June 1944. The only significant success our *Gruppe* had in Normandy was actually on this transfer flight, when flying over France we still had reasonable numbers (over 20 aircraft), and we encountered and fought against an approximately equal-sized force of Mustangs over the Forest of Rambouillet on 7 June at about 08h00. In a short space of time we had scattered the Mustangs. I was also able to shoot down a Mustang in this combat. In the landing after the combat we suffered large losses, as the airfield had just been heavily bombed. We never really recovered from these losses and from then on were always at a disadvantage.' Illustration 47 shows the relevant victory confirmation certificate (*Abschussbestätigung*) awarded to Fritz Engau for this Mustang claim.

Luftwaffe fighter operations over Normandy were concentrated on attacking the landing fleets and the beaches initially and then the congested beachheads, and apart from that they also flew many free chase missions. Due to a vast Allied air superiority (the fruits of the Battle of Germany) German losses were crippling, and the impact of the *Luftwaffe* on events in the air and on the ground was insignificant to the big picture. The Normandy aerial campaign discussed here includes also the period of the Allied breakout on the ground from the initial lodgement area, and the advance of their armies firstly to the River Seine and subsequently into Belgium; aerial operations were always in service of the ground operations, a brief summary of which is detailed below.

Key Allied ground advances, Normandy campaign, June to September 1944[2]	
Date	Event
6 June	Allies land in Normandy on three British/Canadian and two American beaches
8	Three British/Canadian beaches linked up
9	First Allied landing ground in beachhead operational
10	Two American beachheads linked up
17	American forces cut off Cotentin Peninsula
27	Cherbourg taken
9 July	Northern part of Caen taken
18	St. Lo largely in American hands
25	Large American drive south out of restricted beachhead, *Operation Cobra*, begins
30	American forces enter Avranches as part of *Cobra*
2 August	3rd American Army advances into Brittany
3	Mortain falls to American forces
4	Rennes (Brittany) taken
5	Vannes (Brittany) taken
6	Laval taken
7–11	German counterattack at Mortain – fails

8	Le Mans taken
14	St. Malo (Brittany) taken
15	Battle of Falaise Pocket begins, pocket closed 18 August
	Allies land in southern France
16	Chartres taken
17	Dreux, Chateaudun and Orleans taken
19	Résistance begins uprising in Paris (city largely taken by them by 23 August)
20	River Seine reached north and south of Paris
21	Rapid Allied advance towards Seine begins
24	In the south, Grenoble taken
25	General Le Clerc's French armoured division enters Paris
28	Marseilles and Toulon in the south taken
29	Reims and Chalons-sur-Marne taken
1 September	Dieppe and Verdun taken
3	British enter Brussels; Tournai and Abbeville taken; Mons and Lyons taken

Opposing the Germans in the Normandy campaign, in the beginning were 3,467 heavy bombers, 1,645 medium-light bombers, and 5,409 fighters and fighter-bombers – a truly amazing assembly of massive air power; on D-Day itself they put up a total of 14,674 operational sorties (losses = 113, mainly to flak)[3] as against 319 *Luftwaffe* sorties.[4] During June 1944 the Allies flew 130,000 sorties over the invasion beachhead, with their German opponents managing 13,829; June's losses for the *Luftwaffe* totalled 931 aircraft in combat.[5] By the end of June available German fighters in France numbered only 425 machines.[6]

6 June 1944 found the *Luftwaffe* fighter units stationed in northern France poorly placed to help repel the invasion.[7] *I/JG* 2 had been moved away from its base at Creil (north of Paris) on 3 June to the Nancy area (in the far east of France); *II/JG* 2 was in Germany re-equipping with new aircraft; *III/JG* 2 was in the Nantes area on the Atlantic coast.[8] *Hauptmann* Georg Schröder became *Gruppenkommandeur II/JG* 2 on 4 May 1944 and led them over the Invasion Front from June till early September 1944.

His account of the chaos just before and just after the invasion makes for interesting reading. Schröder also became one of the many casualties over Normandy:

Already in April–May 1944 it became clear to us at the front, through the increase in enemy escort fighters, now also with much greater range, and thus also the expansion of the four-engined bomber attacks on the German motherland, that a definite change was approaching. In our higher command echelons the words 'home defence' must have had absolute priority. At least this was my impression, as we were ordered in the last few days of May 1944, that the Me 109s of *II/JG* 2 were to be handed over to *Jafü Süd* in Lyon. While our first thoughts were that this was to enable our re-equipment with the Fw 190, these only lasted a few minutes, as then the next order arrived: 'The *II Gruppe* of *JG* 2 is transferred to Gütersloh for operations in the Home Defence.' I must add here that we were the only *Jagdgruppe* with our own fully equipped workshops. For the transfer we required at least three large goods trains. But this instruction from on-high was already there, and while we flew southwards on the next day, the packing up and loading began in Creil. After we had handed over our aircraft and parachutes to *Jafü Süd*, we became aware that there was no train connection to Paris and further on to Creil. In addition, the available lorries were not enough to transport almost 30 pilots from Lyon. After spending a night in the more than primitive quarters given us, the next morning early we decided to acquire the status of railway officials. Over the telephone we established when on this morning the Marseilles-Paris train reached our district. We also found out where the next railway signal was situated. So there was an early morning march to this signal station, which was soon showing the 'Halt' signal. Thus the train had to stop, and within seconds we were on the train, and the last person put the signal back on free traffic. Within a minute the train was on the move again.

In Paris we were met at the station by our own vehicles. This all happened in the last days of May 1944. Our three trains with the workshop and ground staff needed at least two if not three days running time. In Gütersloh we moved into quarters; everything was unpacked, and feelers were extended about our new aircraft. And then came the 6 June 1944, with the radio announcement of the invasion landings. But we were several hundred kilometres distant from that, and thus in that moment only foot soldiers. The telephone lines to our *Geschwader Kommodore* in France and to the *Reichsluftfahrtministerium* in Berlin ran red hot. Our immediate return was ordered, and the packing and loading began once more. In the meantime we were informed by Berlin of where we could go to fetch new aircraft. Most of the railway distances were about 300–600 km to these locations. We needed four days for this bustle. When the first new birds landed in Gütersloh, our dreams of effective new aircraft vanished. In addition only one of these aircraft was equipped with a radio. This meant that all our aircraft first had to fly to Mannheim/Sandhofen so that necessary operational equipment could be built in and adjustments made. The *Gruppe* thus became divided. From Sandhofen we flew to our prepared anti-invasion landing strip in France which had been set up months before already, which lay about 10 km east of Senlis. Thus the *II/JG 2* was not in French skies on the day of the invasion. However this delay was limited and soon we were in the fray, and several times a day at that. This was a very difficult time for us, and the Allies had a *c.* seven times material advantage over us.

During this period after leaving Gütersloh our losses inevitably increased markedly. I was one of them, downed on 5 July at 7,000 m in the southern Normandy area in a dogfight with seven Thunderbolts. In this we got lower and lower until we were below 1,000 m. When now my elevators were shot away I had no choice but to bail out. As my 'chute became entangled with the tail and rudder, I lost consciousness. I came to again lying on one of the typical high carts of the local farmers. How much time had passed between my bailing out and waking up on the cart has forever remained unknown to me. Two French farmers told me that they had hauled me out of a fruit tree, and now they were taking me to hospital. I will always remember this journey of something over an hour. The hospital was the normal large and modern infirmary typical of a city. At that time it was mostly used as a German military hospital. My recovery there lasted 23 days until I was collected by the *II Gruppe* of our *Geschwader* once more. The next morning I again had a high fever, so that our doctor took me off to hospital once more. The following morning I suddenly saw the medical *Feldwebel* of our *II Gruppe* outside the window of my ward. He had just brought in an accident casualty (overturned on landing). Within three minutes I was in his ambulance and we drove back to the *Gruppe*, now at St. Trond, to where a successful retreat had been achieved. Under the eye of our unit doctor I slowly got better, but could not yet fly. After another four to five days we moved further back via Köln-Butzweilerhof to Wiesbaden. Our aircraft flew directly to these airfields which had been indicated by our local *Jafü*. We were given Nidda/Oberhausen as an alternate base. This was a purely replacement field equipped only with a headquarters, but no hangars for ground staff nor any aircraft either. We made do with small barracks buildings and tents. Quarters for all ranks were obtained in the surrounding villages as well as in Nidda itself. *I* and *III Gruppen* of our *Geschwader* were on fields within about 15 km of us. We had reached Nidda in the first 10 days of September 1944.

The other *Geschwader* based in France before the invasion, *JG 26*, had its *III Gruppe* stationed around Nantes; *II/JG 26* was just west of Paris, and *I/JG 26* was east – south-east of Rouen.[9] Thus of the six fighter *Gruppen* actually based in France, only two were near enough to the invasion beaches to react on the first day, *I* and *II/JG 26*. *III/JG 26* returned on 7 June, to the Paris area, while leading elements of *I* and *III/JG 2* had reached the same area on

6 June already. *Oberleutnant* Hans-R. Hartigs, 4/JG 26 was one of the *JG 26* pilots who experienced what it was like to fly over the invasion area from 6 June onwards, until being badly wounded two months later:

> The operations from 6 June 1944 in Operation Overlord, to invade Northern France, were particularly costly for us. Little more than 200–400 fighters were serviceable. We were hopelessly inferior to the English and Americans. During this time I flew many low level attacks. We had two extra 2 cm cannons built into the outer wings and beneath the wings two 21 cm rockets that were very effective against tanks and flak positions. More than once I flew the weather reconnaissance in the early morning as far as the mouth of the River Orne. In this campaign I also flew as *Schwarm-*, *Staffel-* and even *Gruppenführer*, though never with more than four to sixteen machines, except for a couple of missions where we flew with the entire *Jagdverbänden* in the area north-west of Paris with between 10 and 12 *Gruppen* with 20–100 aircraft at a time. I was shot down twice in this campaign over Northern France, and bailed out the second time in August 1944. On this latter occasion I was surprised by American fighters while landing at my own base, and before I bailed out I pulled my aircraft up steeply and then, when I was out, I collided with the trimming tabs on the tailfin; I suffered a broken pelvis, broken jaw and broken ribs, and was in hospital until October, followed by leave and then a transfer to the flak branch as a battery commander. However I managed to get back to *JG 26* and was declared fit for flying again there; my transfer to the flak was withdrawn.

The German plan was to dispatch massive fighter reinforcements from Germany, in fact most of those available to *Jagddivisions 1, 2, 3* and *7* were to join those already in France (4th and 5th *Jagddivisions – JG 2* and *JG 26*).[10] A total of 17 *Jagdgruppen* was transferred.[11] Arriving on 6 June 1944: *III/JG 1* went to the Paris area; *II/JG 11* flew into the area east of Rouen, close to the eastern edge of the landings; *II/JG 53* went to the Vannes area just south of Brittany; *III/JG 27* was dispatched quite far east of Paris away from any immediate action but available as a reserve.[12] The next day, nine more *Gruppen* arrived in northern France:[13] *I* and *II/JG 1* were sent to the area south of Falaise, close to the south of the landings; *I/JG 27* east of Paris close to *III/JG 27*; *III/JG 3* and *III/JG 54* in the Paris area itself; *II/JG 3* to the Rouen area; *I/JG 11* to Rennes; *I/JG 5* to the Amiens area; *IV/JG 27* to the Reims area, again this *Gruppe* like those east of Paris, was in immediate reserve. Assuming all incoming *Gruppen* were at full strength (64 aircraft)[14] on arrival in France, this should have given a force of 832 fighters to add to the six *Gruppen* of JG 2 and 26. Next, *IV/JG 3* arrived on 8 June but returned to Germany already on 13 June[15] (as a *Sturmgruppe*, they were much better suited to fighting over the *Reich*). On 9 June *10/JG 11* reinforced *I/JG 11* at Rennes.[16] Within a few days therefore, a small force of just over six *Gruppen* was stationed relatively close to the landings: one *Gruppe* and a *Staffel* to the south-west, two to the south and three *Gruppen* to the east thereof; a larger force of eight *Gruppen* lay around Paris, and one *Gruppe* near Amiens, all nine also within range of the Allied landings, while further away, not in immediate range were four further *Gruppen*.[17] Additional reinforcements arrived on 12 June: *I/JG 3* to Reims, *I/JG 301* to the Paris area but this *Gruppe* operated solely at night as *Wilden Sau*;[18] and on 15 June *II/JG 5* to the Rouen area;[19] these arrivals thus completed the 17 *Jagdgruppen* dispatched to the Normandy battle. Right towards the end of the entire campaign *II/JG 6* arrived near Laon (north-west of Reims) on 22 August 1944.[20]

Leutnant Gerd Schindler, an experienced pilot who had flown with *III/JG 52* in Russia for many months, was one of those in *IV/JG 27* who flew in to Romilly, *c.* 100 km to the east of Paris, on 7 June 1944. In correspondence, he related how they flew their first operations the same day and immediately became embroiled in combat with Allied fighters – Typhoons, Thunderbolts and Mustangs. The days were long, with first take-offs at 05h00 and last landings at 22h00. Schindler survived three days of this and in the meantime they had moved to Paris Guyancourt. On 10 June, only his fourth day in this theatre, he was shot down over Lisieux by a Thunderbolt, hit in the thigh with splinters and bailed out; he landed in an active resistance area but was rescued by a French farmer that brought him to a local doctor, who operated on him and thereafter sent him to the Germans.

The aerial fighting over Normandy was vicious and resulted in terrible casualties for the *Jagdgruppen*; during June 1944 three *Gruppen* returned to Germany/Holland (excludes *IV/JG 3*, which returned to Germany on 13 June to reinforce the rump Home Defence) and another six in July, for replenishment of aircraft and pilots.[21] *JG 1* was particularly hard hit, all three *Gruppen* returning while both *JG 11 Gruppen* operating over Normandy did as well.[22] Five of the nine *Gruppen* returning for replenishment were from the units lying closest to the Allied beachhead, and one *Gruppe* (*II/JG 5*) did not return to Normandy, unlike the other eight, which did.[23] For many pilots, Normandy was fatal. The lucky few survived, mostly wounded and some fighting careers were brought to an end by the severity of those wounds. *Oberleutnant* Fritz Engau, *Staffelkapitän 2/JG 11*, was one of those who was out of operations for many months as a result of flying over Normandy: 'From 7 June 1944 I was with the *I Gruppe* of *JG 11* in France, on the Invasion Front, based at Rennes and later a field base near Le Mans. From June–July 1944 due to having been wounded I was in hospital and not able to fly operationally again till the end of the war.'

One of the *Gruppen* that returned to Germany in July 1944 to replenish was Hans Hartig's unit, *II/JG 26*. Ottomar Kruse was one of their new replacement pilots, and I met him during his visit to South Africa in early 1993. The former *Unteroffizier* in the 8th *Staffel* of *II/JG 26* joined the *Gruppe* in late July 1944, after they had been withdrawn from their first stint in Normandy, to replenish with new aircraft and pilots (20 July–12 August 1944).[24] When he arrived in Rheinsehlen the *Gruppe* had just been stocked up to its full establishment of 16 pilots and aircraft per *Staffel*; four *Staffeln*, a *Stabschwarm* as well as 10 reserve aircraft made up the *Gruppe's* total of 78 brand new Fw 190s. He had volunteered to join a frontline unit before his training was complete at *Jagdergänzungsgruppe Süd*, but he had the advantage of having already completed his Me 109 training before converting onto the Fw 190. He was thus better prepared than most replacement pilots. When they returned to France, 8/JG 26 were led by their *Staffelkapitän Leutnant* Wilhelm Hofmann, a pilot who had suffered an eye injury resulting in his flying combat with an eye patch and who was credited with 26 victories at the time; he was later awarded the *Ritterkreuz* and was killed in action in March 1945 having raised his claims total to 44.[25] Ottomar Kruse remembered him as an excellent pilot who could turn his Fw 190 tighter than anyone else. Hofmann had once found one of his best friends hanging in his parachute harness from a tree, having been riddled with bullets while descending helpless on the 'chute.

Once they had returned to Normandy, two *Staffeln* of II/JG 26 were based at Guyancourt (7th and 8th) while the other two were dispersed to Villacoublay, and they flew operations from these bases for about six days. As a new pilot, Kruse was not allowed to fly on these missions. Then they were transferred to Mons aux Chaussée, and on the transfer flight while flying the oldest aircraft in the *Staffel*, Blue 6, Kruse was able to shoot down one of several Mustangs they encountered – his first victory on his first mission! Hofmann could not believe the success at first and when he had Kruse's weapons checked, it was discovered that the two outboard cannons had not even been switched on and only 25% of the ammunition in the remaining four guns had been expended. After this *Staffelkapitän* Hofmann realised he could shoot well and gave him one of the four-gun machines to fly. *Gruppenkommandeur Hauptmann* Lang cut a hole into Kruse's leather jacket to attach his *EK 2* to mark his achievement. Of the operations which Kruse flew on the Invasion Front (from *c.* 26 July to 12 August) all except two were free chases, the other two being attacks on tank spearheads on the ground.

Kruse also recalled that at this time in the points system used in the *Luftwaffe* for victories scored, that one Western fighter shot down gave one point, while one Russian fighter only gave one quarter of a point; for the Iron Cross 2nd class (*EK 2*) one point sufficed and for the *EK 1* five points were required. Kruse and his fellow pilots on the Invasion Front spent much of their time on the ground, playing cards and gambling, as missions were quite limited; this galled the mechanics who had to work very long hours. The mechanics restrained their gripes if a pilot was lost, but soon started complaining again; the pilots were unsympathetic as they risked their lives every time they flew. Not a healthy relationship between pilots and ground crews. Kruse remembers their living conditions on the ground on the Invasion Front as having been very good, with every possible foodstuff on the table, but understandably he had no appetite and lost weight during his combat flying time.

'Otto' Kruse also had very distinct memories of his *Gruppenkommandeur*, the famous Emil Lang, known as 'Bully', who had been a well-known athlete before the war, and taking part in the 1936 Berlin Olympics. Bully Lang was not someone who stood on military ceremony and he let his pilots wear operational dress largely of their own choice; he himself was famous for his leather jacket and his suitably crushed and disreputable operational officer's hat.

Lang had flown with *JG* 54 in the East where he claimed a total of 144 successes, including the *Luftwaffe* record of 18 in one day, in four missions on 3 November 1943; until his death he was never hit in combat at all.[26] A former transport pilot, Lang was an excellent shot but not the best pilot. A natural, hands-on and ebullient leader who was universally loved in the *Gruppe*, he had luck also, the unit being successful when he was up front (unlike when Hofmann occasionally led the *Gruppe* when losses were higher).

On 3 September 1944 when *II/JG* 26 took off from Melsbroeck in Belgium for the transfer flight back to Germany at the end of the campaign in Northern France, three aircraft remained behind that were still being worked on by the ground crew to make them serviceable. *Gruppenkommandeur* Bully Lang and two other pilots had remained behind to fly these lame ducks back to Germany. Finally the three aircraft were able to take off and flew towards Germany at low level; however, they were intercepted by P-51s low down and, as the combat began, the undercarriage in Lang's Fw 190 dropped down. Rendered thus helpless in the dogfight, he was shot down and killed. This was a great shock to *II/JG* 26 and the loss of a truly great fighter pilot and leader, who was the German top scorer in this campaign. That *Gruppenkommandeur* Lang had stayed back to fly one of the three lame duck aircraft back to Germany was also a sign of a true leader, one who didn't shirk the unpleasant and dangerous jobs.

As the Americans advanced, initially southwards from the western (American) sector of the landing area, in the 'Cobra' offensive, then spread first westwards into Brittany, and then south–south-east to Laval and Le Mans where they turned north to close off much of the German ground forces in the Falaise Pocket, so the British-Canadian forces advanced south to Falaise to close off the pocket from the north.[27]

The battle related to this pocket raged for several days from 15 August 1944 (table above), the same day the Allies invaded southern France.[28] Following this the advance went largely eastwards, firstly closing up to the River Seine; Paris fell by 25 August after a successful uprising of the *Résistance*, and by early September 1944 Brussels also fell as the Allies entered Belgium and closed up to the eastern borders of France.[29] The campaign against the Germans in northern France was thus over by the end of August; Montgomery placed the end of the Battle of Normandy with the fall of Paris and the seizure of Allied bridgeheads across the Seine (*c.* 20 August 1944).[30] As these events took place on the ground, the *Jagdgruppen* perforce retreated, essentially to the east and to the south, from their original locations. The *Gruppen* initially stationed south-west of the landings retreated to the south-east to the general Le Mans area while most of the rest went east–south-eastwards via the Paris region to bases closer to the Belgian border – in the areas of Reims, Laon, St. Quentin, Arras and Metz.[31]

German fighter losses in June to July 1944 (table below) exceeded their own claims total, which underlines the measure of their defeat, never mind that they had little real effect on Allied ground forces and their ability to advance and destroy much of the German forces opposing them, and retake most of France within the space of about three months.

Statistics for German day fighters over Normandy, June to July 1944[32]					
Month	*Abschüsse* claimed	Fighters destroyed in combat	Fighters damaged in combat	Fighters lost on ground	Pilots killed, missing, POW	Pilots wounded
June	526	551	290	65+	238	88
July	382	423	85	?	222	128
Total	908	974	375	65++	460	216

Notes: Data for June from 6 June 1944. In August 1944 the *Luftwaffe* lost 482 more fighters in France.[33]

One example of the losses suffered by a single *Staffel* is provided by 7/JG 51 which was transferred from the Russian Front to Germany, arriving on 3 June 1944 and placed under II/JG 1; the *Staffelkapitän Hauptmann* Karl-Heinz Weber, highly experienced and victor in 136 combats in Russia,[34] was appointed as the new *Gruppenkommandeur* of III/JG 1 while *Leutnant* Friedrich Krakowitzer took over as *Staffelführer* 7/JG 51.[35] On the evening of 6 June 'Benjamin' Weber led his new *Gruppe* to their predetermined base in France to counter the Normandy invasion, at Beauvais-Tillé.[36] The very next day on his first operation over Normandy, Weber led the III/JG 1 into a fight with about 30 P-51s south of Rouen from which he did not return.[37] 7/JG 51 arrived in Normandy with 15 pilots and within the first month of operations there, nine had been lost (eight dead, one POW) including the new *Staffelführer*.[38] The 7th *Staffel* of JG 51 was incorporated into II/JG 1 as its 8th *Staffel* on 10 July 1944 and lost another two pilots (one a POW) with five more wounded by the time II/JG 1 withdrew to Germany on 16 August 1944.[39] Total casualties to JG 1 (three *Gruppen*) and JG 11 (two *Gruppen*, one *Staffel*) over Normandy (6 June–31 August 1944) encompassed: 154 pilots lost, 42 wounded, 278 aircraft destroyed and 60 damaged, in combat.[40]

One of the pilots with JG 11 over Normandy was *Feldwebel* Ernst Richter, former wingman of the famous Walter Nowotny in I/JG 54 in Russia; he was amongst a small group of experienced *Rotten-* and *Schwarmführern* transferred from the over-stretched

East to the over-stretched Home Defence, joining *4/JG 11* in early April 1944.[41] He flew over Normandy with 4th *Staffel* and later 8th *Staffel* of *JG 11* (and by then promoted to *Oberfeldwebel*), shooting down six Allied fighters there (to add to his 12 Eastern and two Home Defence victories already achieved):[42] 'In *JG 11* in the Home Defence and on the Invasion Front I took part in a total of 23 *Feindflüge* and had eight confirmed victories. My last mission in the battles over Northern France ended in a belly-landing in Belgium on 2 September 1944.' He had belly-landed due to an engine problem.[43] Another *JG 11* pilot was *Oberleutnant* Fritz Engau, *Staffelkapitän 2/JG 11* who found himself rapidly promoted in air leadership terms due to casualties in his *Gruppe*. 'On 7 June 1944 our *I Gruppe/JG 11* transferred to France to the Invasion Front. *Hauptmann* Simsch led the *Gruppe* and I led the 2nd *Staffel*. Already on the transfer flight over the Forest of Rambouillet near Paris we had combat with Mustangs, and I shot down one of them. From 8 June we flew operations from Rennes. On 9 June *Hauptmann* Simsch was shot down and killed and I had to take over leading the *I Gruppe* in the air again. In the middle of June (15 June 1944)[44] my aircraft was shot up in combat and I crash-landed at Rennes, turning the aircraft over as I went through a bomb crater. I had to be cut out of the wreck with hacksaws. After a short stay in hospital I flew again. On 20 June we moved to Beille near Le Mans (actually just a meadow). Now well camouflaged, I flew missions at the head of the *Gruppe* until I was taken off flying combat due to my injuries (inflicted on 15 June) at the end of June. After that I was admitted into hospital, and that was also the end of my active war.'

Despite being apparently well prepared beforehand for the inevitable and awaited invasion, *II/JG 3* found themselves hindered by the almost axiomatic confusion of war. Below *Leutnant* Hans Grünberg, the *Staffelkapitän* of *5/JG 3* describes what it was like to be thrown in at the deep end over Normandy, including hearing comments made by a surprisingly open *Feldmarschall* Sperrle, who commanded the *Luftwaffe* forces deployed against the invasion:

From May 1944 till the beginning of the invasion of the Allies in France the *II/JG 3* was stationed in Gardelegen and nearby Sachau. Operations were flown against the four-engined bombers that attacked in the area of Berlin. The *II Gruppe* was already being prepared in Sachau for the expected landing of the Allies in France. The strength of the individual *Staffeln* was increased. From Generals and General Staff officers we were assured how impregnable the coast of France was supposed to be. It was ordered that the *Gruppe* should only take the minimum of key technical personnel to France; the rest would stay in Sachau. The transfer to France was to last at most for a week only. On 7 June 1944, before lunch, the *Gruppe* flew in to Evreux in France. We had already flown the first few operations with high losses when we were visited by *Feldmarschall* Sperrle. He asked us how things were looking at the coast and in the air. *Kommodore Oberstleutnant* Bär told him that we had too few ground staff. When Sperrle learnt that part of the ground staff were still in Germany he became annoyed and asked who had ordered this. Now he also learnt from us that the landings in France would be defeated within a week. After all, this is what Generals and General Staff officers in Germany had told us. Sperrle replied by telling us that the Allies would march into Germany if the landings and the break in our own front lines were not totally defeated within eight to 10 days. The *Kommodore*, *Oberstleutnant* Bär and his adjutant, *Gruppenkommandeur* Frielinghaus and his adjutant and we *Staffelkapitäne* were speechless at such openness.

The rest of our technical staff in Germany were now dispatched to join us. In the first few days after arriving in Evreux each *Staffel* had to prepare one *Schwarm* for dropping bombs as *Jabos*. The targets were the Allied fleets, which gave such effective artillery protection for the landed troops, and the landing craft. There were no successes we could report. It was almost impossible that we would be able to drop bombs in the landing zone. The enemy fighters controlled the airspace and the larger ships carried barrage balloons for extra protection. Losses to the units of *II/JG 3* were continuous. When we found ourselves in our Me

109s in dangerous situations, we used the methanol bottle (injected into the fuel) to increase power for short periods. Then we moved from Evreux to Dreux (the *Gruppe* was withdrawn from the Evreux fields from 25–29 June and flew to Guyancourt to get new aircraft and get their breath back, before moving to Nogent-le-Roi near Dreux on 30 June, and then stayed there till 10 August).[45] On both airfields (Evreux and Dreux) we were constantly subjected to strafing and bombing; the fighter aircraft and bases were constantly attacked and, after the next transfer, each *Staffelkapitän* picked out their own meadow to operate from. The moves now came more often and we got closer and closer to the border of the *Reich*. By the beginning of August 1944 the *II Gruppe* was completely finished. When *Gruppen* attacks were ordered on the enemy's supply routes only 10 to 15 aircraft took off. In the time we were on the Invasion Front, we received reinforcements of 10 pilots from *JG 51 'Mölders'* as well as an entire *Staffel* from *JG 52* (4/*JG 52*, arrived in early July 1944),[46] led by *Leutnant* Waldmann. The *JG 52 Staffel* was divided up amongst the *Udet Staffeln*. The pilots transferred to 5/*JG 3* had no prior experience in the West or in the Home Defence and thus suffered very high losses. By early August the *II/JG 3* had almost no pilots left capable of flying missions. With a small number of Me 109s I flew back to Ziegenhain (in Hesse) (in late August)[47] and a period of rebuilding followed. A few wounded pilots from operations over the Invasion Front were discharged from hospitals and returned to us. On the Invasion Front we had the following *Kommandeure*: *Hauptmann* Frielinghaus (exhausted and left 25 June 1944),[48] *Major* Hans-Ekkehard Bob (26 June till sometime between 20 and 27 July 1944),[49] *Hauptmann* Kutscha; *Staffelkapitäne* were: 4th *Staffel* – *Oberleutnant* Ruhl (apparently no longer capable of operations and off sick after *c.* six missions, but returned again when Kutscha got the *Gruppe* command),[50] *Hauptmann* Kutscha; 5th *Staffel* – *Leutnant* Grünberg; 6th *Staffel* – *Leutnant* Zimmermann.

Unit	Aircraft lost	Aircraft damaged	Pilots lost (POW)	Pilots wounded	Victory claims
Stab II/JG 3	2	-	o	1	o
4/JG 3	18	-	14	3	21
5/JG 3	16	-	10 (+1)	2	13
6/JG 3	14	-	10	6	17
4/JG 52	6	-	3	4	12
No *Staffel* shown	28	22 (+11 on ground)	-	-	-
Total, *Gruppe*	84	33	37 (+1)	16	63

II/JG 3 losses over Northern France, Normandy Campaign 7 June to 20 August 1944[51]

Notes:[52] On 15 August *4/JG 3* renumbered as *7/JG 3*, and *2/JG 52* as *8/JG 3*. All damaged aircraft due to air action as far as known with one exception, damaged by flak. Aircraft lost mainly due to air combat, a few to flak and some just missing.

As can be seen above, despite reinforcements from several other units, *II/JG 3* suffered enormous losses on the Invasion Front, losing more aircraft than their claimed victories. Hans Grünberg was responsible for six of the 13 claims made by his 5th *Staffel*.[53]

The last *Jagdgruppe* to become involved in Northern France was *II/JG 6*.[54] *Feldwebel* Fritz Buchholz, up till July 1944 a Home Defence pilot flying Me 410s in *II/ZG 26*, suddenly found himself transformed into a single-engine fighter pilot and posted to the Invasion Front towards the end of August, very poorly prepared for this new role. Due to their rushed conversion, the *Gruppe* only lasted for a few days before being effectively destroyed, as described by Fritz Buchholz:

In August 1944 we re-equipped with the Fw 190 and were renamed *II/JG 6*. After 18 flights to convert onto the new aircraft, including local airfield flights and those devoted to shooting practice, we transferred on 21 August 1944 to the Invasion Front, close to Reims, equipped with *c*. 40 brand new Fw 190s (with rocket tubes and four wing cannons).

On our fifth operation there on 25 August, in a few minutes in an air combat with Lightnings, we lost 16 Fw 190s. From the entire 8th *Staffel* under *Leutnant* Dassow, nobody at all returned. From the relevant combat reports 19 Lightnings had been shot down. On the sixth mission, on 26 August, I took off in a group of four aircraft on a *Jabo* (fighter-bomber) operation to the Le Havre area; only *Oberleutnant* Friedemann returned (he was later killed on the New Year mission, 1945). I landed by parachute in a German bridgehead still existing west of the Seine. An armoured car of the SS brought me back as far as Juvincourt. Here they were packing everything up to leave and had already prepared all the immovable material for demolition. I grabbed an orphaned Fw 190 (black 5) that had been slated for destruction as no pilot was available to fly it out any more. I took off in the direction of Lüttich without any parachute or helmet and earphones/microphone. As the undercarriage could not be retracted, I flew as low as possible. As I reached Namur, the engine coughed and then failed altogether, and I put the aircraft down just the other side of the River Maas into the vegetation. Luckily in the forced landing the engine detached itself, thus saving me from an inferno. I was rescued out of the wreckage by Belgian farmers (thank God not resistance members) who brought me to a pharmacist where I was bandaged and eventually I was picked up by German soldiers in a horse cart. This sacrifice of a *Jagdgruppe* in five days was the result of a rushed conversion onto the Fw 190. In such a short time no worn-out *Zerstörer* pilot could be turned into a perfect single-engined fighter pilot. One should rather have allowed some more time for us to get used to the aircraft in the Home Defence theatre. Later I became an instructor in *EJG 1*, where I trained fighter pilots until the end of the war.

The arrival of Allied forces in Belgium and the capture of Brussels by 3 September 1944 marked the end of this enormous battle for Northern France, encompassing the vast Normandy Battle, which could be said to have ended with closure of the Falaise Pocket on 18 August (see first table in this chapter). On 7 September the American and French forces which had invaded Southern France linked up with Patton's Third US Army, and by 11 September American forces had reached the western border of Germany proper.[55] German losses on the ground had been about half a million men (dead, missing, POW and wounded) and of the 2,300 tanks with which the Germans had begun the battle on 6 June, only about 100 were available at the end of August (bearing in mind also that many more tanks would have been sent to the front in between those two dates).[56] The defeat of the German armies had thus been decisive and France had been freed effectively within three months. German fighter losses in the air add up to *c.* 1,521 aircraft (based on information detailed in this chapter, with sources), but this figure includes something of a mix of air combat losses, those known to have been destroyed on the ground as well as others lost to non-specified causes, and probably excludes many of the aircraft abandoned on evacuated airfields as un-flyable. The total victory claims for German fighter units (again using a mix of data, from unit histories, and Tony Wood's claims lists)[57] amounts to 1,111 – this figure is difficult to qualify as some of the sources only list claims enjoying official Air Ministry recognition (Wood's lists mostly) with others giving those numbers kept by units themselves; there is thus something of an element of mixing apples and oranges in any such total figure. Also claims by *Jabo* units are not included, while those for *Jagdgruppe 200* over Southern France (n=24) are included. In correspondence with the author, Eduard Isken related that he fought in southern France with 2/JG 200 from early June 1944 until late August to early September 1944. For some of this time he was *Staffelführer* of 2/JG 200 and he claimed at least 12 victories during this period. This provides an example of problems compiling *Luftwaffe* victory totals – of *Oberfeldwebel* Isken's 12 victory claims, only six appear in Tony Wood's lists (which are essentially officially recognised claims); also, the latter lists make no claim to be complete, and problems such as missing records, illegible files and the collapse of the official confirmation process after about October 1944, and its endemic long delays in processing paperwork, must always be borne in mind (from correspondence with Tony Wood himself). What would appear to be clear, however, is that *Luftwaffe* fighter claims were less than their own losses by a reasonably wide margin.

Hauptmann Theo Weissenberger, a famous ace from *II/JG 5* on the *Eismeer* and Northern Fronts in the East did very well on the Invasion Front; he was appointed *Gruppenkommandeur* of *I/JG 5* on 4 June 1944, just in time to lead them in this new and very challenging theatre.[58] One of his colleagues left behind on the Eastern Front, *Leutnant* Ernst Scheufele, *6/JG 5* summed up Weissenberger's record over Normandy: 'In the meantime Weissenberger had become a *Hauptmann* and took over our *I Gruppe*. He transferred to the Invasion Front with this unit. Within only nine days he shot down 25 American and British aircraft there, including Thunderbolts, Lightnings, Typhoons, Spitfires and Mustangs.' Despite this amazing performance, Theo Weissenberger actually appears to occupy second place in the list of the top claimers in the Normandy aerial battles, first place going to *Hauptmann* Emil 'Bully' Lang, initially *Staffelkapitän* of *9/JG 54* there and subsequently *Gruppenkommandeur* of *II/JG 26* (table below) who claimed one more victory, for a total of 26. Only one other pilot is known to have claimed over 20 victories above Northern France in June–August 1944, *Leutnant* Wilhelm Hofmann, *Staffelkapitän* of *8/JG 26*.

Major daytime aces over Northern France, Normandy and follow-up operations: 6 June to early September 1944. Showing top ace per major unit involved (and any other ace with 10 or more claims in all the units).			
JG 1	*Oberstleutnant* Herbert Ihlefeld	*Kommodore JG 1*	10 claims
JG 2	*Leutnant* Heinz Eichhoff *	2 and *3/JG 2, Stab I/JG 2*	9 claims
	Oberleutnant Siegfried Lemke	*Staffelkapitän 1/JG 2, Kommandeur III/JG 2*	9 claims
JG 3	*Leutnant* Hans Grünberg	*Staffelkapitän 5/JG 3*	7 claims
	Leutnant Hans Waldmann	*Staffelkapitän 4/JG 52 (under II/JG 3; later became 8/JG 3)*	7 claims
	Oberleutnant Eberhard Graf von Treuberg	*Staffelkapitän 7/JG 52 (under III/JG 3)*	7 claims

I/JG 5	Hauptmann Theodor Weissenberger	Kommandeur I/JG 5	25 claims
	Leutnant August Mors	Staffelkapitän 1/JG 5	12 claims
JG 11	Oberfeldwebel Ernst Richter	8/JG 11	8 claims
JG 26	Leutnant Wilhelm Hofmann	Staffelkapitän 8/JG 26	23 claims
	Hauptmann Emil Lang	Kommandeur II/JG 26	14 claims (+12 more as Staffelkapitän 9/JG 54)
	Major Klaus Mietusch	Kommandeur III/JG 26	13 claims
	Leutnant Gerhard Vogt	Staffelkapitän 5 and 7/JG 26	10 claims
JG 27 (excludes II Gruppe)	Oberfeldwebel Heinrich Bartels	11/JG 27	9 claims
II/JG 53	Oberleutnant Günther Seeger	Staffelkapitän 4/JG 53	5 claims
III/JG 54	Hauptmann Robert Weiss	Kommandeur III/JG 54	18 claims
	Unteroffizier Erwin Schleef	9/JG 54	10 claims
	Leutnant Alfred Gross	8/JG 54	10 claims
Jagdgruppe 200	Oberfeldwebel Eduard Isken	2/JGr 200	6 claims

Notes: neither II/JG 5 nor II/JG 6 had any pilot claiming 5 or more victories; I/JG 301 scored all their victories at night. *Jagdgruppe 200* flew over Southern France. * *Leutnant* Eichhoff: in Tony Wood's Luftwaffe claims lists[59] he is shown merely as 'Leutnant Eickhoff' and in John Weal's *JG 2* history[60] as '*Oberleutnant* Eickhoff'; aviation historian and author Erik Mombeeck pointed out on a web forum (*forum.12oclockhigh.net*) that his surname had been misspelled and was Eichhoff (not Eickhoff) and that his first name was Heinz. Sources of data in table given in notes.[61]

8

BATTLE OVER GERMANY: THE LAST TWELVE MONTHS, JUNE 1944–MAY 1945

While the battles over Normandy and Northern France raged, effectively destroying the core of the German fighter defence capability within three months, the Battle of Germany still continued. While German fighter resources were stretched so thin that only a rump defence could still be mounted over the Homeland, Allied aerial capabilities allowed them simultaneously to fight a battle over the ground forces engaged in Normandy while sending large escorted four-engined bomber formations over Germany, from both the United Kingdom (8th Air Force) and Italy (15th Air Force). In southern Germany (*Jagddivisions* 7 in southern Germany itself and 8 in Austria, Czechoslovakia, the latter division newly promulgated from 15 June 1944 to replace the previous *Jafü Ostmark*) three of the previous *Wilden Sau Gruppen* (I and II/JG 300, I/JG 302) formed the main single-engined component of the defence, together with four *Zerstörergruppen* (II/ZG1, I and II/ZG 76, III/ZG 26); II/JG 27 became active as their *Höhengruppe* (high altitude fighters) in July 1944, and the *Sturmgruppe IV/JG 3* already returned from Normandy on 13 June.[1] In northern Germany (*Jagddivisions* 1, 2 and 3) there were only III/JG 300 and the *Zerstörern* of I and II/ZG 26 in June, reinforced in late June to July by III/JG 53 from Italy, II/JG 5 and I/JG 3 from Normandy, along with two *Staffeln* of III/JG 11 until late June (when they departed for Russia).[2] The north German *Gruppen* were largely concentrated in *Jagddivision* 1 centred on Berlin, but throughout July and August

1944 fighters were moved as needed, between northern and southern German areas on occasion.[3] The long-suffering *Zerstörergruppen*, by now mostly equipped with the Me 410, were recycled into single-engined units during July 1944 (*I* and *II/ZG 26* became *I* and *II/JG 6*; *I/ZG 76* became *I/JG 76* while *II/ZG 1* morphed into *III/JG 76*).[4] With these conversions to single-seat aircraft, the rear-gunners became redundant; *Unteroffizier* Heinz Ludwig of *3/ZG 26*, for example, was transferred to the fighter controllers of *Jagddivision 1*. *III/ZG 26* survived as a *Zerstörergruppe* until late September 1944 when it formed the basis for *Kommando Nowotny*, the unit destined to test the Me 262 jet fighter operationally.[5] *II/ZG 76* went to East Prussia at the end of July 1944 and only re-equipped with Fw 190s in November, then becoming *II/JG 76* within *Jagddivision 1*.[6] *Hauptmann* Karl-Friedrich Schlossstein, the *Kommandeur* of *II/ZG 76* and its successor *II/JG 76* recalled: 'After flying missions in the Home Defence with the Me 410 as *Kommandeur II/ZG 76* against the Allied bomber formations, in 1945 we re-equipped with the FW 190 (now as *II/JG 76*) and flew operations against the Soviets on the Oder Front and around Berlin. On 2 May 1945 I became a POW of the Americans.'

Feldwebel Fritz Buchholz (*II/ZG 26*) was one of the *Zerstörer* pilots who flew in the much reduced Home Defence ranks while the Battle of Normandy and Northern France raged on. The excerpt below from his logbook gives some insight into this difficult period for the Me 410 flyers:

Example of a *Zerstörer* pilot's operational life, Home Defence, June–July 1944, based on flying logbook, 20 June–6 July 1944: *Feldwebel* Fritz Buchholz *II/ZG 26*, flying Me 410 (based at Königsberg, north-east of Berlin, the entire time, but sometimes landing elsewhere after a combat). *Einsatz* = mission, those with contact or combat with enemy denoted as *Feindflug* (Source: Fritz Buchholz).

June 1944

20: *Einsatz*, 07h55–10h00 (46th *Feindflug*); combat north of the Zingst Peninsula, shot down 1 Consolidated Liberator west of the Island of Rügen

21: *Einsatz*, 08h20–09h40 (47th *Feindflug*); combat north of Lake Müritz

24: *Einsatz*, 12h05–14h00

26: *Einsatz*, 09h10–11h00; landed Jüterbog-W., and returned later same day

29: *Einsatz*, 08h05–10h18 (48th *Feindflug*); landed Magdeburg-Ost

29: return flight to Königsberg, 11h30–12h12; combat in area Dessau at 9,000–8,000 m, after first shot, guns jammed

30: *Einsatz*, 08h25–10h29; landed Ohlau and returned later same day

July 1944

2: *Einsatz*, 09h25–11h40

3: *Einsatz*, 11h00–13h00

6: *Einsatz*, 09h40–11h05

Fritz Buchholz recalls the operation flown on 29 June 1944, for the resentment at his skill in blind flying felt by some of his comrades:

My self-preservation actions (saving himself by flying in clouds to escape attack once a dogfight had begun with US escort fighters) were not appreciated by the *Gruppe*; but I had no damned intention to allow myself to be dispatched through the incapability of others in blind flying. There were other actions providing far worse examples of incapacity; thus, for example, on 29 June 1944 we were vectored onto a bomber stream in the area of Dessau. We were flying at about 8,000 m (with approaching bombers apparently at 6,000 m) and suddenly I saw the bombers below us, and reported by radio '*Dicke Autos* (big vehicles – i.e. four-engined bombers) to the right' and turned on my weapons. For a while absolutely nothing happened. Then suddenly the tails of our aircraft lifted and almost in a vertical dive we shot through the bomber formation in a homewards direction, at an angle making shooting impossible. I pulled up again, followed by eight other brothers and tried to attack the bomber stream from ahead. Due to the long time it took to overhaul the bombers the escort fighters could intervene and made a second attack impossible. I flew into the clouds with my band and landed, under flak fire, at Magdeburg-Ost (the flak auxiliaries and band members were not used to the silhouette of the Me 410). At the evening's discussion of the combat I was the bad boy as I had: (a) not reported the enemy as 'Below us, *Dicke Autos*' (due to the reported height of the bomber stream this was self-evident); (b) broken off the second attack. That the *Gruppenkommandeur* with about 20 aircraft after the abortive first attack (where escort fighters were not yet in evidence) flew home again, was not brought up.

When statistical data for June to August 1944 are compared with those from the first five months of 1944 over Germany the reduced German fighter activity enforced by the battles over Northern France is obvious from sortie totals, claims of US fighters and own aircraft losses, but the claims against four-engined bombers, while still less than in January to May 1944, are, compared to the other statistical data, higher. This probably reflects the influence of the *Sturmgruppe* concept which became effective from July 1944 onwards.

Statistical data for German fighters in Home Defence for June to August 1944; data source.[7]						
1944	German fighter sorties	US four-engined bombers claimed shot down	*Herausschüsse*	US Fighters claimed shot down	Combat losses, German fighters	German crew losses (+ and M)
June	1,407	133	5	33	202	172
July	3,171	273	7	63	359	182
August	2,521	148	2	34	315	152

Notes: All statistics relate to strategic four-engined bomber raids and escorts, and exclude Allied light bomber activity and that of their escort fighters; German fighter sorties an estimate.[8] Losses are total for *Reichs* Home Defence daylight losses (includes also night fighters lost in day sorties, plus a few bombers involved in supporting day fighter operations).[9] Symbols + and M = killed and missing. A small portion of Home Defence operations would have opposed raids in south-eastern Europe and these are included in the above statistics.[10]

Comparable American statistics for the same period show an enormous difference in sorties flown and underline that the Germans had effectively lost control of German air space:

Statistical data for US 8th and 15th Air Force raids on Germany opposed by *Luftwaffe* Home Defence for June to August 1944; data source.[11]					
1944	US Bomber sorties	US Fighter sorties	Operational losses (all causes) of US bombers	Operational losses (all causes) of US fighters	US Fighter claims against German fighters
June	8,113	5,009	226	44	251
July	16,175	9,934	375	115	377
August	15,687	9,564	299	93	350
Notes: Operational losses included those due to fighter action, flak, operational accidents (such as collisions). Excludes all American losses/claims related to tactical operations over Europe – i.e. operations of light bombers and their escorts. Sortie totals reflect aircraft taking off at the start of a mission, not aircraft over target which was always a lower figure. In June 1944 German fighters operating over Normandy played a small role in opposing these raids.[12]					

High levels of US fighter participation in the Normandy battles are obvious in the sorties, losses and claims of the American fighters compared to data from January to May 1944, but U.S. bomber sorties and bomber losses for June to August 1944 are approximately comparable to those for the first five months of 1944. American bomber and fighter losses exceed German claims significantly, bearing in mind the unknown losses suffered to flak fire. American fighter claims against their German opponents (978) are not excessive (876 German fighter losses).[13]

Survival for the German pilots flying over Germany from June 1944 till the end of the war was an unlikely outcome. Some of those among the relatively few survivors beat incredible odds and, blessed by large amounts of luck, managed to see the end of the war. One such was *Oberfeldwebel* Eduard Isken whose combat career dated back to 1940, as related in correspondence with the author. He had earlier flown in *Jagdgruppe 200* in Southern France during the Normandy battles, and then followed this up by joining another unusual unit from 15 September 1944: the *Sonderstaffel Kaatsch* (special *Staffel* led by *Major* Walter Kaatsch)[14] which formed part of the larger reconnaissance unit, *Aufklärungsgruppe (F)/123*. With them he flew armed reconnaissance missions in Me 109s over the Western Front,[15] before being posted to *13/JG 53* in October 1944. He took part in Operation *Bodenplatte* on 1 January 1945 during which he shot down his 50th victory. In April 1945 he shot down his last victory, a B-17, but was himself shot down by the escorting fighters and bailed out wounded. This brought an end to a wartime career which had begun with *JG 77* in autumn 1940 and which encompassed 56 victories (26 East) in all, including 17 four-engined bombers, during operations over the Channel, Balkans, Russian Front, North Africa, Italy, Southern France and the Home Defence. He himself was shot down nine times in all and bailed out on six of those occasions; he flew a total of 946 missions, and was awarded the *Ritterkreuz* on 14 January 1945 (see illustration number 50).

Another survivor of the last year over Germany, *Oberleutnant* Alfred Seidl, *Staffelkapitän 7/JG 53*, was succinct about his experience: 'From July 1944 to November 1944, I was in the Home Defence, stationed at Paderborn. We operated to defend against American and English bomber formations.' His *JG 53* colleague, *Oberleutnant* Alfred Hammer, *Staffelkapitän 6/JG 53* until early January 1945, and thereafter *Gruppenkommandeur IV/JG 53*, flew in the Home Defence from September 1944 till the end of April 1945. He gave more detail: 'From September 1944 onwards the Allied superiority in numbers became so big, that one could only survive air combats if you had a lot of experience, and a lot of luck had to be added if you were to score any victories in this period.' The imbalance between the strength of the Allied air forces and the *Luftwaffe* is reiterated by many pilots of that period. One such was *Oberleutnant* Günther Schwanecke, *Staffelkapitän 7/JG 5* (later renamed *10/JG 5*) and then of *13/JG 4*; he flew in the Home Defence from September–October 1944 and again from November 1944 till late in January 1945. He quantified the enormous odds he had faced in this unequal struggle: 'The battle over the German home country in 1944/1945 was very hard and unequal, especially due to the enormous air superiority of the English and American fighters, at least 1:200.' Some German fighter units, in contrast, were stationed along the new Western Front where they mostly flew in support of the struggling German ground forces; a witness to these missions was *Hauptmann* Georg Schröder, *Gruppenkommandeur II/JG 2* who led his unit in operations from September 1944 to the end of the year: 'We were based at Nidda in the first third of September 1944. High altitude missions against the four-engined bombers were seldom flown. Mostly we were ordered to provide support for our own (western) front, partly through low level attacks on the enemy.' Being shot down or force-landing, if one was lucky, often led to injury rather than death; time spent recovering was also part of surviving this stage of the war as pilots were at least spared combat and danger for a period. *Oberleutnant* Walter Bohatsch, *Staffelkapitän 2/JG 3* remembered his experiences in this regard: 'In a belly-landing (August 1944?) I knocked my teeth out when my face hit the Revi gun site. In the *Luftwaffe* hospital in Vienna I received a general overhaul and then was transferred to *Ergänzungsjagdgruppe West* at Stargard. By now we are talking of October 1944.'

While it was the fighter pilots that faced the gravest dangers in the air battles, they were heavily dependent on the guidance and support provided by the controllers on the ground. One of these was *Oberst* Hanns Trübenbach, *Jagdfliegerführer (Jafü) Mittelrhein*, situated in the northwestern part of the area covered by *Jagddivision 7*. However, in October 1944 there was a reorganisation of the German fighters once more: *Jafü Mittelrhein* was detached from *Jagddivision 7* to become part of *Jagdkorps II*, subordinate to *Luftwaffenkommando West* (new name of the remnants of *Luftflotte 3*); *Jagddivisions 1, 2* and *3* in the north along with *Jagddivisions 7* and *8* in the south were united in *Jagdkorps I*, and this together with *Jagdkorps II* fell under a single headquarters, *Luftflotte* Reich.[16] Hanns Trübenbach describes some of the vicissitudes of being a senior fighter controller and how in wartime, even chess can be a dangerous game:

On 6 June 1944 at three o'clock in the morning I received the report of the start of the invasion, through initial information on landings between Cherbourg and Le Havre. During the night of 16 June the bombardment of London and southern England by the flying bombs began. Due to very strong air attacks on Berlin the headquarters of *Jagdkorps I* moved to Treuenbrizen, where there was a commanders conference on 20 July 1944, at which the Battle Headquarters 'Dachs' (Darmstadt, HQ of *Jafü Mittelrhein*, which Trübenbach commanded) was praised. From 1 June 1944 I was promoted to *Oberst*. By 28 August the enemy already stood on the River Marne, and in the southeast at the gates of Bucharest. In the middle of September, Darmstadt burnt out (a large raid on the night of 11–12 September 1944 devastated the city by fire, causing extensive casualties and massive damage).[17] An aerial mine exploded in the forest close to the Dachs headquarters while I was controlling the night fighter units. The large glass map shattered into a thousand pieces and all I could do was to report the headquarters as destroyed to the *Jagdkorps*. My own room had no more windows and important documentary materials were sent flying out by the pressure wave. The barracks of the communications women in the forest remained unharmed and there were no losses or wounds amongst them. Now we had to pack up quickly and with the command staff move to the alternative headquarters prepared beforehand, 'Dachs-Mitte' where peace still reigned. The radio and telephone connections to the various staffs and flying units were rapidly made; the communications personnel behaved very well! After eight weeks in 'Dachs-Mitte', we moved lock, stock and barrel back to the original, newly repaired Ludwigshöhe headquarters, on 11 November 1944. A day later I was provided with a *Major* as my first (Ia) general staff officer, a very big help to me. Due to the great physical strain imposed, the high command of the *Jagdbrigade* decided to split the controlling of the day and night fighters. At the end of November the recently announced commander of *Jagddivision 8*, *Oberst* Handrick, was sent to our headquarters as the provisional day fighter *Jafü*. Handrick was the gold medal-winner in the decathlon from the

1936 Olympic Games and we had known each other from the beginning of the post-First World War flying activity in Germany. Thus I was able to concentrate ever more strongly on the night fighter controlling and on the always important general aerial situation.

The advancing ground forces of the enemy meant an additional task for Handrick. The Army now began to complain bitterly of the poor protection given them by the German *Luftwaffe*, who concentrated on fighting against the bomber streams with their fighters and saw no chance of also shielding the ground forces against the enemy fighter bombers. Handrick and I worked hand in hand and I was glad during the day occasionally to have the opportunity to be able to play chess with my Ia. We played chess in the lookout tower with its all-round windows. One day while we were sitting at the chess table at about midday, and the bombers had long passed back over the English coastline, two Mustangs actually came by as the tail-end of the raids, and one made a target of our tower. A series of bullets whipped past to the left and right of our little chess table, and one round passed right through the wall 10 cm above a divan where one of the war reporter secretaries was taking a midday nap. Within seconds the excitement was over and once more there was no blood spilt. In the meantime the Commander-in-Chief of the *Luftwaffe* concerned himself with how the ever more threatening war situation in the West could be mastered. Out of this arose the strangest orders, for example, providing the Army with so-called close combat leaders: these posts were to be filled by fighter pilots who could no longer fly operations. They were supposed to report the enemy situation by radio and everything that was happening on the battlefield. The Americans were now flying in with incursions into the *Reich* area of over 1,000 bombers accompanied by hundreds of fighters. The aircraft that the flak arm was able to shoot down over the target areas remained pinpricks. And what the fighter arm shot down could not persuade the enemy's leadership to make any significant pauses. Certainly the losses on both sides were bitterly achieved and regretted. However, Germany was no longer able to influence the war in its favour.

For the German pilots in the Battle of Germany, and its continuation from June 1944 till the end of the war, the purpose of their existence was largely downing four-engined bombers. The armament available to them generally grew stronger as the battle proceeded with multiple 20 mm and later even 30 mm cannons becoming the norm, never mind rockets of even greater destructive power. While this weaponry could shatter and destroy large, well-armed bombers within a few seconds, there were also between nine and 10 human beings within the machine so attacked. The effects of German firepower on the American crews (and on those of British bombers by now also operating by day, partially) were simply horrific, and terrible injuries ensued. An excellent account of the terrors and dangers faced by the American bomber crews is given in a recent history of the 303rd Bomb Group, as well as from a website devoted to this unit.[18] As the destruction of Germany continued, casualties to American and RAF aircrew that had bailed out and been captured on the ground in Germany also rose, and death at the hands of civilians and party functionaries became quite common.[19] Similarly, the account of the 35 missions flown by the American 448th Bomb Group crew led by John Rowe over Germany from late August 1944 to March 1945 is a harrowing record of what it was like to be faced with the relentless succession of missions that made up a combat tour late in the war;[20] casualties were continuous and seeing their comrades and friends' demise as they fell out of formation must have tried the stoutest of hearts. War is seldom one-sided and horrors are visited equally on participants on both sides.

Sometimes a German pilot would feel badly about what he had done in shooting down multiple Allied bombers, fully realising the human cost of such actions, necessary as they were from the German perspective. One such flier was Rudolf Hener of 2/JG 3, a highly experienced ex-instructor and senior NCO, and one of his battles even provides a perspective from the Allied side.

Feldwebel Rudolf Hener, who had flown many transport missions into the Stalingrad pocket, was once again employed as an instructor specialising in instrument flying from May 1943, mostly to train young pilots for *Wilden Sau* single-engined night fighters. Then from summer 1944 until the end of the year, a new challenge confronted him, now as a fighter pilot. By this stage he was an extremely experienced pilot and attributed his surviving the war to this long experience in flying:

> In the almost eight years from 1937 to 1945 I built up over 3,500 hours of flying time. Through this in the course of time I built up the experience but also the confidence, so that I always felt completely at home in the particular aircraft I was flying. In addition I was also fortunate in possessing an outstanding reaction ability, through which I was always able to do the right thing at the right moment. This applied not just in air combat but also in flying generally. As the English, during the course of 1944, used their Lancaster bombers to attack German cities in the daytime more often, especially when there was bad weather with thick cloud cover over Germany and good weather over English bomber bases, German fighters could not respond as their pilots were not trained in instrument flying. Thus in summer 1944 some of the blind-flying instructors were taken from the schools and assigned to different *Jagdgruppen*. They were there to lead the *Gruppe* up through the thick cloud cover to be able to attack high-flying bombers above it. I was once again part of this and together with 11 other comrades, all experienced instrument fliers, I joined the *I Gruppe* of *Jagdgeschwader 3 'Udet'* then stationed in Borkheide, south of Berlin. The *I/JG 3 'Udet'* was a *Höhengruppe* whose job it was to tackle the escorting fighters and tie them up in combat so that the heavy fighters of *II, III* and *IV/JG 3* could attack the bomber formations without interference. We thus had dogfights at altitudes far above 10,000 m in our Me 109 G-14s against a ten-fold numerical superiority of Mustangs, Thunderbolts etc., and generally got home reduced to half the number that took off. These operations were simply a slaughter,

as is illustrated by the fact that of the 60 pilots making up *I Gruppe* after its refurbishment in August 1944, only five survived the war. Due to the heavy losses we suffered on every mission we were often totally flattened. Then as replacements we received very young and poorly trained pilots from the schools and most of these only survived for a single day. Those that remained were always the same handful of old and experienced fighter pilots.

At the beginning of October 1944 we moved to Erfurt-Bindersleben, still in the Home Defence. From here we took off on 2 November 1944 with 32 Me 109s against 1,200 incoming bombers and *c.* 1,000 escort fighters that were to attack industries at Leuna-Merseburg, and also the cities of Leipzig, Halle and Magdeburg. On this day *I/JG 3* had the heaviest losses of all the *Jagdgruppen* sent up against these raids. Of the 32 aircraft that took off only 10 returned. I also returned on foot having travelled back by rail, as several Mustangs attacked my aircraft as I landed and set it on fire. Fortunately there was hardly any fuel left (I had landed away from home due to lack of fuel), so that I was able to stay in the lightly burning aircraft for a full two minutes, until I could finally jump out. The wonderful leather flying suit had protected me against burns, just my flying boots were no longer usable. As we always had enough replacement aircraft, the next day I selected the fastest one for myself. This was the 'black 16' of the 2nd *Staffel* and with her I managed to remain unbeaten until my transfer to *JG 7* in March 1945. The Americans had realised that the German pilots who bailed out would already be back in operation the next day in a new aircraft. Therefore they received orders from their high command, to shoot German pilots hanging in their parachutes. This was pure murder, and such a murder of one of my comrades was witnessed by myself during an aerial combat. I was not able to help him, as I found myself in the greatest danger. My comrade was found later and he, as well as his parachute, were riddled with bullets. Such gangster methods were unknown amongst us and not a single German pilot would have been able to perform such a dastardly deed. Also, the attacks and shooting of German farm workers performing their daily jobs on the land by the Americans were also just pure murder, and when one hears endlessly of the war crimes of the Germans, these war crimes of the Americans should not be forgotten. The English did not do such things – they were always fair enemies.

Feldwebel Hener goes on to describe a mission on 12 December 1944 against RAF Lancaster bombers flying a daylight raid on Witten. Notably, it was this mission for which there is also a graphic account available from the British side:[21]

From Erfurt we moved to Werl (east of Dortmund) in the middle of November, and after a bombing raid four days later, during which we lost only two of our Me 109s, we moved further, to Paderborn. From Werl and then from Paderborn also we still flew Home Defence missions. My job, as blind-flying expert to take the *Gruppe* through solid cloud cover, I was able to fulfil properly on 12 December 1944. On this day I was the only one of the 12 instrument-rated instructors who had joined the *Gruppe* in the summer still left: two lay seriously wounded in hospital, the other nine had all been shot down and killed. So on that day I led the 14 Me's in an arrow formation through the clouds (that was all the aircraft we could muster), and when we came out of the clouds, we found ourselves exactly beneath a British Lancaster formation; this consisted of about 250 aircraft and was approaching the city of Witten in the Ruhr at 6,000 m. Right above the bomber formation were about 200 American Mustangs as the escort who, despite red Very lights being fired by the bombers, only reacted when our 12 aircraft (two had already been shot down) had managed to manoeuvre themselves into a gap in the formation and shoot down 14 of the leading 25 Lancasters. I managed to shoot down three, and then the Mustangs were there and we had to disappear rapidly by diving into the clouds. The wrecks of all 14 Lancasters were found and all confirmed as our victories.

Here I can also stress that claiming an *Abschuss* of an enemy aircraft always had to be supported by a comrade from your own unit if it fell behind the lines in enemy territory, and over one's own territory confirmation by a comrade and from finding the wreck of the shot-down machine on the ground were necessary. Only then would an *Abschuss* be confirmed. It was equally strict with the concept of a '*Feindflug*'. Only missions that encompassed either an aerial combat or when success had been achieved during a strafing attack on enemy aircraft on the ground, were counted as a *Feindflug*. I for example flew about 100 operations against the enemy, but only 45 (and not 34 as given in the book *JG 7*)[22] were counted as official *Feindflüge*. Often one flew for two hours behind the enemy lines without meeting enemy aircraft on the Eastern Front in 1945, on free chase missions, and no *Feindflug* would be recognised for these.

As mentioned, there is also a British account of this raid on Witten, with eyewitnesses of some parts of the combat on 12 December 1944 described by Rudolf Hener. Miles Tripp, who was the bomb aimer on a 218 Squadron Lancaster that flew on this mission, wrote a classic book on the Bomber Command crew experience, *The Eighth Passenger*, in which he recalls this raid as being his hardest mission.[23] Two of the 12 Lancasters of 218 Squadron sent on the raid were missing – one ditched on the way back with the crew fortunately rescued from the sea, but the other which was flying behind and just to port of Tripp's aircraft blew up over the target with the loss of all on board.[24] Rudolf Hener was a direct participant in this tragic event as he describes in a follow-up letter to the author who had told him about Tripp's book. 'This confirmation by Miles Tripp of the enormous efforts of their then-enemies fills me with satisfaction even though it was horrible to know, that I alone through shooting down three Lancasters was most likely responsible for the death of 21 men. On the other hand, I probably thereby saved many people below in the city of Witten from death, as the bombers jettisoned their bombs without having time to fuse them when they were attacked and then shot down. Only one Lancaster forgot to jettison the bombs. This aircraft was hit by rounds from my wingman flying to my right; these must have hit the bombload as it exploded in a giant fireball. Absolutely nothing was left after the explosion, the aircraft and its crew were absolutely atomised. My wingman inadvertently flew through the fireball which stripped all the external paint on his aircraft which was stained pitch black as well. He later had to belly-land. This must be the same explosion that Miles Tripp reported. I myself still wonder that one can remember the events of those far off days so well, as with advancing age one forgets more and more. But when the experiences involve a struggle for life and death, these events remain graven in your memory.'

Oberfeldwebel Richard Raupach, a long-serving member of *JG 54* on the Eastern Front, had been transferred as an instructor to *Ergänzungsjagdgruppe Ost* in Silesia in June 1944 and on one occasion in the second half of that year flew a mission against the four-engined bomber formations (probably August 1944). One might be forgiven for suspecting that he had already seen enough of war by then, as he put the welfare of his *Rottenführer* ahead of his desire to attack a lone bomber. The accepted rule that a wingman never left his element leader appears to have been taken more seriously by Eastern Front veterans than for the average Home Defence pilot, as described by Raupach:

With the *Ergänzungsjagdgruppe Ost* in Liegnitz and Sagan we practised attacks for use against the American B-17 bombers with our students. For this purpose every now and then we received one German twin-engined Do 17 bomber and its crew. We overtook this bomber and flew far in advance of it so that we could still just see it as a small point. Then we turned around 180 degrees and flew at it from head-on, in line astern. The head-on attacks were used because the B-17 formations had a very strong defensive fire rearwards. I myself did not ever fly such an attack against the Americans. Only once did the Americans attack oil-producing hydration plants in Silesia. An old instructor and I took off (a *Rotte*), myself flying as wingman – *Kaczmarek*, as we put it. We caught up with the B-17 formations that had dropped their bombs already and had turned back to fly home to Italy.

One of the bombers was flying a bit behind its formation and we closed with this one. Enemy fighters were not in sight. My *Rottenführer* approached the bomber from behind and at the same altitude. I thought that was a mistake. He should have first gained some height, to then be able to attack the bomber in a shallow dive with greater speed. The bomber shot back at long range. He hit the instrument panel of my *Rottenführer*. Splinters hit him in the one eye and he had to turn away. I then had to make a difficult decision. I would like to have attacked the bomber, but it was a cast iron rule that the wingman must stay with his element leader. Thus I accompanied him homewards, where he made a good landing. He survived the war. We see each other every now and then at the *JG 54* get-togethers.

Another Eastern Front veteran who ended up in the Home Defence in its later stages was Ernst Scheufele, who moved with his *Gruppe* from the *Eismeer* Front in far-northern Norway. He ascribed his survival in the cauldron of the Battle of Germany in 1944 to his experience of bad weather flying in the far north where such conditions were almost endemic, and to having had an excellent mentor in the famous Theo Weissenberger. 'After Weissenberger left I became *Staffelkapitän* (of 6/JG 5, which he led from 28 March 1944 – autumn 1944 when *II/JG 5* became *IV/JG 4* and 6/JG 5 changed to *14/JG 4*)[25] and often led the entire *II Gruppe* in the Home Defence, as the *Gruppenkommandeurs* always only lived for a few weeks – Tetzner, Kettner – I stayed alive because I had learnt how to fly in bad weather in Norway and later at the front I had an outstanding teacher in Theo Weissenberger. "Turn, Scheufele, turn tightly – and no fighter in this world will shoot you down!" Thus it was no coincidence that on 3 December 1944 while making low level attacks on American supply routes, I was shot down by flak, wounded and became a POW. By then I was *Oberleutnant* and *Staffelkapitän* (of *14/JG 4*) with 18 *Abschüsse*.' Ernst Scheufele in his correspondence with the author sent a published account (*c.* 1988, place of publication unknown) of his being shot down on 3 December 1944, from which the following brief summary was prepared. Early that morning they were driven from their quarters about 10 km away from their base at Rhein-Main airfield, where their aircraft were camouflaged by being placed in the forest adjacent to the runway. At about mid-day *JG 4*'s *Kommodore, Major* Gerhard Michalski gave out orders to make low level attacks on American supply routes in the Stollberg-Aachen area, specifically in the Hürtgen Forest. As they then had a live *Gruppenkommandeur, Hauptmann* Wienhusen, Scheufele was able to concentrate on his personal mission and his *Staffel*.

They crossed the Rhine near Bonn at 200–300 m and flew on to the northwest, and as they approached the lines, flew lower and lower. As they crossed the main defence line there were suddenly vehicles everywhere, each firing at least one or two guns at the attacking Me 109s of *JG 4*. Then he saw to the right and ahead of him, *Gruppenkommandeur* Wienhusen diving down like a flaming torch and two further aircraft suddenly developed smoke trails. Ernst Scheufele flew as low as he could, gave the vehicles a fleeting burst and then flew a long right turn to get back to German territory. Then it happened – a hammer blow in his left leg, his ears closed up, and he could see right through the right-hand bottom part of the cockpit. His leg got warm as the blood flowed. As he smelled the aircraft burning and the engine stuttered, he let the cockpit hood go but could not pull up to bail out as the clouds were very low. Then he killed the throttle and pushed the aircraft into the ground on a wonderful muddy and soft field that had suddenly appeared. Despite his wounded leg he managed to get out and hobble away from the wreck, but suddenly shells starting landing around him and he crawled into a shallow hollow. Undaunted by this hazard, an American soldier appeared and risked the shell fire to steal Ernst Scheufele's pilot's watch, and then disappeared again. After about 10 more minutes a medic's jeep arrived and he was taken to a field dressing station.

A New Technique: Advent of the Sturmgruppen (July 1944) and Beyond

On 7 July 1944 the *Luftwaffe* deployed an effective new weapon against the four-engined bomber formations, the *Sturmgruppe*. The first of these units to be converted, *IV/JG 3* flew their first operation this day and in a brief and single massed attack from behind claimed 26 B-24s and one *Herausschuss*; 19 bombers were in fact shot down and not solely by the *Sturmgruppe* itself, with *JG 300* (*IV/JG 3* was flying this day with two *Gruppen* and the *Stab* of this *Geschwader* in a composite *Gefechtsverband*) also playing a significant role.[26] The *Sturmgruppe* and *JG 300* were both part of *Jagddivision 7* and *Oberst* Hanns Trübenbach, commander of *Jafu Mittelrhein* within that *Division* is well qualified to report on the origins and character of these new units (*II/JG 4* and *II/JG 300* formed the other two *Sturmgruppen*, initiated a bit later than *IV/JG 3*).[27] His report is based on personal knowledge, his own documentary archive and personal conversations with *Oberst* Dahl (who led *JG 300* before becoming the last Inspector of Day Fighters near the end of the war in 1945). 'The attacks of the *Sturmjäger* were to be made in tight formation and from very close range; opening fire at very short distances made aiming easy and enabled even young and inexperienced pilots to hit their targets relatively easily. Ramming their opponents was only to be used as a last resort and was to be carried out so that the pilot would always have a reasonable chance of saving himself with his parachute. Self-sacrifice was definitely not intended and the inherent principle of having a chance of survival differentiated these occasional "*Rammjäger*" from the Kamikaze pilots of the Japanese. In the winter of 1943/1944 the first unit, a *Sturmstaffel* that *Major* von Kornatzki set up, was formed, as an experimental *Staffel* to test the proposed new method.' While *Oberst* Trübenbach did not know who in the higher echelons of the *Luftwaffe* made the decision to try out the *Sturmjäger* idea, *Generalmajor* Adolf Galland, the *General der Jagdflieger*, recalled *Major* von Kornatzki presenting his original idea of the *Rammjäger* to him officially in early 1944.[28] Galland was able to persuade von Kornatzki that ramming was unnecessary as the very close-range attack envisaged would ensure the bomber being shot down and provide the pilot with a chance of survival as well.[29] Thus the *Sturmjäger* idea grew from the *Rammjäger* idea, and Galland made it very clear that no self-sacrifice of the pilot was implied, a view later confirmed also by both Göring and Hitler.[30] *Sturmstaffel 1* was actually formed under von Kornatzki in October 1943 and in May 1944 was incorporated into *IV/JG* 3;[31] Galland's meeting with von Kornatzki must thus presumably have taken place somewhat earlier than he recalled.

Hanns Trübenbach knew Hans-Günther von Kornatzki from long before the Second World War, and recounted several times when their paths crossed. 'At the beginning of 1944 the experimental *Staffel* of *Major* von Kornatzki lay in Southern France and in the next few months scored some good initial successes, but not major victories. However, the first practical experiences were achieved, the technical equipment was tested, and a particular attack tactic was worked out. The founder and father of the *Sturm*-idea, *Oberstleutnant* von Kornatzki, was killed on 12 September 1944 as commander of the *Sturmgruppe II/JG* 4, that he had himself set up in August 1944; von Kornatzki died in the second *Sturm* attack of his *Gruppe*, flying at the head of his unit, still true to his *Sturm* ideal. When I was in Stettin-Krekow in 1927 taking the tests for the first certificate needed by professional transport pilots, there was an Armed Forces group of pilots from noble families training there as well, and von Kornatzki was one of them. At Christmas 1927 we met again, at the German Transport Pilots School in Schleissheim near Munich, where we both reported for aerobatic training. After this our paths diverged as I then went on to training on seaplanes at List on the Island of Sylt and in autumn 1928 I sailed to the West Indies. I do not recall him being a passionate fighter pilot, as otherwise I would not have relieved him as *Gruppenkommandeur* just after taking over my *JG* 52 as *Kommodore* on 19 August 1940 (von Kornatzki had trained as a Stuka pilot, before becoming *Kommandeur* of *II/JG* 52 from 1 September 1939–26 August 1940).'[32]

The *Kommodore* of the newly-formed *JG* 4, *Major* Gerhard Schöpfel, remembered the establishment of his new *Geschwader*, which included, in time, the *Sturmgruppe II/JG* 4 led by von Kornatzki. 'In my time as *Kommodore* of *JG* 4 (June to August 1944) my duty was firstly to re-equip, to acquaint the pilots with their new aircraft, and to practise operational flights and for me to oversee these, for a *Geschwader* that had been put together from other, established *Jagdgruppen*. At the time I took over *JG* 4, the *Geschwader* had no *Sturmgruppe*. The *Sturmgruppen* that were in fact established at this same time (July 1944),[33] were made up of pilots who had taken an oath to shoot down at least one enemy aircraft on each mission, even if it meant ramming them. This approach can be compared with the Kamikaze missions of the Japanese.'

Hanns Trübenbach, in extensive correspondence with the author, described in some detail the modifications to the Fw 190 aircraft used by the *Sturmgruppen*, and based much of this description on discussions he had during the war with *Oberst* Walther Dahl and on this pilot's post-war book, *Rammjäger*:[34] (1) increased armour protection – armoured glass in the two small triangular windows either side of armoured windscreen; armour plate behind the engine to stop flames entering cockpit if engine caught fire; both sides of cockpit armoured; armour plate behind pilot's seat with upper part of armoured glass so as to give protection with unimpaired rearward vision. (2) An extra fuel tank in rear fuselage which together with standard internal tank and external drop tank gave *c.* three hours endurance including an action period. (3) In addition to standard Fw 190 armament of two 20 mm cannon and two heavy machine guns, *Sturm* aircraft were fitted with an MK 108 3 cm cannon beneath each wing, using also special armour-piercing incendiary ammunition which easily went through B-17 and B-24 armour plate, and one round of which hitting a fuel tank would explode the bomber. (4) To counter all the added weight implicit in all these adaptations, a BMW 801 radial engine developing 2,400 hp was fitted, which gave adequate speed rather than good manoeuvrability. Each *Sturmgruppe* was accompanied into action by two normal Me 109 *Gruppen* to protect against American escort fighters, and one of these flew about 1,500 m above and behind the heavy Fw 190s as the *Höhengruppe*.[35] Below and in front, the *Sturmgruppe* itself flew in a tight arrowhead formation, and made use of two types of attack: either from head-on and slightly above with a pull-up just over the top of the bomber formation, or otherwise from behind from slightly below, slightly above or less often, from directly behind.[36] The *Sturmjäger* would fly in from behind at *c.* 400 km/h and the tight arrowhead formation opened fire together on the order of the *Kommandeur* at about 200 m range, and the breakaway was made below the bombers, with reassembly alongside the bomber formation and a second attack if enough ammunition remained.[37] *Oberst* Trübenbach noted also that, in their early missions, the *Sturmgruppen* would try to launch an initial head-on attack to break up and disorganize a bomber formation, then reassemble (always difficult) for the real *Sturmangriff* in tight formation from the rear.

The first *Sturmgruppe*, IV/JG 3 had been withdrawn from operations to train and equip with their new aircraft and in May 1944 were presented to their commanding general before whom they took the oath of the *Sturm* pilots in a formal ceremony. Hanns Trübenbach, in his capacity as *Jafü Mittelrhein*, was also present and provided the following description of what occurred on this solemn occasion: 'On a beautiful sunny May morning in 1944, the *Gruppenkommandeur* of the *IV Gruppe* of the *Udet Geschwader*, *Hauptmann* Moritz stood in front of his assembled unit and reported to the Commanding General of *Jagdkorps I*, *Generalleutnant* Schmid: "*Sturmgruppe* of the *Udet Geschwader* reports on parade for ceremonial taking of the oath." There were 68 pilots, on the right-hand flank of the parade the standard-bearer, a young *Feldwebel* with the *Ritterkreuz*, on either side a *Leutnant* wearing the German Cross in Gold. *Hauptmann* Moritz read the oath in a quiet firm voice: "We commit ourselves, in accord with the principles and battle rules of the *Sturmgruppe*, to fight in the Home Defence. We know that as pilots of the *Sturmgruppe* we are particularly expected to offer limb and body to protect our people in the home country and to defend them to the limit of our ability. We vow, on every mission that leads to contact with enemy multi-engined bombers, to attack our opponent from the shortest range, and in case he does not fall by our gunfire, to destroy the enemy by ramming." Every line of the oath that *Hauptmann* Moritz read out had been known to all the pilots for weeks already. Everyone had been given the chance to request a transfer to another unit, but none had made use of this chance. The core of the *IV Gruppe* had been joined by volunteers from other fighter units as well. The *Staffeln* had been on parade in their full numbers in front of their *Kommandeur* and all acknowledged the oath with their own free will. A solemn and serious expression was to be seen on the young faces. They were fully aware of the aerial terror that had broken over the people of Germany and they believed that their courage and operations could deflect this suffering, or at least lessen it. After the reading of the oath, the Commanding General approached the paraded men. Each pilot confirmed his duty with a handshake with the General. The first *Sturmgruppe* of the *Luftwaffe* was now ready for operations in the Home Defence.'

IV/JG 3 was to enter combat in their new guise as part of a special anti-bomber *Gefechtsverband* (battle formation) made up of *I* and *II/JG 300* along with the *Sturmgruppe*, led by the new *Kommodore* of *JG 300* (appointed on 27 June 1944), *Oberstleutnant* Walther Dahl and his *Stabschwarm*.[38] In July 1944, *II/JG 300* itself became a *Sturmgruppe*, and *II/JG 4*, the third of these *Gruppen*, was formed on 12 July 1944 under the leadership of the father of the *Sturmgruppen* idea, *Major* Hans-Günther von Kornatzki.[39] *Oberst* Hanns Trübenbach recalled: 'On 7 July 1944, *JG 300* was under the command of *Jagddivision 7* in Schleissheim near Munich. The *Kommodore* (Dahl) flew in front with his *Stabschwarm*, and *Hauptmann* Moritz with his *IV/JG 3* next to them. Moritz was also the deputy commander of the *Gefechtsverband*. On 15 September 1944, the *Kommodore* of *JG 300* was himself downed. In the critical moments of a *Sturm* attack from behind on a Boeing, his guns jammed, and he rammed the bomber, impacting it just in front of the rear gunner's position; he was able to save himself with his parachute.'

Unteroffizier Ernst Schröder was one of the *Sturmgruppen* pilots who managed to survive the war, unlike most of his comrades; the *Sturmgruppen*, while effective weapons against the bombers, suffered very high losses. He was the exception that proved the rule – a newly joined late-war fighter pilot who had been adequately prepared for what lay before him, as he describes:

I was a pilot in the 5th *Staffel* of *Jagdgeschwader 300* from 1 July 1944 till the end of the war. I was different from most of the pilots of my *Gruppe* in that I had at least in some way received an adequate training as a day fighter pilot: completion of basic flying training at *Flugzeugführerschule A/B 23* in Kaufbeuren 1943, in early 1944 at the *Jagdfliegerschule*

JG 101 in Pau, Southern France and thereafter at the *Ergänzungsjagdgruppe* in Orange, France, and later in Märkisch-Friedland/Pommerania. As a result of the training I was able to follow the actually very few basic rules of the tactics of day fighters, and this, combined with lots of luck, is what I thank for my survival. The vast majority of my comrades had no longer received this training – possibly it was considered unnecessary for the '*Sturmgruppen*' that, after all, 'only' had to shoot down four-engined bombers 'at any cost'. At least those in higher command must have had this impression – as mostly we received ex-instructors from the flying schools of the *Luftwaffe* or hastily and incompletely trained young pilots in our *Staffeln*. In 1945 new pilots came to us who had only flown a couple of circuits with the Fw 190!! Pilot training had suffered chronically from about the beginning of 1944 from the lack of fuel – the result was that the already shortened training programme had to be even further reduced. I, as an example, had flown 91 hours in 1943 before I was considered to be a trained 'pilot', and I had another 96 hours flying time at the fighter school including also my time at the operational training unit; I had about 122 hours of flying in *JG 300* – that gives a total of 310 hours for my entire career! I can give these exact amounts of flying time as I saved my flying log book. In addition I was fortunate that at fighter school and in the *Ergänzungsjagdgruppe West* in Orange I had been fully trained on the Me 109 G-6. Through the fortunate accident that on 20 June 1944 pilots were needed to transfer about 20 Fw 190 aircraft in Avignon, France to Märkisch-Friedland, I was able to convert to this type also. Due to this occurrence I owe my life! This is because with the short training time even I had received, I would never have been able to control the Me 109 adequately in combat! (The Fw 190 was much easier to fly). I am of the opinion that the crazy losses suffered by the German fighter arm in 1944–1945 can be ascribed in the first place, to the fact that from 1943 onwards already no focussed and adequate training of pilots was possible any longer, that would have been the first basis for successes later in action. This reality is mentioned far too seldom in the modern literature on the air war! The technical differences between the German and Allied fighter aircraft were not high enough to explain the rapid downfall of the German air defence!

As far as I remember *II/JG 300* became a '*Sturmgruppe*' in late summer–early autumn 1944. All the pilots had to take an oath that they would bring down a four-engined enemy aircraft on every 'mission' (i.e. every *Feindflug*!). If this could not be done with the guns then they had to ram it! An attack on an American combat box of *c.* 25 B-17s or B-24s only had a chance of success, when at least 15–40 fighters attacked simultaneously – this had become obvious after the big air battles of 1943 and the beginning of 1944. Only then was it possible to at least partially divide up the devastating defensive fire of the bombers. The individual 'fighter' pilots didn't need any tactical or basic shooting training for these attacks (or at least that's what was probably thought in the higher command levels) – he only had to approach within 80–50 m of these large machines, exactly from behind and at the same altitude, and then no great deflection shooting knowledge was needed, only some luck – the devastating German ammunition took care of the rest. The suicidal ramming of the bombers was then no longer needed at all. A sane person anyway avoided this madness from pure instinct for self-preservation! Despite this, some of my comrades did indeed bring down several bombers by ramming, some of them more or less by accident, as at very short range and with the fast approach speeds even from behind, one could find oneself in the tail of such a bomber before wiping your eyes out!! Today (Ernst Schröder was writing in 1990) one can only with difficulty imagine what it was like in purely psychological terms and what passed through individual pilots' minds in those few seconds! The saddest part of it all was that there were always naturally combats between fighters, while even the three 'escort groups' equipped with Me 109s (in *JG 300*: *I*, *III* and *IV Gruppen*) could often not stop the American escort fighters from attacking the *Sturmgruppe* itself during or just after their attack on a bomber formation. And then suddenly all these pilots who had not been trained as fighter pilots found themselves holding very 'bad cards': firstly because they had learned no tactical skills as fighter pilots and secondly because they were flying heavy *'Sturmjäger'* with extra armour and 3 cm wing cannons which were not at all suited to fighter-versus-fighter combat! These MK 108 cannons mostly fired only a couple of rounds before jamming due to the forces experienced in tight turns bearing on these heavy weapons' mechanisms! Having been lucky enough to have achieved several successes against Mustangs, I was privileged to get an unarmoured standard Fw 190 with four 2 cm cannon and two 13 mm MG's, to fly as an <u>exception</u> to the rest of the *Gruppe* (Red 19 *'Kölle-alaaf!'*). What remains in my memory today of these difficult times of the war is the amazing (by today's standards) comradeship and unprecedented self-sacrifice as well as very high morale, despite the miserable war situation, that characterised these fighter units. The youth of that time really made every sacrifice for their country – unfortunately with our criminal and risk-taking leadership, it was all for nothing – or perhaps not!?

In the excerpt from Ernst Schröder's flying logbook given below it is interesting to note that three different types of missions are detailed, each with a distinct notation within the logbook itself. There is *'Einsatz'* which is an intended interception mission without any enemy aircraft being sighted; *'Feind-Einsatz'*, an interception mission where the enemy was sighted but not engaged, and finally *'Feind-Einsatz'* is a mission where the enemy is engaged in combat (details provided by Schröder in notes to table below). Somewhat confusingly, the latter notation was sometimes shortened to simply *Einsatz*. Also of note in this logbook is the relatively few missions flown, reflecting the *Luftwaffe's* fuel state, and that quite a few missions did not lead to the enemy being met at all. On the 17 December 1944 mission, Schröder was flying the aircraft of the *Geschwaderkommodore*; quite something for a lowly *Unteroffizier* to be entrusted with the machine of the *Geschwader's* commanding officer.

Example of a fighter pilot's operational life, Home Defence, October 1944 to April 1945, based on flying logbook, 12 October 1944 to 26 April 1945: *Unteroffizier* Ernst Schröder, *5/JG 300*, flying Fw 190 (based at **Löbnitz**, Germany for almost the entire time, but sometimes landing elsewhere). (Source: Ernst Schröder)

October 1944

12: *Feind-Einsatz*, 11h20–12h30; without meeting enemy

16: *Feind-Einsatz*, 11h15–13h25; met lone Mustangs in Prague area; landed Dresden-Klotsche (and returned to Löbnitz later the same day)

November 1944

5: *Einsatz*, 11h10–13h10; mission against southern incursion, didn't count as *Feind-Einsatz*

21: *Feind-Einsatz*, 10h45–12h45; mission against western incursion, enemy sighted in Braunschweig area. Landed Gardelegen and returned to Löbnitz later same day via Sachau

27: *Feind-Einsatz*, 11h50–13h30; attacked by Mustangs south of Harz Mountains, hit trees and belly-landed

30: *Feind-Einsatz*, 12h25–14h25; met enemy bomber formations and strong escort in Halle-Leipzig-Merseburg area. Landed Altenburg and on return flight later same day bailed out due to engine trouble and darkness

December 1944

11: *Einsatz*, 11h20–13h25; mission against southern incursion without meeting enemy

17: *Feind-Einsatz*, 10h30–12h30; met Liberator formations in Olmütz area. Flying in *Mühle* (crate) of Dahl, *Geschwaderkommodore*. Landed Liegnitz and returned to Löbnitz later same day

24: *Feind-Einsatz*, 13h55–15h40; met strong fighter formations in area of Erfurt-Kassel, shot down a Mustang

29: *Einsatz*, no times recorded; no enemy met, did not count as *Feind-Einsatz*

31: *Einsatz*, 10h55–11h45; sortie aborted due to damaged oxygen system

January 1945

1: *Einsatz*, 10h45–12h30; met enemy bombers and fighters in area of Osnabrück. Landed Hess. Lichtenau, and flew back to Löbnitz later same day

20: *Einsatz*, 12h00–13h40; did not meet enemy

23: transferred to Schönfeld-Seifersdorf for operations against Russian ground troops, which continued until 2 February 1945 from several bases, including Löbnitz from 1 February.

February 1945

14: *Einsatz*, 11h00–12h45; met enemy Mustangs in area Leipzig-Dresden; landed aircraft with many bullet holes (hit 27 times!)

26: *Einsatz*, 10h20–11h30; enemy not met

28: *Einsatz*, 13h55–15h15; enemy not met

March 1945

2: *Einsatz*, 09h20–10h45; met enemy in area of Wittenberg-Jüterbog

24: *Einsatz*, times not recorded; combat with enemy fighters near Göttingen

April 1945

9: *Transfer flight*, 18h50–19h45; combat with 4–5 Mustangs, one shot down. Transfer flight to Pilsen and next day further transfer flight to Adlhorst

12: Einsatz as Jabo, 12h30–13h50; *Jabo* attack on road-railway crossing at Uffenheim; shot down an 'Auster' (see note* at bottom of table)

13: *Einsatz* as *Jabo*, 15h20–16h45; attack enemy ground column-heads north of Bamberg. Landed Windisch-Laibach, returned Adlhorst later same day

14: transferred from Adlhorst to Straubing

15: *Einsatz*, 10h40–11h30. Landed Ansbach and returned to Straubing later same day

19: transferred from Straubing to Holzkirchen

Last flight on 26 April 1945. Missing here between 19 and 26 April another about four – five flights, including one ground attack on American column-heads in area Augsburg and an airfield protection flight in a *Schwarm* one evening, over Holzkirchen.

Total of 39 *Feind-Einsätze*, of which enemy met on 23 (*mit Feindberührung*).

Notes: Ernst Schröder provided the following details in regard to notations applied in his logbook: 'The boxed flight entries were *Feindflüge* with enemy contact (*Feindberührung*) that means there was aerial combat involved. The flight entries which were only underlined counted as missions against the enemy (*Feind-Einsätze*) but without any contact with enemy aircraft. I am giving here the usage at the time for terminology and differentiation of missions. These played a role in the awards of the *Frontflugsspange*! (the mission clasps); and these should not be confused with the Iron Crosses that were awarded solely for victories! That's how it was then.' The term *Einsatz* itself is used in this log book excerpt for a sortie that did not count as a mission. Note *: ' "Auster" – we called them this for simplicity's sake – this victory was actually an artillery spotter of type Stimson Sentinel.'

Unteroffizier Ottomar Kruse, who was with the 8th *Staffel* of II/JG 26 stationed at Kirchhellen, not far north of Essen in the heart of the Ruhr, flew his last mission over Germany on 16 September 1944 which he detailed in correspondence with the author. On this day *Leutnant* Wilhelm Hofmann, *Staffelkapitän* 8/JG 26 led this and the 7th *Staffel* on a free chase over the Aachen area. Kruse and his wingman Erich Klein were flying the *Holzauge* (lookout) *Rotte* behind and about 300–400 m higher than the rest of the formation. Hofmann saw some P-47s and attacked them but Kruse was still above and in a bad position for an attack. They were flying amongst cumulus clouds and suddenly a large number of P-38s and P-47s came out of the clouds. He and Klein then saw a Fw 190 being attacked by P-47s (in his experience the Americans always flew in fours). Klein and Kruse dived onto these four P-47s, but Klein pulled away as Kruse went in and attacked the rear P-47, hit it and then shot at the second one. The P-47 leader then turned suddenly upwards, swinging up to his left, and Otto Kruse passed under him. The P-47 then swung back and was sitting behind him through this sudden manoeuvre.

Kruse then found himself trapped in a bunch of P-47s and, as he fought to turn and stay out of trouble, his shoulders and arms began to ache and then he was hit – a bullet passing through his microphone just missing his throat, and another shot a pocket off his uniform at the knee. Then his engine was hit. He could not dive away from the heavier P-47s and they were too many to out-climb (the Fw 190 could out-climb the P-47) so he decided to bail out. He followed exactly the bail-out procedure laid down in II/JG 26: (1) blow off the cockpit canopy by hitting down on a cartridge; (2) remove microphone, otherwise the small pull as the lead broke on bailing out would make you hit the tail plane, which killed many German pilots; (3) undo seatbelt, then push stick to the left front or right front, thus lifting up the pilot and exposing him to the airflow, so he would be plucked from the cockpit – as the aircraft was in a turn you would miss the tail. When Kruse did this the slipstream knocked his breath out as he was still travelling at 550 km/h; (4) don't pull ripcord for three–four seconds to lose speed and avoid ripping harness – failure to do this also killed many pilots; (5) delay pulling ripcord till you judge the height at about 200 m as the Americans were noted for shooting German pilots as they descended helpless on their 'chutes. When Kruse bailed out he was facing upward and as he descended he could still see his Fw 190 above him. He then turned over to watch the ground and pulled the cord when he judged his height at about 200 m. About 2 m off the ground he pulled on his lines and fell out of the harness; as the P-47s were looking for him, he hid in a ditch. His comrades had not seen his parachute opening so low and reported him killed. Hofmann wrote a letter to his mother who, however, maintained that he was still alive. He was taken prisoner and, while ensconced in Lancashire, once escaped from his camp and was on the run for a few days before being recaptured.

Gefreiter Karl-Heinz Hirsch had joined the *Luftwaffe* aged only 16 in 1940, with the very reluctant permission of his father; he was already an experienced glider pilot. After the war he settled in South Africa and we met twice in 1988–1989. He had spent years in the system in different training courses, including a full schooling as a bomber pilot (multi-engine aircraft, instrument rating etc.) and also spent a couple of months at the Rechlin test centre flying the Spitfire 9 and the Mustang in comparative trials against the Me 109. By the time he eventually got to a front-line unit he was a very experienced pilot with 3,000 hours flying time to his name. He joined *III/JG 27* under *Gruppenkommandeur* Peter Werrft in southern France in early August 1944 but the unit returned to Germany after only about a week, and then he flew in the Home Defence from Achmer in September/October until being shot down and seriously wounded on 24 December 1944. On active service pilots of all ranks lived in the same quarters and messed together, and Peter Werrft insisted on his pilots addressing him with the informal '*du*' and using his nickname '*Bodo*'.

Hirsch experienced this last part of the Battle over Germany as a combination of slaughter and confusion. Almost every take-off resulted in action against vast US bomber formations escorted by hordes of fighters, odds of 40:1 and even 60:1 were the rule. Often a lone *Geschwader* would be pitted against 1,000 or 2,000 American aircraft. Most times as they tried to get at the bombers in *Gruppen* formations the enemy fighters would be on them before they could get near the bombers. On the few occasions when they did manage to get past the escort, a head-on attack was always attempted – they would get 3 to 5 km ahead of the bombers and then turn in, and at the very high closing speeds it took only seconds before they were on the bombers, and then they flew as a *Gruppe* straight through the bomber formations. Following this rather suicidal behaviour they would pull up to about 1,000 m above the bombers, then drop vertically through them and, as they pulled up underneath them, each man picked out an individual bomber to fire on. He recalls one such occasion in September or October 1944 when, using this method, he closed in to only about 10 m from the rear gunner of his target bomber and could clearly see his terrified face for a split second before the petrified gunner jumped, just missing the Me 109's propeller. He tried to get the now rather helpless bomber (to rear attack anyway) as it descended, to land or force-land by flying with his wheels down and waggling his wings, but to little avail. He had first attacked the bomber near Hannover and as they neared Hamburg it was down to 1,000 m – he had not yet actually fired on it. Now he opened up and shot it down, otherwise it would have continued on to the UK. Hirsch found the Battle over Germany very hard going. He and his fellow pilots mostly started the day with a bottle of brandy underneath their chairs at breakfast, and after breakfast, on *Sitzbereitschaft* strapped into their cockpits, the bottle would be finished off with their mechanics. Over Germany and later over Czechoslovakia he saw five or six of his fellow pilots finished off on their parachutes by American pilots.

On 24 December 1944 the *III/JG 27* took off from Achmer at about 13h00 to intercept a bomber formation and thereafter to attack ground targets in Belgium, but Hirsch's Me 109 K-4 had a defective supercharger and he could not keep up with his *Staffel*, so the *Staffelkapitän* ordered him to fly to Bonn-Hangelar to have it fixed. He turned away but over Steinfeld saw eight Mustangs coming at him head-on in line astern. Normally the Me 109 K could out-climb a Mustang but not with a defective supercharger. He was not yet too worried as his single aircraft should be more manoeuvrable than eight aircraft acting together. He flew head-on at the left-hand Mustang and then turned sharply away going into a tight right turn – the P-51s turned inside him but were not yet too close. By the third turn Hirsch was turning much tighter, had achieved the inside track and, after four to six turns, he was in a position to shoot at one of the P-51s which left the circle issuing white smoke. These eight Mustangs seemed to be beginners. As Hirsch got into a firing position on a second Mustang, a further set of Mustangs attacked him from vertically above and he was hit badly. At a height of 8,000 m his engine was dying, oil covered the windscreen and flowed into the cockpit. Over the Eifel the engine finally quit and, as a forced-landing was impossible in such mountainous terrain, he prepared to bail out.

In the *Luftwaffe* he had been taught the procedure of climbing at 150 km/h to a stall, and then to kick the stick hard forward, thus shooting the pilot out vertically as the aircraft went on down and away. However, when Karl-Heinz Hirsch tried this, it didn't work out that way due to his elevators having been damaged, and instead he slid back along the fuselage and hit the tail section very hard, becoming stuck with his back and outstretched arms against the tail fin and his legs under the tail. His injuries amounted to a seriously shattered forearm, both ankles broken, and his fifth and sixth vertebrae also broken. While stuck thus on the tail, Hirsch and the Me 109 fell from 8,000 m to 4,000 m and, during this short time, his life really did flash before his eyes, from having been a three year-old till their take-off that day. Although he could not move he did not yet feel any pain. The slipstream forced his mouth open. Finally at about 4,000 m the elevators broke off and he fell free of the Me 109. As the ground temperature on take-off had been -16°C he didn't want to open the parachute too high otherwise he would freeze to death. After falling to about 1,000 m (still no pain) as he started to move his right arm to pull the ripcord (in the *Luftwaffe* this was located on the left upper chest, and pilots were encouraged to hang on to it, there being a 5 DM reward for it because the 'chute was then immediately reusable), he felt massive pain in his right arm and, for the first time, saw what a bloody mess it was and that blood was dripping off his flying boots. Then, still falling, he kept his head, tested his left arm, found it worked and deliberately pulled very hard with this arm, pulling the ripcord right out and, as the 'chute opened, felt terrible pain in his legs, back and right arm. The 'chute opened about 400–500 m above the ground and he landed in pine trees, being suspended about 8–9 m off the ground.

He hung there for about two and a half hours in total silence and ate some of his emergency rations, suffering terrible pain from the least movement. After this, crazed with pain, he pulled out his pistol to shoot himself and end it quickly, when he heard German voices. A number of foresters had seen him come down and came to find him, complete with stretcher. One of them climbed free-hand up the tree and wanted to carry him down on his back, but Hirsch declined because of his wounds. They then cut down a number of surrounding trees and attached a cable to his tree which they were then able to cut and lower gently to the ground. In addition to all of this he had landed in the middle of no-man's land, being only 400–600 m from the lines. He then spent some hours in the foresters' barracks, and his stretcher was packed with presents, mostly bottled! At dusk they took him to Steinfeld to a dressing station where he received first aid and remained till about 23h00. Then an ambulance took him to the station where he was put on a train, complete with still-laden stretcher. After two days on the train he reached Helmstädt and a hospital. Here a high-ranking military doctor (a major) wanted to amputate his right arm but, after a flaming row, Hirsch crawled out of the hospital and was lucky enough to meet a *Luftwaffe* man in the street who got him on a train to Braunschweig where there was a big *Luftwaffe* hospital. Here he was operated on, the surgeons picking more than 200 pieces of bone out of his arm and fitting him with one of the very early metal pins as well. He remained in hospital until 10 April 1945 when the Americans came, and thereafter left the hospital in the same clothes and damaged flying boots in which he had been shot down.

Karl-Heinz Hirsch was in the 7th *Staffel* of III/JG 27. Its *Staffelkapitän* at the time was *Oberleutnant* Emil Clade who was fortunate to spend much of 1944 *hors de combat* due to having been wounded in the air. Although this spared him much of the terrible fighting of 1944 over Germany, when he did return to action late in the year, he was so rusty that he was almost immediately shot down again. He is a direct witness to American fighter pilots shooting at their helpless opponents while hanging in their parachutes:

My fifth and last jump. For almost the whole of 1944 I was out of action due to a bullet which broke my thigh bone. When I took over my *Staffel* again in November 1944, I flew the first missions in the Home Defence against American bombers as a wingman so that I could get used to the new air war over Germany. One had already told us beforehand that possibly some new twin-engined aircraft of our own, that had not been seen up till then, could appear; the Me 262 was meant by this. When it came to air combat, I did see the described aircraft. We could not then imagine that an aircraft could fly without a propeller. I admired this bird much too long until I noticed that the imagined underwing (jet) engines were in reality the drop tanks of Mustangs and were being jettisoned. In the next moment I was alone in a dogfight with eight Mustangs. As I was also in an inferior position, it did not take long before I had to jump out (at 6,000 m). I knew the American bomber escort was flying at three levels, 6,000, 4,000 and 2,000 m. As a result I decided not to open my 'chute immediately and thus made my first free fall until I opened my parachute at *c.* 500 m. On the way down during my free fall I saw several enemy fighters. When I opened my 'chute, low-flying Mustangs were already there and shot at me in my parachute. This practice up till then was not normal, as with our friends and enemies the rule was: a pilot on his parachute is taboo. I swung backwards and forwards perhaps three–four times after the 'chute opened before landing in a field south of Oldenburg. Due solely to the presence of a light flak battery nearby, I was spared the Mustangs also attacking me on the ground. On the next day I flew another mission in the Osnabrück area. By then my friend 'Poldi' (*Herr* Hirsch) was also flying with me.

Feldwebel Rudolf Hener, who appears earlier in this chapter and again several times below, was a pilot in 2/*JG* 3 and amongst his comrades was *Leutnant* Theodor Schirmers, who had been an instructor for about three years before seeing action. Thus, like Karl-Heinz Hirsch of 7/*JG* 27, he was highly experienced as a pilot but not in combat. He lasted for some months due to his experience but was shot down and badly wounded on 2 November 1944, one of many casualties on that day, as was typical for most days at this stage of the battle. 'I joined *JG* 3 *"Udet"* as a pilot in the so-called Home Defence only in summer 1944 as the air war over Germany reached its high point. However my membership of this *Geschwader* came to an end soon enough. After several missions against raids in the central German region, I was shot down on 2 November 1944 while landing at an air base in the Potsdam area, by four American P-51 Mustangs. On this day *JG* 3 and other units suffered 27 dead and 11 wounded pilots, according to Edward H. Sims in his book *"Jagdflieger"*. I was one of those wounded. I lost my right lower leg and the right hand. I spent the rest of the war in a hospital near Potsdam. There I was taken prisoner by the Russians in April 1945, and was released in October 1946.' In the unit history of I/*JG* 3 it is reported that Schirmers was flying in a *Schwarm* led by Rudolf Hener and that three of the four Messerschmitts were shot down as they came in to land at Borkheide, seriously wounding two of the wingmen with Hener being lucky enough to get away from the crash of his fighter without having been wounded.[40] The *Jagdflieger* casualties given above by Theodor Schirmers were actually much greater on 2 November: fighter losses amounted to a staggering 133 aircraft, 71 dead/missing and 31 wounded pilots.[41]

The Ardennes Offensive

During Hitler's last-gasp Ardennes offensive in December 1944, many of the Home Defence pilots became embroiled in this battle, but still also tackled the high-flying four-engined bomber formations and their escorts when need arose. Theodor Schirmer's *Gruppe*, I/*JG* 3, received a new *Kommandeur* in late November 1944, *Oberleutnant* Alfred Seidl who recalled: 'In November 1944 I was transferred to the *Kommandeursreserve der Jagdflieger* and at the end of November I moved to *JG 3, I Gruppe* as *Kommandeur*. During December, missions were flown in support of the Ardennes Offensive with heavy combats over Belgium and the Ruhr area. Our home base was again Paderborn. Our last big operation was "*Bodenplatte*" on 1 January 1945, marked by heavy losses.' One of Alfred Seidl's pilots in *I/JG 3* was *Feldwebel* Rudolf Hener in the 2nd *Staffel*, who saw much fighting over the Ardennes as related below:

Then, from 16 December 1944, we provided fighter cover for our ground troops during the 'Ardennes Offensive'. This offensive only lasted two and a half weeks weeks. After being defeated by the Allied troops, not only was the fighting power of the German army units broken, but also that of the German fighter pilots. On one of these days, 16 December, we flew an escort mission for a few Ju 52s that dropped paratroopers behind the enemy lines in bad weather. The paratroopers were all very young boys and most of them were captured almost immediately after jumping and landing. Still, in the beginning the Ardennes Offensive was successful and the tanks of the *Waffen-SS* reached almost to the Maas River in Belgium within a few days. But there they were stopped, as they were largely destroyed by enemy fighter-bombers, or because the logistic support no longer functioned to provide them with fuel and ammunition. The Allies had been prepared, having been informed through treachery (this memory might reflect wartime German propaganda, as there is no truth to it at all – the onset of the Ardennes Offensive was a total surprise to the Allies who were caught flat-footed).

The Allies cut off the supply lines of the advanced German troops from two sides and some were trapped. To put an end to these trapped troops the Allied air forces sent in all their available forces and we, who were supposed to protect our ground troops from the air, always had to deal with hundreds of enemy aircraft while we flew in small formations of eight, 12 or sometimes 24 fighters to combat them. It is thus no wonder that on two separate days when I took off with eight aircraft to combat enemy *Jabos*, I returned home after combats over Belgium quite alone. The pilots who had accompanied me were all very young and had only recently come to us from the training schools. They were an easy prey for the American and English fighter pilots. On 26 December I flew one such operation in the region of Bastogne where I was able to shoot down a Thunderbolt fighter-bomber that was attacking German tanks. But as all seven of my comrades were shot down by other Thunderbolts that were flying cover to the *Jabos*, I had no witness for my *Abschuss*. Despite this, two days later an army unit reported that they had observed my *Abschuss* and could confirm it, but also unfortunately confirmed the loss of my seven comrades. On that occasion 12 Thunderbolts tried very hard to shoot me down as well, and chased me from the Maas to the Rhine. But I had a very fast machine (650 km/h and, for short times when the pure methanol injection was used, it was even faster) and the Thunderbolts were not faster than me, so that by using a few aerobatic tricks I was able to keep them at some distance. Only after we passed Koblenz did I get rid of them, after I had dived down into the valley mist of the Lahn River repeatedly.

Despite the critical importance of protecting the German ground troops involved in the Ardennes offensive, the fighter *Gruppen* were still involved in repelling continuing high level bomber attacks on the German homeland, as related below, in the continuation of Rudolf Hener's narrative:

Two days before, on 24 December 1944, it was a wonderful sunny day. Not a cloud in sight, no haze or mist, and a marvellous range of vision. No wonder that the Allies again this day sent in many bomber formations that concentrated on railway junctions and stations, to cut off supplies to the troops who had advanced in the Ardennes. Our *IV Gruppe*, the so-called '*Sturmgruppe*' (equipped with the Fw 190) had taken off to intercept a Marauder formation of the Americans and, after assembly, we of the *I Gruppe* flew high above them to protect the *IV Gruppe* of *JG 3* and involve the escorts in combats. The Marauder formation was indeed sighted but, as they had already dropped their bombs and were on their return flight, we flew after them in a westerly direction. Now we were far over Belgium already and, in the meantime, we had been joined by other German *Jagdgruppen* below us and left and right of us, all about as strong as us, namely 24 aircraft, and all flying on a westerly heading. Then came the moment that froze the blood in our veins: coming towards us was a bomber formation of enormous size and all around a massive number of enemy fighters. As was later established there were over 2,000 bombers(!) with over 700 fighters.

Our *IV Gruppe* were able to shoot down a large number of bombers but then were, like we had been, caught up in combat with the escort fighters. And the same thing happened to all the German *Gruppen* around us as well. As far as one could see, high up with condensation trails, lower down, but also close to the ground, an aerial battle of enormous scale raged and everywhere burning aircraft dived down to destruction. This image of burning and crashing aircraft stayed with me in my dreams for years afterwards. Those who did not see this massive confusion of fighting themselves, cannot be expected to comprehend it. Our unit was split up immediately by the first attack of *c.* 60 Thunderbolts who attacked us from two sides. I turned steeply with my *Schwarm* into this attack, but one of my comrades was already hit and had to go down for a belly-landing. He returned unwounded from English imprisonment after the war. A reassembly of our *Gruppe* was out of the question, as all the rest were caught up in dogfights. For this reason I climbed, together with my two companions, up to 12,000 m where the condensation trails began, and we remained for a while up there untouched, so that I could get an overview of the whole event. I could not see any German machines I could join up with except those already caught up in combat. Nevertheless my moment of peace up high did not last long, as several *Schwarme* of American Mustangs climbed up and all wanted to attack us.

I avoided these by climbing up into the sun every time that Mustangs got into an attacking position, and then they could no longer see us. Only once we got over Paderborn could we lose height and then land undamaged.

Of our 24 aircraft only 12 returned, but some of those missing had been able to bail out and returned later on foot. On 25, 26 (as already described) and 27 December 1944 we flew operations with only a few aircraft to protect our ground troops. Each time our losses were high and when I had to fly another mission on the afternoon of the 27 December (the second on this day) we had a combat between six of our machines and Spitfires, who shot down four of our inexperienced beginners, we were once again completely washed out. But now we received a bunch of replacement pilots, amongst them fortunately some old and experienced ones from the hospitals, so that on 1 January 1945 we could make the attack on Eindhoven with 30 aircraft.

Oberleutnant Hans Hartigs of 4th *Staffel*, II/JG 26 was another pilot involved in the strenuous Ardennes missions. During this time he was flying the new Fw 190 D long-nosed fighter, but was not very impressed by this aircraft:

The Fw 190 D *'Langnase'*, I did not enjoy flying: I found the earlier fighter types much better in dogfights and turning ability. The radial engine in the D-model in fact ran more roughly and it was very insensitive when shooting. In December 1944 I flew various missions from Fürstenau against the four-engined bombers and against American and English fighters, as *Staffelführer* and *Gruppenführer*. On 26 December 1944 I had the instruction to take the *Gruppe* over the leading elements of the Hitler Youth (*HJ*) Division in the Ardennes – at low level – to counter the enemy fighter-bomber attacks on them. In this area (southern tip of Belgium, near Charleroi) with 14 of my 16 new aircraft (it had been very cold overnight and the mechanics had struggled to start the new Fw-*'Langnase'* aircraft, as they did not have enough experience of them yet and many would not start;

I could not keep circling over the base waiting for them due to fuel with time limitations) we found the leading elements of the *HJ* division. The tanks were abandoned and partly dug in. Apparently their supplies of fuel and ammunition had not reached them.

At that time, for such missions, there was a standing order forbidding a return without engaging the enemy, so I climbed from low level in the direction of Luxembourg and into the sun, towards the south. Unfortunately soon after take-off my radio had failed and I could not communicate with my men. They could not hear me either, as I soon established by hand signals with my wingman. While still climbing I saw Allied fighters and counted about 60 'Indians'. A fighter group climbing above me led by Major Emmeroy (whom I later got to know personally and who treated me so well in England in his group when I was already a POW, and who made it possible for me to attend a symphony concert in the Albert Hall) attacked me in the precise moment that I made a half-turn away to attack four Thunderbolts below me. I shot down a Thunderbolt and in the same moment my aircraft burst into flames. Emmeroy had shot me down. I bailed out at *c.* 5,000 m and landed in a very high pine tree in dense forest. My parachute caught in the top of one of the trees and, after some swinging and struggling, I got loose from my harness and slid down the very thick trunk like a monkey. That was the end of my war experiences, the beginning of my life as a POW and then later, sadly, as a Russian captive!

Operation 'Bodenplatte', 1 January 1945

Oberleutnant Alfred Heckmann, *Staffelkapitän 3/JG 26* was one of the participants in this New Year's Day mission and succinctly gave its primary aim: 'We carried out low level strafing attacks on the enemy airfields in Belgium and France.' *Oberst* Hanns Trübenbach, the senior night fighter controller at *Jafü Mittelrhein* watched from afar as his colleague directed the assault: 'At the turn of the year 1944/1945 the crazy order was given, for all available German fighter units to attack the enemy air force on their

European airfields and to destroy them in a single blow. *Oberst* Handrick (the ranking day fighter controller at *Jafü Mittelrhein*) was tasked with carrying out operation "Bodenplatte", through which the greater part of the remaining German fighters and their outstanding leaders were sacrificed. As it was thought that the surprise attack could be carried out at low level, many of our own fighter pilots were killed by our own flak.'

During the second half of 1944, after the Normandy battles were over, the *General der Jagdflieger*, Adolf Galland, began to accumulate a large reserve of German fighters and pilots with the idea of launching a single and massive blow ('*Grosse Schlag*' – Great Blow) against the daytime four-engined raiders, encompassing some 2,000 fighters in one fell swoop.[42] By November 1944, Galland had some 3,700 fighters ready, but this all came to nought as the majority were taken away to support the Ardennes offensive where losses were very high. The remainder were sent in on *Operation Bodenplatte*, the large coordinated attack on Allied airfields on the Western Front where again losses were extensive.[43] Overall in *Bodenplatte*, 18 airfields are known to have been attacked, mainly in Belgium and Holland, by *c.* 900 German fighters from *JG 1*, *JG 3*, *JG 6*, *JG 26* (plus *III/JG 54*), *JG 27*, *IV/JG 54*, *JG 77*, *JG 2*, *JG 4*, *JG 11*, *JG 53*, with also some aircraft from *JG 104*, *SG 4*, *NSGr 20* and *KG(J) 51*.[44] Despite tactical surprise having been achieved by this early morning massed attack, German losses were very high, largely due to pilot inexperience, but also due to Allied as well as German flak, and some due to Allied fighters which were airborne at the time of the attacks: 151 German pilots were killed and missing, 63 became POWs.[45] German fighter losses are thought to have been *c.* 300 in total.[46] Estimates of casualties included 137 German fighter wrecks located in Allied territory (80 interpreted as flak losses, the other 57 as shot down by Allied fighters); in addition 48 aircraft were missing and remain so, and 18 returned damaged with wounded pilots.[47] This would leave something of the order of 100 German fighters lost to their own flak.[48] More serious than the aircraft losses were the three *Geschwaderkommodoren*, six *Gruppenkommandeure* and 10 *Staffelkapitäne* who failed to return,[49] a loss that could ill be afforded at this late stage in the war. Allied losses are estimated at 305 aircraft destroyed and 190 damaged, of which, respectively, 15 and 10 occurred in aerial combat, the rest on the ground.[50]

That ubiquitous pilot, *Feldwebel* Rudolf Hener of *2/JG 3*, was one of the many participants in *Operation Bodenplatte*. 'This major operation involving all available German *Jagdgeschwader* under the codename "*Bodenplatte*" is well known. The *Jagdgeschwader 3 "Udet"* at last flying united as a single unit under the leadership of its *Kommodore*, *Oberstleutnant* Bär, was the only *Geschwader* to achieve a complete success in this large undertaking. In the low level attack on the airfield at Eindhoven, three Spitfire squadrons and eight of Typhoons were completely destroyed. *Oberstleutnant* Bär shot down two Typhoons that were just taking off as we arrived. Our losses were also heavy: through flak and also from enemy fighters on the return flight, of the 60 pilots who had originally started in the entire *Geschwader* (*I, III* and *IV Gruppen*) we lost 20, thus a third. Our *I Gruppe* to which I belonged, alone lost 10, also a third of those who had taken off. On the evening of 1 January 1945 in Paderborn we held a New Year's party with an enormous amount of liquid refreshment.'

Among the *Bodenplatte* casualties, and one of the unit leaders lost on this ill-fated mission, was *Hauptmann* Georg Schröder, *Kommandeur* of *II/JG 2*. 'In particular I cannot leave out the beginning of 1945 in my story. On New Year's Day at almost eight o'clock I escaped the Grim Reaper. This was due to the fact that I had a large engine in front of me that came close to being equivalent to a tank. Our friend the enemy assailed us from ahead with shells of 4 cm calibre. My bird was a Me 109 G-14, and I remained undamaged. This all happened at the lowest level, just a few metres above the ground. Flying at high speed and with clear concentration, based also on 16 years of experience of such aircraft, I suddenly had to pull up slightly, turn to the right a bit and a classic belly-landing followed. My aircraft had received a direct hit, but no explosion, and lay fallen on its belly. And in its lower parts still lots of fuel and a full load of ammunition. After arming the built-in incendiary device, I tiptoed off to the south. Just 200 m away from my aircraft the New Year's fireworks began and soon the ammunition started to explode. After about six hours the U.S. military police picked me up in a forest. Thus in the Jeep I came past the remains of my aircraft once again. The whole thing happened near the Belgian town of Huy. From this day my freedom was taken away for a period of three years and over four months – as a guest of his Majesty in the British Isles!'

Flying the Jets: Final Flourish of the Jagdwaffe

While *JG 7* 'Nowotny' was the main fighter unit to use the Me 262 in combat, there was a long and complex pre-history to the establishment of that *Geschwader*.[51] The first Me 262 unit was *Erprobungskommando 262* (*Ekdo.* 262) which was formed very early on, in autumn 1943, to develop the Me 262 into an operational fighter and to evaluate its suitability (Horst Geyer in discussion with author). *Hauptmann* (*Major* by the end of the war) Geyer, previously General Udet's adjutant and *JG 51* fighter pilot over Russia, who had also led *Erprobungskommando* (Experimental Unit) 25 to test methods to use in the battle against the four-engined bombers, was given command of *Erprobungskommando 262* in Lechfeld in July 1944. His role was to develop the Me 262 as a jet fighter, and he took over after *Hauptmann* Thierfelder's death (their first *Kommandeur*), and in time was relieved by *Oberstleutnant* Heinz Bär. Geyer recalled that *Major* Nowotny's *Erprobungskommando Nowotny* (which was meant to evaluate the jet fighter <u>in action</u>) was detached from *Erprobungskommando 262* later in 1944. Horst Geyer found the Me 262 a pleasure to fly, but there were some technical problems to be overcome. One was that the throttle was basically too open and uncontrolled – if it was opened up too fast the engines tended to burst into flames. Pilots also had to avoid reaching the speed of sound as the Me 262 was capable of 1,200 km/h in a dive. When flown in action, care had to be taken not to engage in dogfights with enemy fighters, as at low speeds the Me 262 had poor flying characteristics and was not able to turn tightly at all. It also suffered from very poor acceleration, thus making it very vulnerable when attacked on take-off or landing. Its high speed was its major advantage and after a firing pass it was wisest not to try and turn in for a dogfight. Tactics used by the Me 262 against four-engined bombers were to attack from behind from a higher altitude. They could also attack from above and ahead but then the firing time was very limited. Due to their very high speed it was most sensible for the Me 262s to attack the bomber formations singly rather than in formations.

Amongst *Hauptmann* Geyer's pilots in *Ekdo.* 262 was *Leutnant* Josef Neuhaus who was one of its earliest recruits. 'From autumn 1943 *Hauptmann* Werner Thierfelder took over the *Erprobungskommando* 262 in Lechfeld. Thierfelder, who had been my *Staffelkapitän* in Russia, and later *Kommandeur*, organised my transfer to *Erprobungskommando* 262 – evaluation and test flights, weapons tests (MK 108 30 mm cannon) and shooting trials. Against my wishes and also those of Thierfelder, on 19 July 1944 I was ordered on an officer's course from which I returned only in November. By this time *Hauptmann* Thierfelder had been killed in aerial combat, and *JG* 7 was being set up under *Oberst* Steinhoff. The *I Gruppe* moved to Parchim, the *III Gruppe* that I joined, moved to Brandenburg-Briest. Through successes and losses we approached the end of the war. During one mission – I found myself in the Dessau area – our bases were bombed. I landed at the Junkers Works airfield, and received a message to fly via Leipzig to Prague-Rusin. From Prague, when fuel allowed, we still flew missions as far afield as Berlin. Here and lastly in Saatz the *Geschwader* was disbanded.'

Horst Geyer scored three victories with the Me 262 including a B-24 and a P-38, two of them at least in 1945. In February 1945 he was posted to lead yet another experimental unit, *Erprobungskommando He 162*. Although this unit had good pilots, losses were very high due to the over-rapid development of the Heinkel He 162 aircraft; they never saw action.

While *EKdo.* 262 did engage in some combat and claimed 12 victories in all,[52] *Kdo. Nowotny* was (for its size – about a weak *Gruppe* in strength) not overly successful, reflecting insufficient training and also being stationed too far to the West;[53] they were ready for operations from the end of September 1944 and saw approximately six weeks of action (3 October to 19 November 1944).[54] In the first month they claimed 19 victories (of a final total of 22)[55] while losing six Me 262s in combat and a further seven (and nine damaged) in accidents.[56] The high accident rate of the Me 262 would continue – something to be expected in a revolutionary new aircraft which was put into combat before being fully developed, and with the combination of short training and some difficult flying characteristics. With the death of its *Kommandeur*, *Major* Nowotny, the famous *JG* 54 ace, on 8 November 1944 in combat, *Kdo. Nowotny* essentially became ineffective, and *Major* Erich Hohagen took it over.[57] On 19 November this *Kommando* was renamed *III/JG* 7, forming the nucleus thereof and being led by Hohagen until 26 December 1944, following which *Major* Rudolf Sinner took over (1 January 1945) until 4 April 1945.[58] Sinner enjoyed flying the Me 262. 'The Me 262 was easy to fly and was a well-balanced aircraft, and was very well suited to fighting against the four-engined bombers due to its fire power and its high speed. The proper usage of its fighting power needed new tactical thinking and some changes. Its use in combat required greater inputs from the higher commands and the ground organisations. The book published on *JG* 7[59] refutes some of the widely believed legends about apparent failings and wrong decisions of the German leadership; however, in describing personal victory claims and alleged experiences, this author (Manfred Böhme) has also been taken in by some isolated tall tales.' Rudolf Sinner was also acting *Kommodore* of *JG* 7 for a short time, from 19 February 1945 to some time in March 1945.[60]

III/JG 7's last *Kommandeur* was *Hauptmann* Johannes Naumann[61] who previously figured in a companion volume[62] to this book as a member of *JG* 26 on the Western Front. *I/JG* 7, though formed in August 1944, was renumbered *II/JG* 7 in November, and never reached full strength.[63] *Oberfeldwebel* Rudolf Hener was amongst its pilots. 'After *I/JG* 3 was dissolved, I was transferred at the end of March 1945 to *JG* 7, and after instruction in Lager Lechfeld on flying the Me 262, I was assigned to *II/JG* 7. On one occasion during a practice flight, I had to do with some Mustangs, but easily got away due to my high speed, and landed safely. I did not get to fly a "*Feindflug*" any more, as our Me 262s were almost all destroyed by bombing attacks.'

A new *I/JG* 7 was formed from *II/JG* 3 on 25 November 1944, and led successively by Majors Theo Weissenberger

(25 November 1944 to 14 January 1945), Erich Rudorffer (14 January to 4 April 1945) and Wolfgang Späte (April 1945 to 8 May 1945; Oblt. Stehle was acting *Kommandeur* briefly before Späte arrived).[64] *Oberleutnant* Hans Grünberg, a *Staffelkapitän* in *II/JG 3*, then became the leader of *1/JG 7*. He describes the changeover and his experiences in the new jet *Gruppe* below:

At the beginning of November 1944 the *II/JG 3 Udet* found itself stationed at Stotterheim airfield near Erfurt. There, quite unexpectedly, we received a visit from *General der Jagdflieger* Galland. After a brief greeting we were informed that the 5th *Staffel* led by *Oberleutnant* Grünberg, 7th *Staffel* (the ex-4th *Staffel*, led by a *Hauptmann*), the 8th *Staffel* (previously 4/JG 52) led by *Oberleutnant* Waldmann, as well as the *Stabskompanie* (ground component of the *Gruppe*) led by *Hauptmann* Kriegshammer, were to become the *I Gruppe* of *JG 7* with immediate effect and were to convert to the Me 262. The pilots were immediately ordered to report to Lechfeld, to convert to the Me 262. The ground staff were moved to Kaltenkirchen/Holstein. In Lechfeld we received initial technical instruction, and then we went to Landsberg/Lech. There we flew 10 hours on the Me 110 and also practised take-offs and landings in twin-engined and single-engined aircraft. We had still not flown an Me 262 when we moved once more, to Unterschlauersbach, where we eventually got to know the wonderful bird. After 10 familiarisation flights it was off to Kaltenkirchen. Here we awaited the arrival of our wonder-aircraft impatiently, but they only arrived in dribs and drabs. We made sure we kept our shooting eyes in by hunting rabbits and hares morning and evening. My new *Kommandeur*, *Major* Weissenberger, I had got to know briefly in Landsberg. In Kaltenkirchen, at last, *I/JG 7* was officially set up: *Kommandeur*, Adjutant, wingmen and additional *Staffelkapitäns* all came from *JG 5* (*Eismeerjäger*) or were friends of the *Kommandeur*. Leaders were: *Oberleutnant* Grünberg (1st *Staffel* of *JG 7*), *Oberleutnant* Stehle (2nd *Staffel*), and *Oberleutnant* Waldmann (3rd *Staffel*; after his fatal crash, *Oberleutnant* Schuck).

With few exceptions the *Staffeln* consisted of very young pilots who came from the *Ergänzungsgruppen* and who had little flying time and less combat exposure. Thus there was no suitable replacement if I was to fall out. Then I thought of my old flying comrade from *JG 3 Udet*, *Oberleutnant* Bohatsch – known as 'Bonzo' – who I had got to know in Russia and with whom I enjoyed a very close and cordial friendship. He had taken over the 1st *Staffel* of *JG 3* in 1943 as *Staffelkapitän*, and more recently had been an instructor in the *Ergänzungsgruppe* led by *Hauptmann* Sannemann. *Hauptmann* Sannemann himself had previously been my *Kommandeur* and I called him up and requested the transfer of *Oberleutnant* Bohatsch to *I/JG 7*. *Herr* Sannemann agreed to my request and on the next morning Bonzo appeared in Kaltenkirchen. Now our big problem arose: Bonzo had to be converted onto the Me 262, and to get him onto a conversion course at Lechfeld at the beginning of 1945 was almost impossible. We thus had to fall back on self-help. I explained the aircraft to him as well as its handling. He had to familiarise himself with all the handles and buttons, and eventually he was practising finding them blindfolded. After two days Bonzo made his first flight with the Me 262, and we were both delighted when aircraft and pilot made it back without any damage. From this time on until the capitulation in May 1945 we flew operations together. After our re-equipment in Kaltenkirchen the *Staffeln* relocated: 1st *Staffel* to Brandenburg, 2nd *Staffel* to Burg, and 3rd *Staffel* to Oranienburg. It wasn't long before the airfields of all three *Staffeln* were bombed out, all on the same day. On the next day all the *Staffeln* moved to Prague; there we suffered losses while landing and taking-off. Up till the capitulation on 8 May 1945 we continued to fly missions, up to eight o'clock at night. Then came the very last flight when we took the remaining serviceable Me 262s and handed them over to the English at Fassberg/Lünenburger Heide.

Walter Bohatsch briefly described these events as well: 'In January 1945 after *c.* three months of instructing, my transfer to *JG 7* followed. Another circle closed with this move.

My original *Staffel, 5/JG 3 Udet* became *1/JG 7*, whose *Staffelkapitän* was "Specker", *Oberleutnant* Grünberg, my old comrade from *5/JG 3*. One evening he phoned me up and asked if I was interested in flying the Me 262 and in taking over a *Schwarm* in his *Staffel*. An old friendship was thus renewed which lasts till this day (writing in 1990). With the Me 262 we were able to survive the war. On 8 May 1945 Specker and I took off from Saatz in the West; this was our last flight in the German *Luftwaffe*.'

Another ex-*JG 3* pilot to join *I/JG 7* was *Oberleutnant* Alfred Seidl. 'At the end of March 1945 I was transferred to the *Gruppe* of *Major* Späte (*I/JG 7*) for conversion onto the Me 262. Together with other pilots from different units, we were six to eight officers. We tried to convert on the airfield at Brandenburg. We were using the operational machines of the *I Gruppe* and when a mission was announced, the conversion naturally had to be broken off. Thus I did not fly any missions in the Me 262.' *Kommodoren* of *JG 7* were, firstly *Oberst* Johannes Steinhoff (1–26 December 1944), *Major* Weissenberger (January to 8 May 1945) with *Major* Sinner acting in his stead between 19 February and March 1945; *JG 7* was by far the most successful unit to fly the Me 262 in combat, claiming something in the order of 500 victories.[65]

The balance of *EKdo. 262* (which did not go to form *Kommando Nowotny*) became the basis of *III/Ergänzungsjagdgruppe 2*, formed on 2 November 1944 until its incorporation into *Jagdverband 44* (*JV 44*) on 27 April 1945; *III/EJG 2* was initially commanded, briefly by *Hauptmann* Horst Geyer, then by *Oberleutnant* Wörner as acting *Kommandeur* until January 1945, followed by *Oberstleutnant* Heinz Bär (14 February to 23 April 1945).[66] This *Gruppe* claimed 40 successes.[67] *Hauptmann* Rudolf Engleder, *Staffelkapitän* of 10th *Staffel* in *III/EJG 2* served as Bär's deputy: '*Oberstleutnant* Bär was *Kommandeur* of *III/EJG 2* (the first German jet fighter unit) from February 1945. I was his deputy. In April 1945 the entire *Gruppe* became part of *JV 44*. *Oberstleutnant* Bär achieved 216 *Abschüsse* in total. On about 10 March 1945 I shot down a Marauder over Augsburg with the Me 262; Bär and Herget were witnesses for this victory.'

Two bomber units equipped with the fighter version of the Me 262 also saw action: *KG(J) 51* and *KG(J) 54* (first operation on 9 February 1945),[68] claiming at least eight and 50 victories respectively.[69] Finally, there was *JV 44* (*Jagdverband* 44), formed on 10 January 1945 around the person of the sacked *General der Jagdflieger*, Adolf Galland, who led it until 26 April 1945, after which Heinz Bär took over.[70] This elite unit, which included many highly experienced pilots, achieved at least 55 victories.[71] *Major* Hans-Ekkehard Bob was one of its expert members and recalled: 'This jet was capable of cruising at 850 km/h, at least 200 km/h faster than the fastest enemy aircraft. In purely flying terms, this was the high point of my flying career at that time. Due to the lack of vision of our leaders and due to the situation then, this, the first jet fighter in the world, was not built in large numbers, so that its potential for success was not reached. With a speed of over 200 km/h greater than the fastest enemy aircraft, the Me 262 was suitable to address the suffering and destruction that the German people were going through by at least being able to hinder the masses of four-engined American bombers in their task. The operations of a few Me 262 fighters against thousands of bombers resulted in large successes.' Known daytime victories accredited to Me 262 day-fighter units totalled at least 687 in number;[72] losses of Me 262s on Home Defence missions amounted to 74 destroyed, 37 damaged, with 47 pilots killed and 17 wounded.[73]

The excellence of the Me 262 allowed quite a number of experienced pilots to achieve jet-ace status despite the overwhelming Allied air superiority late in the war. Amongst them was *Oberfeldwebel* Hermann Buchner, who had earned the *Ritterkreuz* as a *Schlacht* pilot over Russia. 'On 1 November 1944 I was transferred to *Erprobungskommando* Lechfeld and converted onto the Me 262 "Swallow". In *Ekdo*. Lechfeld (a conversion unit) I scored my first jet *Abschuss*, a P-38 Lightning on 26 November 1944. From December 1944 I flew in the 9th *Staffel*, III/JG 7 "*Nowotny*", and from 18 March 1945 in 10/JG 7 out of Parchim, all within the Home Defence. By the end of the war (5 May 1945) I had flown a total of 640 *Feindflüge*, scored 58 *Luftsiege* and also destroyed 46 tanks. Of my *Luftsiege*, 12 were achieved with the Me

262 against US bombers and fighters, and I was amongst the most successful fighter pilots in the Me 262 units of the Home Defence.' Top Me 262 ace was the redoubtable *Oberstleutnant* Heinz Bär with 16 victories, closely followed by *Hauptmann* Franz Schall (*Kommando Nowotny* and *JG 7*; killed in action 10 April 1945) with 14, three pilots each with 12 (Buchner; *Major* Georg-Peter Eder and *Major* Erich Rudorffer, both of *JG 7*), and *Leutnant* Karl Schnörrer (one of the members of Nowotny's famous *Schwarm* of *I/JG 54* in Russia in 1943; *Ekdo. 262, Kdo. Nowotny* and *JG 7*) who scored 11.[74]

1945, the Final Months

And so the hopeless battle over an ever shrinking homeland continued, and as it did so, German fighter pilots were shot down in droves, standing little chance to avoid such a fate unless flying the revolutionary Me 262. Some lucky few did manage to preserve themselves, such as *Obergefreiter* Pay Kleber who had previously served in 7/JG 2 along the Channel in late 1943 – early 1944:[75] 'From the end of March 1945 I returned (from *Ergänzungsjagdgruppe Süd*, part of *EJG 1*, with whom he flew ground operations against the advancing Russians from late January 1945) to 7/JG 2 and accompanied them in the retreat via Lepizig, Eger, Cham, Straubing, Holzkirchen, Prien/Chiemsee; final destination was the end of the war and becoming a POW of the Americans.' *Unteroffizier* Kurt Beecken, who had previously flown in the East in 6/JG 54, later served in IV/JG 54 over Germany where, unlike many others, he survived being shot down and later flew jets as well (IV/JG 54 became incorporated into II/JG 7 in early February 1945).[76] He recalled: 'On 14 January 1945 I was shot down for the third and last time. This was my last mission in the Fw 190, in the Home Defence.'

As the German war machine crumbled and the country tottered to inevitable defeat, so morale began to suffer and not all leaders were able to maintain a calm and encouraging authority over their unfortunate subordinates. *Oberleutnant* Gerd Schindler, veteran of III/JG 52 in Russia and of IV/JG 27 over Normandy, where he had been shot down and wounded on 10 June 1944, finally returned to IV/JG 27 in December

1944; here he was appointed *Staffelkapitän* of *11/JG 27* by the *Gruppenkommandeur, Hauptmann* Dudek. Having not flown an Me 109 for about six months, on his first flight in one again on 16 December 1944, he crashed on landing and was injured. As he related in correspondence to the author, this accident probably saved his life as he missed participation in the *Bodenplatte* operation which led to the loss of many German fighter pilots, including Dudek who was taken prisoner after being shot down.[77] By the time he returned to *IV/JG 27* again in January 1945, Schindler was sent as spare officer to the *10/JG 27*, the *Gruppe* now under *Hauptmann* Ernst-Wilhelm Reinert. This leader showed the worst part of his character at this time, gave out orders he himself ignored, and expressed himself freely before each mission. Schindler's memory of this situation is given below:

There were exceptions to the good leadership we generally enjoyed in the *Jagdwaffe*. I got to know one of them, thank God only in 1945. I can say nothing against the achievements of *Herr* Reinert, winner of the Swords to the Knights Cross, but his leadership abilities with people scored a zero in my opinion: he just shouted, forbade many pleasant things to us but did not apply this to himself. This all made him very unpopular, and even today (writing in 1990) such feelings persist, even at the veterans' get-togethers. Very likely in 1945 he was anxious about the future. As far as I remember his profession before the war was that of a turner – I have nothing against such people, but during the war he was treated as something like a god, today he is a sort of miracle healer (Karl-Heinz Hirsch of *III/JG 27* recalled that Reinert became a homeopath after the war). Possibly it was a mistake in the *Luftwaffe* that the higher command promoted highly successful fighter pilots with lots of victories from senior NCOs (often from relatively basic professions) to officers on account of their bravery at the front (which practice I have nothing against). Often they did not possess the requirements for an officer and good leader. That Reinert was appointed *Gruppenkommandeur* in the last months of the war was probably due to shortage of experienced personnel.

In his correspondence with the author, Schindler said he was glad, in view of the situation in *IV/JG 27*, that he was not to fly for very long in this unit any more. The conditions at Achmer, their base, were almost impossible. There were continuous fighter-bomber attacks, bombers flying overhead, up to 1,000 at a time, low level attacks, aerial combat above the base, and all of this led to high losses and high levels of stress and anxiety. At about this time his transfer to a jet unit became known, and he and others were already studying the theory of the Me 262, but nothing came of this (due to Reinert also). In these days, often the *Gruppe's* pilots could not even take off at all. And then came 22 February 1945: on this occasion the *Gruppe* did actually manage to get off, and intercepted a Mitchell formation at high altitude, then became involved in combats and, finally, Schindler was able to attack and hit a Marauder in another bomber formation, and managed to get away from the escorts. However, flying at low level after this, he met eight Tempests flying in the opposite direction, who went after him and, following quite a long chase at very low level, hit him in the tail, disabling most of the controls; but he was able to use the elevator trim to gain some height and bailed out successfully at only 150–200 m. The Tempests circled round his chute but left him alone, unlike many another German pilot shot on his parachute. He landed in the soft soil of a ploughed field but was unable to stand up as his one knee had been injured, either hitting the tail on bailing out or on hitting the ground. As he was rescued and carried away by local home guards (*Volkssturm*) they saw another Me 109 force-land close by, cabin roof already jettisoned; and before the pilot could climb out an American fighter shot it up on the ground, killing the pilot in his cockpit. Schindler did not fly again before the war ended.

As German-held territory shrank, the vast organisation that supported active *Luftwaffe* operations also came under attack, and as their activities were increasingly curtailed, so the knock-on effect further decreased the efficiency of flying operations. *Oberst* Hanns Trübenbach, *Jafü Mittelrhein*, was a senior witness to the increasing chaos, the madness of over-zealous courts martial, and the destruction and abandonment of his own massive headquarters, Dachs, as detailed below:

On 23 January 1945 *Oberst* Handrick was transferred out of *Jafü Mittelrhein* and I once more had the honour to be controller of day and night fighters again. Although the end of the war was staring everyone in the face, my staff were further increased. Part of it included a court martial unit that had to be fully ready for duty. There were courts martial continuously. If a *Kommodore* could not take off with his *Gruppen* due to snowfalls at the bases, then there was an automatic court martial. There were many such cases and similar ones that never led to punishment by me. So at the end of March I ordered the disbandment; it was only a matter of days before the Americans would arrive at the foot of the Ludwigshöhe. In the general situation, on 17 February 1945, the Russians had taken the whole of East Prussia and Upper Silesia. The Oder Front was already at Küstrin. Our troops defended desperately. Everything that could shoot and defend was put into operation, at times with pointless losses. The area of the German home defence grew ever smaller. On 23 March the Americans had already crossed the Rhine at Oppenheim and their advance columns were close to Darmstadt. From our lookout tower on the Ludwigshöhe at night I had a good view of the battlefield lying in front of us. Just one day later, events overtook us. At 16h00 on 24 March 1945 I received the order to disband *Jafü Mittelrhein* and to transfer the control of the day and night fighters to *Jagddivision* 7 in Munich. We were to prepare the Dachs headquarters for demolition. One of my staff officers, *Major* M. was tasked with getting our 4,000 female communications auxiliaries out of the danger zone, and this occurred without any hindrances. My senior general staff officer got the columns together that drove off to Spessart to the east. As I was the last to leave our demolished headquarters, I drove through the still unoccupied forests with a small BMW motorbike to the Aircraft Reporting Station Aphrodite, where my staff met up once again. On the roads to the east a picture of dissolution met us everywhere. The war was close to the end!

In this chaotic climate with everything falling apart, fanaticism by some few believers who still held to their National Socialist convictions raised its ugly head. Despite the ramming idea implicit as a last resort in the *Sturmgruppen* ethos, and its rejection as a tactic by *General der Jagdflieger* Adolf Galland, with Göring and even Hitler also excluding any concepts of self-sacrificing operations equivalent to the Japanese Kamikazes, in the second half of 1944, *Oberst* Hajo Hermann (the initiator of the *Wilden Sau* night fighters) again presented the ramming idea to Galland.[78] When Galland asked him what role Hermann would play personally in any such operations, Hermann replied that he would not be leading any such unit in the air[79] (in contrast to the *Wilden Sau* missions, where Hermann did participate and lead).[80] In early 1945 Hermann's proposal again came up, this time with a new *General der Jagdflieger*, *Oberst* Gordon Gollob, and when *Oberst* Hermann telephoned Gollob and the newly appointed (April 1945) Inspector of Day Fighters, *Oberst* Walther Dahl, they both rejected any suicide missions when Hermann proposed a special mission once more. This was reported to the author in correspondence with Oberst Hanns Trübenbach, who recalled further: 'I wish here to report very briefly on *"Schulungslehrgang Elbe"*, that later became renamed as *"Sonderkommando Elbe"*. The call for pilots to volunteer for a decisive but dangerous mission, did not go unheard. They came forward: old experienced pilots for whom life had lost all meaning after their loved ones had been buried in the rubble of their cities, young men convinced of their cause to save the Fatherland and who had deep faith in the value of their possible sacrifice, and there were also the fanatics. When they reported for duty with this special unit, they first signed an oath of silence and thereafter they were able to proceed unhindered to their ten-day-long ram-training. *Oberfähnrich* Stumpf and his comrades travelled to Stendal, the collection point of the special command. After being welcomed by the *Kommandeur* (identity no longer known), there came the first surprise – special rations! On the next day an *Oberfeldwebel* decorated with the *Ritterkreuz* and a member of a *Sturmgruppe* told the pilots how he had successfully rammed a four-engined bomber.' From this it is clear that somehow *Oberst* Hajo Hermann had indeed been allowed by some high authority in the *Luftwaffe* to create such a special ramming-commando, and that this unit was set up well in advance of his phone call to *Oberst's* Gollob and Dahl, as described above. In fact this unit had been conceived in January 1945.[81]

Oberst Trübenbach goes on to describe how some of these '*Elbe*' pilots were recruited, as related to him confidentially by *Oberfähnrich* Stumpf, who was one of them. 'On a day in March 1945 a senior officer gave a talk to the assembled pilots of *EJG 1* on the political and military situation that led up to a call for participation in a unique and war-decisive special mission. From the group of pilots that *Oberfähnrich* Stumpf belonged to, amongst those who stepped forward were Pollmeyer from Hamm in Westphalia, Pöschel from Silesia, Günther from Güstrow and *Unteroffizier* Hopp from Schwegenheim in Pfalz; they volunteered for a mission that was not further defined for them in any detail. They were young, they were passionate about flying and they loved their country that was being turned into a heap of ruins by the enemy bomber fleets. And they believed that with all the power of their youth that their participation in such a mission, even if it cost their lives, would help their fatherland. True to their military oath and true to their voluntary undertaking to fly on this special mission, the "*Elbe*" pilots took off on the next mission against the US bomber fleets on 7 April 1945. They were volunteers without any external pressure forcing them to do this. The most interesting witnesses of this mission of volunteers have become very rare (writing in 1992); *Oberfähnrich* Stumpf crashed fatally while flying a glider on 12 August 1962 at Walldürn airfield.'

In the end, on 7 April 1945, when the *Sonderkommando Elbe* was set in motion, 143 fighter aircraft actually took off. While they managed to knock down 14 four-engined bombers by ramming, 45 of the '*Elbe*' fighters were lost at a cost of 24 of their pilots killed and a further eight missing.[82] It was thus by no means a success and the hoped-for shock to American aircrew morale was not achieved. The debate on this special mission of *Sonderkommando Elbe* on 7 April 1945 carried on in Germany for a long time after the war. Hajo Hermann himself, initiator of this more extreme 'ramming-type' mission, long proclaimed the '*Elbe*' pilots as being the best of the best, and deserving of greater respect than the rest of the surviving *Luftwaffe* fighter pilots. Other members of the community saw it as a needless waste of young lives at a time when the war was definitely lost and in its last stages, brought on by a few fanatics such as *Oberst* Hermann. Hanns Trübenbach has a final comment on all of this: 'Just looking back to the 150-odd fighter pilots killed in *Operation Bodenplatte* on 1 January 1945, that was controlled from my *Jafü* headquarters by *Oberst* Handrick, assigning over-much glory to the "Elbe" pilots is not justifiable.'

9

THE CAMPAIGN IN NORWAY: AN OFT FORGOTTEN THEATRE OF THE SECOND WORLD WAR

While the original *I/JG 77* had been incorporated into *JG 51* as its *IV Gruppe* in 1940,[1] a new *I/JG 77* was set up in Norway at the turn of the year 1940–1941 and scored their first victory there on 24 May 1941.[2] The next month, this unit was renamed *Jagdgruppe Stavanger* and in January 1942 had a final name-change to *I/JG 5*.[3] This *Gruppe* actually shot down the very first four-engined bombers over Western Europe on 8 September 1941 when *Unteroffizier* Woite and *Leutnant* Jakobi each managed to down an early model B-17 over Norway, belonging to a small contingent supplied to the RAF from America.[4] Mostly this unit met single or small formations of British aircraft over or near Norway, with large actions being the exception; one such took place on 17 May 1942 when 54 RAF bombers closed with the Norwegian coast, in an attack on a German naval group, including the heavy cruiser *Prinz Eugen*.[5] *I/JG 5* claimed 18 confirmed victories as well as five more without witnesses.[6] The *Prinz Eugen* had been seriously damaged by a Royal Navy submarine in March and, after temporary repairs in Norway, was sailing back to Germany.[7] RAF Coastal Command sent out two groups of aircraft to attack her and only the second group of 52 machines made an attack: while losing nine aircraft missing, they claimed five German fighters in return.[8] As in almost all larger air battles, both sides were guilty of rather high over-claiming. At the beginning of August 1943, *I/JG 5* left Norway for Denmark and later flew over Romania and in the Home Defence.[9]

The other main unit of *JG 5* serving over Norway was *IV/JG 5*, formed on 26 June 1942 with Me 109s, and which re-equipped with the Fw 190 in August 1942.[10] With the exception of *c.* three months from August to the beginning of November 1944 (when they were sent to Finland to reinforce the *Eismeer* units), *IV/JG 5* served continuously in Norway.[11] The relatively low intensity of enemy activity can be gauged from their claims and losses in 1942–1943; 16 victories claimed against 50 of their own aircraft lost, with 21 pilots killed and 17 wounded.[12] With the poor weather conditions in Norway and the mountainous nature of the country, many of the losses would have been accidental rather than in combat. One of the pilots serving in *IV/JG 5* in Norway from late 1944 to the end of the war was *Unteroffizier* Karl-Heinz Erler, who recalled flying against the British over southern Norway, as well as the excellence of the Me 109 G-14 fighters:

Our Messerschmitts were all G-14 types. The Me 109 G-14 was the best '109' that we ever had. It had a compressor on the engine that, at high altitude, was supposed to supply adequate oxygen to the petrol-air mixture. The compressor ran at 10 times the revolutions of the engine and, if placed under too much strain, the compressor gear could melt. As a result direct injection of methyl alcohol was added to cool the gear; the result of this was not only cooling of the gear but also an increase in aircraft speed of 100 km/h, up to 700 km/h (after cooling the gear, the methyl alcohol became added to the air-fuel mixture in the engine thereby increasing the speed). One was only supposed to use the compressor and methyl alcohol injection for a maximum of five minutes at most. The armament of the Me 109 was good: two heavy machine guns of 13 mm that shot through the propeller blades with an interrupter gear and one 2 cm cannon that shot through the propeller hub; one could use them separately or together. One could make tight turns at high speed with the '109': I loved this aircraft, there was nothing better than flying it. She was superior to the Mustangs, more manoeuvrable and faster. Our opponents were the English; only in northern Norway were the Russians our opponents (but after October 1944, *JG 5* no longer maintained a presence there or in Finland).[13] My own operations (late 1944 to end of war) were initially flown from Stavanger and finally from Oslo fjord, at Rygge near Moss. The Norwegians at that time had requested air cover for Oslo, as the 'Tommies' were bombing the port. I can well understand the Norwegians asking for fighter protection, because it was very difficult for the English to differentiate between a German and a Norwegian ship, as from above they all looked the same.

We lost a good comrade in *Leutnant* Gillet (*Staffelkapitän 16/JG 5* very briefly, in April, killed on 11 April 1945);[14] the *Staffel* was then led by *Feldwebel* Heinz Halstrick (a 13-victory ace)[15] and I flew as his wingman (*Katschmarek*). When our *Staffel* moved to Rygge, on one mission we managed to surprise the Tommies who flew straight into our 'open blades' and we shot six of them down. Our new operational area was the Oslo fjord and the Skagerak. We also had a base at Forus on the south-west coast of Norway. Our duties were mainly to protect the shipping and general air cover for southern Norway. The air combats against the Tommies were fair, which one could no longer say of the Americans. Our rations were always very good. We hardly had any contact with the Norwegians. However, I had a Norwegian girlfriend as did my one friend also. As we did not live in a barracks there were no problems. We of *Jagdgeschwader 5* meet every year (writing in 1995) on Ascension Day in Oberauroff (near Frankfurt/Main) at the Hotel 'Heinz Kern', who himself was also a pilot in *JG 5*. In this way the tradition is kept alive; obviously the 'pilots' brides' are always there too. Our *Staffel* always has the most pilots there.

Other *JG 5* units flying over Norway against the Western Allies were *III/JG 5* from 8 November 1944 till the end of the war, and *13(Z)/JG 5* from 16 February to 18 July 1944.[16] *I/ZG 76* was stationed in Norway from the invasion of that country in April 1940 until September of the same year, when it became *II/NJG 1*; its place in Norway was taken by *III/ZG 76* in October and they remained there until April 1941, when this unit was transformed into *II/SKG 210* and left the theatre.[17] *Stab/ZG 76* had also arrived in October 1940, remaining till June 1941.[18] However, there was one *ZG 76* unit, 2nd *Staffel* of *I/ZG 76*, which had a different history to the rest of the *Gruppe*.[19] This *Staffel* remained behind in Norway and was put under the new *I/JG 77* (later *I/JG 5*), becoming *1(Z)/JG 77* in about summer 1941, and then took part in the *Barbarossa* invasion in June 1941.[20] In March 1942 the *Zerstörerstaffel* was renamed once more, becoming *10(Z)/JG 5* and thus also becoming part of *JG 5 'Eismeer'*.[21] A final metamorphosis to *13(Z)/JG 5* took place in June 1942; it remained in action against the Russians on the *Eismeerfront* and in Lappland until 1944.[22]

Leutnant Karl-Friedrich Schlossstein was one of the pilots in *1(Z)/JG 77* and flew operations over western Norway in the first half of 1941: 'We flew convoy patrols over the shipping off the coast, to protect them against English aircraft attacking them, and shot down some Blenheims and Hudsons.' In correspondence with the author he described a rather unique combat with the Royal Navy over far northern Norway on the *Eismeerfront*. Shortly before the beginning of the Barbarossa campaign against the Soviet Union, the *Staffel* transferred to Kirkenes, equipped with the Me 110 E model and comprising 10 crews. On 30 July 1941, *1(Z)/JG 77* were tasked with escorting Ju 88s of *KG 30* in an attack on Murmansk. As the bombers were to overfly Kirkenes to pick up their escort, eight Me 110s took off and assembled over their base in mid-afternoon, when suddenly Schlossstein saw strange aircraft over the harbour below them, British biplanes (Albacores) attacking shipping with torpedoes. Deciding to defend the harbour, the Me 110s joined some Ju 87s of *I/StG 5* (returning fortuitously from a mission over the

Russian lines) in attacking the interlopers. In a combat at very low level, Schlossstein managed to shoot down one retiring Albacore and then, in attacking a second, got too close and had to pull up rapidly, exposing his aircraft to the rear gunner who promptly shot his right-hand engine into flames.

A desperate attempt to reach land on one engine didn't pan out and he and *Gefreiter* Gutsche his gunner were forced to ditch in the freezing water, with only their mae wests. With no land in sight their chances looked hopeless, but after some time they were very lucky to hear a boat, shoot off some flares, and be picked up. According to British records, which a historian had sent to Karl-Friedrich Schlossstein, the attack on Kirkenes had been mounted by 20 Albacores escorted by nine Fulmar fighters (from the aircraft carrier HMS *Victorious,* one of two carriers attacking *Eismeer* targets to try and relieve some of the pressure on the Russians). While claiming one Ju 87, one Me 109 and 2 Me 110s, the naval aircraft suffered 11 Albacores and two Fulmars shot down: according to Schlossstein, only one Me 110 and one Ju 87 were in fact lost, and total German claims amounted to 27 aircraft. Typical of larger-scale actions, over-claiming on both sides involved would remain almost endemic.

A complete post-war account of this carrier raid from the British side is available in a Supplement to the *London Gazette* published in 1948,[23] detailing that two Royal Navy carriers were involved: HMS *Furious* attacking Petsamo, and HMS *Victorious* raiding Kirkenes. No shipping was present at Petsamo and this force (18 Albacores escorted by six Fulmars) lost an Albacore and a Fulmar to German fighters, with one other Fulmar missing. Details of the attack on Kirkenes were as given by Schlossstein above.[24] While the Royal Navy Fulmars over Kirkenes claimed two Me 110s shot down,[25] only that of Karl-Friedrich Schlossstein was lost and, as described by him above, appears to have been shot down by a retiring Albacore when he got too close during his attack on this rather slow aircraft.

Oberstleutnant Günther Scholz, who had flown in the Spanish Civil War and throughout the Second World War, most recently as *Kommodore* of JG 5, ended his time in the *Luftwaffe* as *Jafü*

Norway in late 1944. 'In 1944 – I cannot recall exactly when now – Finland made a separate peace with the Soviet Union (armistice on 19 September 1944), the Germans left Finland and two *Gruppen* of JG 5 remained in Norway. I myself became *Jagdfliegerführer* Norway (responsible for defence of supply shipping on the Norwegian coast and Denmark) with headquarters in Stavanger; I now saw very little active flying but rather spent my time in the *Jafü* control centre. The attacks of the English, particularly on the heavy water plants near Oslo and in the north, and on the battleship *Tirpitz*, became more intense. The *Tirpitz* was later sunk, a great victory for the cleverly led and skilfully used British flying units.'

IO

THE END OF THE WAR AND IMPRISONMENT: WEST AND EAST

The end of the war in Europe was a time for great celebration in Great Britain, America and the Soviet Union, and also of course in all the liberated countries freed from the Nazi yoke. However, those in Eastern Europe exchanged their previous masters for new Russian ones, who were repressive but not anywhere near as murderous as the Germans had been. For the Germans themselves, they were not only utterly defeated and their country ruined but, for the fighting men, nothing better than imprisonment, frequently long, lay ahead. Capture by Soviet forces often, but not always, implied years of forced labour and poor conditions, leading to very high casualties from exposure, disease and hunger. Prisoners of the Western powers, while much better treated, also suffered deprivation and indeed severe casualties due to exposure and starvation because the occupying forces were not adequately prepared to feed and house such huge numbers of prisoners. For the German fighter pilots, relief at the end of a long and terrible war was tempered by the disgrace of defeat, by a nation that had no regard for former soldiers, sailors or airmen, and discriminated against them obtaining higher education (especially for officers), and by continued imprisonment, in some cases for years. Also problematic in the post-war world was the oft-delayed repatriation of the many prisoners who had been accommodated in North America back to a ruined Germany.

The numbers of prisoners taken in the various campaigns fought by the Luftwaffe varied greatly. While no prisoners are reported from the Polish campaign (where survivability would probably have been low anyway), the campaign in France and the Low Countries in May to June 1940 resulted in many short-term POWs. This was due to the terms of the armistice imposed on a defeated France that included a proviso that all prisoners had to be released.[1] These included approximately 400 German aircrew, including at least 43 fighter pilots who would go on to claim 549 known victories after re-joining the *Luftwaffe* (research credited to Laurent Rizzotti in an appendix to source).[2] Amongst them was the incomparable Werner Mölders, at the time the top German ace, and later the first to reach 100 victories.[3] Prisoners who were removed from France by the British before the armistice were few; for example, three lost in *JG 26*, four in *JG 51*, one in *III/JG 52* and five in *JG 77*.[4]

It was in the fighting in the Battle of Britain that numbers of captives grew rapidly, when many German fighter pilots crash-landed or bailed out over British territory or in the surrounding seas, and were rescued to become British POWs. Examples were *JG 51*, who had 29 pilots captured (as against 46 recorded for the entire war) in the battle itself and another four by May 1941;[5] *JG 26* suffered 21 and nine prisoners in the same two periods respectively.[6] A contrasting example is *III/JG 52*, later the most successful fighter *Gruppe* of the *Luftwaffe,* whose operational time over England lasted only a few days before they suffered heavy casualties, including most of their leadership; their one POW, an NCO, provided minutely detailed information to his British interrogators, deliberately or inadvertently, as is obvious from study of his 'K report'[7] from British archives (copy supplied to author by Nigel Parker, writer of the noted *Luftwaffe Crash Archive* volumes from the Battle of Britain and beyond).[8] After being shot down in the Battle of Britain on 28 August 1940, *Oberfeldwebel* Artur Dau of *7/JG 51* was captured on reaching the ground with his parachute by a police constable and some soldiers, and then taken to Hawkinge airfield near Folkestone where he spent two nights in their cells. He recalled: 'After two days I was taken to the interrogation camp in London. Here I was questioned night and day; the questioning was without result and after three weeks of this, I was taken to a POW camp near Manchester. For *Oberfeldwebel* Dau, thus, imprisonment began – in England, Canada and then once again in England, ending in February 1947. Only at the end of that month did the journey back to Germany take place. It was also the end of my flying experiences.'

Oberleutnant Josef Bürschgens, occasional *Staffelführer* 7/JG 26 in the Battle of Britain, was shot down over England and crash-landed badly, being wounded, on 1 September 1940. In correspondence with the author he related how, on the way to the interrogation centre in London from his hospital, he had amused his guards and a photographer on telling the ticket collector for the train that he unfortunately did not have a ticket. He further noted that this journey into foreign skies cost him six years as a guest of the British King. After being shot down over southern England on 12 October 1940, *Oberleutnant* Günter Büsgen of 1/JG 52 spent a long time as a POW: 'During the years of my captivity (six years in England and Canada) I was treated fairly and decently.' Like many others, he was promoted during captivity, to *Hauptmann*.

Rudolf Miese was actually taken prisoner twice, having been repatriated to Germany in the course of the war as part of an exchange of grievously wounded captives. After being shot down and badly wounded over England on 15 November 1940, *Gefreiter* Miese of 4/JG 2 finally went to a POW camp in August 1941 after a long convalescence:

In March 1942 we sailed in an old tub originally from New Zealand, named *Rankitiki*, which had been converted to a troop transport as part of a convoy from Glasgow to Halifax in Canada. There followed a year in Camp Espanola in Ontario and a year in Lethbridge in Alberta. I can add that my initial treatment in the private hospital in Littlehampton was very good, and after that in the military hospital, also good; in Camp Number 2 in Oldham in the UK, hunger was a constant companion, but at that time the English also had little enough to eat. Canada in comparison was a land of milk and honey, as it is called in the Bible. I do not want to talk about Germany in the last year of the war or the first three years thereafter. On 2 May 1944, with other badly wounded prisoners, we were to be exchanged and sailed in the Swedish *Gripsholm* from New York via Algiers to Barcelona, where the actual exchange took place. In Germany after the harrowing bombing attacks and with the shortages resulting from the war, things looked very different. After a stay in hospital, leave and a convalescence in the Tyrol, I was sent to the *Frontfliegersammelgruppe* (front flyers collection group) in Quedlinburg, Harz. As, following the Geneva Convention I was not allowed to fly in combat any more, I was trained as an instructor from December 1944 to March 1945, and then, when fuel was available and when there were no incursions of American bombers and fighters reported, I was able for the last time to enjoy flying in light aircraft and doing aerobatics. After much hither and thither on 3 May 1945, and as the Russians advanced to within 200 m of us, I got away over the Elbe River and entered captivity under the Americans. Together with 80,000 men confined to a swampy meadow, and after some days without any food, people started to keel over like flies. After being handed over to the English, I was released from captivity on 2 August 1945.

Smaller numbers of *Luftwaffe* fighter pilots fell into British (and later American) hands in the Mediterranean theatre. Another Battle of Britain veteran, Heinz Altendorf (illustration 62) was a pre-war pilot who was a *Leutnant* with 5/JG 53 when the war broke out. In correspondence with the author, he noted that he was transferred to 7/JG 53 on 8 February 1940, a unit he stayed with until 16 December 1941. He led 7/JG 53 as *Staffelkapitän* and *Oberleutnant* from September 1940, the height of the Battle of Britain, until becoming a POW in North Africa in December 1941. 'I achieved 24 recognised *Abschüsse* (four over France, three in the Battle of Britain and 17 over Russia), both fighters and bombers.' He was awarded the Iron Cross second and first class in 1940, and the *Ehrenpokal* (Honour Goblet) on 30 July 1941. *III/JG 53* was transferred to the Western Desert on 8 December 1941, and was only to fly there for 10 days until 17 December when they moved to Sicily for the Malta operations.[9] It was one day too late for Altendorf who was taken prisoner on 16 December: 'On 16 December 1941 I was shot down by British tanks 150 km south of Derna and became a POW of the British in North Africa; I only returned to Germany in November 1946.' He was awarded the German Cross in Gold in captivity on 25 February 1942 and was promoted to *Hauptmann* on 1 July 1943 while still a prisoner. *Leutnant* Heinz Riedel had flown briefly as wingman to *Major Freiherr* von Maltzahn, *Kommodore* of *JG 53*, over the island of Malta. He was shot down over Luca airfield there on 11 July 1942 and became a POW; his experiences are detailed briefly below:

> After about a week, together with a comrade from the *Pik-As Geschwader*, Dr Heiner Jörg from Bamberg (a *Leutnant* in *II/JG 53*, shot down on 10 May 1942),[10] I was removed from the small little camp on Malta and taken to Cairo by a C-47 aircraft. From there it was off to an interrogation camp at Gizeh for 14 days. Six weeks in a camp at Latrun in Palestine followed. On the journey back to Egypt, from where we were to be taken to Canada for final incarceration, the two of us, Dr Jörg and I, made ourselves scarce. However, after three days on the loose, we were caught again near El-Arisch and then locked up at the Bitter Lake for four weeks. When we emerged, the transport to Canada was naturally long gone. In Suez a new convoy was being put together and we (by now 18 officers and 50 men) landed in Durban after a two-week voyage. The South Africans enjoyed us so much that they kept us in a transit camp in Pietermaritzburg (about 80 km inland from Durban; coincidentally where the author lives). We were not very well behaved and I think that they were pleased when they got rid of us again. After six weeks in South Africa, where we were fell fed and well treated, we sailed from Durban in the *Isle de France* via Australia, Tasmania, New Zealand, Hawaii to San Francisco, where the English handed us over to the Americans. A four days' train journey brought us to Tennessee, where we stayed until the end of the war. In January 1946 we returned to the ruins of Germany and, in

August 1956, I entered a refresher flying course in Landsberg am Lech on Pipers and T-6s. I later became a flying instructor on the T-6 and Fouga Magister. I ended my military career at age 53 and went on pension as an *Oberstleutnant*.

In correspondence and conversation with Hans-Ulrich Kornstädt, a *Leutnant* in *II/JG* 27 flying from Sicily in the first half of 1943, he told me about his final mission on 7 June 1943, when he was shot down on a reconnaissance flight over Pantelleria by Spitfires, and bailed out into the sea; here he drifted in his dinghy for 17 hours before being rescued by a British destroyer which had seen his flares at night. To his great disappointment, after being landed in Bizerta, he was handed over to the Americans for a short while, and then to the French who took control of all prisoners in North Africa. He remained a prisoner of the French for four years in a camp 500 km south of Oran in Algeria, at the edge of the Sahara Desert, followed by a further year as a prisoner in France before being released in February 1948.[11] Surprisingly few prisoners were taken around the Mediterranean: JG 77, for example, lost six pilots to captivity in the brief Balkans campaign of April to May 1941, one over Malta in October 1942, and 15 over North Africa from late 1942 till May 1943.[12]

The enormous air battles over Germany produced few *Luftwaffe* fighter-pilot prisoners. This was hardly surprising for an essentially continental campaign fought over friendly territory in the main. Prior to that, in 1941–1942 over the Channel and Northern France, prisoners were also few and far between as most of the fighting was over German-held France; *JG* 26, for example, only had seven pilots captured from 22 June 1941 till the end of 1943, with another five over the Invasion Front in mid-1944.[13] Once the Allied armies were properly established ashore and advancing westwards to the German borders, aerial fighting produced more prisoners for the Allies. *Hauptmann* Georg Schröder, in command of *II/JG* 2, was shot down and made prisoner during *Operation Bodenplatte* on New Year's Day 1945. Captured by American troops after force-landing near Huy in Belgium, he ended up in English captivity: 'After that unfortunately, the unattractive core of the English came to the fore. I was flown to England in a

DC-3, where I was imprisoned for three years and four months. It is better to remain silent on this time. I learnt there about the English soul!'

The end of the war in Europe saw most surviving fighter pilots taken prisoner either by the British and Americans, or by the Soviet forces. *Oberleutnant* Gerd Schindler of *IV/JG* 27 having been shot down and wounded by Tempests on 22 February 1945, did not fly again because he was still recovering from his wounds when the war ended. He stayed with his *Gruppe* during his convalescence and, about a month before the end of the war, had a very lucky escape from Mustangs strafing his *Gruppe's* airfield. Being able by now to get about a bit, he had grabbed a rifle to shoot back at the P-51s but one of them saw him and loosed off a burst of machine gun fire at Schindler, missing him by only a few metres. In correspondence with the author he described how, as the war drew to a close, he was put in charge of some of the ground personnel and over time they travelled southwards, through Munich and into the Alpine region, and then to Graz in Austria, and finally to the *Jagdflieger* rest and convalescent home on Lake Tegern where he spent a restful 10 days. Then he was sent to the hospital at Bad Wiessee but instead arrived at Bad Aibling, where he was reunited with the remains of *JG* 27 and was granted 14 days of leave to recover fully. He went into the Alps once again and visited friends there, where he also found his parents who had been evacuated from Graz; during this time the war ended. He was taken into captivity by the Americans who sent him to a huge open-air camp at Mauerkirchen, where he spent about six weeks before being discharged, only to be 'captured' by the British who soon discharged him for the second time, in Graz, his home town!

With few units of piston-engined fighters still active at the end of the war, prisoners were taken from the training establishments (some were still running even then) and, especially, from the jet fighter units. Battle of Britain veteran with *JG* 51, *Oberfeldwebel* Georg Pavenzinger, who had briefly been a POW of the French in 1940, was one such instructor, who had the good fortune to enjoy a quiet transition into short-lived British captivity in Denmark. He recalled: 'In March 1945, with my commissioned student pilots, we were doing a high altitude flight at about 9,500 m when, suddenly, a dot appeared in the distance which rapidly grew into an enemy aircraft. I was about 500 m higher and was able to get within 150 m of the Mosquito. To increase its speed the crew of the Mosquito jettisoned various objects. As I could get no closer I shot at long range and saw that the tracer was striking home. The enemy aircraft began to break up and crashed into the sea near Flensburg. My combat report was accepted but I never heard anything more about it, most likely due to the end of the war being close.

My last training post was at Flensburg where, towards the end of the war, officers and NCOs collected, some of them with high decorations, and who had been flying as bomber and reconnaissance pilots. They were to be subjected to a test to determine whether they were capable of converting to fighter pilots. To decide this issue a two-man committee was created with the commander of the school, an *Oberleutnant*, and myself as *Oberfeldwebel* and instructor. This pointless business was soon terminated as everyone could see the end was near. On 20 April 1945 the *Führer*'s birthday was celebrated for the last time, but very simply, and then the fighter school was closed down. At the end of April 1945 I was transferred for the last time, to Aalborg in Denmark, to await the end of the war. On 10 May 1945 we marched in formation and fully armed to the German border, where we gave up our arms and entered a POW camp in Meldorf. After about six weeks I was discharged and was at home again by the end of July 1945. With that, the war was finally over for me.'

In contrast, a much more complex end to the war was experienced by *Oberst* Hanns Trübenbach, *Jafü Mittelrhein*, as a senior fighter controller with wide-ranging responsibilities. He was flown to England for interrogation before being passed over to the French, whose treatment was less salubrious:

When the Americans crossed the Rhine in 1945 I received orders from my commanding *Jagdkorps General* to blow up my large headquarters near Darmstadt and to retreat to Nürnberg-Fürth, from where I was to get in touch with the

General der Jagdflieger, Oberst Gollob. While my senior staff officer, Fritze Schaffer, was to wait for me with my service car and chauffeur at the River Main, I journeyed with a small BMW motorbike, alone through the forests towards the East. In a clearing I was attacked by two enemy fighters at low level and was able to protect myself behind a thick oak tree. When dissolving my headquarters I had given my *Ia*, an elderly *Major*, orders well in advance to send all 4,000 female auxiliaries of the day- and night-fighters home. This took place in an exemplary fashion and many of these women later wrote to me to thank me that they all got home safely, even though it was just my damned duty.

Thus I met up with Fritze Schaffer at the Main, where we spent the night with a farmer. Then we went on to Fürth to my family, who were staying in the gardener's cottage on the estate of the Countess of Resseguier, to where we were anyway only able to journey after some days had passed. The estate lay in the area of Murnau/Obb. When I telephoned the *General der Jagdflieger* in Innsbruck, where he had just been operated on for his appendix, I received the order to give myself up when the Americans or the French advanced to where we were. The daughter of the elderly Countess von Hochried was married to an American and thus things went very well for my family (my wife anyway spoke perfect English). Thus I was taken into custody by the friendly Americans and registered. After saying goodbye to my family I was sent to Wiesbaden after a few days and later flown to England. When I was recognised as also being an international aerobatic team leader, I received splendid quarters with everything one could desire. Only with the transfer of our officers group from England to France, did things get worse. We were accommodated in tents, 34 to 40 men per tent. And the guards of this camp were really criminal NCOs whom we had to threaten to hang if they did not behave decently.

Weeks later we were moved by train to the infamous Camp Attichy, where there were thousands of prisoners. One day a large group of German prisoners arrived from Canada, and the camp authorities needed a large number of tarpaulins to fence off their compound as they had no more wire. But who knew how to splice tarpaulins together in the sailor's way? A good joke, as I was the only one – as an experienced small-boat sailor and voyager to the West Indies – who could report himself as able to do the job. I thus received all the relevant material and a nice tent to myself, where I was allowed to splice all the canvas together. After finishing this work, I reported its completion to the French commander of the camp. Very happy with me, he asked if I also could understand French and, if I could, I was to join the medical section immediately to write out the medical reports.

There were many prisoners in the camp who were keen to work in the agricultural sector as they would be well treated and also paid. I thus became the medical clerk and was astonished at the number of young men who came for a check-up and then wanted to be taken away. Many of them found the loves of their lives at their farms, and returned to Germany very happy!

And so the time passed rapidly by and I was able to write many letters to my wife and friends, also in the justified hope of an imminent release. One day we were taken to the generals' camp and heard that the generals were soon to be moved to Dachau, to the concentration camp there. We staff officers up to the rank of *Oberst* were to go with the Hungarians to Rosenheim/Obb, where we were also going to be released. They were a nice and comradely bunch, but many of them knew nothing about their families or other relations. While I was passing the time studying maps, many of them became curious, and many only wanted to know what their future would be like. Thus I did what my mother had done for me as an older child, and helped my comrades back on to their spiritual legs again; those that wanted to. On 26 March 1946 the Americans discharged me with a two-page discharge document with thumbprint, back to my family at Murnau on the Hochried estate, where I was able to celebrate the happy return home on my birthday. On 28 March I was confirmed as a free and unblemished citizen.

Compared to many fighter units, those who had been flying the latest Me 262 jet fighters were generally rather well treated in a special camp set aside for these uniquely qualified opponents, who were to be questioned closely on their experiences. *Hauptmann* Rudolf Engleder, *IV/JG* 7 recalled: 'The *Geschwader* surrendered south of Mühldorf to the 14th American Armoured Division on about 8–10 May 1945; after about 10 days we were transported and entered captivity as a unit in Obertraubling near Regensburg. The *Geschwader* had its own separate camp! I was released in September 1945.' *Oberfeldwebel* Rudolf Hener, *II/JG* 7 enjoyed a similarly brief incarceration: 'We stuck around railway stations in the Mühldorf am Inn area (after bombing had deprived *II/JG* 7 of their Me 262 aircraft) and as a unit went into American captivity on 7 May 1945. The captivity only lasted five or six weeks. The American General Patton did not know how he was going to feed the many German and Hungarian prisoners, and in the Camp at Bad-Kreuznach many prisoners had died of hunger, so he ordered the discharge.' Another of the relatively privileged members of *JG* 7 was *Oberleutnant* Alfred Seidl, of the *I Gruppe*: 'Not having had the chance to fly missions in the Me 262, I was instructed to lead the ground column of *I/JG* 7 from Brandenburg, via Leipzig-Pilsen-Eisenstein to Landau. I experienced the 12 April 1945, my birthday, on the *Autobahn*. At Pilsen we pilots were put on to a bus and taken, via Lechfeld, to Mühldorf/Inn where, with large numbers of the rest of the *Geschwader*, we waited for the advancing Americans. At Metten, a field airbase, we entered American captivity and, after days of being transported in trucks, we were taken to a special camp in Regensburg.'

However, not all the *JG* 7 pilots were that lucky and, in common with quite a few other members of the flying personnel of the *Luftwaffe*'s fighter arm, found themselves serving in hastily conceived ground units, fighting against Western or Eastern foes. After his Me 262 aircraft had been damaged by Russian flak, *Unteroffizier* Kurt Beecken of *II/JG* 7 managed to return to Prague-Rusin, but there was neither a new aircraft nor repairs to his existing one. Despite some unpleasant times, he actually had rather a lucky break compared to many other POWs of the Russians: 'I was assigned to the infantry for ground operations and had some nasty experiences; I fled alone from Prague-Rusin and managed to reach the Americans near Karlsbad, to whom I gave myself up. Sadly, after about a week, the Americans delivered myself and my POW comrades to the Russians one night. Thus began a time of suffering, which one really does not want to remember. As I became very sick, I was, thank God, released back home towards the end of 1945.' *Leutnant* Josef Neuhaus of the *III Gruppe* belonged to the same group of unlucky *JG 7* pilots assigned to ground duty, but had a much more fortunate fate, largely of his own making: 'At Prague-Rusin and in Saatz, *JG 7* was dissolved. As the youngest *Leutnant*, I received the order to relieve the *Luftwaffe* Division Staff with a platoon of young soldiers: this was on 8 May 1945. Prague-Rusin on 9 May was very empty. I searched for a serviceable aircraft and, with the help of a mechanic, found a Me 108 *Taifun*. Together we took the fuel from a Siebel 204, transferred about 24 buckets of petrol and took off across the runway. Flying over "enemy territory" we flew close to my home in Münster in Westphalia. A smooth belly-landing ended my wartime flying and allowed me to escape any captivity.'

Some pilots, taking to the Alpine regions to await the end of the war, were only incarcerated for brief periods before being released. *Oberfeldwebel* Ernst Richter, who had flown in Russia with *JG 54* and over Normandy with *JG 11*, found himself an instructor from September 1944 onwards. 'I was ordered to *Ergänzungsjagdgruppe 1* as an instructor. There I trained about 50 pilots up till the beginning of April 1945. Most were ex-bomber or *Zerstörer* pilots, or had been instructors in basic flying schools or fighter schools; there were also some young pilots there who had been trained to fly on a fast-track (about 60 hours), whose chances of survival on active operations were very small! On my last mission on 29 April 1945, which I flew in company with another instructor and two good students from Bad Aibling, we were instructed to reconnoitre the Munich and Landshut area, to see how far the American tanks had advanced. This was only with the aim of an orderly retreat of our own troops! I had volunteered for this mission as I was very familiar with this area as seen at low level. We took off at 19h45 and landed at 20h20 in Mühldorf.

On the evening of 1 May 1945, together with eight comrades, I took off for my last flight in the German air force, from Bad Aibling to Salzburg. From there, with weapons and workshop vehicle, we moved to the mountains in Saalbach im Pinzgau, where we awaited the end of the war. In the middle of May we were interned there and then taken to the Munich area; the Americans had set up a processing and release camp on the airfield at Bad Aibling where I obtained my official release document at the beginning of August 1945. This was signed in Wunstorf by the English on 6 August 1945; on 8 August I was at home again with my wife in Oldenburg.'

Those flying personnel transferred to ground units enjoyed highly variable fates. Some were very lucky and avoided captivity completely, including *Oberfeldwebel* Joachim Robel, ex-gunner/radio-operator in *I/ZG 1*: 'Our flying came to an end in December 1944 (at the *Zerstörer* Training School) as we had no more fuel. I was transferred to the paratroops in Austria. On 8 May 1945 the war ended. I was able to avoid becoming a prisoner and was able to make my way to Dresden (my home). For this 700 km journey I needed three weeks. My flying log book with all my detailed notes and many photos was lost in February 1945 in a British raid on Dresden.' Others were only kept captive for very short periods and then released; this applied more easily to NCOs than officers. *Oberfeldwebel* Josef Ederer had flown with *I/JG 53* over England in 1940 and then over Malta and Russia, before returning to Sicily in late 1942 from the Stalingrad front. Here he caught malaria, which affected his eyesight, and he was utilised thereafter as an instructor and later a Messerschmitt works test pilot. After a bad crash on 25 October 1944 due to sabotage he was not able to fly any longer. He was then posted to the flak arm: 'On 20 March 1945 I was ordered to join the flak protecting rail transport, Regiment 54 "Hermann Göring". Here I was part of the protection for transport trains carrying V2 rockets. On 8 May 1945 I was captured by the English in Schleswig-Holstein and identified as a fighter pilot. After a short interrogation I was detained. The interrogating officer was particularly interested to know if I was prepared, in time, to fly against the Russians once more. When I declared my willingness to do so, I was discharged with the friendly advice to "Go Home".' Others had to endure strenuous ground fighting against the Russians but nevertheless managed to break away and retreat westwards into American or British captivity. One such was *Unteroffizier* Heinz Ludwig, ex-gunner/radio-operator in *I/ZG 26*, then part of the fighter control personnel: 'When I entered American captivity on the Elbe River near Stendal, all my possessions were taken away from me, except for what we had already thrown away while fleeing from the Russians; we had been involved in house-to-house fighting in Rathenow but I was able to reach the Elbe successfully with 14 men.'

Many of the pilots who had flown in the so-called 'Eastern *Jagdgeschwadern*' (*JGs 51, 52, 54*), even though they had managed to surrender to the Western Allies, found themselves handed back to the Russians. In *JG 52*, the *II Gruppe* managed to avoid this fate[14] and enjoyed an early release, as the *Staffelkapitän 7/JG 52*, *Leutnant* Heinz Ewald related very succinctly: 'POW from 8 May 1945–22 June 1945 in a camp at Fürstenfeldbruck.' However, the rest of the *Geschwader*, including its famous ace and last *Kommodore*, *Oberst* Hermann Graf, as well as *Major* Erich Hartmann (the *Luftwaffe's* top ace), last *Gruppenkommandeur* of *I/JG 52*, disobeyed high command orders to fly westwards and give themselves up to the Allies, and to their great credit Graf and Hartmann joined their men in lengthy and horrendous Russian captivity.[15] After having been shot down and seriously wounded on 16 January 1945, *Feldwebel* Günther Granzow of *Stabstaffel/ JG 51* suffered the additional hardship of Soviet imprisonment: '2 May 1945 to 16 May 1948, prisoner of war in Russia.'

Unteroffizier Johann Heinrich, who first joined a frontline unit as a *Zerstörer* radio-operator/gunner in *ZG 76* at the end of August 1940, later flew as a crewman in bomber, transport and communications units, as well as with the night-fighters and reconnaissance *Staffeln*; he also had the misfortune to become an infantryman at the end of the war. 'On 15 January 1945 in Berlin/ Kladow I was discharged from the flying personnel and transferred to the Hermann Göring Regiment in Berlin/Reinickendorf. Then from 16 January 1945 to 24 April 1945 I endured hard battles in the 6th Company, 1st Regiment, of the 1st Hermann Göring

Division in Poland and Silesia, and during street fighting in the town of Bautzen, Niederlausitz on 24 April 1945 at about 08h00 I was seriously wounded. I was in hospitals at Löbau/ Saxony, Zittau/Silesia, and Jermer/Sudetenland where I was taken prisoner by the Russians on 10 May 1945. On this day we (*c.* 4,000 Germans, including refugees from Silesia and the Sudetenland) were captured in Dobriic/Czechoslovakia by a Russian tank unit where we suffered brutal torments from the accompanying Czech partisans. This was a horrible imprisonment with beatings, shootings etc. as well much hunger and hard labour. On 16 June 1945 I was supposed to be shot by the Russians, but was pardoned by a Russian Guards Major with a final warning: at the slightest report of any misbehaviour of mine, he would put me in a cellar half-filled with water where I would have to stand until I starved! I was in various prisoner of war camps in Czechoslovakia and Poland. On 17 July 1945 in Poland, with 2,000 German soldiers and 400 German civilians, we were loaded onto railway waggons for heavy labour at Murmansk in North Russia. On the journey I caught a chill and fever, but managed to escape from the train and had the good fortune to make it back home to Tobisegg (Austria). On 8 October 1945 I was discharged at the demobilisation centre in Deutschlandsberg.'

Another of those German Eastern Front pilots handed back to the Russians after reaching Allied territory was Horst Petzschler. After flying out of East Prussia on 4 May 1945 and landing in Denmark, *Oberfeldwebel* Petzschler of *3/JG 51* ended up being handed over to the Soviet forces. 'In January 1946 we were sent from Trellerborg to Libau in Latvia – why? – 2,700 German and 300 Latvian and Estonian soldiers were sold out to the Soviet Union, and we thus became their prisoners after the war was over! The officers of the Latvian and Estonian soldiers were hanged immediately after our arrival in Riga. We were merely told that they were enemies of the Soviet Union! Their NCOs and men were transported to Siberia, which was later confirmed by the Polish railway staff who had returned from there to Libau in Latvia. We German POWs worked in the shipping yards on the most modern submarines, on the ex-German heavy cruiser

Prinz Eugen, and the light cruisers *Leipzig* and *Nürnberg* –
repairing all of them! In October 1947 we were transported over
10 days in cattle trucks (100 men to a truck, 60-ton Pullmans)
from Libau to, dare we forget it, Shdanov, today again known
as Mariupol. For almost two years our work ran at a high
productivity rate – three shifts of eight hours each, each shift
producing about 80 tons of steel from tanks, guns and other steel
scrap. In September 1949 we were given our lives back at last!
We were released from the forced labour camp at Mariupol in
southern Russia – where we constructed an American steelworks
with 6,000 German and 12,000 Russian slave labourers. On
22 September 1949 I arrived in Berlin, my home town, weighing
118 pounds, half dead but having survived!'

11

CONCLUSIONS

Hitler's long-term war plans had always envisaged expansion to the east at the expense of the smaller East European nations and, particularly, of the Soviet Union. The intention was to destroy the Soviet state and occupy enough space to provide the *Lebensraum* the Germans wanted, as well as enormous resources of raw material and slave labour. Altogether a wonderful scenario from the German nationalistic perspective, which Hitler espoused quite openly in *Mein Kampf*, but what eventuated was a genocidal war that resulted in massive destruction, an enormous military and civilian casualty bill in Russia, and atrocities on an almost unimaginable scale, focussed on the Jews, 'partisans' and communist functionaries of any sort; it was also the death knell of the Third Reich and a very large proportion of its forces, particularly ground assets. Hitler never intended his hegemony over Eastern Europe to extend further southwards than Bulgaria and Yugoslavia. He had no desire to occupy Greece, nor to become involved in a maritime-influenced war over and around the Mediterranean Sea. In contrast, this was very much the desire of his fascist partner, Mussolini, whose ill-advised and poorly executed invasion of Greece forced Hitler's hand to invade Greece and Yugoslavia in April to May 1941. *Il Duce*'s equally incompetent military leaders in Italian-occupied Libya, having suffered catastrophic defeat in the Egyptian-Cyrenaican (Western) desert, also forced him to allocate a small force to save their tottering North African empire, and thus the *Afrikakorps* (and the Rommel legend) were born. While the *Korps* itself was never large (*c.* four and a half divisions in the end) they were all of the *panzer* and mobile-type units, which were in endemically short supply in the German army and thus a significant divergence from Hitler's main war aims.

Like it or not, the Germans were now fully involved in a war around the Mediterranean Sea; Hitler was never comfortable with naval and maritime campaigns and battles, yet all the logistics of his North African forces (and the considerable numbers of their Italian allies) had to come by sea from Sicily, southern Italy and Greece. Sitting right astride the shortest supply route lay the tiny British island group of Malta, whose light naval, submarine and aerial attack forces could and did seriously interdict the flow of military necessities of all sorts to the Western Desert. The very heavy losses to the German paratroop and air-landed forces in their occupation of the island of Crete (May 1941), off southern Greece, put Hitler off ever allowing these limited elite forces to be used in an attempted conquest of Malta. The role of the *Luftwaffe* thus became paramount in several ways: (1) to bomb Malta and drive away British naval forces as well as reduce its air defence and attack potential to relative impotence, thus allowing adequate supply of Axis land forces in North Africa; (2) to stop British supply convoys, naval and merchant marine operations of considerable size and complexity, reaching the oft-beleaguered Maltese islands, with emphasis on hindering carrier-delivered fighter aircraft; (3) when needed, which was quite often, to utilise air transport to ferry critical supplies, especially of fuel to the *Afrikakorps*.

In the Western Desert, the advances of the ground forces of that energetic general, Rommel, needed significant aerial support for their success, especially as the increasingly sophisticated cooperation of British aerial and ground forces (with strong Commonwealth participation in both) often saved the day for their generals. Aerial reinforcements for Rommel were usually taken from those placed to subdue Malta, and these in their turn came almost exclusively from the Russian front, especially over the winter and the following thaw-mud period there from *c*. December 1941 to April 1942, which greatly reduced *Luftwaffe* efficiency on the Eastern front. Once this period was over, most German aerial forces departed Sicily for the East again, leaving few units behind that could either continue attacking Malta or assist Rommel, and never adequately do both at the same time. In the end this inexorably led to failure everywhere. However, despite these constraints on the *Luftwaffe* and especially on fighter operations over the desert, probably the greatest ace of them all, whom no less an authority than *General der Jagdflieger* Adolf Galland called the 'unrivalled virtuoso' amongst all the *Jagdflieger*,[1] Hans-Joachim Marseille of *I/JG* 27, won 151 of his never-to-be-beaten total of 158 victory claims against Western opponents, over the desert. Despite excellent tactical leadership of *JG* 27 by *Major* 'Edu' Neumann, the *Luftwaffe* once again were misled by their fixation on kill-rate and victory claims, major aces and propaganda stars, and neglected to emphasise tackling the very effective light-medium bombers of the British, many belonging to the South African Air Force, and with increasing American participation towards late 1942.

With the resounding defeat of the Italian-German forces at the Battle of Alamein (23 October to 4 November 1942) and almost concomitant Allied landings in French North Africa (8 November), the conflict rapidly shifted to Tunisia, where major Allied air forces were opposed by *Jagdgruppen* drawn largely from Russia, the Mediterranean area itself, and even from occupied France. Overall, the Mediterranean theatre reflected the major drawdown of Russian front fighter power, before the Home Defence in turn drew units from the Mediterranean theatre, Russia and Norway from 1943 onwards. Units taken from the Russian front and sent to the Mediterranean theatre encompassed *Stab*, *II* and *III/JG* 27; the whole of *JG* 53; the whole of *JG* 77; *II/JG* 51. In contrast only *7/JG* 26 and *II/JG* 2 were transferred from France. The Mediterranean theatre was thus no sideshow and reflects that British war strategy was working.

With victory in the Western Desert and the invasion of French North Africa, Malta's isolation was thereby also at an end, and German reinforcements and logistics into Tunisia were largely by aerial means. The *Jagdgruppen* were overwhelmed in time, and strategic bombing of both Tunisian and Sicilian/Italian air bases, mainly by growing US bomber units, including the dreaded four-engined bomber formations, crippled their abilities. With the Axis surrender in North Africa on 13 May 1943, the cross-Mediterannean war was finally at an end. The next campaigns, the invasions of Sicily (and its rapid conquest) and of Italy (and its slow and agonizing conquest) still encompassed major maritime power, now exclusively Allied, but Allied aerial superiority rendered *Luftwaffe* and Italian fighter units rapidly impotent, once again with even greater influence from Allied (particularly American) bombing of their bases. The fall of Sicily and that of Mussolini went hand in hand, leading to a divided Italy (fascist north and co-belligerent south) with rump air forces supporting both sides. The landings at Salerno (Naples) and Anzio in Italy did not achieve the desired breakthroughs for the Allies, who were in turn surprised by the *Luftwaffe's* use of radio-controlled anti-shipping bombs to good effect. Remaining fighter forces in Italy dwindled constantly, under the demands, largely, of the Home Defence, finally exiting the theatre altogether in autumn 1944.

Initial rapid advances in southern Italy brought the Allies to the Foggia airfield complex by October 1943 and, a month later, the US 15th Air Force was able to initiate four-engined bomber raids on southern Germany, Austria and the Balkan countries, especially Romania with its critically important Ploiesti oil fields. Attacks on this prime target were launched from Italy from April 1944 till the Russian invasion of Romania in late August that year, upon which the country changed sides. Limited German and local fighter forces from Romania and the Balkan region were no more able to master these large bomber formations than their colleagues had been able to do over Sicily and then Italy. The wisdom and methods learned the hard way from Northern France and the Home Defence were not adequately applied in these

Italian and Balkan theatres, resulting in Göring's accusations of cowardice against Sicilian-based *Jagdgeschwadern*, leading even to the temporary arrest there of a few randomly chosen pilots in mid-1943.

Following the massive invasion of Normandy launched on 6 June 1944, the six *Jagdgruppen* in that region plus the 17 rapidly transferred from the Home Defence, were simply overwhelmed by Allied air superiority, which also played a significant role in the defeat of the German ground forces, large parts of which were eventually trapped in the Falaise pocket. The rump Home Defence during this period was manned largely by Me 410 *Zerstörer* units, *Wilde Sau* single-engine night-fighters fighting in a daytime role, and the newly launched *Sturmgruppen*. The latter units caused some serious loss to US bomber formations on occasion, but suffered high losses of largely poorly trained neophyte pilots, as did the entire German fighter arm over Germany after September 1944 when the campaign in France was effectively ended. The last-ditch *Bodenplatte* raids on Allied air bases in France and the Low Countries on 1 January 1945, while again achieving a measure of Allied losses at high cost to themselves (and as always to the few remaining experienced leaders), made only a small dent in the Allied aerial juggernaut now consuming Germany. The latter now encompassed the shorter ranged, strongly escorted medium bombers of the RAF and USAAF plus the enormous four-engined bomber formations of the 8th (UK-based) and 15th (Italian-based) Air Forces, often accompanied now by RAF heavy bomber daylight raids as German fighter opposition paled. One thousand attacking heavy bombers and even double that number became a commonplace. The only bright spot against this stark reality was the promise of the Me 262 jet fighter, with initial tests of combat suitability from autumn 1943 and the first regular *Jagdgruppen* operational by late 1944, until the end of the war. But as with any radically new aircraft, and with the small and ever-decreasing pool of experienced pilots, its successes were relatively limited and counted for little against the massive aerial strength of the Allies in the West and the advancing Russians in the East, while the catastrophic ground situation in 1945 ensured an end to the Third Reich.

It is ironic in a way that the *Luftwaffe*, which so successfully complemented the German ground forces in the early Blitzkrieg invasions, that also saw the defeat of Poland, France, the Low Countries, Yugoslavia and Greece, and which devastated Russia in 1941–1942, in its own later campaigning consistently underestimated the importance of the bombers of their enemies. While, early in the war, the Germans attacked and largely destroyed the air forces of their opponents in very effective bombing of enemy air bases in the first few days of a campaign, following which their bomber capability was largely devoted to direct support of ground advances, they appeared to ignore the threat of these methods being turned back on them later on. In Russia (where the Sturmovik Il-2s were a deadly weapon against the *Wehrmacht*), in North Africa where medium bombers helped stop Rommel several times in Egypt and where heavy US bombers pounded German fighter fields in Tunisia, *Jagdgruppen* remained fixated on achieving high scores, largely against fighter aircraft, and the cult of the ace and the kill-rate reigned supreme in their tactical and, to a degree, even strategic thinking. These realities only became worse over Sicily and Italy and reached their nadir in Normandy, by which time the *Luftwaffe* was already a spent force from the unending strategic battle over the home country. It is not as if they lacked warning of what was coming – the first two RAF-manned B-17 Fortresses, early models of less defensive capability than their successors, were shot down over that operational sideshow, Norway, in September 1941. Although the *Jagdflieger* managed to effectively make the bombing of Germany too expensive until adequately-ranged escort fighters were available to the Allies, this was at the cost of concentrating their available fighter forces very largely over the home country. Once the American P-51 Mustang came on the scene they were doomed.

While General of Fighters Galland and many other fighter leaders had earlier warned of the necessity of an adequate aerial defence capability, Hitler would never subscribe to a defensive mindset, and Göring, ever subservient to his leader's wishes, was not one to stand against what he must have known deep down was a coming catastrophe. Thus the Germans were fundamentally defeated in the air (and partly on the ground) by Allied airpower, including that of the Russians, and it was the escorted bomber that did the damage. It was this very type of force the Germans themselves had applied so effectively at the battlefield scale early in the war. Strategic application of airpower, as used by the Allies in the East, North Africa, and in the West, was the *Luftwaffe's* downfall. The first failure of the considerable German air forces in this context, was that over the United Kingdom in 1940.

Whatever their experiences as prisoners of war (as described in the last chapter of this book), whether relatively benign or like those described by Horst Petzschler, and whether lasting many years or only a short time, these men faced an uncertain future upon their release and return to Germany. Their country and its infrastructure and industry were ruined, the economy on its knees and jobs initially were few and far between. Starvation of the populace was a close-run thing during that first post-war winter and for several years after. The Allied bombing onslaught, especially the RAF night-bombing campaign, had reduced most cities to ruin and accommodation was at an absolute premium. Most of the fighter pilots had entered the *Luftwaffe* direct from school and knew no other trade; the German air force was only resuscitated in the mid-1950s within the framework of the 'Cold War'. Ex-officers were generally denied entry into universities to obtain training to contribute usefully to the life of their country.

Post-war Germany had seen enough of war to last for a very long time and there was little respect for veterans of any ilk at all, least of all elites such as the *Jagdflieger*; this has continued right till today, still affecting the very few veterans still alive. However, most of them were able to re-establish themselves within German society and to live useful lives, contributing to the rebirth of their economy, today the strongest in Europe. Many *Geschwader* associations and the *Gemeinschaft der Jagdflieger* veteran's organisation kept the flame of remembrance flickering;

they are often better supported by foreign visitors from their erstwhile enemies' countries than by the German populace, although there are exceptions at local level. In recent years, the Russian and Ukrainian veterans have also become part of this welcome interaction. Traditions within the modern *Luftwaffe* have tended to sideline or totally ignore Second World War personalities and traditions; even someone as revered in his day as Werner Mölders, the first *General der Jagdflieger*, did not escape this politically enforced excision, as discussed in the *Gemeinschaft*'s bi-monthly magazine *Jägerblatt*, and its more modern successor title, *Fliegerblatt*.

NOTES

Preface

1. Eriksson, Patrick G., *Alarmstart* (Stroud: Amberley, 2017).

2. Eriksson, Patrick G., *Alarmstart East* (Stroud: Amberley, 2018).

3. Gilbert, Martin, *Second World War* (London: Weidenfeld and Nicolson, 1989); Young, Peter (Editor), *The World Almanac Book of World War II* (New York: World Almanac Publisher, 1981).

4. *ibid.*

5. Bekker, Cajus, *Angriffshöhe 4000. Die deutsche Luftwaffe im Zweiten Weltkrieg* (Munich: Wilhelm Heyne Verlag, 1967).

6. *ibid.*

7. Gilbert, Martin, *op. cit.*

8. Wood, Tony and Gunston, Bill, *Hitler's Luftwaffe: A pictorial and technical encyclopedia of Hitler's air power in World War II* (London: Salamander Books, 1977); Prien, Jochen, *Geschichte des Jagdgeschwaders 77, Teil 1, 1934–1941* (Eutin: Struve-Druck, 1992).

9. Gilbert, Martin, *op. cit.*

10. Shores, Christopher, Massimello, Giovanni and Guest, Russell, *A History of the Mediterranean Air War 1940–1945; Volume One: North Africa June 1940–January 1942* (London: Grub Street, 2012); Shores, Christopher, Massimello, Giovanni and Guest, Russell, *A History of the Mediterranean Air War 1940–1945; Volume Two: North African Desert February 1942–March 1943* (London: Grub Street, 2012).

11. Shores, Christopher and Cull, Brian with Malizia, Nicola, *Malta: the Hurricane years 1940–41* (London: Grub Street, 1987); Shores, Christopher and Cull, Brian with Malizia, Nicola, *Malta: the Spitfire year 1942* (London: Grub Street, 1991).

12. Greene, Jack and Massignani, Alessandro, *The Naval War in the Mediterranean 1940–1943* (London: Frontline Books, 2011).

13. Shores, Christopher, 2012, vol. 1, *op. cit*; Shores, Christopher, 2012, vol. 2, *op. cit*; Shores, Christopher, 1987, *op. cit*; Shores, Christopher, 1991, *op. cit.*

14. Gilbert, Martin, *op. cit.*

15. Macintyre, Donald, *The Battle for the Mediterranean* (London: Pan Books, 1970).

16. Shores, Christopher, 1987, *op. cit*; Shores, Christopher, 1991, *op. cit.*

17. Shores, Christopher, 2012, vol. 1, *op. cit*; Shores, Christopher, 2012, vol. 2, *op. cit*; Shores, Christopher, 1987, *op. cit*; Shores, Christopher, 1991, *op. cit.*

18. Shores, Christopher, 2012, vol. 2, *op. cit.*

19. Shores, Christopher and Ring, Hans, *Fighters over the Desert* (London: Neville Spearman, 1969).

20. Montgomery, Field Marshal The Viscount, *Montgomery of Alamein, Volume I, El Alamein to the River Sangro* (London: Corgi Books, 1974).

21. *ibid.*

22. Shores, Christopher, 1987, *op. cit*; Shores, Christopher, 1991, *op. cit.*

23. Shores, Christopher, 2012, vol. 1, *op. cit*; Shores, Christopher, 2012, vol. 2, *op. cit*; Holm, Michael, *The Luftwaffe, 1933–1945*; www.ww2.dk

24. Shores, Christopher, 2012, vol. 1, *op. cit*; Shores, Christopher, 2012, vol. 2, *op. cit.*

25. Shores, Christopher, Cull, Brian and Malizia, Nicola, *Air war for Yugoslavia, Greece and Crete 1940–41* (London: Grub Street, 1987); Baker, E.C.R., *Ace of aces M St J Pattle* (Rivonia: Ashanti Publishing, 1992).

26. Ring, Hans and Girbig, Werner, *Jagdgeschwader 27, Die Dokumentation über den Einsatz an allen Fronten 1939–1945* (Stuttgart: Motorbuch Verlag, 1975); Skawran, Paul Robert, *Ikaros; Persönlichkeit und Wesen des deutschen Jagdfliegers im Zweiten Weltkrieg* (Steinbach am Wörthsee: Luftfahrt-Verlag Walter Zuerl, 1969).

27. Shores, Christopher, 1987, *Air war for Yugoslavia, op. cit.*

28. Gilbert, Martin, *op. cit*; Young, Peter, *op. cit.*

29. Shores, Christopher, *Dust clouds in the Middle East* (London: Grub Street, 2010).

30. Shores, Christopher, 2010, *op. cit*; Gilbert, Martin, *op. cit*; Young, Peter, *op. cit.*

31. Shores, Christopher, 2010, *op. cit.*

32. *ibid.*

33. Montgomery, Field Marshal The Viscount, *op. cit.*

34. *ibid.*

35. Gilbert, Martin, *op. cit.*

36. Gilbert, Martin, *op. cit*; Montgomery, Field Marshal The Viscount, *op. cit.*

37. Gilbert, Martin, *op. cit.*

38. Shores, Christopher, Ring, Hans and Hess, William N., *Fighters over Tunisia* (London: Neville Spearman, 1975).

39. Shores, Christopher, 2012, vol. 2, *op. cit.*

40. Shores, Christopher, Massimello, Giovanni with Guest, Russell, Olynyk, Frank and Bock, Winfried, *A History of the Mediterranean Air War 1940–1945; Volume Three: Tunisia and the end in Africa November 1942– May 1943* (London: Grub Street, 2016); Holm, Michael, *op. cit.*

41. Shores, Christopher, 1975, *op. cit.*

42. *ibid.*

43. Shores, Christopher, 2016, *op. cit.*

44. Prien, Jochen, *Pik-As: Geschichte des Jagdgeschwaders 53, Teil 2* (Eutin: Struve-Druck, 1990); Prien, Jochen, *Geschichte des Jagdgeschwaders 77, Teil 3, 1942–1943* (Eutin: Struve-Druck, undated).

45. *ibid.*

46. Steinhoff, Johannes, *The straits of Messina: Diary of a fighter commander* (London: Corgi Books, 1973). Although not a fully factually accurate account (see details in Prien, Jochen, undated) it does provide a comprehensive picture of this sorry crisis.

47. Prien, Jochen, 1990, *op. cit*; Steinhoff, Johannes, *op. cit.*

48. Prien, Jochen, 1990, *op. cit*; Prien, Jochen, undated, *op. cit.*

49. Gilbert, Martin, *op. cit.*

50. Montgomery, Field Marshal The Viscount, *op. cit.*

51. Gilbert, Martin, *op. cit.*

52. Holm, Michael, *op. cit*; Wood, Tony, *op. cit.*

53. Wood, Tony, *op. cit.*

54. Young, Peter, *op. cit.*

55. Tillman, Barrett, *Forgotten 15th: the daring airmen who crippled Hitler's war machine* (Washinton DC: Regnery Publishing, 2014).

56. Wood, Tony, *op. cit*; Young, Peter, *op. cit.*

57. Gilbert, Martin, *op. cit.*

58. Holm, Michael, *op. cit*; Prien, Jochen, *Pik-As: Geschichte des Jagdgeschwaders 53, Teil 3* (Eutin: Struve-Druck, 1991).

59. Morgan, Hugh and Seibel, Jürgen, *Combat Kill: The drama of aerial warfare in World War 2 and the controversy surrounding victories* (Sparkford: Patrick Stephens Ltd., 1997).

60. *ibid.*

61. Tillman, Barrett, *op. cit.*

62. Holm, Michael, *op. cit.*

63. Wood, Tony, *op. cit*; Gilbert, Martin, *op. cit.*

64. Martin, H.J. and Orpen, Neil, *Eagles Victorious; South African Forces World War II (Volume 6): The SAAF in Italy and the Mediterranean, 1943/45* (Cape Town: Purnell and Sons, 1977).

65. Newby, Leroy W., *Into the guns of Ploesti* (Osceola: Motorbooks International, 1991); Ring, Hans, *op. cit.*

66. Neulen, Hans Werner, *In the skies of Europe: air forces allied to the Luftwaffe 1939–1945* (Ramsbury: The Crowood Press, 2005).

67. Eriksson, Patrick G., 2017, *op. cit.*

68. Holm, Michael, *op. cit.*

69. Holm, Michael, *op. cit*; Caldwell, Donald, *Day Fighters in Defence of the Reich; a War Diary, 1942–45* (Barnsley: Frontline Books, 2011).

70. Murray, Williamson, *Luftwaffe* (London: Grafton Books, 1988).

71. Murray, Williamson, *op. cit*; Prien, Jochen and Rodeike, Peter, *Jagdgeschwader 1 und 11. Einsatz in der Reichsverteidigung von 1939 bis 1945, Teil 2, 1944* (Eutin: Struve Druck, undated).

72. Montgomery, Field Marshal The Viscount, *Montgomery of Alamein, Volume II, Normandy to the Baltic – Invasion* (London: Corgi Books, 1974); Montgomery, Field Marshal The Viscount, *Montgomery of Alamein, Volume III, Normandy to the Baltic – Victory* (London: Corgi Books, 1974).

73. Caldwell, Donald, *op. cit.*

74. *ibid.*

75. Dahl, Walther, *Rammjäger – das letzte Aufgebot* (Offenbach am Main: Orion-Heimreiter-Verlag, 1973).

76. deZeng, Henry L. IV and Stankey, Douglas G., *Luftwaffe Officer Career Summaries* (2014 updated version). Accessed via Michael Holm's website, The Luftwaffe 1933–1945: www.ww2.dk; this source at www.ww2.dk/lwoffz.html

77. Girbig, Werner, *Start im Morgengrauen* (Stuttgart: Motorbuch Verlag, 1973).

78. Caldwell, Donald, *op. cit.*

79. Eriksson, Patrick G., 2017, *op. cit*; Eriksson, Patrick G., 2018, *op. cit.*

80. Holm, Michael, *op. cit.*

81. Obermaier, Ernst, *Die Ritterkreuzträger der Luftwaffe* (Mainz: Verlag Dieter Hoffmann, 1966).

82. Holm, Michael, *op. cit.*

83. Eriksson, Patrick G., 2018, *op. cit.*

84. Neitzel, Sönke and Welzer, Harald, *Soldaten: on fighting, killing and dying* (London: Simon and Schuster, 2012).

85. Eriksson, Patrick G., 2017, *op. cit*; Eriksson, Patrick G., 2018, *op. cit.*

1 The Balkan Campaign, April–May 1941

1. Bekker, Cajus, *Angriffshöhe 4000. Die deutsche Luftwaffe im Zweiten Weltkrieg* (Munich: Wilhelm Heyne Verlag, 1967).
2. Prien, Jochen, *Geschichte des Jagdgeschwaders 77, Teil 1, 1934–1941* (Eutin: Struve-Druck, 1992).
3. Prien, Jochen, *op. cit*; Bekker, Cajus, *op. cit.*
4. Wood, Tony and Gunston, Bill, *Hitler's Luftwaffe: A pictorial and technical encyclopedia of Hitler's air power in World War II* (London: Salamander Books, 1977).
5. Wood, Tony, *op. cit*; Prien, Jochen, *op. cit.*
6. Dierich, Wolfgang, *Kampfgeschwader 51 "Edelweiss"* (Stuttgart: Motorbuch Verlag, 1974); Shores, Christopher, Cull, Brian and Malizia, Nicola, *Air war for Yugoslavia, Greece and Crete 1940–41* (London: Grub Street, 1987).
7. Prien, Jochen, *op. cit*; Dierich, Wolfgang, *Die Verbände der Luftwaffe 1935–1945* (Stuttgart: Motorbuch Verlag, 1976); Shores, Christopher, *op. cit.*
8. Dierich, Wolfgang, 1974, *op. cit*; Gilbert, Martin, *Second World War* (London: Weidenfeld and Nicolson, 1989).
9. Prien, Jochen, *op. cit.*
10. en.wikipedia.org/wiki/History_of_the_Hellenic_Air_Force
11. Richards, Denis, *The Royal Air Force 1939–1945, volume 1: The Fight at Odds* (London: HMSO, 1953); Prien, Jochen, *op. cit.*
12. Richards, Denis, *op. cit.*
13. en.wikipedia.org/wiki/Royal_Yugoslav_Air_Force
14. www.aeroflight.co.uk/waf/yugo_af1_hist_orbat41.htm
15. Note 13, *op. cit.*
16. Shores, Christopher, *op. cit.*
17. *ibid.*
18. *ibid.*
19. Shores, Christopher, *op. cit*; Möbius, Ingo, *Am Himmel Europas: Der Jagdflieger Günther Scholz erinnert sich* (Chemnitz: Eigenverlag Ingo Möbius, 2009).
20. Shores, Christopher, *op. cit.*
21. Möbius, Ingo, *op. cit.*
22. Shores, Christopher, *op. cit.*
23. Trautloft, Hannes, *Grünherzjäger im Luftkampf 1940–1945: Die Geschichte des Jagdgeschwaders 54; Kriegs-Tagebuch von Hannes Trautloft (edited by Bob, Hans Ekkehard)* (Zweibrücken: VDM Heinz Nickel, 2006).
24. *ibid.*
25. *ibid.*

26. Gilbert, Martin, *op. cit.*
27. Shores, Christopher, *op. cit.*
28. Note 14, *op. cit.*
29. Möbius, Ingo, *op. cit.*
30. Shores, Christopher, *op. cit.*
31. *ibid.*
32. *ibid.*
33. Prien, Jochen, *op. cit.*
34. *ibid.*
35. Prien, Jochen, *op. cit*; Shores, Christopher, *op. cit*; Wood, Tony, *Tony Wood's Combat Claims and Casualties Lists*. Accessed via Don Caldwell's website: don-caldwell.we.bs/claims/tonywood.htm (Data for confirmed victory claims from the lists first published on the web by Tony Wood, with many succeeding repeats and relatively minor edits by fellow historians). These claims lists are not complete and contain gaps, some large also, especially for certain Me 110 units in 1940; however, they do reflect accredited victory claims and not just submitted and unverified claims; Prien, Jochen, *Geschichte des Jagdgeschwaders 77, Teil 4, 1944–1945* (Eutin: Struve-Druck, undated).
36. Note 14, *op. cit.*
37. en.wikipedia.org/wiki/Invasion_of_Yugoslavia
38. Full electronic copy of the *Luftwaffe* Quartermaster General Loss Returns (which is a very large document) kindly provided by Nigel Parker, from original obtained from the Imperial War Museum, London.
39. Ring, Hans and Girbig, Werner, *Jagdgeschwader 27, Die Dokumentation über den Einsatz an allen Fronten 1939-1945* (Stuttgart: Motorbuch Verlag, 1975).
40. Note 38, *op. cit*; Ring, Hans, *op. cit.*
41. Baker, E.C.R., *Ace of aces M St J Pattle* (Rivonia: Ashanti Publishing, 1992).
42. Ring, Hans, *op. cit.*
43. Shores, Christopher, *op. cit.*
44. Note 38, *op. cit*; Prien, Jochen, 1992, *op. cit.*
45. Note 38, *op. cit.*
46. The Kracker Luftwaffe Archive: Axis Powers, on the Aircrew Remembered website: www.aircrewremembered.com
47. Ring, Hans, *op. cit.*
48. Prien, Jochen, 1992, *op. cit*; Holm, Michael, *The Luftwaffe, 1933-1945*; www.ww2.dk
49. Holm, Michael, *op. cit.*
50. Shores, Christopher, *op. cit*; Ring, Hans, *op. cit.*

51. Shores, Christopher, *op. cit.*
52. Prien, Jochen, 1992, *op. cit*; Baker, E.C.R., *op. cit.*
53. Baker, E.C.R., *op. cit.*
54. *ibid.*
55. Prien, Jochen, 1992, *op. cit*; Shores, Christopher, *op. cit.*
56. Prien, Jochen, 1992, *op. cit.*
57. Baker, E.C.R., *op. cit.*
58. Prien, Jochen, 1992, *op. cit.*
59. Baker, E.C.R., *op. cit.*
60. *ibid.*
61. Håkans Aviation Page, Biplane fighter aces from the Second World War; surfcity.kund.delnet.se
62. Shores, Christopher, *op. cit*; Baker, E.C.R., *op. cit.*
63. Shores, Christopher, *op. cit*; Wood, Tony, Combat Claims, *op. cit.*
64. Shores, Christopher, *op. cit.*
65. Note 38, *op. cit.*
66. Prien, Jochen, 1992, *op. cit.*
67. *ibid.*
68. *ibid.*
69. *ibid.*
70. Wood, Tony, 1977, *op. cit*; Dierich, Wolfgang, 1974, *op. cit*; Dierich, Wolfgang, 1976, *op. cit.*
71. Pissin, D.W., *The Battle of Crete* (Maxwell Air Force Base, Alabama: USAF Historical Division, Research Studies Institute, Air University, 1956). USAF Historical Studies No. 162 (229 pp.). Accessed via webpage of the Air Force Historical Research Agency: www.afhra.af.mil/studies/numberedusafhistori calstudies151-200.asp
72. Pissin, D.W., *op. cit*; Prien, Jochen, 1992, *op. cit.*
73. Pissin, D.W., *op. cit.*
74. *ibid.*
75. *ibid.*
76. *ibid.*
77. *ibid.*
78. *ibid.*
79. Dillon, John, website, Battle of Crete: www.my-crete-site.co.uk/raf.htm
80. *ibid.*
81. *ibid.*
82. *ibid.*
83. *ibid.*
84. *ibid.*
85. *ibid.*

86. *ibid.*
87. Prien, Jochen, 1992, *op. cit.*
88. *ibid.*
89. *ibid.*
90. *ibid.*
91. Pissin, D.W., *op. cit.*
92. *ibid.*
93. *ibid.*
94. Prien, Jochen, 1992, *op. cit.*
95. Pissin, D.W., *op. cit.*
96. Prien, Jochen, 1992, *op. cit.*
97. Shores, Christopher, Massimello, Giovanni and Guest, Russell, *A History of the Mediterranean Air War 1940–1945; Volume One: North Africa June 1940–January 1942* (London: Grub Street, 2012).
98. *ibid.*
99. Barbas, Bernd, *Die Geschichte der III. Gruppe des Jagdgeschwaders 52* (Überlingen: self-published, undated).
100. Pissin, D.W., *op. cit.*
101. Young, Peter (ed.), *The World Almanac Book of World War II* (New York: World Almanac Publications, 1981).
102. Murray, Williamson, *Luftwaffe* (London: Grafton Books, 1988); Pissin, D.W., *op. cit.*
103. Woods, Tony, Combat Claims, *op. cit*; Prien, Jochen, 1992, *op. cit.*
104. Pissin, D.W., *op. cit.*
105. Shores, Christopher, *Dust clouds in the Middle East* (London: Grub Street, 2010).
106. *ibid.*
107. *ibid.*

2 Western Desert, February 1941–January 1943

1. Shores, Christopher, Massimello, Giovanni and Guest, Russell, *A History of the Mediterranean Air War 1940–1945; Volume One: North Africa June 1940–January 1942* (London: Grub Street, 2012); Shores, Christopher and Ring, Hans, *Fighters over the Desert* (London: Neville Spearman, 1969).
2. Shores, Christopher, 1969, *op. cit.*
3. Ring, Hans and Girbig, Werner, *Jagdgeschwader 27, Die Dokumentation über den Einsatz an allen Fronten 1939–1945* (Stuttgart: Motorbuch Verlag, 1975).
4. Shores, Christopher, 2012, *op. cit*; Shores, Christopher, 1969, *op. cit*; Ring, Hans, *op. cit*; Holm, Michael, *The Luftwaffe, 1933–1945*; www.ww2.dk
5. Holm, Michael, *op. cit.*

6. Shores, Christopher, 1969, *op. cit.*

7. *ibid.*

8. Caldwell, Donald, *JG 26 Luftwaffe Fighter Wing Diary, Volume 1: 1939–1942* (Mechanicsburg: Stackpole Books, 2012).

9. Shores, Christopher, 1969, *op. cit*; Ring, Hans, *op. cit.*

10. Ring, Hans, *op. cit.*

11. Shores, Christopher, 1969, *op. cit.*

12. Caldwell, Donald, *op. cit.*

13. Shores, Christopher, 2012, *op. cit.*

14. Galland, Adolf, *The First and the Last* (London: Fontana/Collins Books, 1970). The quote on Marseille being the 'unrivalled virtuoso' amongst all *Luftwaffe* pilots is on page 122 of this edition of the book.

15. Ring, Hans, *op. cit.*

16. Shores, Christopher, 2012, *op. cit*; Shores, Christopher, 1969, *op. cit*; Ring, Hans, *op. cit.*

17. Shores, Christopher, 1969, *op. cit.*

18. Shores, Christopher, 2012, *op. cit.*

19. *ibid.*

20. *ibid.*

21. *ibid.*

22. *ibid.*

23. *ibid.*

24. Ring, Hans, *op. cit.*

25. Shores, Christopher, 2012, *op. cit.*

26. Ring, Hans, *op. cit.*

27. Shores, Christopher, 1969, *op. cit.*

28. Heaton, Colin D. and Lewis, Anne-Marie, *The Star of Africa: The story of Hans Marseille, the rogue Luftwaffe ace who dominated the WW II skies* (Minneapolis: Zenith Press, 2012).

29. *ibid.*

30. Wikipedia; specifically on Hans-Joachim Marseille: https://en.wikipedia. org/wiki/Hans-Joachim_Marseille; Metapedia; specifically on General Siegfried Marseille, father of Hans-Joachim Marseille: de.metapedia. org/wiki/Marseille_Siegfried; *Lexikon der Wehrmacht, Gliederungen, Kommandantur OK 1324,* www.lexikon-der-wehrmacht.de/Gliederungen/ Kommandantur/OKI324-R.htm

31. Wikipedia; specifically on Marseille's step father, Carl Reuter: https:// de.wikipedia.org/wiki/Carl_Reuter

32. Wikipedia, Hans-Joachim Marseille, *op. cit.*

33. *ibid.*

34. *ibid.*

35. Prien, Jochen, *Geschichte des Jagdgeschwaders 77, Teil 1, 1934–1941* (Eutin: Struve-Druck, 1992).

36. Wikipedia, Hans-Joachim Marseille, *op. cit*; Prien, Jochen, *op. cit.*

37. *ibid.*

38. *ibid.*

39. Prien, Jochen, *op. cit.*

40. *ibid.*

41. *ibid.*

42. Wikipedia, Hans-Joachim Marseille, *op. cit.*

43. Heaton, Colin, *Interview with World War II Luftwaffe eagle Johannes Steinhoff*; text of a post-war interview of General Johannes Steinhoff, initially published in World War II Magazine (February 2000 issue; WorldWarII. com of the Weider History Group). This text is widely available on the web.

44. www.jg52.net (website of the *Traditionsgemeinschaft Jagdgeschwader 52*)

45. www.jg52.net, *op. cit*; Barbas, Bernd, *Die Geschichte der II. Gruppe des Jagdgeschwaders 52* (Überlingen: self-published, undated).

46. Barbas, Bernd, *op. cit.*

47. www.jg52.net, *op. cit.*

48. *ibid.*

49. *ibid.*

50. Gardner, E.R., *Military justice in the German Air Force during World War II.* Journal of Criminal Law, Criminology, and Police Science, volume 49/3, 1958, pp. 195–217.

51. *ibid.*

52. www.jg52.net, *op. cit.*

53. Barbas, Bernd, *Die Geschichte der III. Gruppe des Jagdgeschwaders 52* (Überlingen: self-published, undated).

54. A copy of the relevant RAF intelligence report (K report) on this *III/JG 52* pilot was provided to the author by well known aviation historian and author Nigel Parker (noted for his multiple volume set of *Luftwaffe Crash Archive* books published by Red Kite Books, Air Research Publications).

55. Barbas, Bernd, *II/JG 52, op. cit.*

56. *ibid.*

57. Prien, Jochen, *op. cit.*

58. Barbas, Bernd, *II/JG 52, op. cit.*

59. Wikipedia, Hans-Joachim Marseille, *op. cit.*

60. Shores, Christopher, 2012, *op. cit*; Shores, Christopher, 1969, *op. cit*; Ring, Hans, *op. cit*; Wikipedia, Hans-Joachim Marseille, *op. cit.*

61. Ring, Hans, *op. cit.*

62. Shores, Christopher, 2012, *op. cit.*

63. Shores, Christopher, 2012, *op. cit*; Ring, Hans, *op. cit.*

64. Wikipedia, Hans-Joachim Marseille, *op. cit.*

65. Shores, Christopher, 2012, *op. cit*; Ring, Hans, *op. cit*; Wikipedia, Hans-Joachim Marseille, *op. cit.*

66. *ibid.*

67. Shores, Christopher, 2012, *op. cit.*

68. Wikipedia, Hans-Joachim Marseille, *op. cit*; Nowarra, Heinz J., *The Messerschmitt 109 – A famous German fighter* (Letchworth: Harleyford Publications Ltd., 1966).

69. Wikipedia, Hans-Joachim Marseille, *op. cit.*

70. Shores, Christopher, 2012, *op. cit*; Ring, Hans, *op. cit.*

71. Wikipedia, Hans-Joachim Marseille, *op. cit.*

72. Shores, Christopher, Massimello, Giovanni and Guest, Russell, *A History of the Mediterranean Air War 1940–1945; Volume Two: North African Desert February 1942 to March 1943* (London: Grub Street, 2012).

73. Wikipedia, Hans-Joachim Marseille, *op. cit.*

74. Shores, Christopher, 2012, vol. 2, *op. cit.*

75. Ring, Hans, *op. cit*; Wikipedia, Hans-Joachim Marseille, *op. cit.*

76. Ring, Hans, *op. cit.*

77. Heaton, Colin D., 2012, *op. cit.*

78. Shores, Christopher, 2012, vol. 2, *op. cit.*

79. Ring, Hans, *op. cit*; Wikipedia, Hans-Joachim Marseille, *op. cit.*

80. Ring, Hans, *op. cit*; Shores, Christopher, 2012, vol. 2, *op. cit.*

81. Ring, Hans, *op. cit*; Wikipedia, Hans-Joachim Marseille, *op. cit*; Shores, Christopher, 2012, vol. 2, *op. cit.*

82. Ring, Hans, *op. cit.*

83. Wikipedia, Hans-Joachim Marseille, *op. cit.*

84. Ring, Hans, *op. cit*; Holm, Michael, *op. cit.*

85. Obermaier, Ernst, *Die Ritterkreuzträger der Luftwaffe* (Mainz: Verlag Dieter Hoffmann, 1966).

86. *ibid.*

87. Shores, Christopher, 1969, *op. cit.*

88. *ibid.*

89. Shores, Christopher, 2012, vol. 2, *op. cit.*

90. Skawran, Paul Robert, *Ikaros; Persönlichkeit und Wesen des deutschen Jagdfliegers im Zweitem Weltkrieg* (Steinbach am Wörthsee: Luftfahrt-Verlag Walter Zuerl, 1969).

91. *ibid.*

92. *ibid.*

93. Ring, Hans, *op. cit*; Wikipedia, Hans-Joachim Marseille, *op. cit*; Skawran, Paul, *op. cit.*
94. Skawran, Paul, *op. cit.*
95. *ibid.*
96. Nowarra, Heinz, *op. cit.*
97. Skawran, Paul, *op. cit.*
98. Galland, Adolf, *op. cit.*
99. Shores, Christopher, 2012, vol. 1, *op. cit.*
100. Holm, Michael, *op. cit.*
101. Copy of *Kriegstagebuch I/JG 77* (25 October 1942–19 August 1943), made in the field by Professor Paul Robert Skawran in Italy in about August 1943. Copy of this provided to author by Professor Skawran.
102. *ibid.*

3 Malta, January 1941–October 1942

1. Shores, Christopher and Cull, Brian with Malizia, Nicola, *Malta: the Hurricane years 1940–41* (London: Grub Street, 1987); Shores, Christopher and Cull, Brian with Malizia, Nicola, *Malta: the Spitfire year 1942* (London: Grub Street, 1991).
2. Greene, Jack and Massignani, Alessandro, *The Naval War in the Mediterranean 1940–1943* (London: Frontline Books, 2011).
3. *ibid.*
4. Shores, Christopher, 1987, *op. cit*; Shores, Christopher, 1991, *op. cit.*
5. Shores, Christopher, 1987, *op. cit.*
6. Moulson, Tom, *The Flying Sword: The story of 601 Squadron* (London: Macdonald, 1964); Malta: War Diaries; https://maltagc70. wordpress.com
7. Shores, Christopher, 1991, *op. cit.*
8. Shores, Christopher, 1987, *op. cit*; Shores, Christopher, 1991, *op. cit.*
9. Shores, Christopher, 1987, *op. cit*; Shores, Christopher, 1991, *op. cit*; Bekker, Cajus, *Angriffshöhe 4000. Die deutsche Luftwaffe im Zweiten Weltkrieg* (Munich: Wilhelm Heyne Verlag, 1967).
10. Holm, Michael, *The Luftwaffe, 1933–1945*; www.ww2.dk; Shores, Christopher, 1987, *op. cit*; Shores, Christopher, 1991, *op. cit.*
11. Green, Jack, *op. cit*; Caldwell, Donald, *JG 26 Luftwaffe Fighter Wing Diary, Volume 1: 1939–1942* (Mechanicsburg: Stackpole Books, 2012).
12. Greene, Jack, *op. cit.*
13. *ibid.*
14. Caldwell, Donald, *op. cit.*
15. Holm, Michael, *op. cit*; Caldwell, Donald, *op. cit.*

16. Shores, Christopher, 1987, *op. cit*; Caldwell, Donald, *op. cit*; Wood, Tony, *Tony Wood's Combat Claims and Casualties Lists*; accessed via Don Caldwell's website: don-caldwell.we.bs/claims/tonywood.htm (data for confirmed victory claims from the lists first published on the web by Tony Wood, with many succeeding repeats and relatively minor edits by fellow historians). These claims lists are not complete and contain gaps, some large also, especially for certain Me 110 units in 1940; however, they do reflect accredited victory claims and not just submitted and unverified claims. The probable victories noted in the text were annotated with *ASM* (*Anerkennung später möglich* – recognition possible later) or *VNE.ASM* (*Vernichtung nicht erwiesen* – destruction not proven – *ASM*) in Tony Wood's *Luftwaffe* claims lists.

17. Shores, Christopher, 1987, *op. cit*; Caldwell, Donald, *op. cit*; Wood, Tony, *op. cit.*

18. Caldwell, Donald, *op. cit*; Wood, Tony, *op. cit.*

19. *ibid.*

20. Shores, Christopher, 1987, *op. cit.*

21. *ibid.*

22. *ibid.*

23. *ibid.*

24. Holm, Michael, *op. cit.*

25. Wood, Tony, *op. cit.*

26. Shores, Christopher, 1987, *op. cit.*

27. Shores, Christopher, 1987, *op. cit*; Greene, Jack, *op. cit*; Wood, Tony, *op. cit.*

28. Holm, Michael, *op. cit.*

29. Wood, Tony, *op. cit.*

30. Shores, Christopher, 1987, *op. cit.*

31. Caldwell, Donald, *op. cit*; Wood, Tony, *op. cit.*

32. Shores, Christopher, 1991, *op. cit.*

33. Holm, Michael, *op. cit.*

34. Prien, Jochen, *Pik-As: Geschichte des Jagdgeschwaders 53, Teil 1* (Illertissen: Flugzeug Publikations, 1989).

35. Holm, Michael, *op. cit*; Prien, Jochen and Stemmer, Gerhard, *Messerschmitt Bf 109 im Einsatz bei der II./Jagdgeschwader 3, 1940–1945* (Eutin: Struve-Druck, 1996).

36. Holm, Michael, *op. cit*; Prien, Jochen, 1989, *op. cit*; Prien, Jochen, *Pik-As: Geschichte des Jagdgeschwaders 53, Teil 2* (Eutin: Struve-Druck, 1990).

37. Shores, Christopher, 1991, *op. cit.*

38. *ibid.*

39. *ibid.*

40. *ibid.*

41. Prien, Jochen, 1989, *op. cit.*

42. Shores, Christopher, 1991, *op. cit.*

43. Shores, Christopher, 1991, *op. cit*; Prien, Jochen, 1989, *op. cit.*

44. Shores, Christopher, 1991, *op. cit*; Prien, Jochen, 1989, *op. cit*; Wood, Tony, *op. cit.*

45. Shores, Christopher, 1991, *op. cit.*

46. *ibid.*

47. *ibid.*

48. Prien, Jochen, *Pik-As: Geschichte des Jagdgeschwaders 53, Teil 3* (Eutin: Struve-Druck, 1991).

49. *ibid.*

50. Shores, Christopher, 1991, *op. cit.*

51. Prien, Jochen, 1991, *op. cit.*

52. Prien, Jochen, 1989, *op. cit.*

53. Shores, Christopher, 1991, *op. cit*; Prien, Jochen, 1989, *op. cit*; Prien, Jochen, 1991, *op. cit.* Discussion on the aerial combat resulting in Hermann Neuhoff being shot down is given at: https://juhansotahistoriasivut.weebly.com; concurrently it also offers an example of how multiple claims on a single loss, made in all sincerity, can lead to over-claiming.

54. Prien, Jochen, 1996, *op. cit.*

55. Buzzati, Dino, *The shipwrecked airman, a German soldier, Marine combat outpost X, June 1942* (Milan: *Corriere della Sera* newspaper, 1942). Newspaper first published in 1876, it is still going strong (*https://en.wikipedia.org/wiki/Corriere_della_Sera*).

56. Holm, Michael, *op. cit*; Prien, Jochen, 1989, *op. cit*; Prien, Jochen, 1990, *op. cit.*

57. Holm, Michael, *op. cit.*

58. Prien, Jochen, 1991, *op. cit.*

59. Holm, Michael, *op. cit.*

60. Prien, Jochen, 1990, *op. cit*; Prien, Jochen, 1991, *op. cit.*

61. *ibid.*

62. *ibid.*

63. Prien, Jochen, *Geschichte des Jagdgeschwaders 77, Teil 3, 1942–1943* (Eutin: Struve-Druck, undated).

64. *ibid.*

65. Holm, Michael, *op. cit*; Shores, Christopher, 1991, *op. cit.*

66. Holm, Michael, *op. cit.*

67. Shores, Christopher, 1991, *op. cit.*

68. *ibid.*
69. Prien, Jochen, 1990, *op. cit*; Prien, Jochen, 1991, *op. cit.*
70. Prien, Jochen, 1990, *op. cit.*
71. Prien, Jochen, 1990, *op. cit*; Prien, Jochen, 1991, *op. cit.*
72. Prien, Jochen, undated, *op. cit.*
73. Shores, Christopher, 1991, *op. cit*; Holm, Michael, *op. cit*; Ring, Hans and Girbig, Werner, *Jagdgeschwader 27, Die Dokumentation über den Einsatz an allen Fronten 1939–1945* (Stuttgart: Motorbuch Verlag, 1975).
74. Shores, Christopher, 1991, *op. cit*; Prien, Jochen, 1990, *op. cit*; Prien, Jochen, 1991, *op. cit*; Prien, Jochen, undated, *op. cit.*
75. Shores, Christopher, 1991, *op. cit.*
76. *ibid.*
77. Holm, Michael, *op. cit.*
78. *ibid.*

4 Tunisia: The End in Africa, November 1942–May 1943

1. Calvocoressi, Peter and Wint, Guy, *Total War: causes and courses of the Second World War* (Aylesbury: Pelican Books, 1974).
2. Montgomery, Field Marshal The Viscount, *Montgomery of Alamein, Volume I, El Alamein to the River Sangro* (London: Corgi Books, 1974); Gilbert, Martin, *Second World War* (London: Weidenfeld and Nicolson, 1989).
3. Gilbert, Martin, *op. cit.*
4. *ibid.*
5. *ibid.*
6. Montgomery, Field Marshal, *op. cit*; Gilbert, Martin, *op. cit.*
7. Montgomery, Field Marshal, *op. cit.*
8. Montgomery, Field Marshal, *op. cit*; Gilbert, Martin, *op. cit.*
9. Montgomery, Field Marshal, *op. cit.*
10. *ibid.*
11. *ibid.*
12. *ibid.*
13. Montgomery, Field Marshal, *op. cit*; Gilbert, Martin, *op. cit.*
14. Holm, Michael, *The Luftwaffe, 1933–1945*, www.ww2.dk; Dierich, Wolfgang, *Die Verbände der Luftwaffe 1935–1945* (Stuttgart: Motorbuch Verlag, 1976); Shores, Christopher, Ring, Hans and Hess, William N., *Fighters over Tunisia* (London: Neville Spearman, 1975).
15. Holm, Michael, *op. cit*; Prien, Jochen, *Pik-As: Geschichte des Jagdgeschwaders 53, Teil 2* (Eutin: Struve-Druck, 1990).
16. Holm, Michael, *op. cit.*

17. Gilbert, Martin, *op. cit*; Shores, Christopher, Massimello, Giovanni with Guest, Russell, Olynyk, Frank and Bock, Winfried, *A History of the Mediterranean Air War 1940–1945; Volume Three: Tunisia and the end in Africa November 1942 to May 1943* (London: Grub Street, 2016); Holm, Michael, *op. cit.*

18. Prien, Jochen, *Geschichte des Jagdgeschwaders 77, Teil 3, 1942–1943* (Eutin: Struve-Druck, undated).

19. *ibid.*

20. *ibid.*

21. *ibid.*

22. *ibid.*

23. *ibid.*

24. *ibid.*

25. Prien, Jochen, *JG 77, Teil 3, op. cit*; Prien, Jochen, *Geschichte des Jagdgeschwaders 77, Teil 4, 1944–1945* (Eutin: Struve-Druck, undated).

26. Prien, Jochen, *JG 77, Teil 3, op. cit*; Holm, Michael, *op. cit.*

27. *ibid.*

28. Holm, Michael, *op. cit.*

29. Prien, Jochen, *JG 77, Teil 3, op. cit*; Holm, Michael, *op. cit*; Shores, Christopher, 1975, *op. cit*; Prien, Jochen, 1990, *op. cit.*

30. *ibid*

31. Copy of *Kriegstagebuch I/JG 77* (25 October 1942–19 August 1943), made in the field by Professor Paul R. Skawran in Italy in about August 1943. Copy of this provided to author by Professor Skawran.

32. Holm, Michael, *op. cit*; Prien, Jochen, 1990, *op. cit.*

33. Holm, Michael, *op. cit.*

34. Prien, Jochen, 1990, *op. cit*; Prien, Jochen, *Pik-As: Geschichte des Jagdgeschwaders 53, Teil 3* (Eutin: Struve-Druck, 1991).

35. Kornstädt, Hans-Ulrich, *Als Jagdflieger beim JG 27 über dem Mittelmeer: Vom englischen Zerstörer gerettet – vier Jahre Kriegsgefangenschaft im Algerien; ein Erlebnisbericht* (Munich: self-published, 1988). Self-published for friends and family.

36. *ibid.*

37. *ibid.*

38. *ibid.*

39. Shores, Christopher, 1975, *op. cit.*

40. Kornstädt, Hans-Ulrich, *op. cit.*

41. *ibid.*

42. Shores, Christopher, 1975, *op. cit.*

43. Prien, Jochen, 1990, *op. cit.*

44. Prien, Jochen, *JG 77, Teil 3, op. cit*; Prien, Jochen, *JG 77, Teil 4, op. cit.*
45. Prien, Jochen, *JG 77, Teil 3, op. cit.*
46. Aders, Gebhard and Held, Werner, *Jagdgeschwader 51 'Mölders'* (Stuttgart: Motorbuch Verlag, 1985).
47. Shores, Christopher, 1975, *op. cit.*
48. *ibid.*
49. Wikipedia; specifically on the Tunisian campaign: https://en.wikipedia.org/wiki/Tunisia_Campaign
50. Prien, Jochen, *JG 77, Teil 4, op. cit*; Shores, Christopher, 1975, *op. cit.*
51. Obermaier, Ernst, *Die Ritterkreuzträger der Luftwaffe* (Mainz: Verlag Dieter Hoffmann, 1966).

5 Sicily and Italy, May 1943–September 1944

1. Prien, Jochen, *Geschichte des Jagdgeschwaders 77, Teil 3, 1942–1943* (Eutin: Struve-Druck, undated); Prien, Jochen, *Pik-As: Geschichte des Jagdgeschwaders 53, Teil 2* (Eutin: Struve-Druck, 1990); Holm, Michael, *The Luftwaffe, 1933–1945*; www.ww2.dk.
2. Prien, Jochen, undated, *op. cit*; Holm, Michael, *op. cit.*
3. *ibid.*
4. Prien, Jochen, 1990, *op. cit*; Holm, Michael, *op. cit.*
5. Prien, Jochen, undated, *op. cit.*
6. Holm, Michael, *op. cit.*
7. *ibid.*
8. *ibid.*
9. *ibid.*
10. Prien, Jochen, 1990, *op. cit*; Holm, Michael, *op. cit.*
11. Prien, Jochen, undated, *op. cit*; Holm, Michael, *op. cit.*
12. Copy of *Kriegstagebuch I/JG 77* (25 October 1942–19 August 1943), made in the field by Professor Paul Robert Skawran in Italy in about August 1943. Copy of this provided to author by Professor Skawran.
13. Prien, Jochen, undated, *op. cit.*
14. Holm, Michael, *op. cit.*
15. Prien, Jochen, undated, *op. cit*; Prien, Jochen, 1990, *op. cit.*
16. Prien, Jochen, 1990, *op. cit.*
17. Prien, Jochen, 1990, *op. cit*; Prien, Jochen, *Pik-As: Geschichte des Jagdgeschwaders 53, Teil 3* (Eutin: Struve-Druck, 1991).
18. Kornstädt, Hans-Ulrich, *Als Jagdflieger beim JG 27 über dem Mittelmeer: Vom englischen Zerstörer gerettet – vier Jahre Kriegsgefangenschaft im Algerien; ein Erlebnisbericht* (Munich: self-published, 1988). Self-published for friends and family.

19. *ibid.*
20. *ibid.*
21. *ibid.*
22. *ibid.*
23. Prien, Jochen, 1990, *op. cit*; Prien, Jochen, undated, *op. cit.*
24. Prien, Jochen, undated, *op. cit.*
25. Prien, Jochen, undated, *op. cit*; Prien, Jochen, 1990, *op. cit.*
26. Prien, Jochen, undated, *op. cit*; Prien, Jochen, 1990, *op. cit*; Steinhoff, Johannes, *The straits of Messina: Diary of a fighter commander* (London: Corgi Books, 1973). Although not a fully factually accurate account (for details see Prien, Jochen, undated) it does provide a comprehensive picture of this sorry crisis.
27. Prien, Jochen, undated, *op. cit*; Prien, Jochen, 1990, *op. cit.*
28. Prien, Jochen, undated, *op. cit*; Prien, Jochen, 1990, *op. cit*; Steinhoff, Johannes, *op. cit.*
29. Prien, Jochen, 1990, *op. cit.*
30. Prien, Jochen, 1990, *op. cit*; Steinhoff, Johannes, *op. cit.*
31. Prien, Jochen, undated, *op. cit*; Prien, Jochen, 1990, *op. cit*; Steinhoff, Johannes, *op. cit.*
32. Steinhoff, Johannes, *op. cit.*
33. Prien, Jochen, undated, *op. cit.*
34. *ibid.*
35. *ibid.*
36. Holm, Michael, *op. cit.*
37. Prien, Jochen, undated, *op. cit*; Prien, Jochen, 1990, *op. cit*; Holm, Michael, *op. cit.*
38. Prien, Jochen, undated, *op. cit.*
39. *ibid.*
40. *ibid.*
41. *ibid.*
42. *ibid.*
43. Prien, Jochen, 1990, *op. cit.*
44. *ibid.*
45. *ibid.*
46. Prien, Jochen, undated, *op. cit.*
47. Prien, Jochen, undated, *op. cit*; Holm, Michael, *op. cit.*
48. Prien, Jochen, undated, *op. cit.*
49. Wood, Tony and Gunston, Bill, *Hitler's Luftwaffe: A pictorial and technical encyclopedia of Hitler's air power in World War II* (London: Salamander Books, 1977).

50. Holm, Michael, *op. cit.*
51. *Kriegstagebuch I/JG 77, op. cit.*
52. Holm, Michael, *op. cit.*
53. Murray, Williamson, *Luftwaffe* (London: Grafton Books, 1988).
54. *ibid.*
55. *Kriegstagebuch I/JG 77, op. cit.*
56. Murray, Williamson, *op. cit.*
57. *ibid.*
58. Prien, Jochen, undated, *op. cit.*
59. Young, Peter (Editor), *The World Almanac Book of World War II* (New York: World Almanac Publisher, 1981).
60. *ibid.*
61. *ibid.*
62. Wood, Tony, *op. cit*; Holm, Michael, *op. cit.*
63. Wood, Tony, *op. cit.*
64. *ibid.*
65. *ibid.*
66. *ibid.*
67. Young, Peter, *op. cit.*
68. *ibid.*
69. Wood, Tony, *op. cit.*
70. *ibid.*
71. Wood, Tony, *op. cit*; Young, Peter, *op. cit.*
72. Holm, Michael, *op. cit.*
73. *ibid.*
74. *ibid.*
75. *ibid.*
76. Prien, Jochen, 1990, *op. cit.*
77. *ibid.*
78. *ibid.*
79. *ibid.*
80. *ibid.*

6 South-eastern Europe and the Balkans, 1943–1944

1. Neulen, Hans Werner, *In the skies of Europe: air forces allied to the Luftwaffe 1939–1945* (Ramsbury: The Crowood Press, 2005).
2. Holm, Michael, *The Luftwaffe, 1933–1945*; www.ww2.dk
3. *ibid.*
4. *ibid.*
5. Aders, Gebhard and Held, Werner, *Jagdgeschwader 51 'Mölders'* (Stuttgart: Motorbuch Verlag, 1985).

6. Wood, Tony and Gunston, Bill, *Hitler's Luftwaffe: A pictorial and technical encyclopedia of Hitler's air power in World War II* (London: Salamander Books, 1977).

7. *ibid.*

8. Martin, H.J. and Orpen, Neil, *Eagles Victorious; South African Forces World War II (Volume 6): The SAAF in Italy and the Mediterranean, 1943/45* (Cape Town: Purnell and Sons, 1977).

9. Wood, Tony, *op. cit.*

10. *ibid.*

11. Martin, H.J., *op. cit.*

12. *ibid.*

13. *ibid.*

14. *ibid.*

15. Ring, Hans and Girbig, Werner, *Jagdgeschwader 27, Die Dokumentation über den Einsatz an allen Fronten 1939–1945* (Stuttgart: Motorbuch Verlag, 1975).

16. Martin, H.J., *op. cit.*

17. *ibid.*

18. *ibid.*

19. *ibid.*

20. *ibid.*

21. *ibid.*

22. *ibid.*

23. Ring, Hans, *op. cit.*

24. *ibid.*

25. *ibid.*

26. Neulen, Hans Werner, *op. cit.*

27. *ibid.*

28. Holm, Michael, *op. cit*; Neulen, Hans Werner, *op. cit.*

29. Holm, Michael, *op. cit.*

30. Neulen, Hans Werner, *op. cit.*

31. *ibid.*

32. *ibid.*

33. Holm, Michael, *op. cit*; Aders, Gebhard, *op. cit.*

34. Holm, Michael, *op. cit.*

35. Ring, Hans, *op. cit.*

36. *ibid.*

37. *ibid.*

38. *ibid.*

39. Holm, Michael, *op. cit*; Aders, Gebhard, *op. cit.*

40. Aders, Gebhard, *op. cit.*

41. Wikipedia; specifically on the Allied bombing of Yugoslavia: https://en.wikipedia.org/wiki/Allied_bombing_of_Yugoslavia_in_World_War_II

42. Neulen, Hans Werner, *op. cit.*

43. Holm, Michael, *op. cit.*

44. Neulen, Hans Werner, *op. cit.*

45. Eriksson, Patrick G., *Alarmstart East* (Stroud: Amberley, 2018).

46. Neulen, Hans Werner, *op. cit.*

47. Newby, Leroy W., *Into the guns of Ploesti* (Osceola: Motorbooks International, 1991).

48. Ring, Hans, *op. cit*; Neulen, Hans Werner, *op. cit.*

49. Ring, Hans, *op. cit*; Newby, Leroy W., *op. cit.*

50. Ring, Hans, *op. cit*; Neulen, Hans Werner, *op. cit*; Newby, Leroy W., *op. cit.*

51. Neulen, Hans Werner, *op. cit.*

52. Holm, Michael, *op. cit.*

53. *ibid.*

54. Holm, Michael, *op. cit*; Reschke, Willi, *Jagdgeschwader 301/302 "Wilde Sau"* (Atglen: Schiffer, 2005).

55. Prien, Jochen, *Pik-As: Geschichte des Jagdgeschwaders 53, Teil 3* (Eutin: Struve-Druck, 1991).

56. Neulen, Hans Werner, *op. cit.*

57. Neulen, Hans Werner, *op. cit*; Young, Peter (Editor), *The World Almanac Book of World War II* (New York: World Almanac Publisher, 1981); Prien, Jochen, JG 53, *op. cit*; Prien, Jochen, *Geschichte des Jagdgeschwaders 77, Teil 4, 1944–1945* (Eutin: Struve-Druck, undated).

58. Eriksson, Patrick G., *op. cit.*

7 The Normandy Invasion and Subsequent Allied Re-conquest of France

1. Eriksson, Patrick G., *Alarmstart* (Stroud: Amberley, 2017).

2. Young, Peter (Editor), *The World Almanac Book of World War II* (New York: World Almanac Publisher, 1981).

3. Terraine, John, *The Right of the Line* (Ware: Wordsworth Editions Ltd., 1997).

4. Prien, Jochen and Rodeike, Peter, *Jagdgeschwader 1 und 11. Einsatz in der Reichsverteidigung von 1939 bis 1945, Teil 2, 1944* (Eutin: Struve Druck, undated).

5. Murray, Williamson, *Luftwaffe* (London: Grafton Books, 1988).

6. *ibid.*

7. Holm, Michael, *The Luftwaffe, 1933–1945*; www.ww2.dk

8. Weal, John, *Jagdgeschwader 2 'Richthofen'* (Oxford: Osprey Publishing, 2000).

9. Young, Peter, *op. cit*; Caldwell, Donald L., *JG 26 Luftwaffe Fighter Wing Diary, 1943–1945*, Vol. 2 (Mechanicsburg: Stackpole Books, 2012).

10. Caldwell, Donald, *Day Fighters in Defence of the Reich; a War Diary, 1942–45* (Barnsley: Frontline Books, 2011); Weal, John, *op. cit*; Caldwell, Donald, 2012, *op. cit*; Holm, Michael, *op. cit.*

11. Caldwell, Donald, 2011, *op. cit.*

12. Holm, Michael, *op. cit.*

13. *ibid.*

14. Caldwell, Donald, 2012, *op. cit.*

15. Holm, Michael, *op. cit.*

16. *ibid.*

17. Holm, Michael, *op. cit*; Weal, John, *op. cit*; Caldwell, Donald, 2012, *op. cit.*

18. Reschke, Willi, *Jagdgeschwader 301/302 "Wilde Sau"* (Atglen: Schiffer, 2005).

19. Holm, Michael, *op. cit.*

20. *ibid.*

21. Holm, Michael, *op. cit*; Weal, John, *op. cit*; Caldwell, Donald, 2012, *op. cit.*

22. Holm, Michael, *op. cit.*

23. *ibid.*

24. Holm, Michael, *op. cit*; Caldwell, Donald, 2012, *op. cit.*

25. Caldwell, Donald, 2012, *op. cit*; Obermaier, Ernst, *Die Ritterkreuzträger der Luftwaffe* (Mainz: Verlag Dieter Hoffmann, 1966).

26. Caldwell, Donald, 2012, *op. cit*; Obermaier, Ernst, *op. cit*; Priller, Josef, *J.G. 26: Geschichte eines Jagdgeschwaders* (Stuttgart: Motorbuch Verlag, 1980); Wood, Tony, *Tony Wood's Combat Claims and Casualties Lists*; accessed via Don Caldwell's website: don-caldwell.we.bs/claims/tonywood. htm (data for confirmed victory claims from the lists first published on the web by Tony Wood, with many succeeding repeats and relatively minor edits by fellow historians). These claims lists are not complete and contain gaps, some large also, especially for certain Me 110 units in 1940; however, they do reflect accredited victory claims and not just submitted and unverified claims.

27. Montgomery, Field Marshal The Viscount, *Montgomery of Alamein, Volume II, Normandy to the Baltic – Invasion* (London: Corgi Books, 1974).

28. Montgomery, Field Marshal, *op. cit*; Young, Peter, *op. cit.*
29. *ibid.*
30. Montgomery, Field Marshal, *op. cit.*
31. Holm, Michael, *op. cit.*
32. Prien, Jochen, *op. cit.*
33. Murray, Williamson, *op. cit.*
34. Eriksson, Patrick G., *Alarmstart East* (Stroud: Amberley, 2018).
35. Prien, Jochen, *op. cit.*
36. *ibid.*
37. *ibid.*
38. *ibid.*
39. Prien, Jochen, *op. cit*; Holm, Michael, *op. cit.*
40. Prien, Jochen, *op. cit.*
41. *ibid.*
42. *ibid.*
43. *ibid.*
44. *ibid.*
45. Holm, Michael, *op. cit*; Prien, Jochen and Stemmer, Gerhard, *Messerschmitt Bf 109 im Einsatz bei der II./Jagdgeschwader 3, 1940–1945* (Eutin: Struve-Druck, 1996).
46. Prien, Jochen, 1996, *op. cit.*
47. Holm, Michael, *op. cit.*
48. Prien, Jochen, 1996, *op. cit.*
49. *ibid.*
50. *ibid.*
51. *ibid.*
52. *ibid.*
53. *ibid.*
54. Holm, Michael, *op. cit.*
55. Prien, Jochen, undated, *op. cit.*
56. *ibid.*
57. Caldwell, Donald, 2012, *op. cit*; Prien, Jochen, undated, *op. cit*; Prien, Jochen, 1996, *op. cit*; Wood, Tony, *op. cit*; Prien, Jochen and Stemmer, Gerhard, *Messerschmitt Bf 109 im Einsatz bei Stab und I./Jagdgeschwader 3* (Eutin: Struve-Druck, 1997); Prien, Jochen and Stemmer, Gerhard, *Messerschmitt Bf 109 im Einsatz bei der III./Jagdgeschwader 3* (Eutin: Struve-Druck, 1995); Prien, Jochen, *Pik-As: Geschichte des Jagdgeschwaders 53, Teil 3* (Eutin: Struve-Druck, 1991); Acred, Matthew Laird (website editor), *Jagdgeschwader 5 Abschussliste*; www.asisbiz.com/Luftwaffe.html

58. Holm, Michael, *op. cit.*

59. Wood, Tony, *op. cit.*

60. Weal, John, *op. cit.*

61. Prien, Jochen, undated, *op. cit*; Weal, John, *op. cit*; Wood, Tony, *op. cit*; Prien, Jochen, 1996, *op. cit*; Reschke, Willi, *op. cit*; Prien, Jochen, 1997, *op. cit*; Prien, Jochen, 1995, *op. cit*; Prien, Jochen, 1991, *op. cit*; Caldwell, Donald, 2012, *op. cit*; Acred, Matthew Laird, *op. cit.*

8 Battle over Germany: The Last Twelve Months, June 1944–May 1945

1. Holm, Michael, *The Luftwaffe, 1933–1945*; www.ww2.dk; Caldwell, Donald, *Day Fighters in Defence of the Reich; a War Diary, 1942–45* (Barnsley: Frontline Books, 2011).

2. *ibid.*

3. Caldwell, Donald, *op. cit.*

4. Holm, Michael, *op. cit*; Caldwell, Donald, *op. cit.*

5. Holm, Michael, *op. cit.*

6. *ibid.*

7. Caldwell, Donald, *op. cit.*

8. *ibid.*

9. *ibid.*

10. *ibid.*

11. *ibid.*

12. *ibid.*

13. *ibid.*

14. deZeng, Henry L. IV and Stankey, Douglas G., *Luftwaffe Officer Career Summaries* (2014 updated version); www.ww2.dk/lwoffz.html (hosted on Michael Holm's webpage: *The Luftwaffe, 1933–1945*; www.ww2.dk)

15. The Western Front referred to here is that formed following the Allied breakout and victory in Normandy, followed by a rapid advance towards the Low Countries and the German frontier, thereby forming a new western-most front for the German forces, facing these Allied advances from the west.

16. Caldwell, Donald, *op. cit.*

17. Middlebrook, Martin and Everitt, Chris, *The Bomber Command War Diaries; an operational reference book, 1939–1945* (Harmondsworth: Viking Penguin Books, 1985).

18. Stout, Jay A., *Hell's Angels: The true story of the 303rd Bomb Group in World War II* (New York: Berkley Caliber, 2015); see also the website of this unit: Moncur, Gary L., *Hells Angels; 303rd Bomb Group (H)*; www.303rdbg.com

19. Stout, Jay A., *op. cit.*

20. Rowe, John C., *448ʰᵗ Bomb Group replacement crew #46's Eighth Air Force mission records – World War II*; pdf file entitled *John C. Rowe WWII aircrew log* on website www.willisrowe.com

21. Tripp, Miles, *The Eighth Passenger* (London: Corgi Books, 1971). The relevant descriptions of the Witten raid are on pages 58 and 144 of this edition of the book, where the city's name is given incorrectly as Watten.

22. Böhme, Manfred, *Jagdgeschwader 7. Die Chronik eines ME 262-Geschwaders 1944/45* (Stuttgart: Motorbuchverlag, 1983).

23. Tripp, Miles, *op. cit.*

24. *ibid.*

25. Holm, Michael, *op. cit*; Girbig, Werner, *Jagdgeschwader 5 "Eismeerjäger"* (Stuttgart: Motorbuch Verlag, 1976).

26. Caldwell, Donald, *op. cit.*

27. Holm, Michael, *op. cit.*

28. Galland, Adolf, *Zum Thema "Rammjäger-Selbstaufopferer"; eine Stellungnahme des ehemaligen Generals der Jagdflieger*. Statement published in *Jägerblatt*, number 2/XL, May-June 1991, page 17.

29. *ibid.*

30. *ibid.*

31. Holm, Michael, *op. cit.*

32. Barbas, Bernd, *Die Geschichte der II. Gruppe des Jagdgeschwaders 52* (Überlingen: self-published, undated) (official edition of the *Traditionsgemeinschaft JG 52*).

33. Holm, Michael, *op. cit.*

34. Dahl, Walther, *Rammjäger – das letzte Aufgebot* (Offenbach am Main: Orion-Heimreiter-Verlag, 1973).

35. *ibid.*

36. *ibid.*

37. *ibid.*

38. Lorant, Jean-Yves and Goyat, Richard, *Jagdgeschwader 300 "Wilde Sau"*, vol. 1, *June 1943–September 1944* (Hamilton: Eagle Editions, 2005).

39. Holm, Michael, *op. cit.*

40. Prien, Jochen and Stemmer, Gerhard, *Messerschmitt Bf 109 im Einsatz bei Stab und I./Jagdgeschwader 3* (Eutin: Struve-Druck, 1997).

41. Caldwell, Donald, *op. cit.* The earlier German loss figure cited by Schirmers is from: Sims, Edward H., *Jagdflieger, die grossen Gegner von einst* (Stuttgart: Motorbuch Verlag, 1994).

42. Galland, Adolf, *The First and the Last* (London: Fontana/Collins Books, 1970).

43. *ibid.*

44. Girbig, Werner, *Start im Morgengrauen* (Stuttgart: Motorbuch Verlag, 1973).

45. *ibid.*

46. *ibid.*

47. *ibid.*

48. *ibid.*

49. *ibid.*

50. Manrho, John and Pütz, Ron, *Bodenplatte: the Luftwaffe's last hope – the attack on Allied airfields, New Year's Day 1945* (Ottringham: Hikoki Publications, 2004).

51. Böhme, Manfred, *op. cit.*

52. Morgan, Hugh and Weal, John, *German jet aces of World War 2* (Osprey Aircraft of the Aces No. 17) (Botley: Osprey Publishing, 2004).

53. Galland, Adolf, 1970, *op. cit*; Böhme, Manfred, *op. cit.*

54. Holm, Michael, *op. cit.*

55. Morgan, Hugh, *op. cit.*

56. Price, Alfred, *The last year of the Luftwaffe: May 1944 to May 1945* (Osceola: Motorbooks International, 1991).

57. Holm, Michael, *op. cit*; Böhme, Manfred, *op. cit*; Price, Alfred, *op. cit.*

58. Holm, Michael, *op. cit.*

59. Böhme, Manfred, *op. cit.*

60. Holm, Michael, *op. cit.*

61. *ibid.*

62. Eriksson, Patrick G., *Alarmstart* (Stroud: Amberley, 2017).

63. Holm, Michael, *op. cit.*

64. *ibid.*

65. Holm, Michael, *op. cit*; Morgan, Hugh, *op. cit.*

66. Holm, Michael, *op. cit.*

67. Morgan, Hugh, *op. cit.*

68. Price, Alfred, *op. cit.*

69. Holm, Michael, *op. cit*; Morgan, Hugh, *op. cit.*

70. Holm, Michael, *op. cit*; Price, Alfred, *op. cit.*

71. Morgan, Hugh, *op. cit.*

72. *ibid.*

73. Caldwell, Donald, *op. cit.*

74. Morgan, Hugh, *op. cit.*

75. Eriksson, Patrick G., *op. cit.*

76. Holm, Michael, *op. cit.*
77. Girbig, Werner, 1973, *op. cit.*
78. Galland, Adolf, 1991, *op. cit.*
79. *ibid.*
80. Lorant, Jean-Yves, *op. cit.*
81. Caldwell, Donald, *op. cit.*
82. *ibid.*

9 The Campaign in Norway: An Oft Forgotten Theatre of the Second World War

1. Aders, Gebhard and Held, Werner, *Jagdgeschwader 51 'Mölders'* (Stuttgart: Motorbuch Verlag, 1985).
2. Girbig, Werner, *Jagdgeschwader 5 "Eismeerjäger"* (Stuttgart: Motorbuch Verlag, 1976).
3. *ibid.*
4. *ibid.*
5. *ibid.*
6. *ibid.*
7. Cherrett, Martin (editor), *Heavy losses as Coastal Command attacks Prinz Eugen*; article under 17 May 1942 on World War II Today website; ww2today.com
8. *ibid.*
9. Girbig, Werner, *op. cit.*
10. *Lexikon der Wehrmacht, Gliederungen, Jagdgeschwader, IV/JG 5*; www.lexikon-der-wehrmacht.de/Gliederungen/Jagdgeschwader/Inhalt.htm
11. *ibid.*
12. *ibid.*
13. Holm, Michael, *The Luftwaffe, 1933–1945*; www.ww2.dk; Girbig, Werner, *op. cit.*
14. Girbig, Werner, *op. cit.*
15. *ibid.*
16. Holm, Michael, *op. cit.*
17. *ibid.*
18. *ibid.*
19. Girbig, Werner, *op. cit.*
20. *ibid.*
21. *ibid.*
22. *ibid.*
23. Tovey, Admiral Sir John C., *The carrier borne aircraft attack on Kirkenes and Petsamo* (London: HMSO, 1948). This was the Despatch

submitted by Admiral Tovey, Commander in Chief of the Home Fleet, to the Admiralty on 12 September 1941. It was published in a post-war Supplement to the London Gazette of 25 May 1948, which appeared the next day.

24. *ibid.*
25. *ibid.*

10 *The End of the War and Imprisonment: West and East*

1. Cull, Brian, *First of the Few* (Stroud: Fonthill Media, 2013).
2. Cull, Brian, *op. cit.*
3. Obermaier, Ernst, *Die Ritterkreuzträger der Luftwaffe* (Mainz: Verlag Dieter Hoffmann, 1966).
4. Priller, Josef, *J.G. 26: Geschichte eines Jagdgeschwaders* (Stuttgart: Motorbuch Verlag, 1980); Aders, Gebhard and Held, Werner, *Jagdgeschwader 51 'Mölders'* (Stuttgart: Motorbuch Verlag, 1985); Barbas, Bernd, *Die Geschichte der III. Gruppe des Jagdgeschwaders 52* (Überlingen: self-published, undated) (official edition of the *Traditionsgemeinschaft JG 52*); Prien, Jochen, *Geschichte des Jagdgeschwaders 77, Teil 4, 1944–1945* (Eutin: Struve-Druck, undated).
5. Aders, Gebhard, *op. cit.*
6. Priller, Josef, *op. cit.*
7. The so-called 'K reports' were the RAF interrogation reports, based on evidence from the crash site itself and early interrogation of surviving aircrew prisoners.
8. Parker, Nigel, *Luftwaffe Crash Archive*, Vol. 1 (Walton on Thames: Red Kite Books, Air Research Publications, 2013). This, the first volume amongst many, includes brief description of the circumstances of the loss of this particular III/JG 52 POW over England in July 1940.
9. Prien, Jochen, *Pik-As: Geschichte des Jagdgeschwaders 53, Teil 2* (Eutin: Struve-Druck, 1990).
10. Prien, Jochen, *Pik-As: Geschichte des Jagdgeschwaders 53, Teil 3* (Eutin: Struve-Druck, 1991).
11. Kornstädt, Hans-Ulrich, *Als Jagdflieger beim JG 27 über dem Mittelmeer: Vom englischen Zerstörer gerettet – vier Jahre Kriegsgefangenschaft im Algerien; ein Erlebnisbericht* (Munich: self-published, 1988).
12. Prien, Jochen, undated, *op. cit.*
13. Priller, Josef, *op. cit.*
14. Barbas, Bernd, *Die Geschichte der II. Gruppe des Jagdgeschwaders 52* (Überlingen: self-published, undated) (official edition of the *Traditionsgemeinschaft JG 52*).

15. Barbas, Bernd, *III Gruppe*, *op. cit*; Toliver, Raymond F. and Constable, Trevor J., *Holt Hartmann vom Himmel!* (Stuttgart: Motorbuch Verlag, 1976).

11 Conclusions

1. Galland, Adolf, *The First and the Last* (London: Fontana/Collins Books, 1970). The quote on Marseille being the 'unrivalled virtuoso' amongst all *Luftwaffe* pilots is on page 122 of this edition of the book.

LIST OF ILLUSTRATIONS

1. Percentages of German fighter *Gruppen* stationed in the different main theatres from June 1941 till the end of the war; black line on graph at 50% level. It is clear that the North African-Malta campaign absorbed significant fighter forces from late 1941 till the end of the Tunisian campaign (April-May 1943). Thereafter operations over Sicily and Italy locked up fewer *Gruppen* until about mid-1944 when they were essentially withdrawn. June-August 1944 saw a massive transfer of fighter units from German Home Defence to Normandy. From late 1942 till late 1944 the Balkans region was served by several *Jagdgruppen*, remaining relatively constant in number while never becoming over-significant. Following the German defeat in Normandy the Home Defence once more became the prime theatre, only reaching approximate parity with the Eastern Front in 1945.

2. *Oberleutnant* Günther Scholtz and *Leutnant* Max Clerico of 7/JG 54 enjoy a lighter moment during the Balkans campaign in 1941. Max Clerico commented on this photograph at some length. 'I still have a photo of *Oberleutnant* Scholtz (*Staffelkapitän 7/JG 54*) and myself wearing nightcaps, that we often wore when we had spare time to fly in open-cockpit sports aircraft (Kl 35 – wonderful!), which we wore as a joke so as not to appear so military! When I bought mine in France in 1941 prior to going to the Balkans, I did not know the French word for these nightcaps, and I had to draw what I wanted on a piece of paper. The sales lady laughed and called out "A nightcap [*bonnet de nuit*] for the customer". Mine had a tassel made of wood wrapped in textile (clearly visible in the picture) and this unfortunately bounced around

in the Kl 35's slipstream and hit me on the back of the head often; that way I could not fall asleep.' (Dr Max Clerico)

3. A formal portrait of *Leutnant* Günther Schwanecke, 7/JG 77 taken in 1941. He flew mainly low-level attacks on shipping in the Balkans campaign of that year. (Günther Schwanecke)

4. Formation flight practice over Germany for a *Schwarm* of four Me 110s from *III/ZG 26*. This *Gruppe* saw action over Yugoslavia and later over the island of Crete during the 1941 Balkan campaign. (Werner Ludwig)

5. Graph showing the wastage in the Ju 52 transport aircraft fleet used in the invasion of Crete. The wastage encompasses losses through combat directly, operational losses and accidents to these aircraft. Very steep losses characterised the first few days of the operations after which a steady decrease in machines available for operations continued. It was a close-run situation and would not have been able to continue for too much longer if the defenders of the island could have imposed some more delay on the invasion. For source of data, see note 71 for Chapter One.

6. *Unteroffizier* Johann Pichler of 7/JG 77 commented on this photograph: 'One of my hardest forced-landings, on 22 May 1941 on my airfield in the Peloponnese, during the operations over Crete.' This followed combat damage suffered during a *Schwarm* attack on the British battleship *Valiant* north of Crete at about lunchtime, with as is obvious, the Messerschmitt being destroyed (graded as 85% damage, some parts salvageable) with extensive damage to the cockpit area (note windscreen pointing vertically upwards in the middle of the photo) – his survival was a miracle. (Johann Pichler)

7. *Leutnant* Martin Drewes and his gunner flying to Iraq on 14 May 1941 as part of 4/ZG 76. Despite carrying Iraqi markings and the crews wearing Iraqi uniforms, the famous shark's mouth emblem on the nose of *II/ZG 76* ('*Haifischgruppe*') aircraft was maintained; note also the long-range fuel tanks. (Martin Drewes)

8. *Hauptmann* Joachim Müncheberg who led 7/JG 26 over the Western Desert. Photo taken after his time in Africa, late 1941 or beginning of 1942, after the award of the *Eichenlaub*. (Lothair Vanoverbeke)

9. New experiences for most German fighter pilots in North Africa: the Arabic people, palm trees, desert and camels. The touristic experience soon gave way to more serious pursuits. All three photos taken around Castel Benito airfield, south of Tripoli. *Feldwebel* Werner Ludwig of *III/ZG 26* gets close to a camel in the top right-hand photo. (Werner Ludwig)

10. *Oberfeldwebel* Heinrich 'Henri' Rosenberg, 9/JG 27, or as he put it, 'the "Phantom" in Africa, 1942'. Note the ubiquitous fighter pilot's scarf to reduce chafing around the neck with the constant swivelling of their heads looking for the enemy possibly approaching from above and behind. (Heinrich Rosenberg)

11. Gerhard Keppler, who flew in the Western Desert as a *Feldwebel* with 1/JG 27. This shows him later in the war after promotion to *Leutnant*. He commented on the medal hanging next to his C-licence badge for gliding (three white swallows on a blue background, above the Iron Cross First Class): 'The badge hanging next to the C-licence is something Italian, whose name I can no longer remember.' The latter was likely the Italian Africa Service Medal. (Gerhard Keppler)

12. Missions flown by *Feldwebel* Hans Fahrenberger, 8/JG 27 over the Western Desert, mid-1942. One of the *Aufklärerschutz* (reconnaissance escort) missions here was actually an *Aufklärung* (reconnaissance mission) by Fahrenberger himself near his own base. *Seenoteinsatz* = air sea rescue mission; *Panzer Tiefangriff* = low level attack on tanks. He was already an experienced pilot before arriving in the Western Desert, his prior operations encompassing the following *Feindflüge*: Channel (cf., late Battle of Britain) – two; Balkan campaign – ten; Russia 1941 – 106; prior missions over Africa – nine. His grand total of operational missions had thus reached 234 by 5 August 1942.

13. A graphic summary of *Hauptmann* Hans-Joachim Marseille's combat career, illustrating that it comprised alternating operational flying and leave periods throughout. Note also that the leave periods tended to become longer as time went on and as exhaustion became ever more prevalent. In the end the candle that was Marseille inevitably burnt itself out. Sources of data given in text and notes to Chapter 2.

14. Professor Paul Robert Skawran, the *Luftwaffe's* 'Seelenspion', trained psychologist who spent much of the war observing German pilots on active service. (Paul Skawran)

15. A Me 110 N of *III/ZG 26* loaded with two 250 kg bombs and four 50 kg bombs, takes off on a fighter-bomber mission in the Western Desert. Note *Geschwader* badge on nose. (Georg Christl)

16. A Me 110 of *III/ZG 26* providing escort of supply convoy for Rommel over the Mediterranean Sea. The aircraft carries the ZG 26 badge on its nose. (Georg Christl)

17. The sad remains of a Me 110 of *III/ZG 26*, burnt out after being attacked on the ground at Fuka in Egypt. (Werner Ludwig)

18. Take-off from Derna in the Western Desert, Me 110 of *III/ZG 26*. (Werner Ludwig)

19. A Me 110 of *8/ZG 26* being warmed up on Cagliari airfield in Sardinia. *III/ZG 26* was the first *Luftwaffe* fighter unit to fly into Sicily for operations over Malta, arriving from 14 December 1940. (Werner Ludwig)

20. *Unteroffizier* Dr Felix Sauer, then with *6/JG 53*, taken in Bergen, northern Holland in September 1941 three months before he moved to Sicily to fly over Malta. (Dr Felix Sauer)

21. Two photographs of *Major* Günther Freiherr von Maltzahn, *Kommodore* of the *'Pik As'* (Ace of Spades) *Geschwader*, *JG 53*. In the right hand picture, *Major* von Maltzahn (second from left) and *Oberleutnant* Otto Böhner (at right; *Staffelkapitän 6/JG 53* over Malta, December 1941–March 1942; wounded over Malta 7 March 1942). Photographs taken in September 1941, Bergen airfield in northern Holland, before the move to Sicily. (Dr Felix Sauer)

22. *Oberstleutnant* Helmut Bennemann, who succeeded *Kommodore* von Maltzahn, and led *JG 53* over the Italian theatre from 9 November 1943 till 27 June 1944. (Helmut Bennemann)

23. *Oberfeldwebel* Josef Ederer, *3/JG 53* captioned this photograph: 'Home leave, July-August 1942, after leaving hospital following my crash in Sicily.' (Josef Ederer)

24. Chart showing *Luftwaffe* daytime losses over Malta, as well as those of defending British fighters (only losses to aerial combat and anti-aircraft fire shown). In May 1942, two 'other' type German and eight Italian aircraft were also lost, which are not included. Source of data: note 32 for Chapter 3.

25. The Italian destroyer *Turbine* which rescued *Unteroffizier* Dr Felix Sauer, *10/JG 53* from the sea after eight days, on 23 May 1942. (Dr Felix Sauer)

26. *Unteroffizier* Dr Felix Sauer, *10/JG 53* said of this photograph: 'The 10th *Staffel* of the *Pik-As-Geschwader* was the "*Jabo*" (*Jagdbomber*, fighter-bomber) *Staffel*. Four pilots of this *Staffel* next to the emblem of the unit, the *Jabo*-symbol, a bomb pointing towards Malta. Despite their primary *Jabo* role they also flew some ordinary fighter missions when required.' (Dr Felix Sauer)

27. *Unteroffizier* Dr Felix Sauer, *10/JG 53* posing in his dinghy: 'In my dinghy for eight days on the Mediterranean Sea, 16–23 May 1942. The yellow signalling flag also served as a sail.' (Dr Felix Sauer)

28. 'An original photo from the rescuing vessel: German fighter pilot *Unteroffizier* Dr Felix Sauer, drifting in the Mediterranean Sea for eight days, is found 200 km east of Malta and rescued on 23 May 1942 by the Italian destroyer *Turbine*.' (Dr Felix Sauer)

40. *Major* (*Oberst* by the end of the war) Gustav Rödel, *Geschwaderkommodore* JG 27 titled this photograph: 'A photo from the war.' (Gustav Rödel)

41. The Balkans, 1943, *Oberfeldwebel* Johann Pichler, 7/*JG*77: 'Heavily laden Ju 87 dive bombers off on a new mission.' (Johann Pichler)

42. *Oberleutnant* Emil Clade, *Staffelkapitän* 7/*JG* 27, Greece 1943–1944. (Emil Clade)

43. One of the ever more scarce veterans flying over the Balkans in 1943–1944, *Oberfeldwebel* Johann Pichler, 7/*JG* 77 in the foreground, in a photo from earlier in the war, taken in southern Russia in winter 1941–1942. 'Shortly before departing on leave, with the Me 108, December 1941. The Me 108 could seat four people.' (Johann Pichler)

44. 'Mizil/Romania, 10 June 44: after the first victory in air combat; in the middle is *Unteroffizier* Martin Hain 8th *Staffel*, *JG* 77'. Right, 44b: Award certificate for the Iron Cross 2nd Class (*EK* 2) awarded to *Unteroffizier* Martin Hain for the aforementioned achievement. (Martin Hain)

45. *Unteroffizier* Martin Hain, 8/*JG* 77: copy of a page from his *Leistungsbuch* showing his three claims. Columns headed, left to right: running number of claim; aircraft type shot down; date; time; grid square reference/place; height; witnesses (that for number 3 is a ground witness); remarks. (Martin Hain)

46. *Unteroffizier* Martin Hain, 8/*JG* 77: award certificate for the *Verwundetenabzeichen* or Wound Badge (Black) signed by the acting *Gruppenkommandeur* of III/*JG* 77, *Hauptmann* Bresoscheck, an ethnic German from Yugoslavia. (Martin Hain)

47. Copy of official confirmation certificate (*Abschussbestätigung*) for a victory claim by *Oberleutnant* Fritz Engau, *Staffelkapitän* 2/*JG* 11, achieved on 7 June 1944 during the transfer flight of I/*JG* 11 to the Invasion Front. Handwritten note added by Fritz Engau. The original of the certificate went to the *Staffel* (to whom the victory was always credited, not the individual pilot) and stayed there, the unit itself issuing a stamped copy of the certificate originally sent out by the *Reichsluftfahrtministerium*, on to the relevant pilot. Note that issue of the certificate post-dated the claim by three months. (Fritz Engau)

48. A *JG* 26 pilot sits in his Fw 190. (JG 26 veteran, via Lothair Vanoverbeke)

49. *Oberleutnant* Wilhelm Hofmann, in an earlier photograph taken probably at either Wevelghem or Moorsele in Belgium, in about 1941; obviously in hot summer weather, during *Sitzbereitschaft* in his Fw 190. (JG 26 veteran, via Lothair Vanoverbeke)

50. *Oberfeldwebel* Eduard Isken receives the *Ritterkreuz* on 14 January 1945; he ended the war as a *Leutnant*. (Eduard Isken)

60. Karl-Heinz Erler drew these *JG 5* badges: 'The *"Eismeer"* badge was the official emblem of *Jagdgeschwader 5*; the other badge is the one for our 16th *Staffel* – I designed the latter myself. It represents, humorously the day fighters with their weapon and flying helmet.' (Karl-Heinz Erler)

61. *16/JG 5* dispersal area at Forus, Norway 1944 (headquarters at left). Note the boardwalk in foreground and wooden-paved parking places for individual aircraft, all to avoid the mud. (Karl-Heinz Erler)

62. One of the many *Luftwaffe* prisoners of war, *Oberleutnant* Heinz Altendorf, *Staffelkapitän* of 7th *Staffel, JG 53* – '*Pik As*' in a photograph taken in September 1940. One tends to forget how young almost all the combat pilots of World War 2 were; at 23 in 1940, Heinz Altendorf was bordering on being considered 'older'! (Heinz Altendorf)

BIBLIOGRAPHY

Aders, Gebhard and Held, Werner, *Jagdgeschwader 51 'Mölders'* (Stuttgart: Motorbuch Verlag, 1985)

Baker, E.C.R., *Ace of aces M St J Pattle* (Rivonia: Ashanti Publishing, 1992)

Barbas, Bernd, *Die Geschichte der II. Gruppe des Jagdgeschwaders 52* (Überlingen: self-published, undated) (official edition of the *Traditionsgemeinschaft JG 52*)

Barbas, Bernd, *Die Geschichte der III. Gruppe des Jagdgeschwaders 52* (Überlingen: self-published, undated) (official edition of the *Traditionsgemeinschaft JG 52*)

Bekker, Cajus, *Angriffshöhe 4000. Die deutsche Luftwaffe im Zweiten Weltkrieg* (Munich: Wilhelm Heyne Verlag, 1967)

Böhme, Manfred, *Jagdgeschwader 7. Die Chronik eines ME 262-Geschwaders 1944/45* (Stuttgart: Motorbuchverlag, 1983)

Buzzati, Dino, *The shipwrecked airman, a German soldier, Marine combat outpost X, June 1942* (Milan: *Corriere della Sera* newspaper, 1942)

Caldwell, Donald, *Day Fighters in Defence of the Reich; a War Diary, 1942–45* (Barnsley: Frontline Books, 2011)

Caldwell, Donald, *JG 26 Luftwaffe Fighter Wing Diary, Volume 1: 1939–1942* (Mechanicsburg: Stackpole Books, 2012)

Caldwell, Donald, *JG 26 Luftwaffe Fighter Wing Diary, 1943–1945, Vol. 2* (Mechanicsburg: Stackpole Books, 2012)

Calvocoressi, Peter and Wint, Guy, *Total War: causes and courses of the Second World War* (Aylesbury: Pelican Books, 1974)

Cull, Brian, *First of the Few* (Stroud: Fonthill Media, 2013)

Dahl, Walther, *Rammjäger – das letzte Aufgebot* (Offenbach am Main: Orion-Heimreiter-Verlag, 1973)

Dierich, Wolfgang, *Kampfgeschwader 51 "Edelweiss"* (Stuttgart: Motorbuch Verlag, 1974)

Dierich, Wolfgang, *Die Verbände der Luftwaffe 1935–1945* (Stuttgart: Motorbuch Verlag, 1976)

Eriksson, Patrick G., *Alarmstart* (Stroud: Amberley, 2017)

Eriksson, Patrick G., *Alarmstart East* (Stroud: Amberley, 2018)

Galland, Adolf, *The First and the Last* (London: Fontana/Collins Books, 1970)

Galland, Adolf, *Zum Thema "Rammjäger-Selbstaufopferer"; eine Stellungnahme des ehemaligen Generals der Jagdflieger, Jägerblatt* (May-June 1991)

Gardner, E.R., *Journal of Criminal Law, Criminology, and Police Science* (49/3, 1958)

Gilbert, Martin, *Second World War* (London: Weidenfeld and Nicolson, 1989)

Girbig, Werner, *Start im Morgengrauen* (Stuttgart: Motorbuch Verlag, 1973)

Girbig, Werner, *Jagdgeschwader 5 "Eismeerjäger"* (Stuttgart: Motorbuch Verlag, 1976)

Greene, Jack and Massignani, Alessandro, *The Naval War in the Mediterranean 1940–1943* (London: Frontline Books, 2011)

Heaton, Colin, *World War II Magazine* (February 2000)

Heaton, Colin D. and Lewis, Anne-Marie, *The Star of Africa: The story of Hans Marseille, the rogue Luftwaffe ace who dominated the WW II skies* (Minneapolis: Zenith Press, 2012)

Kornstädt, Hans-Ulrich, *Als Jagdflieger beim JG 27 über dem Mittelmeer: Vom englischen Zerstörer gerettet – vier Jahre Kriegsgefangenschaft im Algerien; ein Erlebnisbericht* (Munich: self-published, 1988)

Lorant, Jean-Yves and Goyat, Richard, *Jagdgeschwader 300 "Wilde Sau", vol. 1, June 1943–September 1944* (Hamilton: Eagle Editions, 2005)

Macintyre, Donald, *The Battle for the Mediterranean* (London: Pan Books, 1970)

Manrho, John and Pütz, Ron, *Bodenplatte: the Luftwaffe's last hope – the attack on Allied airfields, New Year's Day 1945* (Ottringham: Hikoki Publications, 2004)

Martin, H.J. and Orpen, Neil, *Eagles Victorious; South African Forces World War II (Volume 6): The SAAF in Italy and the Mediterranean, 1943/45* (Cape Town: Purnell and Sons, 1977)

Middlebrook, Martin and Everitt, Chris, *The Bomber Command War Diaries; an operational reference book, 1939–1945* (Harmondsworth: Viking Penguin Books, 1985)

Bibliography

Möbius, Ingo, *Am Himmel Europas: Der Jagdflieger Günther Scholz erinnert sich* (Chemnitz: Eigenverlag Ingo Möbius, 2009)

Montgomery, Field Marshal The Viscount, *Montgomery of Alamein, Volume I, El Alamein to the River Sangro* (London: Corgi Books, 1974)

Montgomery, Field Marshal The Viscount, *Montgomery of Alamein, Volume II, Normandy to the Baltic – Invasion* (London: Corgi Books, 1974)

Montgomery, Field Marshal The Viscount, *Montgomery of Alamein, Volume III, Normandy to the Baltic – Victory* (London: Corgi Books, 1974)

Morgan, Hugh and Seibel, Jürgen, *Combat Kill: The drama of aerial warfare in World War 2 and the controversy surrounding victories* (Sparkford: Patrick Stephens, 1997)

Morgan, Hugh and Weal, John, *German jet aces of World War 2* (Osprey Aircraft of the Aces No. 17) (Botley: Osprey Publishing, 2004)

Moulson, Tom, *The Flying Sword: The story of 601 Squadron* (London: Macdonald, 1964)

Murray, Williamson, *Luftwaffe* (London: Grafton Books, 1988)

Neitzel, Sönke and Welzer, Harald, *Soldaten: on fighting, killing and dying* (London: Simon and Schuster, 2012)

Neulen, Hans Werner, *In the skies of Europe: air forces allied to the Luftwaffe 1939–1945* (Ramsbury: The Crowood Press, 2005)

Newby, Leroy W., *Into the guns of Ploesti* (Osceola: Motorbooks International, 1991)

Nowarra, Heinz J., *The Messerschmitt 109 a famous German fighter* (Letchworth: Harleyford Publications, 1966)

Obermaier, Ernst, *Die Ritterkreuzträger der Luftwaffe* (Mainz: Verlag Dieter Hoffmann, 1966)

Pissin, D.W., *The Battle of Crete* (Maxwell Air Force Base, Alabama: USAF Historical Division, Research Studies Institute, Air University, 1956)

Price, Alfred, *The last year of the Luftwaffe: May 1944 to May 1945* (Osceola: Motorbooks International, 1991)

Prien, Jochen, *Pik-As: Geschichte des Jagdgeschwaders 53, Teil 1* (Illertissen: Flugzeug Publikations, 1989)

Prien, Jochen, *Pik-As: Geschichte des Jagdgeschwaders 53, Teil 2* (Eutin: Struve-Druck, 1990)

Prien, Jochen, *Pik-As: Geschichte des Jagdgeschwaders 53, Teil 3* (Eutin: Struve-Druck, 1991)

Prien, Jochen, *Geschichte des Jagdgeschwaders 77, Teil 1, 1934–1941* (Eutin: Struve-Druck, 1992)

Prien, Jochen and Stemmer, Gerhard, *Messerschmitt Bf 109 im Einsatz bei der III./Jagdgeschwader 3* (Eutin: Struve-Druck, 1995)

Prien, Jochen and Stemmer, Gerhard, *Messerschmitt Bf 109 im Einsatz bei der II./Jagdgeschwader 3, 1940–1945* (Eutin: Struve-Druck, 1996)

Prien, Jochen and Stemmer, Gerhard, *Messerschmitt Bf 109 im Einsatz bei Stab und I./Jagdgeschwader 3* (Eutin: Struve-Druck, 1997)

Prien, Jochen and Rodeike, Peter, *Jagdgeschwader 1 und 11. Einsatz in der Reichsverteidigung von 1939 bis 1945, Teil 2, 1944* (Eutin: Struve Druck, undated)

Prien, Jochen, *Geschichte des Jagdgeschwaders 77, Teil 3, 1942–1943* (Eutin: Struve-Druck, undated)

Prien, Jochen, *Geschichte des Jagdgeschwaders 77, Teil 4, 1944–1945* (Eutin: Struve-Druck, undated)

Priller, Josef, *J.G. 26: Geschichte eines Jagdgeschwaders* (Stuttgart: Motorbuch Verlag, 1980)

Reschke, Willi, *Jagdgeschwader 301/302 "Wilde Sau"* (Atglen: Schiffer, 2005)

Richards, Denis, *The Royal Air Force 1939–1945, volume 1: The Fight at Odds* (London: HMSO, 1953)

Ring, Hans and Girbig, Werner, *Jagdgeschwader 27, Die Dokumentation über den Einsatz an allen Fronten 1939–1945* (Stuttgart: Motorbuch Verlag, 1975)

Shores, Christopher and Ring, Hans, *Fighters over the Desert* (London: Neville Spearman, 1969)

Shores, Christopher, Ring, Hans and Hess, William N., *Fighters over Tunisia* (London: Neville Spearman, 1975)

Shores, Christopher and Cull, Brian with Malizia, Nicola, *Malta: the Hurricane years 1940–41* (London: Grub Street, 1987)

Shores, Christopher, Cull, Brian and Malizia, Nicola, *Air war for Yugoslavia, Greece and Crete 1940–41* (London: Grub Street, 1987)

Shores, Christopher and Cull, Brian with Malizia, Nicola, *Malta: the Spitfire year 1942* (London: Grub Street, 1991)

Shores, Christopher, *Dust clouds in the Middle East* (London: Grub Street, 2010)

Shores, Christopher, Massimello, Giovanni and Guest, Russell, *A History of the Mediterranean Air War 1940–1945; Volume One: North Africa June 1940–January 1942* (London: Grub Street, 2012)

Shores, Christopher, Massimello, Giovanni and Guest, Russell, *A History of the Mediterranean Air War 1940–1945; Volume Two: North African Desert February 1942–March 1943* (London: Grub Street, 2012)

Shores, Christopher, Massimello, Giovanni with Guest, Russell, Olynyk, Frank and Bock, Winfried, *A History of the Mediterranean Air War 1940–1945; Volume Three: Tunisia and the end in Africa November 1942–May 1943* (London: Grub Street, 2016)

Bibliography

Sims, Edward H., *Jagdflieger, die grossen Gegner von einst* (Stuttgart: Motorbuch Verlag, 1994)

Skawran, Paul Robert, *Ikaros; Persönlichkeit und Wesen des deutschen Jagdfliegers im Zweiten Weltkrieg* (Steinbach am Wörthsee: Luftfahrt-Verlag Walter Zuerl, 1969)

Steinhoff, Johannes, *The straits of Messina: Diary of a fighter commander* (London: Corgi Books, 1973)

Stout, Jay A., *Hell's Angels: The true story of the 303rd Bomb Group in World War II* (New York: Berkley Caliber, 2015)

Terraine, John, *The Right of the Line* (Ware: Wordsworth Editions, 1997)

Tillman, Barrett, *Forgotten 15th: the daring airmen who crippled Hitler's war machine* (Washinton DC: Regnery Publishing, 2014)

Toliver, Raymond F. and Constable, Trevor J., *Holt Hartmann vom Himmel!* (Stuttgart: Motorbuch Verlag, 1976)

Tovey, Admiral Sir John C., *The carrier borne aircraft attack on Kirkenes and Petsamo* (London: HMSO, 1948)

Trautloft, Hannes, *Grünherzjäger im Luftkampf 1940–1945: Die Geschichte des Jagdgeschwaders 54; Kriegs-Tagebuch von Hannes Trautloft (edited by Hans Ekkehard Bob)* (Zweibrücken: VDM Heinz Nickel, 2006)

Tripp, Miles, *The Eighth Passenger* (London: Corgi Books, 1971)

Weal, John, *Jagdgeschwader 2 'Richthofen'* (Oxford: Osprey Publishing, 2000)

Wood, Tony and Gunston, Bill, *Hitler's Luftwaffe: A pictorial and technical encyclopedia of Hitler's air power in World War II* (London: Salamander Books, 1977)

Young, Peter (Editor), *The World Almanac Book of World War II* (New York: World Almanac Publisher, 1981)

Websites

Acred, Matthew Laird (website editor), *Jagdgeschwader 5 Abschussliste*; www.asisbiz.com/Luftwaffe.html

Aeroflight Website for Aviation Enthusiasts; specifically on Royal Yugoslav Air Force; www.aeroflight.co.uk/waf/yugo_af1_hist_orbat41.htm

Cherrett, Martin (website editor), World War II Today; *Heavy losses as Coastal Command attacks Prinz Eugen*; article under 17 May 1942; ww2today.com

deZeng, Henry L. IV and Stankey, Douglas G., *Luftwaffe Officer Career Summaries* (2014 updated version); www.ww2.dk/lwoffz.html (hosted on Michael Holm's webpage: *The Luftwaffe, 1933–1945*; www.ww2.dk)

Dillon, John, *Battle of Crete*; www.my-crete-site.co.uk/raf.htm

Eriksson, Patrick G., Buchanan, Rob with Vaittinen, Juha, *Malta 10th April 1942: a German ace is vanquished; Hermann Neuhoff versus George Buchanan*; (article on website) https://juhansotahistoriasivut.weebly.com

Håkans Aviation Page, *Biplane fighter aces from the Second World War*; surfcity. kund.delnet.se

Holm, Michael, *The Luftwaffe, 1933–1945*; www.ww2.dk

Kracker *Luftwaffe* Archive: *Axis Powers*, on the Aircrew Remembered website; www.aircrewremembered.com

Lexikon der Wehrmacht, Gliederungen, Jagdgeschwader, IV/JG 5; www.lexikon-der-wehrmacht.de/Gliederungen/Jagdgeschwader/Inhalt.htm

Lexikon der Wehrmacht, Gliederungen, Kommandantur OK 1324; www. lexikon-der-wehrmacht.de/Gliederungen/Kommandantur/OKI324-R.htm

Malta: War Diaries; https://maltagc70.wordpress.com

Metapedia; specifically on General Siegfried Marseille, father of Hans-Joachim Marseille; de.metapedia.org/wiki/Marseille_Siegfried

Moncur, Gary L., *Hell's Angels; 303rd Bomb Group (H)*; www.303rdbg.com

Rowe, John C., *448th Bomb Group replacement crew #46's Eighth Air Force mission records – World War II*; pdf file entitled *John C. Rowe WWII aircrew log* on website www.willisrowe.com

Traditionsgemeinschaft Jagdgeschwader 52; www.jg52.net

Wikipedia; specifically on the history of the Royal Hellenic Air Force: https://en.wikipedia.org/wiki/History_of_the_Hellenic_Air_Force; specficially on the history of the Royal Yugoslav Air Force: https://en.wikipedia.org/wiki/Royal_Yugoslav_Air_Force; specifically on the invasion of Yugoslavia, April 1941: https://en.wikipedia.org/wiki/Invasion_of_Yugoslavia; specifically on Hans-Joachim Marseille: https://en.wikipedia.org/wiki/Hans-Joachim_Marseille; specifically on Marseille's step father, Carl Reuter: https://de.wikipedia.org/wiki/Carl_Reuter; specifically on the Tunisian campaign: https://en.wikipedia.org/wiki/Tunisia_Campaign; specifically on the Allied bombing of Yugoslavia: https://en.wikipedia.org/wiki/Allied_bombing_of_Yugoslavia_in_World_War_II

Wood, Tony, *Tony Wood's Combat Claims and Casualties Lists;* don-caldwell. we.bs/claims/tonywood.htm

Bibliography

Archives

Imperial War Museum, London: *Luftwaffe* Quartermaster General Loss Returns (a very large document). Electronic copy kindly provided by Nigel Parker, from original at the Museum.

Private document archive of Professor Paul Robert Skawran, wartime *Luftwaffe* psychologist, who collected copies of various extant wartime records, the originals of many of which were destroyed at the end of the war. Includes a copy of the war diary or *Kriegstagebuch I/JG 77* (25 October 1942–19 August 1943), made in the field by Professor Paul. R. Skawran in Italy in about August 1943. Copy of this provided to author by Professor Skawran.

The National Archives, Kew, Richmond, Surrey: records of the Air Intelligence Department, Assistant Directorate of Intelligence (K), the Air Intelligence 'K' reports, detailing information obtained during interrogation of captured *Luftwaffe* aircrew. A copy of the relevant RAF intelligence report on a *III/JG 52* pilot captured in late July 1940 was provided to the author by Nigel Parker, from original in the National Archives.

ACKNOWLEDGEMENTS

Without the many veterans, from all *Geschwadern* and all levels of responsibility therein, this book would not have been possible at all. All of these men were extremely generous in giving me of their time, their documentation and in providing their recollections of experiences suffered in a global war almost all of them wanted only to forget. A full list of all the *Luftwaffe* fighter-pilot veterans who provided valuable material for this book is given below. Many of them also contributed to the two preceding volumes, *Alarmstart* and *Alarmstart East*, both to be found within the Bibliography here. One such was *Oberst* Hanns Trübenbach, who began flying in the 1920s, led the German pre-war aerobatic team, and began his war as *Gruppenkommandeur I/LG 2* in France in 1940, followed by the Battle of Britain. He was promoted to *Kommodore* of *JG 52*, which he also led in Romania and then over Russia in the second half of 1941. More directly related to the current volume, he was for a long time one of the two senior controllers in charge of the large *Jafü-Mittelrhein* headquarters near Darmstadt, situated approximately in western central Germany in the path of many day (and night) raids. He had detailed first-hand knowledge of the important *Sturmgruppe* innovation, and also of the tragic events surrounding *Sonderkommando Elbe* at the end of the war. We corresponded for many years, almost until he passed away. Not only did he provide perspective from the *Gruppenkommandeur* level right up to Göring himself, but he also gave freely of his logbooks and gave me his personal copies of several critical books long out of print. Hanns Trübenbach was a true old-world gentleman, someone of impeccable integrity whose insights and factual recollections, backed up by many documents, provided an irreplaceable foundation for many aspects of this book.

Another person whose support was truly treasured was Josef Kronschnabel who helped me despite being bed-ridden and unable to type, and thus wrote everything out laboriously in longhand. He was an ex-*Oberfeldwebel* from *III/JG 53*, who had been shot down by flak on the opening day of the attack on Russia, *Operation Barbarossa*, force-landed behind the lines and walked back. He later saw action over Malta and was shot down over El Alamein in the Egyptian desert in August 1942, becoming a prisoner.

Dr Felix Sauer, another member of *JG 53* who flew over Malta (with 6th and 10th *Staffeln*), managed to survive eight days drifting in the Mediterranean Sea after being shot down; he was most generous with his recollections of the war.

Professor Paul Robert Skawran was another quite exceptional witness. He was a trained psychologist working in South Africa and consulting for the South African Air Force on aircrew selection criteria. During a research trip to Germany shortly before the war, he had become trapped there by the outbreak of hostilities; being German-born he was drafted into the *Luftwaffe* where he was generally known as the *Seelenspion* ('soul spy', cf. 'shrink'). His duties there were initially also in the field of aircrew selection procedures. He had spent a large part of the war with diverse units and famous pilots, and being an experienced psychologist was able to provide insights into their characters, achievements and failings in great depth. He also had considerable documentary material with which he was exceptionally generous. As an Emeritus Professor from my own workplace at the University of Pretoria, he and I had common ground, and as he lived in the same city, I was able to bother him a good deal. A truly wise man, he was able to open up perceptions of that great German ace, 'Jochen' Marseille who plied his trade over the Western Desert in 1941–1942 and who lies buried there as well.

I was fortunate to be able to visit Bavaria twice on official trips and during my spare time on these, managed to see quite a bit of the old *Jagdfliegern* in that area, including a hospitable evening which included one of the regular meetings of *Jägerkreis Süd* (as it then was, the Munich area chapter of the *Luftwaffe* fighter pilot veterans). Here I was able to meet about 30 of the 'old pilots' (*alte Flieger*) and enjoy a good meal and a jolly evening in their company.

Amongst them was one of my regular correspondents, Hans-Ulrich Kornstädt who had joined *II/JG 27* as a freshly-baked *Leutnant* in Sicily in January 1943, to be thrown into the deep end of conflict against heavy odds. In the few months he lasted, he was able to down a B-17 with two head-on attacks, and a Beaufighter later, before himself being shot down over the Mediterranean in June 1943 and finding himself in a tiny dinghy with no land in sight. He was fortunate to be rescued by a British destroyer but was imprisoned by the French deep in the desert of North Africa for years afterwards. While in Munich I also spoke to local resident *Oberst* Edu Neumann, another correspondent of mine, on the telephone. He had been *Kommodore* of *JG 27* over the Western Desert theatre.

A later *Kommodore* of *JG 27*, *Oberst* Gustav Rödel who had also been a famous pilot in the 'Desert' told me specifically about fighting against the four-engined bomber formations over the Balkans in 1943–1944. The gravitas which such senior officer veterans bring to their testimony cannot be overstated. At the other end of what might be termed the 'rank spectrum', Heinrich Rosenberg had also flown in *JG 27*, as an *Oberfeldwebel* in the *III Gruppe* in Russia and the Western Desert; he was shot down in October 1942 and wounded, bringing an end to his combat career. After the war 'Henri' as he liked to be called, married for a second time, had a young family and for years flew his own light aircraft between his adopted home in the Canary Islands and the European mainland; another great character.

Amongst the important contributions he made to this book, quite apart from his own recollections, was to persuade his *8/JG 27* colleague *Feldwebel* Hans Fahrenberger to provide me with an extensive excerpt from his flying logbook. This in turn precipitated some possibly mistaken interpretation by myself, which was roundly criticised by Rudolf Sinner, who had himself flown over the 'Desert' also, as an *Oberleutnant* and *Staffelkapitän* in *I* and *II/JG 27*; together these views and debates contributed substantially to a better understanding and hopefully to the veracity of the totality of this volume. *Hauptmann* Erhard Braune, longtime *Staffelkapitän* of *7/JG 27* and *Oberleutnant* Emil Clade who led the same unit later in the war, both flew in the Battle of Britain and in various Mediterranean campaigns. Emil Clade also provided excellent accounts of serving in Sicily in 1943 and thereafter in the Balkans (1943–1944) and over Germany in the last year of the war.

Karl-Heinz Hirsch, who lived in South Africa after the conflict, spent a large portion of the war in many different training courses (the military has distinct talents in posting some people all over the place – in German this well-tried military practice is known as *bummeln*) finally arrived at the front, a mere *Gefreiter* but one with something like 2,000 flying hours. Arriving in *JG 27* for Home Defence operations in the second half of 1944 was close to a death sentence for any new pilot. His experience saved him but the stark description he gave me when we met (I entertained him twice to lunch at the University of Pretoria) of how each pilot at breakfast early every morning was provided with a bottle of brandy under their chairs, gave a taste of the savage reality of being in the front line. My contacts with the German veterans had by then long destroyed any illusions I may have still harboured about glorious aerial combat, but this picture he drew of his daily life at the front remains graven on my mind.

He was shot down in December 1944, badly injured and landed high in a forest, and the tree had to be cut down by the foresters who found him, to get the badly injured pilot to the ground. Shortly before war's end he was released from hospital, in the same uniform he had been shot down in, still bloodied and unwashed. In South Africa, Hirsch worked initially in high rise construction and then ran a gliding club out in the country.

Unteroffizier Ernst Schröder, a member of *5/JG 300* which formed part of one of the three *Sturmgruppen* provided valuable material on his training and especially on his operations against the four-engined bombers over Germany in the closing months of the war. His logbook extracts were especially valuable. *Unteroffizier* Karl-Heinz Erler flew with *16/JG 5* over southern Norway late in the war and was generous with his memories and particularly his fine photographs of his service in this oft-forgotten theatre.

Another pilot I was able to meet face-to-face in South Africa was Horst Geyer, who had managed to sandwich in several secondments to frontline flying, west and east, in *II/JG 51*, while serving as adjutant to *Generaloberst* Ernst Udet. After Udet's suicide he commanded various experimental units including one to test all weaponry in action against the four-engined bombers. Of greatest interest for this volume, he led the test unit examining the combat suitability of the Me 262 jet, and at the end of the war a similar unit testing the He 162 jet fighter. *Major* Geyer was very forthcoming on all his varied experiences and important tactical responsibilities. *Oberleutnant* Gerd Schindler, from Austria, had flown in the famous 9th *Staffel* of *JG 52* for two tours in Russia. Later he flew in *IV/JG 27* over the Invasion Front and in the late part of the Home Defence. Somehow he survived being shot down four times (wounded three of them), force-landing five times, and being injured twice in landing accidents. His recollections were detailed, very open and honest and provided a vivid picture of the reality of war flying.

The *Zerstörer* crewmen also assisted my quest for information and personal experiences greatly. *Oberstleutnant* Georg Christl led *7/ZG 26* in fighter-bomber missions over the Western Desert and over Malta, and amongst many fascinating accounts described the special tactics used in bombing targets on Malta. *Feldwebel* Fritz Buchholz also provided logbook excerpts, having seen action as a Me 410 pilot over Germany in 1944, in *II/ZG 76*, and later converted onto single-seaters when the *Gruppe* became *II/JG 6*. *Unteroffizier* Heinz Ludwig experienced over 100 *Feindflüge* over the Eastern Front with *I/ZG 1* including a devastating attack on a Russian airbase, where he saw a comrade blown out of the sky by flak. He later came back to Germany where he flew in the Home Defence in both Me 110s and Me 410s as gunner/rear seat man; during a training exercise his aircraft collided with another and he was thrown out by the impact, fracturing his skull. Some months later he was back in the air in this most dangerous of theatres.

Oberfeldwebel Rudolf Hener, another of the veterans with a Russian front pre-history, was a blind flying instructor initially, and was roped in like so many highly qualified instructors to fly transport aircraft on the Stalingrad supply run in the terrible winter of 1942–1943; one of the few survivors amongst his instructor comrades, he later flew in the Home Defence in *JG 3*, fighting against RAF Lancaster bombers on daylight raids late in the war. He ended up with *JG 7* on the Me 262 jet fighters, and also related his experiences being taken prisoner at the end of the war, as did quite a few other witnesses, including those captured earlier in the conflict.

Another prisoner was *Hauptmann* Georg Schröder, shot down on New Year's Day 1945 in *Operation Bodenplatte*. His recollections of flying in the campaign over Normandy in 1944 and thereafter in the Home Defence made for riveting reading. Two other people meriting special mention and thanks are Juha Vaittinen, Finnish air historian and fellow enthusiast (who supplied documents from the Finnish archives for both Finnish and German air forces), and Lothair Vanoverbeke, Belgian historian, well published author and enthusiast (who kindly sent me much material and many photographs from his own extensive *Luftwaffe* contacts and researches, particularly for *JG 26*). I owe both of them a large debt of gratitude.

Another *Luftwaffe* researcher of note is Tony Wood, responsible for *Tony Wood's Combat Claims and Casualties Lists* (see references), an enormous data base of all known confirmed German claims of enemy aircraft, put together from surviving *Reichsluftfahrtministerium* records, often of poor quality and difficult to read. The service he has thereby provided to all *Luftwaffe* historians is simply enormous. I am also grateful to him for taking the time to explain some of the relevant details and pitfalls in the available records, in correspondence with myself.

Last, but by no means least, I also offer my heartfelt thanks to my wife, Mariánne, who for years tolerated my retreats into my study to pursue my researches and eventually to write this book. She is a talented writer and illustrator of her own series of children's books, and provided not only great support but also much inspiration; she is a much better writer than I and in our house carries a 'rank' of at least *Generaloberst*. My appreciation also goes to my brother, Dr. Andrew Eriksson, who helped considerably in many ways, especially in encouragement, clear-headedness and in assisting with computer-related matters at many levels.

The full list of *Luftwaffe* fighter pilot witnesses who made this book possible is shown below. Ranks are those attained by the end of the war (note that several of them joined the new, post-war *Luftwaffe* rising even higher in rank) and all units they served in within the *Jagdwaffe* are also given: *Hauptmann* Heinz Altendorf, II and III/JG 53; *Unteroffizier* Kurt Beecken, II and IV(?)/JG 54, JG 7; *Major* Hans-Ekkehard Bob, III/JG 54, IV/JG 51, JV 44; *Oberleutnant* Walter Bohatsch, I and II/JG 3, I/JG 7; *Major* Erhard Braune, III/JG 27; *Feldwebel* Fritz Buchholz, II/ZG 76, II/JG 6; *Oberfeldwebel* Hermann Buchner, III/SG 1, II/SG 2, III/JG 7; *Hauptmann* Josef Bürschgens, I and III/ JG 26; *Oberleutnant* Günter Büsgen, I/JG 52; *Oberstleutnant* Georg Christl, ZG 2, III/ZG 26, JGr 10; *Hauptmann* Emil Clade, I, II, III and IV/JG 27; *Leutnant* Dr Max Clerico, III/ JG 54; *Oberfeldwebel* Artur Dau, I/JG 26, III/JG 51; *Major* Martin Drewes, II/ZG 76; *Oberfeldwebel* Josef Ederer, I/JG 53; *Oberleutnant* Fritz Engau, I/JG 11; *Hauptmann* Rudolf Engleder, I/JG 1, III/EJG 2, JG 7; *Unteroffizier* Karl-Heinz Erler, IV/JG 5; *Leutnant* Heinz Ewald, II/JG 52; *Feldwebel* Hans Fahrenberger, III and IV/JG 27; *Major* Horst Geyer, *Stab* and II/JG 51, EKdo 25, EKdo Me 262, EKdo He 162; *Feldwebel* Günther Granzow, Stabstaffel/JG 51; *Oberleutnant* Hans Grünberg, II/JG 3, I/JG 7, JV 44; *Unteroffizier* Martin Hain, III/JG 77; *Hauptmann* Alfred

Hammer, *II* and *IV/JG 53*; *Hauptmann* Hans-R. Hartigs, *JG 2*, *I/JG 26*; *Oberleutnant* Alfred Heckmann, *II/JG 3*, *I/JG 26*; *Unteroffizier* Johann Heinrich, *II/ZG 76*; *Oberfeldwebel* Rudolf Hener, *I/JG 3*, *II/JG 7*; *Gefreiter* Karl-Heinz Hirsch, *III/JG 27*; *Unteroffizier* Heinz Hommes, *I* and *III/JG 53*; *Leutnant* Eduard Isken, *III/JG 77*, *JG 200*, *IV/JG 53*; *Leutnant* Gerhard Keppler, *I/JG 27*; *Unteroffizier* Werner Killer, *III/JG 77*; *Obergefreiter* Pay Kleber, *III/JG 2*, *EJG 1*; *Leutnant* Hans-Ulrich Kornstädt, *II/JG 27*; *Oberfeldwebel* Josef Kronschnabel, *III/JG 53*; *Unteroffizier* Ottomar Kruse, *II/JG 26*; *Oberleutnant* Erwin Leykauf, *III/JG 54*, *III/JG 26*, *IV/JG 54*, *II/JG 3*, *JG 7*; *Unteroffizier* Heinz Ludwig, *I/ZG 1* and *I/ZG 26*; *Oberleutnant* Werner Ludwig, *III/ZG 26*; *Gefreiter* Rudolf Miese, *II/JG 2*; *Leutnant* Josef Neuhaus, *II/ZG 26*, *I/JG 7*; *Oberst* Eduard Neumann, *II/JG 26*, *Stab* and *I/JG 27*; *Oberfeldwebel* Georg Pavenzinger, *I/JG 51*; *Feldwebel* Horst Petzschler, *Stabstaffel* and *I/JG 51*, *I/JG 3*; *Leutnant* Johann Pichler, *III/JG 77*; *Leutnant* Alfred Rauch, *II*, *IV* and *Stabstaffel/JG 51*; *Oberfeldwebel* Richard Raupach, *I* and *IV/JG 54*; *Oberfeldwebel* Ernst Richter, *I/JG 54*, *II/JG 11*; *Leutnant* Heinz Riedel, *Stab/JG 53*; *Oberfeldwebel* Joachim Robel, *II/ZG 76*, *III/ZG 26*, *I/ZG 1*; *Oberst* Gustav Rödel, *III/JG 54*, *Stab* and *II/JG 27*; *Oberfeldwebel* Heinrich Rosenberg, *III/JG 27*; *Leutnant* Dr Felix Sauer, *II/JG 53*, *10/JG 53*; *Oberleutnant* Ernst Scheufele, *II* and *IV/JG 5*, *IV/JG 4*; *Oberleutnant* Gerd Schindler, *III/JG 52*, *IV/JG 27*; *Leutnant* Theodor Schirmers, *I/JG 3*; *Hauptmann* Karl-Friedrich Schlossstein, *Zerstörerstaffel JG 77* and *Zerstörerstaffel JG 5*, *II/ZG 76* and *II/JG 76*; *Oberstleutnant* Günther Scholz, *III/JG 54*, *III* and *Stab/JG 5*, *Jagdfliegerführer* Norway; *Major* Gerhard Schöpfel, *III* and *Stab/JG 26*, *Stab/JG 4*, *Stab/JG 6*; *Unteroffizier* Ernst Schröder, *II/JG 300*; *Hauptmann* Georg Schröder, *I* and *II/JG 2*; *Hauptmann* Günther Schwanecke, *III/JG 77*, *I*, *II* and *III/JG 5*, *Stab* and *IV/JG 4*; *Oberleutnant* Alfred Seidl, *III/JG 53*, *I/JG 3*, *I/JG 7*; *Major* Rudolf Sinner, *I*, *II* and *IV/JG 27*, *III* and *IV/JG 54*, *I* and *III/JG 7*; *Leutnant* Erich Sommavilla, *III/JG 77*, *I/JG 53*; *Oberleutnant* Otto Stammberger, *II* and *III/JG 26*; *Oberst* Hanns Trübenbach, *I/LG 2*, *Stab JG 52*, *Jagdfliegerführer Mittelrhein*.

INDEX